Digital SLR Photography

ALL-IN-ONE

FOR

DUMMIES®

Digital SLR Photography

ALL-IN-ONE

FOR DUMMIES®

by Robert Correll

WILEY

Wiley Publishing, Inc.

Digital SLR Photography All-in-One For Dummies®

Published by
Wiley Publishing, Inc.
111 River Street
Hoboken, NJ 07030-5774
www.wiley.com

WILEY

About the Author

Robert Correll is an author, a photographer, and an artist with a lifetime of film and digital photography experience. He is a longtime expert in photo editing and the use of graphics software such as Adobe Photoshop, Adobe Photoshop Elements, and Corel PaintShop Photo Pro (formerly Paint Shop Pro). He is also an expert in the areas of photo management and HDR applications.

Robert's latest published works include *High Dynamic Range Digital Photography For Dummies*, *HDR Photography Photo Workshop* (with Pete Carr; published by Wiley), *Photo Restoration and Retouching Using Corel PaintShop Photo Pro,* Second Edition, and *Your Pro Tools Studio.*

The author of creative tutorials for Corel Corporation and the Virtual Training Company on titles ranging from HDR, graphics, and photo topics to music applications, Robert has been published in the Official *Corel PaintShop Pro Photo* magazine, *Music Tech* magazine, and *Macworld* magazine.

Robert provides professional authoring, software testing (on Windows and the Mac), tutorial and manual writing, advertising copywriting, and other services. He retouches and restores photos.

A music producer, an audio engineer, and a musician who makes his music on the electric guitar and bass, Robert graduated with a bachelor of science degree in history from the United States Air Force Academy and has worked in the publishing, education, and marketing and design industries.

Dedication

For all you digital SLR photographers out there.

For my family: Anne, Ben, Jake, Grace, and Sam.

Author's Acknowledgments

Thanks to David Fugate, my agent. David, you're my trusted advisor, friend, and confidant.

Thanks to everyone at Wiley who's associated with the *For Dummies* series, including Steve Hayes, executive editor; Nicole Sholly, project editor; Anne Sullivan and Becky Whitney, copy editors; Michael Sullivan, technical reviewer; Composition Services; and many others.

Steve, thanks for giving me the room to do this book and trusting me to get it done. I value your instincts and direction. Nicole, you are a joy to work with. Thank you for your delightful collaboration and editing efforts. I not only benefited from your wise editorial expertise but also made a good friend in the process.

My very special thanks go to Roger Cicala, the owner of LensRentals.com. Roger, you and your team made this book possible. Thank you for your timely support and assistance, not to mention your professional and trustworthy service. I wholeheartedly recommend you to everyone who reads this book. And yes, I want to buy everything I rented!

Thanks to Rick Hawks and Kathy Wagner of The Chapel, Michelle Gray and Amy Sipe of Tower Bank, Bob Krafft and Emily Fisher of the Kruse Automotive and Carriage Museum and the National Military History Center, and Bruce Gaylor and Mike Bergum of New Castle Chrysler High School. Thank you all for your permission to set up and shoot interior shots at your wonderful locations.

Thanks also to all the manufacturers out there who make the gear I use and the gear I write about: Nikon, Sony, Canon, Olympus, Pentax, Sigma, Tamron, Manfrotto, LumiQuest, Sto-Fen, Coken, Tiffin, Westcott, and many more.

Thanks to everyone at the Sunny Schick Camera Shop, for your assistance and support.

Thanks to Don and Mary Anne. And, thanks to my wife and kids, for your faith and support.

Publisher's Acknowledgments

We're proud of this book; please send us your comments at http://dummies.custhelp.com. For other comments, please contact our Customer Care Department within the U.S. at 877-762-2974, outside the U.S. at 317-572-3993, or fax 317-572-4002.

Some of the people who helped bring this book to market include the following:

Acquisitions, Editorial

Project Editor: Nicole Sholly

Executive Editor: Steve Hayes

Copy Editors: Rebecca Whitney, Anne Sullivan

Technical Editor: Michael Sullivan

Editorial Manager: Kevin Kirschner

Editorial Assistant: Amanda Graham

Sr. Editorial Assistant: Cherie Case

Cartoons: Rich Tennant (www.the5thwave.com)

Composition Services

Project Coordinator: Sheree Montgomery

Layout and Graphics: Claudia Bell, Timothy C. Detrick

Proofreaders: Jessica Kramer, Lisa Young Stiers

Indexer: BIM Indexing & Proofreading Services

Publishing and Editorial for Technology Dummies

    Richard Swadley, Vice President and Executive Group Publisher

    Andy Cummings, Vice President and Publisher

    Mary Bednarek, Executive Acquisitions Director

    Mary C. Corder, Editorial Director

Publishing for Consumer Dummies

    Diane Graves Steele, Vice President and Publisher

Composition Services

    Debbie Stailey, Director of Composition Services

Contents at a Glance

Table of Contents

Book IV: Lighting Strikes 233

Chapter 1: Flash Fundamentals 235

Chapter 2: Of Speedlights and Speedlites .253

Introduction

A digital SLR is a fancy camera that has lots of buttons, knobs, and LCD monitors on it. It's beefier and more capable than a compact digital camera. The digital SLR has interchangeable lenses, and it looks like a *professional* camera.

It has a reputation for being intimidating. For this reason, many people prefer to use a mild-mannered compact digital camera that has as few buttons as possible. I used to be one of these people. When I made the transition from digital compact to digital SLR, I was surprised at how much happier I was — happier with my camera and happier with my pictures.

My wife and I used to take pictures with compact digital cameras and thought they were good. We have thousands of photos to show for it. When we got our first digital SLR, we were blown away. The pictures we both took with our entry-level Sony Alpha 300 were that much better than any compact we had ever used. And, that was when we were just starting out. In fact, it was a few months later before I even tried taking the camera off Auto exposure mode. The pictures we took with our dSLR had less noise and were clearer, sharper, and more colorful. We found ourselves saying "Wow."

You too can be a happier photographer. The task doesn't have to be super difficult or intimidating. Digital SLRs aren't meant *just* for professionals (although they use dSLRS for many good reasons). If you can drive a car, use an iPod, or operate a modern washing machine, you have what it takes to shoot great photos with a dSLR.

About This Book

Digital SLR Photography All-in-One For Dummies is about unveiling digital SLRs and the seemingly complex world around them and taking the mystery out of the process. I show you how to take professional-looking pictures with a digital SLR, even if you're not a professional photographer. In short, this book is practical, topical, and real-world.

I know a lot of people who have questions about the digital SLR — what it is and what it does — enough questions that I had a clear vision, from the beginning, of who I was writing this book for:

- ✔ **The curious:** If you use a compact digital camera and are wondering what the dSLR hubbub is about, this book is for you. I show you what a dSLR is, where it came from, and how to use one. I go well beyond those topics, but there's a lot here to get you started.

✔ **The frustrated:** If you have a digital SLR and need help to use it more effectively, this book is for you. The entire book is loaded with tips, tricks, and helpful tidbits of knowledge. I've poured all I can into it, to show you how to improve your photography skills using your dSLR.

✔ **The adventurous:** If you're looking to broaden your knowledge and venture into new dSLR territory, this book is for you, too. It challenged me in writing it. I had to leave my own comfort zone and get out there and experience new ways of taking photos with different lenses and techniques. Flash, video, and telephoto and macro lenses are all areas in which I had to grow a little.

Whether you're curious, frustrated, or adventurous, this book was designed and written from the ground up to teach you about the technology and help you take better pictures with your digital SLR.

Basic Assumptions

I assume that you aren't a professional photographer looking for highly specialized, professional techniques using advanced, full-frame digital SLRs and lighting gear. Along those lines, this book doesn't specifically target portrait photographers, landscape photographers, or building and architecture photographers, for example.

I assume that you want to find out about digital SLRs and are willing to put into practice what you read here. The experience you gain from going out and experimenting with things like different lenses, apertures, depth of field, flash modes, and other topics will lock into your mind the words you read on these pages and make it that much easier to go out the next time.

Knowledge is cumulative. Read about apertures today; read about shutter speeds tomorrow. Review the next day what you find out about apertures today. Continue until you've discovered all you want to know about digital SLRs and can take the photos you want in the situations you're in.

To avoid starting at the beginning, where you take the mouse out of the package and plug it in, I have written this book as though you know how to use your computer, install software, and navigate around applications without much trouble.

I haven't taken much for granted in photography. Generally, though, I anticipate that you want more from your digital SLR than the most basic automatic modes provide. Therefore, I don't go into extreme detail to explain the difference between such settings as Portrait and Landscape scene modes, nor do I show sample photos using those settings. I *do* mention them, but then I move on.

Conventions Used in This Book

To help you navigate this book easily and so you can get the most benefit from it, I consistently use a few style conventions. Terms or words that I truly want to emphasize are *italicized* (and defined). Web site addresses, or URLs, are shown in a special monofont typeface, like this. Numbered steps that you need to follow and characters you need to type are set in **bold**. Menu commands are given like this: Transporter Room⇨Energize.

What You Don't Have to Read

As an author, I hesitate to tell you what not to read. I've put all the pertinent information in the book for good reasons, although those reasons aren't universal. A topic that may interest you may not interest someone else. A tip that you may need *today* might not be important tomorrow. At some point, I hope that you read every word of this book. Until then, feel free to skip, jump, browse, peruse, flip, and otherwise read what you need when you need to read it.

If you're seeking a general introduction to a topic, you don't need to read steps with specific procedures. Read the headings and main paragraphs. As an alternative, skim the steps and look for Tip and Remember icons.

If you already know which software you want or you already have it, you don't need to read the "software shootouts" I've put in the book. Skip them.

If you're a diehard Canon user, you can skip the other brands in Book VIII. The same goes for Nikon, Olympus, Pentax, and Sony users.

If you're looking for quick information on different topics, look for tables and lists.

If you couldn't care less about black-and-white photography, panoramas, or HDR (shame on you), you can skip those three chapters in Book VI.

You can also skip all the Technical Stuff icons and return to them when you want.

How This Book Is Organized

Digital SLR Photography All-in-One For Dummies is split into nine minibooks. You don't have to read the book sequentially. Feel free to skip from book to book, forward or backward, between chapters that grab your attention, and from section to section. Make the book work for you. You decide which material you need, and in which order — that's part of the beauty of the *All-in-One For Dummies* series.

I didn't even write this book sequentially. I started in reverse order (which is completely unlike me), and then jumped around toward the middle, went to the front, and finished up with flash and video. Simpatico!

Use the table of contents at the front of this book and the index in back to find the information you need and quickly get your answer. E-mail me at contact@robertcorrell.com if you get stuck or need some friendly advice.

The following sections summarize the information you can find in each minibook.

Book 1: Learning about Digital SLRs

In this "demystifying" minibook, I show you every angle of a digital SLR and its menus so that you can see what the parts are and what they do and not be intimidated. I want you to be able to see and understand the difference between a shutter button and a command dial, for example. I walk you through the process of setting up your camera and taking photos. You also see how to clean your camera, its sensor, and its lenses.

Book II: Through the Looking Glass

Because you can take lenses off and put on new ones, lenses are an important part of the overall world of digital SLR photography. They enable you to customize your camera to suit you and what you want to shoot at the time. You'll see what makes different types of lenses different and check out a number of photographs that were taken with each one. Along the way, I give you tips and tricks for using each lens and finding what it's good for. You'll also read about the difference between single focal length prime lenses and zoom models.

Book III: Hey, Your Exposure's Showing

Don't think of exposure as the "black magic" of photography. If you know a little bit about aperture, shutter speed, and ISO, managing exposure becomes much easier. I explain each of these elements in detail and describe how they work together. I want you to be able to "trade" stops of aperture for stops of shutter speed, or any other combination. You can also read about filters and how to use them so that you can shop for them without being overwhelmed.

Book IV: Lighting Strikes

Flash doesn't have to be a pain to use. This book exposes all those pesky flash settings and gives you the information you need to use all the gear you have, and then some. You'll see examples of different techniques involving the pop-up flash and an external speedlight, and you'll see examples of shots taken with a snoot, a shoot-through umbrella, a diffuser, and a reflector.

Book V: Composing Great Shots

Design is a less subjective topic than you may believe. We humans have a basic sense of what looks good, even if it's at the subconscious level. My goal is to bring your innate ability to the level of your conscious mind so that you can design, frame, and shoot great-looking pictures.

Book VI: "Spiffifying" Photos in Software

Photography isn't just about taking pictures. It's about the whole journey, from setting up on location (even if that's your backyard) to saving a finished JPEG file to post on Flickr. I show you the elements of a digital photography workflow, including raw editing, photo management, and basic photo editing. You'll see how to shoot brackets for High Dynamic Range (HDR) photography, shoot and process panoramas, and convert photos to black and white or colorize them.

Book VII: Shooting Videos

Shooting videos introduces a whole new set of challenges for you as a photographer. In fact, it turns you into a *videographer*. Be forewarned and forearmed. I also show you which digital SLRs shoot video, their differences, and basic instructions for how to shoot movies with each type of camera. To top it off, you can find out how to edit videos using one of the many available video editors.

Book VIII: The dSLR Reference

In some ways, this minibook started out as the heart of this book. I believe that if you know the gear, you have nothing to fear. I chose five of the top dSLR manufacturers and devoted a chapter to each one. You'll see the differences between Canon, Nikon, Olympus, Pentax, and Sony. You'll learn about every digital SLR model these companies sell today, which categories they all fit in, and their strengths, weaknesses, and important specifications. You'll be able to shop for your next dSLR with the knowledge of what you need in a camera. I introduce you to each company's lenses and flashes, and finish off the minibook with a look at notable non-dSLRs.

Book IX: Practical dSLR Tips

This practical guide to digital SLR photography is organized around different types of photos. You can see a number of my photos in each chapter. I explain what's in them, what I was doing when I shot them, and how I did it. This minibook has a little bit of everything, from people to vehicles, landscapes, buildings, odds and ends, different shades of light, and animals.

Icons Used in This Book

What's a *For Dummies* book without icons pointing you in the direction of useful information that's sure to help you along your way? In this section, I briefly describe each icon used in this book.

The Tip icon points out helpful information that's likely to make your job easier. I love tips. If I could make every paragraph a tip, I would. In fact, I try to write as though most statements are tips. But, because I can't label them all that way, I've identified the most obviously helpful ones.

The Remember icon marks a generally interesting and useful fact — one that you might want to remember for later use.

The Warning icon highlights lurking danger. With this icon, I'm telling you to pay attention and proceed with caution. You know, as though you were about to drive off a cliff or stumble across a cache of hidden dynamite. Warnings inject pizzazz into the book, so I've tried to include as many as possible, for no extra charge.

When you see this icon, you know that technical information lurks nearby. If you're not feeling up to it, you can skip these paragraphs.

Where to Go from Here

If you want to dive right into flash photography (who doesn't!), flip on over to Book IV, Chapter 1. If you want to find out about different types of lenses and what they're good for, have a gander at Book II. If you want to see how to handle and clean your digital SLR, read Book I, Chapter 5. To see some cool telephoto and macro photos, read Book II, Chapter 4. If you've been having trouble composing your shots, go immediately to Book V. If you're a little fuzzy about what ISO is and how to use it, try Book III, Chapter 4.

You get the idea. Have fun and let me know how it goes!

Book I
Learning about Digital SLRs

*L*ots of helpful content is scattered throughout this minibook (if I do say so myself). If you just can't help yourself, flip back and forth to mini-books, chapters, or sections that look interesting and read about different subjects at the same time. That's one outstanding quality of the *For Dummies* series, and it holds true also for the *All-in-One* variety: It's designed to be the type of book that you don't have to read from front to back "or else."

Book I introduces you to digital SLRs. If you're new to digital SLR photography, this minibook may be the best place to start. You'll see what digital SLRs are, what they look like, how to set one up and take pictures with it, and how to handle it and clean it.

It sounds like a great start!

Chapter 1: What's So Special about Digital SLRs?

In This Chapter

✏ **Introducing the digital SLR**

✏ **Discovering the origin of the dSLR**

✏ **Determining whether a dSLR is worth the cost**

✏ **Deciding to make the investment**

*I*f you want a professional-looking camera, look no further than the digital single lens reflex (dSLR). In fact, it does more than look professional; it is a professional workhorse. The dSLR has a plethora of controls, knobs, buttons, screens, and features, both manual and automatic, that make it imminently capable of taking gorgeous photographs in just about every situation you will find yourself in. Not only that, the design relies on using interchangeable lenses, which means you can customize the camera to photograph just about anything.

It's a great design. Digital SLRs are great cameras. They take great photos.

The thing is, not everyone is a professional photographer or wants to use a professional camera. Is the dSLR right for you? Can you figure it out and make it work for you, even if you're not a serious professional photographer?

Many people do. Today, there are many levels of digital SLRs. Manufacturers have expanded their vision to include everyone from entry-level photographers on a budget to professionals who demand the highest possible quality and are willing to pay for it. You should be able to find a camera with the right features and price for you, no matter what your skill or interest level.

If you want to explore photography with fewer limits than with a compact digital or other type of consumer digital camera, I encourage you to learn more about dSLRs and how to use them. That's what this chapter, and the rest of the book, is about.

Introducing the Digital SLR

Digital single lens reflex cameras, also known as *digital SLRs* or *dSLRs* (you might also see *DSLR*), are amazing works of engineering and manufacturing. They're much larger and more complex than compact digital cameras, which are small enough to fit in your pocket.

You don't need to be a rocket scientist to use a dSLR. In fact, entry-level dSLRs have enough automatic shooting modes to satisfy the casual photographer in all of us. The truth is that most digital SLRs, even those that cost thousands of dollars, can be configured to act like a simple point-and-shoot camera. Digital SLRs have manual controls and complexity *if you want them.*

They call it single lens reflex

Single lens reflex cameras are characterized by their design, which allows light to pass through a single lens, where it then either bounces up through the viewfinder by a mirror (hence the term *reflex*) or passes directly to the film or sensor. Figure 1-1 illustrates these paths.

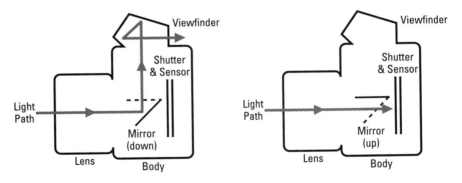

Light bouncing off the mirror.   Light hitting the sensor.

Figure 1-1: Light path through a digital SLR.

This revolutionary (at the time it was invented) design puts your eye inside the lens. It lets you see what the camera sees, which is a tremendous help in *metering* (evaluating how much light is present) and *framing* (deciding what you want the photo to include) a scene.

Compared to film cameras of yore, having one lens that lets you see what the camera sees was a great achievement because everyone looked through a second lens (twin-lens reflex), through what amounted to a hole in the camera body (cereal box top reflex), or through a flimsy framing rectangle that popped up (let's pretend it's reflex). You either focused by walking off the distance to your subject or not at all, and metering was just a wild guess. Rangefinder cameras attempted to make finding the range easier, but without modern ranging techniques (today's dSLRs use phase detection), focusing was still a chore.

Sony has recently announced two new dSLRs (the Alpha 33 and 55) that feature a semi-transparent mirror in place of a traditional moving reflex mirror. It remains to be seen how successful this design change will be, but it offers greater shooting speeds (frames per second) and fewer moving, clunking, banging, noise-making parts. You can reportedly move the mirror out of the way to clean the sensor.

Using interchangeable lenses

Another hallmark of SLR cameras is their flexibility with respect to lenses. To make a long point short, the lenses are interchangeable, which means that the camera is incredibly customizable. Find the lens that is best suited for the subjects you want to photograph and attach it to the camera body. If you need more than one lens (many photographers do), buy them and keep them with you. Switch lenses in order to find the one that produces the shot you want.

Although having an interchangeable lens system isn't a unique property of digital SLRs (or SLRs), it's often thought of as a defining characteristic. Figure 1-2 shows just how flexible this property is. You can modify one camera body (a Nikon D300S, in this case) with as many lenses as you can afford — each with a different purpose and characteristics.

Figure 1-2: A healthy lens stable.

Sensor sizes and crop factors

One thing that separates digital SLRs from their ancestors is sensor size and crop factor. I take a look at the former to explain the latter.

It all boils down to a 35mm frame of film. That is, pardon the pun, the ultimate frame of reference in the digital SLR world. Why? Because, back in the day, SLRs used 35mm film. Their bodies were built around that film format, and the lenses were designed to support it.

When you look at a picture, you see a field of view based on the frame dimensions and the focal length of the lens. Knowing this will help you decide on lenses, understand and be able to compare focal lengths on different platforms, and know the angle of view they capture. (*Hint:* That's what crop factor quickly tells you.)

Comparing sizes

A 35mm frame (see Figure 1-3) of film measures 36mm long by 24mm tall. (I know that hurts. It hurts me too.) *Why do they name 36mm film 35mm?* Because the film strip is 35mm across from top to bottom. Go measure it, if you need to. I just did.

Figure 1-3: A frame of 35mm film.

The *frame* (which is a fancy name for the part of the negative that is the photo) itself is 36mm by 24mm. Table 1-1 compares the sensor sizes of the current crop of dSLRs with a 35mm film frame. Figure 1-4 illustrates it visually.

Table 1-1	**Digital SLR Sensor Dimensions**			
Format	*Length (mm)*	*Width (mm)*	*Diagonal (mm)*	*Crop Factor*
35mm film frame	36	24	43.3	1
Full-frame	36	24	43.3	1
APS-H (Canon)	28.1	18.7	33.8	1.3
APS-C (Nikon DX, Pentax, Sony)	23.6	15.8	28.4	1.5
APS-C (Canon)	22.3	14.9	26.8	1.6
Four Thirds (Olympus)	17.3	13.0	21.6	2.0

* Some cameras have subtly different sensor sizes than listed here, but they fit within the type.

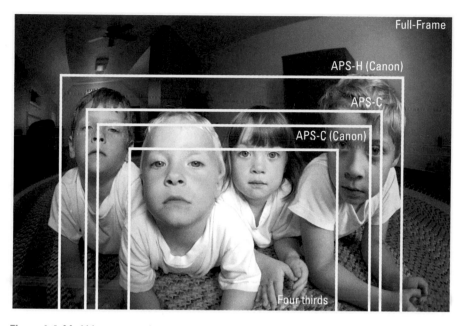

Figure 1-4: My kids, as seen through different sensor sizes.

Looking at crop factors

Crop factor is simply a fixed measure of how much larger a 35mm film frame is than the digital SLR sensor in question. (Both are measured diagonally.) Is the film frame twice as large as the sensor? That sensor would have a crop factor of 2.0. Is the frame one-and-a-half times larger than the sensor? That sensor has a crop factor of 1.5.

The crop factor is sometimes confusing. It's not something you want to be large because the larger the crop factor the smaller the sensor is. Full-frame dSLRs have the smallest crop factor amongst digital SLRs: Larger sensors, as explained in this chapter, are generally preferred over smaller sensors. Practicality rears its head, however, when you realize that most full-frame dSLRs are professional-level cameras that are quite unaffordable to casual photographers. I've put each digital SLR's crop factor in Book VIII. You can also find the crop factor or sensor size in your camera's manual or on the manufacturer's product Web page.

Here's where the crop factor helps you compare lenses and what *field of view* (how wide an angle you can see through the lens) they show on different cameras. A 50mm lens is a 50mm lens — those numbers don't change, no matter what camera it's connected to. It's manufactured so that the distance between the front optical element of the lens and the camera's sensor is 50mm. When you put a 50mm lens on a full-frame digital SLR, it has a 46-degree field of view. The field of view is *different* on a cropped-frame dSLR!

I admit, it would be a nicer world if we didn't have to mess with crop factors. It used to be that way. Every 35mm film SLR ever manufactured that used 35mm film exposed negatives that were the same size. There was no need for crop factors. Likewise, when you bought a 50mm lens, it had the same 46-degree field of view on every film SLR you could attach it to. In this world, a 50mm lens was a 50mm lens. They all acted the same.

Fast-forward to today. There is no single, universal sensor size among digital SLRs. Some are full-frame and have sensors the same size as 35mm film. Some dSLRs have smaller sensors. Even these are not officially standardized. You'll find some sensors that are a few millimeters different than others that are in the same basic size category. Having different sensor sizes is analogous to using differently sized film in different 35mm film cameras. Yeah. Ouch.

The problem is, lens terminology hasn't (and probably shouldn't) change. Even more confusing would be if you had to shop for a 50mm lens named differently based on what camera you plan to put it on, but for all other purposes are identical. No, a 50mm lens is still a 50mm lens.

You have to realize, though, that the field of view of this one lens depends on what camera you have. On a full-frame camera, a 50mm lens takes photos that have a 46-degree field of view. On a cropped-frame dSLR with a crop factor of 1.5, the same lens takes photos of approximately 31.5 degrees.

The long and the short of the field of view is this: Using the same lens, full-frame dSLRs take photos with a greater field of view than cropped-frame dSLRs. So, when you're talking to your friend about your favorite 50mm lens, remember to say what camera you have and what the crop factor is.

Figure 1-5 shows my son Jacob at baseball practice. I took this photo at 200mm with a Nikon D300S, which has an APS-C-size sensor. The field of view is just over 8 degrees, which is represented by the yellow box. (I was about 15 meters away.) The same lens on a full-frame camera would have captured more than 12 degrees of view, represented by the magenta box in the figure.

What a full-frame "catches"

What a
cropped-frame
"catches"

Totality of what the lens sees

Figure 1-5: What a cropped versus full-frame sensor sees.

Don't think that you get "free optical zoom" with a cropped-frame sensor. The photo is *cropped,* not zoomed. Visually, it looks zoomed, but the lens is doing nothing different. In other words, the lens isn't zooming in and providing greater detail or more fidelity. In fact, the lens captures less actual information of the same scene and then pastes it on a tableau of the same size (in pixel dimensions or as a printout).

Understanding this concept helps you "translate" focal lengths and their effects between different cameras. Woohoo!

A 50mm lens on a full-frame dSLR acts like a 75mm lens on an APS-C-size Nikon body. How do I know? Multiply the focal length (50mm) by the crop factor (1.5) to produce the result 75mm!

Similarly, a 35mm prime on a cropped-frame dSLR performs much like a 50mm on a full-frame. However, it acts like a 70mm lens on a four thirds system camera. (Four thirds sensors are a bit smaller and have a different aspect ratio than other cropped-frame dSLR sensors.) The same lens can be a wide angle, standard, or moderate zoom lens, depending on the camera you put it on. (Depth of field isn't the same of the same aperture, however.)

Controls and controllability

One factor that sets dSLRs apart from their main competition (small and inexpensive yet increasingly powerful compact digital cameras) is their devotion to control.

Figure 1-6 shows the controls on my Nikon D200 compared to a tiny Canon PowerShot A480. There's a huge difference in how many controls each camera has.

dSLR   Compact digital

Figure 1-6: dSLRs focus on control.

Son of an SLR

This section is for anyone who may want to know more about the difference between digital and film SLRs. Digital SLRs have *history* to them. They didn't just pop up overnight at a retailer. Lots of refinement to the design and manufacturing have occurred over the years, plus the invention of new and creative ways to take photos. Figure 1-7 shows my Nikon FE2 (vintage, from the mid-1980s) next to a Nikon D300S (new, 2010).

Figure 1-7: Old school versus new school.

Here are some key differences between a 35mm film SLR and a digital SLR:

✔ **Film versus sensors and memory cards (see Figure 1-8).**

Digital SLRs sense light with their sensors and store the recorded image on digital memory cards. Film cameras use film to serve both those needs.

Film

✔ **Analog versus digital interface**

My old Nikon FE2 has no LCD monitor in back, electronic gizmos on top, or any way of communicating with the "brains" of the camera. I'm the one who has to supply the brains. It's just me and a few knobs.

Memory cards

Figure 1-8: Film and memory cards.

My Nikon D200 has an LCD monitor on its back side and an LCD monitor on top. I can look at exposure information and other settings, work the camera's software, and review photos. If I want to, I can spend more time messing around with those aspects than taking pictures.

✔ **Film ISO versus dSLR ISO**

Film cameras can't change ISO (the measure of film sensitivity; now applied to digital sensor sensitivity) on the fly because ISO is entirely dependent on the film you buy. You can develop film of one ISO as if it were another by using different times, temperatures, and sometimes developer solution. The two techniques are called *push* (overdeveloping to compensate for film underexposure) and *pull* (underdeveloping to compensate for film overexposure) processing.

With digital SLRs, being able to manage ISO from moment to moment is an important part of elevating your photography game.

✔ **More batteries versus fewer batteries**

Digital SLRs eat batteries. They need them to power up, run the chip inside, sense light, display photos, store exposures on the card, light up buttons or backlight LCD monitors, and more.

Bare-bones film SLRs may use a button battery to power a light sensor, if anything.

Figure 1-9 shows the difference between my D200 and FE2 batteries.

✓ LCD monitors

Film SLRs have no built-in LCD monitors on the back side of the camera. They generally have a little slot in which to put the end of the box the film came in, to remind you what type it is, how many exposures are on the roll, and the ISO.

These monitors serve quite a few purposes. Reviewing photos after you take them, composing using Live view before you take them, and accessing the camera's menu system to control options and settings are among the most helpful. Figure 1-10 shows the articulated LCD monitors on the Sony Alpha 300.

Figure 1-9: Guess which one powers the digital camera!

✓ Videos (also known as Movies)

Film SLRs lack the ability to shoot movies, of course. What you might not realize is that it has taken some time for digital SLRs to make the

Figure 1-10: Some LCD monitors swing out.

transition from shooting still photos only to shooting both still photos and videos. Although not all dSLRs can shoot video, the number that can is growing. (Compact digital cameras have been able to shoot movies for several years.) For more information on shooting video, hop over to Book VII.

Here are some similarities between film and digital SLRs:

✓ **SLR:** Digital and film SLRs share the same basic design. They use a mirror to divert light coming into the lens up and out of the viewfinder. You see what the camera sees. When you take the picture, the reflex mirror (the *R* in SLR) flips up and out of the way to expose the shutter, which is free to expose the film or digital sensor.

✓ **Interchangeable lens systems:** Film and digital SLRs both take advantage of interchangeable lens systems. Although newer lenses use newer technology (such as processors, vibration reduction mechanisms, and digital contacts to communicate with the camera body) and mounts, the concept of being able to change lenses is the same.

✔ **Photo quality:** Both digital and film SLRs shoot fantastic photos that are worthy of being published and otherwise used professionally. Much of this is because of the interchangeable lens system and the basic SLR design.

✔ **Professional workhorse:** SLRs, digital and otherwise, are and have been used by professionals worldwide. They're rugged and take high-quality pictures.

✔ **Hot shoe:** Both types of cameras have an accessory mount, often called a hot shoe, on top of their viewfinder. A hot shoe is used primarily to mount external flashes. Top-of-the line dSLRs (the super professional models) do not normally have built-in, pop-up electronic flashes, but they do have hot shoes on which you can mount external flashes and accessories. Most old 35mm cameras did not have built-in flashes.

✔ **Accessible to enthusiasts and hobbyists:** Despite being professional cameras, SLRs and digital SLRs are widely used by enthusiasts and amateurs, which should give you pause. That SLRs and dSLRs can be used both professionally and by backyard photographers is a testament to excellent design.

Why Bother?

Is going to the trouble of shopping for, buying, and learning how to use a digital SLR worth it? Should I bother? If everyone else is running around with a snazzy compact digital camera with a touchscreen in their hip pockets or purses, digital SLRs can't be *all that,* can they?

I help you resolve these questions by addressing the pros and cons of buying into the digital SLR scene. Here are some benefits:

✔ **Better pictures:** Ultimately, it's about the pictures. That doesn't mean dSLRs are better than other camera types in every situation and scenario, but they're effective platforms with which to take potentially amazing pictures. When my family upgraded from a compact digital camera to an entry-level dSLR, we were immediately amazed at how much better the photos were, even using Auto shooting mode.

As a matter of fact, your photos will get worse when you venture away from your dSLR's Auto shooting mode and start trying to take photos that require you to set up the camera, evaluate the exposure, and handle all the controls. It takes time to learn how to use your dSLR fully and develop as a photographer. Don't give up. Your photos will get better with practice!

Figure 1-11 is an example of this excellent picture quality. I grabbed a macro lens, teleconverter, and flash and went outdoors to shoot water drops on plants. When I got there, I saw a tiny spider, about the size of a small drop of water, and was able to get a few good shots of him. Shots like these are what makes the effort worth it.

Figure 1-11: Smile and look (with all your eyes) at the camera.

✔ **Fast response:** I don't like waiting to take photos. I don't like waiting for the camera to "boot up." I don't like pressing the shutter button and having to wait (without moving) to hear the shutter click.

If you're like me, that makes dSLRs a perfect fit for you.

dSLRs start up faster and have less shutter lag (the time between pressing the shutter release button and when the photo gets taken) than compact digitals.

✔ **Versatility:** Digital SLRs are incredibly flexible. You can shoot close-up macros or sweeping landscapes, ultra-wide angle or telephoto, intimate portraits, family gatherings, fast-action sports, slow waterfalls, and everything in between — large, small, fast, slow. What more could you want from a camera?

✔ **Sensor size:** Even cropped-body dSLRs have larger sensors than compact digitals and super zooms.

✔ **Large viewfinder:** The worst dSLR viewfinder is still larger and better than the one most compacts have. Well, that's if a compact even has a viewfinder. Most don't, which makes you rely exclusively on the LCD monitor on the back of the camera. Figure 1-12 shows the tiny viewfinder on the back side of an older Canon PowerShot A75. It's tiny (compare this viewfinder to the one shown in Figure 1-10).

Figure 1-12: You're lucky nowadays if you even get a viewfinder on a compact camera.

LCD monitors aren't as precise as seeing the "real thing" through a view-finder and can wash out when you're outdoors in strong light.

✓ **Interchangeable lenses:** Although being able to change lenses isn't a cure-all, it means that you have the flexibility to tailor your camera to take the photos you need. To me, that's an enormous benefit.

✓ **Manual control:** I can't tell you how many times I've been frustrated with compact digital cameras. They never seem to have *just the right* automatic scene I need at the time. That, and it takes me ten minutes to find it.

Automatic shooting modes can make photography easier, but being able to exercise manual or semimanual control over your camera when you need it is priceless. *You* make the creative decisions. *You* set the priorities. *You* manage your shots.

You don't have to be a brainiac to do it. You just need a little knowledge and some practice.

✓ **Tough:** dSLRs, which are much more rugged than compact digital cameras, are designed and built to stand up to more punishment without breaking. That doesn't mean you should go out and hammer nails with them. But they're well-built cameras.

High-end dSLRs emphasize the fact that their bodies are made from magnesium alloy, but even low-end dSLRs with plastic (also known as polycarbonate) bodies are rugged.

People with magnesium bodies tend to claim that theirs are better, and people with polycarbonate bodies tend to say that theirs are better.

✓ **Cool factor:** Nothing says cool like walking into a cocktail party with your significant other and a huge dSLR slung around your neck.

With that discussion out of the way, it's time to look at a few costs, or challenges, of owning a digital SLR.

For example, digital SLRs are heavier than smaller cameras (how much varies; some pretty light dSLRs are available). Knowing that going in can help you decide whether or not it's worth the price. If weight is your *primary* or *only* criteria, digital SLRs might not be for you. On the other hand, the weight issue may just be something to note and move on. Check out weights for dSLRs in Book VIII.

✓ **Cost:** When you start shopping for most dSLRs, you run into the fact that most of them cost more than compact digitals and super zooms. In some cases, they cost far more, and that doesn't account for lenses, which can also be quite expensive, or a bag, tripod, extra batteries, filters, and other accessories.

Depending on the brand, the cheapest entry-level digital SLR can be about the same price as the most advanced, expensive compact digital camera.

If cost is a significant issue, don't expect to be able to buy into the digital SLR world at the professional level. Shop between brands and compare their inexpensive, entry-level models. They're more reasonably priced than ever. Think about buying a used body and picking up new or used lenses as you can. Look for great deals on bodies that manufacturers are getting ready to retire and replace. For very little difference in capability (most times), you can score the camera for almost half-price. I did!

✔ **Bulk:** Digital SLR bodies are much larger than digital compact cameras, and that's before you attach a lens to them. Figure 1-13 shows an extreme example.

Not every digital SLR is the same size, though. The super-professional models with built-in vertical grips are massive, but entry-level models are far less bulky.

Figure 1-13: A Nikon D300S digital SLR with a superduper telephoto lens.

It gets even better. Olympus is staking out the awesomely cool and thriftily nifty niche with its tiny line of digital SLRs. Their E-420 and E-450 are the world's smallest digital SLRs. How's that work for ya!

✔ **Weight:** If you look at the tables in Book VIII, you can see the precise weight of a number of dSLRs expressed in grams and in 12-ounce cans of soda.

For comparison, the lightest Canon dSLR — the EOS Rebel XS — weighs in at 450 grams. That's its body only. One of the advanced compacts, the Canon PowerShot SX210 IS, weighs in at 215 grams.

Before you go writing off dSLRs, realize that 450 grams isn't all that heavy. Sure, 215 is half as much, but a Big Mac sandwich from McDonald's weighs about 214 grams. You wouldn't call that too heavy. That means the XS weighs as much as 2 Big Macs. If you're concerned, buy a few Big Macs and carry them around to see whether it bothers you. Just don't eat them.

✔ **The perception of being difficult to use:** Sometimes you want to be able to point the camera at something and just take a picture. You can do exactly that with most digital SLRs.

Digital SLRs have a reputation for being complex. They can be complicated, but they don't always have to be. You don't have to manually focus all the time. You don't have to have 15 lenses lying around. You can get an entry-level digital SLR that has plenty of automatic modes and treat it as a "super point-and-shoot" camera.

In fact, this is what I do. My first digital SLR, the Sony Alpha 300, has all the advantages of being a digital SLR yet has an automatic shooting mode that makes it a breeze to use. I can unleash every manual mode I want to one day and then switch to Auto mode and take it to the zoo the next day and not think, just take pictures.

✔ **Complexity:** Even the most basic dSLRs are more complex than most compact digitals. dSLRs are designed for you to be able to take full control of the camera. To do that, you need as many buttons, knobs, and other doodads as possible. The system software needed to set up the camera adds a layer of complexity as well.

If you can work an iPhone, you can work a dSLR. In general, manufacturers have tried to work these problems out of their entry and lower-level lines of dSLRs. They cost less, are smaller and lighter, and have more automatic controls than do more advanced dSLRs.

Buying into the dSLR System

When you buy a digital SLR, you're buying into an entire system whether you like it or not. It's not like picking up a compact digital camera from Panasonic and then wanting one from Fuji. With those cameras, everything is self-contained. If you wanted, you could have a collection of compacts from different manufacturers and not miss a beat.

When you purchase a digital SLR, you're buying into a system that includes compatible lenses, flashes, and other accessories that aren't necessarily compatible between brands. In fact, most of the time, they aren't. You can't put a Canon lens on a Nikon camera body. By the same token, you can't put a Sony flash on an Olympus dSLR.

The upshot to this situation is that it makes "changing teams" harder the more gear you have that fits a single camera system. It's not impossible, especially given the wealth of online auctions and photography communities, but it will take time and effort.

Chapter 2: Anatomy of a Digital SLR

In This Chapter

- Looking at the parts of the D300S
- Viewing from the front
- Viewing from the backside
- Looking down at the top
- Looking up at the bottom
- Discovering what's on the sides
- Peering inside
- Figuring out lenses

The point of this chapter is to show you around a digital SLR. I barrage you with photos, labels, and descriptions. Why? Because I think that's one of the most effective ways to learn photography.

Photography, especially digital SLR photography, is based on gear. Love your gear. Know your gear. If you know it, you can use it. If you can use it, you can get increasingly better at taking pictures.

I'm not talking pansy half-measures here. I'm talking about every button, knob, lever, display, cover, optical, and other doohickey on your camera.

Now, before you panic, throw this book down, and run screaming in the opposite direction, realize that it isn't difficult. It may take some *effort*, but that's different from asking you to be smarter than everyone else.

Can you drive a car? Can you work your cellphone? Can you use iTunes and load your iPod with music? Then you can figure out how to work a digital SLR.

Your camera might be different from those I show you here — no matter. They all have similar pieces and parts. In fact, they all share a remarkably similar basic design.

Dissecting a D300S

I use the Nikon D300S as my primary model for this chapter and toss in shots of a Sony Alpha 300 for alternative looks.

The D300S is a good example of a fairly complex dSLR with lots of bells and whistles and knobs and buttons and switches and monitors. When you handle the D300S, you *know* that you have a sophisticated piece of machinery in your hands.

Figure 2-1 shows a photo I recently took with a D300S. It's a quirky shot (we're renovating) of me taking a photo of myself taking a photo of myself. (I flipped it horizontally so that it looks normal.) I'm using the NIKKOR 10.5mm f/2.8G fisheye lens, which is fun and creative. I look fairly undistorted, but the closet door frame is completely bowed out and you can see quite a bit of the room behind me.

©Sigma Corp.

Figure 2-1: *Say hello to the Nikon D300S.*

If you're used to thinking of the camera as the entire package, stop. When you're working with dSLRs, think of the body as the camera and the lens as the lens. When you put a new lens on your camera, it doesn't cease to be a Canon EOS Rebel T2i. It's an EOS Rebel T2i with a different lens. They work together to take pictures.

I've organized this chapter around the sides of a D300S rather than try to group items functionally. All digital SLRs have a front, back, top, bottom, and sides. Each area of the camera performs different tasks, and different cameras may have different controls, but dSLR design has a good degree of commonality.

Here's how digital SLRs are generally configured:

- ✔ **Front:** The business end. This is where lenses mount and where you might find certain autofocus controls (the type depends on the camera). It might also have some optional buttons and elements you don't have to mess with (such as the microphone).

- ✔ **Back:** The command center, where you find the viewfinder, LCD monitor, and lots of other controls (typically metering modes, focus modes, review controls, menu buttons, and possibly more).

✔ **Top:** At minimum, the top contains controls or dials to set the shooting mode and the shutter button. The pop-up flash (if applicable) and hot shoe are located here.

✔ **Bottom:** Where you put the battery and mount a tripod.

✔ **Sides:** Where you grip the camera. It's where the memory card is located, along with some input and output ports.

✔ **Inside:** Where the magic happens. Approach the inside with care to clean it. Otherwise, don't mess with it.

Taking the Full Frontal View

The front of the camera is the side you rarely see when you're in action. After you attach your lens and make any connections, you have to use your sense of touch to work it.

Here's what's on the front left of the D300S (see Figure 2-2):

✔ **Lamp:** This lamp performs several chores. It's an autofocus assist illuminator, self-timer lamp, and red-eye reduction lamp. Make sure not to cover lamps like this with your finger or get them dirty.

✔ **Dial:** Technically, this dial is the Sub-command dial on this camera. Depending on the camera's mode, it has a number of purposes. For example, when in Aperture priority, it changes aperture.

Pay special attention to generic dials and buttons that change operation. Camera designers try to consolidate functions to make operating the camera possible.

✔ **DOF preview button:** This button is the depth of field (DOF) preview button. When you have all settings except the aperture dialed in, snake your index finger over and press it — the result is an instant DOF preview.

✔ **Function button:** This Function button (Fn) defaults to bracketing parameters on the D300S but can be programmed by itself or used in conjunction with dials. Think about that for a minute. You can customize cameras with buttons so that they respond to *your* needs — pretty cool.

✔ **Grip:** The grip is a prominent protrusion (in this case, beneath the red triangle — a Nikon design element) that fits in your hand sort of like a joystick. It has room for three to four fingers to hold on to the camera from the front. The index finger works the dial and preview button, and travels to the top to work those controls. The pinky hits the function button.

Dial   Lamp

Grip   Function

DOF preview

Figure 2-2: The D300S front left side.

The right front side of the camera (see Figure 2-3) has about the same amount of items:

- ✓ **Pop-up button:** This button pops up the flash. Try removing any hot shoe accessories or flash beforehand.

- ✓ **Flash modes and compensation button:** Below the pop-up button is a button where you change flash modes and adjust flash compensation.

  Most of the time, I have to look for these buttons to push them, which means that I hold the camera in my right hand and push buttons with my left. Ideally, you can use your left index finger.

- ✓ **Lens release button:** Push this button to release the lens from the mount.

   Don't press the lens release button unless you have a hand on the lens and intend to change it.

Flash modes

Pop-up | Cover & teminals

Lens release

Focus mode

Figure 2-3: The D300S right front side.

✓ **Focus-mode switch:** This selector enables you to change between two autofocus modes and one manual focus mode. Although you can push it with one finger, I like to use two, so I have positive control over the little bugger.

✓ **Covers and terminals:** The D300 has a few terminals on the front of the camera. They're beneath a rubberized cover. Underneath, you find the flash sync terminal and the ten-pin remote terminal.

I use a remote shutter release all the time, so I use this terminal regularly. My D200 had a much less practical cover — a little cap that comes completely off. It's designed to be lost in fewer than 5 minutes.

✓ **Lens mount:** Behind the lens is the lens mount, which securely attaches the lens to the camera body.

dSLR Got Back

The back of a digital SLR is your office. It's where you do most of your work. You frame, compose, adjust, review, and set options. That means you need to be quite familiar with all the buttons, knobs, levers, and screens and be able to work them fluidly.

This camera has a busy backside, as shown in Figure 2-4. The top area of the back has the following elements (from left to right):

✏ **Playback button:** The playback button kicks the camera into Playback mode, or if the camera is already in Playback mode, it returns you to Shooting mode. This is sometimes referred to as Review button and Review mode.

I use this button all the time. Press it to check a photo. Press it to quickly get back to work.

✏ **Delete button:** Deletes the selected photo.

When pressed and held for a few seconds with the Mode button, it enters Card Format mode. When pressed simultaneously again, the duo reformats the memory card. I love that combination and use it all the time because it saves me from having to laboriously go through the menu system and find Format Disk.

✏ **Optical viewfinder:** Look through the viewfinder to see the scene. Lots of helpful information is available in the viewfinder. The most important information relates to the shooting mode, exposure details, and the focus and metering modes you're in. The exact type and location depend on the camera and the mode that's active at the time.

The viewfinder "blinks" when you take a photo because the mirror has swung up and out of the way so that the light can pass directly to the sensor. When taking quick shots, it's hardly noticeable. For longer exposures, it becomes quite noticeable. Relax and it will come back when the exposure is over.

✏ **Diopter adjustment:** The diopter adjustment control lets you correct the viewfinder to match your vision. On older cameras, you had to buy small corrective lenses that screwed onto the viewfinder. dSLRs have the ability to correct on the fly.

Larger adjustments may still require external diopter lenses.

You may not even need this control. If you need to adjust the viewfinder and are the only person who uses the camera, it's a "set it and forget it" situation. On the other hand, if you share the camera with people who have different eyesight, you may have to adjust the control back and forth every time you use the camera.

Viewfinder   Diopter adjustment

Delete   Combo

Playback   AF-ON

Main command dial

Menu

Protect

Zoom out

Zoom in

OK

Multi selector

Focus selector lock

Monitor   Live view   Speaker

Info   Card access

AF area

Figure 2-4: You see a lot from this side.

✔ **Combination button:** This button is an interesting one on Nikon cameras. It's a dial surrounding a button. The dial selects any one of the camera's three metering modes while the button activates AE lock or AF lock (lock the exposure and focus while in auto modes, respectively).

Both this and the AF-ON button are conveniently located so that you can press them when looking through the viewfinder.

✔ **AF-ON button:** This button activates the autofocus, just like depressing the shutter button halfway. The big exception is that it doesn't engage vibration reduction like the shutter button does.

✔ **Main command dial:** The main command dial is a control type that Nikon and Pentax dSLRs favor putting on the back of the camera. The recessed dial is a quick way to scroll through shooting options and parameters, such as aperture and shutter speed. Canon, Olympus, and Sony (with the exception of the Alpha 850 and 900) do not place a dial on the back. Rather, they put command dials on the front of the grip or the top of the camera on the right side.

Dials in particular are best suited for scrolling through a lot of modes and options. This dial is often conveniently located so that your right thumb (or index finger, if the dial is on the front of the grip) can easily access it.

The lower-left side houses many of the buttons that are active when reviewing and playing back photos. As such, you don't use them when you have the camera up to your face but, rather, after you've taken the photo. This list describes the buttons:

- **Menu button:** Opens the menu system — handy.

- **Protect button:** Locks photos to keep them from being deleted accidentally. This button is helpful if you review and delete lots of bad photos from the camera before you download them. Protecting photos will not save you from deleting all photos in case you choose to format the card (except that it does lock out the Nikon 2-finger format that uses the delete button).

- **Zoom out/Thumbnail button:** Shows thumbnails of the photos you have on the memory card rather than one at a time. Different levels of zoom are available, from 1 (full-frame playback) to 4, 8, and 72.

- **Zoom in button:** The reverse of zoom out. I find this button helpful when I'm reviewing photos to see whether they're in focus. It's not enough to see them full-frame — even bad photos look good at this magnification. You have to zoom in to a detailed feature to be able to tell.

- **OK button:** Used to commit most operations. In other words, if you back out of the menu without pressing OK, you don't change anything.

The lower-right side has these controls:

- **Multi selector:** The multi selector is the Nikon navigation button. Use it when navigating the menus and when moving *autofocus points* (small areas in the viewfinder that you can tell the camera to autofocus on) around in the viewfinder.

  - *Center button:* The center button selects options such as the OK button in the lower-left corner. I guess they figure you need two buttons for this task.

  - *Focus selector lock:* When the index mark points at the dot, you can use the multi selector to change autofocus points. When pointing to the L, the autofocus point is locked and the multi selector can't change it. This is helpful when you've established a focus point for a shoot and don't want it accidentally changed when you hit the multi selector.

- **Live view button:** Press this button to enter Live view, which turns on the LCD monitor on the back of the camera for you to compose and focus shots (just like if you were using a compact digital camera). The optical viewfinder is blocked and cannot be used when you enter Live view.

  Some cameras (such as my Sony Alpha 300) have a switch that toggles between the optical viewfinder and Live view. Some camera switch from phase-detection autofocus to contrast-detect autofocus when in a tripod Live view mode (like the D300S). Contrast-detect, as the name suggests, focuses by maximizing contrast and takes longer to achieve than standard autofocus, making it unsuitable for handheld photography.

Currently, all dSLRs that shoot video require you to use Live view when in movie mode.

✔ **Autofocus area mode selector:** Sets the AF-area mode of the D300.

I previously confused this selector with the metering selector on my D200 because they both have little squares and rectangles in the icon. I had to sit down and review the icons several times before I was able to lock it into my memory.

You may run into similar problems when you find out how to use your camera. Relax and consult the manual. You might have to spend some extra time, like I did, to get past the confusing parts. You don't have to "get it" all at once.

✔ **Info button:** Display shooting information on the monitor, like lots of other cameras do.

Some cameras are different. Unless it's in Live view, my Sony Alpha 300 displays by default a nice summary of shooting information on the LCD monitor. My Nikon D200 doesn't and can't. The D200 puts it on the LCD monitor on top of the camera or in the viewfinder.

✔ **Memory card access lamp:** This lamp turns when the camera is writing to the memory cards. Make sure that this lamp is off before removing the card.

✔ **Speaker:** You know what a speaker is, right?

✔ **LCD Monitor:** Slightly to the left side and under the viewfinder is, of course, the large LCD monitor.

Looking at the Top

Depending on the camera, you might have a few or a lot of controls on the top. The Nikon D300S, shown in Figure 2-5, has a lot: an LCD control panel, ISO button, white balance button, image quality button, drive mode wheel, shutter release button, exposure mode button, and more. Other cameras have a power button, mode dial, flash, and shutter button.

If your camera has a simple top, you don't need to practice using it much. You can pretty much work it by touch. For a camera like the D300S, practice with how you want to work the buttons and wheels until your fingers know where things are.

Figure 2-5 shows the top of the D300S.

Here's a breakout of the top-left side of the D300S:

Camera strap eyelet

Lock release

Quality   Pop-up flash

Shutter release

Power

Mode   Exposure compensation

ISO   Hot shoe

Release mode dial

White balance

Control panel

Camera strap eyelet

Figure 2-5: Looking down.

✔ **Release mode dial:** Some cameras call it drive mode. This dial changes between single-shot and continuous.

✔ **Release mode dial lock release:** It's a name that only an engineer could love. This keeps the release mode dial from accidentally being moved. It reminds me of the Camera Back Lock Lever on my old FE2. I have to pull it out to pop the film rewind crank to open the back of the camera.

✔ **Quality button:** Pressing this and rotating the main command dial sets the photo quality.

For me, this button is wasted because I never change the photo quality. It's like having a COM port (an old transfer method) on the side — useless.

✔ **White balance button:** Pressing this and rotating the main command dial scrolls through different white balance presets. White balance is a control that, ideally, makes white look white in photos by compensating for lighting that has different temperatures. Our eyes and brain perform this task automatically. Aside from Auto, you can select from options such as sunshine, clouds, shade, incandescent, and fluorescent.

Commit to mastering one feature or button on your camera at a time. Look your dSLR over periodically and ask yourself whether you're neglecting anything. You might be, and it might make your photos better if you used it more.

✓ **ISO button:** Pressing this and rotating the main command dial changes the ISO settings. After you set this for a particular shoot, you shouldn't have to mess with it.

Moving to the top-center:

✓ **Pop-up flash unit:** Under that cover in front of the hot shoe is the pop-up flash. It stows nicely out of the way when you aren't using it. Higher-end dSLRs may not have a pop-up flash.

✓ **Hot shoe (or accessory shoe):** Attach external flashes and other accessories such as levels or remote flash triggers.

Speaking of accessories, if only they could find a way to put a cupholder up there for when it's hot and you get thirsty!

Finally, the buttons and switches on the top right get continual use:

✓ **Power switch:** For the Nikon D300S, this switch toggles the camera on or off and illuminates the LCD monitor on the camera's top, making it possible for you to read the settings in the dark. Other cameras have a simpler on-off switch or button.

Sometimes, this switch is on the left. Sometimes, it's on the right. There seems to be no best design practice.

✓ **Shutter-release button:** This is *the* button. Hopefully, it's the most-often-used button on your camera. Press halfway to autofocus and all the way down to take the picture.

When you press the shutter (or shutter-release) button, don't stab at it or you jiggle the camera. Squeeze it like you're pulling a trigger.

✓ **Mode button:** When used with the main command dial, this button changes shooting (or exposure) modes.

The Mode button is an important button. It changes form and position from camera to camera. Lots of cameras have a chunky dial on the top left or right sides with modes printed on top of the dial. Spin the dial to change modes.

Table 2-1 shows main exposure modes you'll find on command dials. If you have a button, you will probably have fewer modes to choose from. At a minimum, you should be able to select from Programmed Auto, Aperture priority, Shutter priority, and Manual modes.

✔ **Exposure compensation button:** This button is another one that uses the main command dial to scroll through options, such as exposure compensation values.

✔ **Control panel:** Nikon likes displaying items on the top LCD monitor. Other cameras put everything on the back side and have no second LCD monitor.

✔ **Eyelets:** The top of the camera also has two camera strap eyelets.

Table 2-1		**Common Mode Dial Settings**
Mode	*Abbreviation*	*Description*
Auto	Auto	Automatic operation. The camera evaluates the exposure and configures the controls to take the best photo.
Program AE	P	Also called Programmed Auto.
Aperture priority	A or Av	Enables you to set a desired aperture and have the camera handle the other exposure elements.
Shutter priority	S or Tv	Similar to Aperture priority, but you set the shutter speed instead of aperture.
Manual	M	You are in charge of setting the camera's controls.
Bulb	B	A special shutter mode that opens the shutter when you press the shutter button and closes it when you release it.
Scene	Graphical icons	Automatic exposure modes where you tell the camera what you're shooting so it knows how best to take the photo. Landscape, portrait, night, and fireworks are examples of scenes.
Movie	Graphical icon	Enter movie mode, if applicable, to shoot videos with your dSLR.

Reviewing from the Bottom Up

You hardly ever see pictures of dSLR bottoms. I am committed to rectifying that problem in this section. (See Figure 2-6.) Despite the fact that there's not much to say about the camera bottom, the features are still important:

✔ **Battery compartment door:** Unlatch the door and pop it up to access the battery chamber. That part is fairly standard. Some cameras have a small catch that keeps the battery from falling out. Press the catch to allow the battery to slide in and out.

✔ **Tripod socket:** Screw the tripod or monopod into this socket. This socket is also where vertical grips (if they're available for your camera model) screw in.

Battery compartment door   Tripod socket

Figure 2-6: The underbelly.

Quick-release plates, which screw into the camera bottom and then mount on the tripod head, are great time-savers. These plates are easier and safer to use than having to literally screw your camera down onto a tripod every time you mount it. I always feel like I'm going to drop it or strangle myself with the strap.

Simply Sides

Every camera has two sides: right and left (naturally). Sides are generally boring. They contain one or more covers and few if any controls.

On the right side is the grip, where your right hand will rest most of the time. Because your right palm covers this side of the camera, there are no controls. Figure 2-7 shows the right side of the D300S, which has these features:

- ✔ **Memory card slot cover:** Most cameras have the card slot and cover on the right side. If yours doesn't (such as some of the new Sony dSLRs), it's on the left side.

- ✔ **I/O (not shown):** Some cameras have input and output connectors in the memory card area. This one doesn't.

For some cameras, the left side is bare. For others (see Figure 2-8), it's more complicated. For the most part, your left hand covers the left side or is under the lens, leaving room for connectors and ports that you don't use when shooting.

Memory card slot cover

Figure 2-7: Memory card access.

- ✔ **Terminal cover:** The D300S has one large, rubberized connector cover that occupies the entire left side of the camera. Beneath it are lots of goodies explained in the next bullet.

- ✔ **Terminals:** The D300S has A/V, HDMI mini-pin, external microphone, DC-in, and USB connectors located in one easily accessible location.

If you're holding the camera, having the cover open and items plugged in is cumbersome. Using a tripod would be a lot easier.

Terminals
(underneath)

Terminal cover

Figure 2-8: Terminal central.

Looking Inside

Your camera also has an inside. The parts you can access are located by using the lens mount.

REMEMBER

The only reason you should have for opening your camera and not immediately putting a lens on is to clean it. Otherwise, leave it closed with a body cap or with a mounted lens and lens cap.

✔ **Mirror:** The mirror, shown in Figure 2-9, is the most obvious feature you see when you remove the lens from your digital SLR. It's in the down position by default. It needs to be down to bounce light up and out the viewfinder and into your eye.

Don't touch the mirror, or you might smudge, scratch, or otherwise damage the mirror and make it hard or impossible to see out the viewfinder. That's going to make it harder to sell on eBay. If you damage the mirror, you may not be able to look through the viewfinder and take pictures with your camera.

✔ **Pentaprism:** Inside, beneath the flash and above the mirror and sensor, is the *pentaprism*, a 5-sided reflector (see Figure 2-10). This reflecting mirror redirects light coming into the camera (bounced up to it by the mirror) out the viewfinder in the back.

Don't touch the pentaprism, or you might damage or smudge it, just like the mirror. A smudged or scratched pentaprism might not affect your ability to take photos, but it will make it harder to use the viewfinder.

✔ **Digital sensor:** This is your "film". The sensor (see Figure 2-11) captures the light, records the intensity, and sends the data to be processed. Sensors can get dusty and occasionally need cleaning. For that task, see Chapter 5 of this minibook.

Don't touch the sensor with anything other than a brush or another cleaning device (swab) specifically intended for the precise purpose of cleaning a digital SLR sensor.

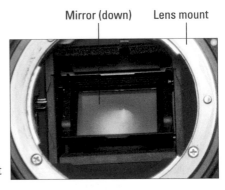

Mirror (down)   Lens mount

Figure 2-9: The mirror is one defining element of an SLR.

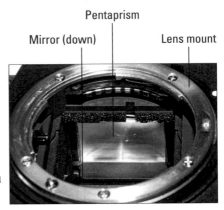

Pentaprism

Mirror (down)   Lens mount

Figure 2-10: The pentaprism is behind the viewfinder.

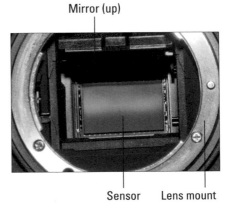

Mirror (up)

Sensor   Lens mount

Figure 2-11: Sensor, sensor, on the wall. . . .

Looking at Lenses

This section takes a quick look at a lens. Although it's a separate component, you should be as familiar with it as you are with your camera body.

Depending on the lens you have, it might have these parts (see Figures 2-12 through 2-14 for reference):

- **Front glass:** Light enters here. Most lenses mount screw-in filters at the front. Filter size is measured in millimeters. Most lenses come with a detachable lens hood, which usually rotates on with a quarter- or half-turn. On some lenses, filters go toward the rear and are dropped in with special trays.

  Keep the front glass clean and covered, as I describe in Chapter 5 of this minibook.

- **Lens hood:** This blocks stray light from entering the lens, but may cause *vignetting* (when the corners of the photo looks darker than the center).

- **Focus ring:** Use this ring to focus manually.

- **Zoom ring:** On zoom cameras, the zoom ring changes the focal length, allowing you to zoom in and out. Depending on the lens, the zoom ring may be larger than the focus ring.

- **Aperture ring:** Older lenses (some newer, but it's becoming rare) have an aperture ring on the lens. Newer, computerized lenses forego it — you have to set the aperture in-camera.

- **Mount:** The rear of the lens is the mount, which locks into the camera. Keep the rear cover on lenses when not in use.

Lens hood

Focus ring   Front glass

Figure 2-12: The front of a lens.

Distance and DOF scale

Filter threads

Front glass   Focus ring

Aperture ring

Figure 2-13: An older lens with older parts — but still quite functional.

✔ **CPU contacts:** These little gizmos send computerized data to the camera from the lens.

CPU contacts are critical to modern lenses. Don't bend them, break them, or otherwise mess with them. Keep them covered.

✔ **Distance or depth-of-field scale:** A scale that shows you the focal plane distance and sometimes the depth of field. Though this feature is handy at times, it's becoming less so with digital SLRs.

✔ **Switches:** You may see switches that switch from manual to autofocus, limit or expand the focus range, or switch on vibration reduction.

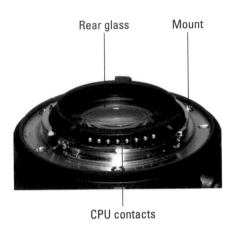

Figure 2-14: The rear of a lens.

Chapter 3: Menus and Settings Extravaganzapalooza

In This Chapter

- The menu system
- A long list of basic menu settings
- A shorter list of advanced menu options

Hidden beneath a maze of menus and tabs lurks your camera's brain. You have the power to change it, mold it, program it. It's there to help you, but you have to figure out how to use it.

Use your menu system and the options within it to customize your camera and use anything other than the default values. In other words, you deny yourself a truckload of ways to make the camera work for you in the specific situation you're in and in the precise manner you choose if you ignore the menu.

It's the truckload part that gets people.

This area is another one where people get scared about dSLRs. The plethora of menus and options intimidated *me* for a long time. I want to break that mystique and show you that you can use these menus to make your camera part of the team.

Perusing the Menu

You can't be a digital photographer without knowing how to work at least some of your camera's system software. You have to know some tricks to get into it, though:

- **Access system software:** Your camera should have a Menu button on its back side. Figure 3-1 shows the similarity in placement between the Nikon D300S and the Sony Alpha 300. Notice the other buttons running down the side of each camera and their differences.

    Press the Menu button to activate the menu system, which is displayed on the camera's LCD monitor.

✔ **Skim your way through menus:**
Spelunking menus quickly takes
some practice. Not only do you
have to know where you're going,
but you also have to be able to
work the controls. These controls
are similar among cameras across
the spectrum of manufacturers.
Broken down by function, they're
described in this list:

Nikon D300S

• *Navigate:* Look at the four
arrow buttons or a circular
controller, shown in Figure 3-2,
on your camera where your
right thumb rests. You use the
buttons to navigate up and
down or left and right in menus
and settings.

Not all navigation controllers
look identical. Some cameras
have separate arrow keys (the
Canon EOS Rebel T1i or both
Pentax dSLR models, for example). Other cameras, such as
the Canon EOS 7D or the Nikon
D300S, integrate them into a
round dial that you press in any
of the four directions. Other
cameras, such as the Sony
Alpha 900 and 850, have
buttons that act like little
joysticks.

Sony Alpha 300

Figure 3-1: The Menu button is usually well
labeled.

Navigation controllers are also named differently. A few sample
names are arrow keys, multiselector, four-way controller, Quick
Control Dial, arrow pad, and cross keys.

• *Select:* After you navigate to where you want to be, you have to be
able to make selections or choices. To do that, you either press
a button in the center of the arrow keys or press the round
multiselector-type button in the center.

On the Canon EOS 7D, this button is named Set. It's right in the
middle of the Quick Control Dial. On Olympus cameras, it's labeled
OK. Nikon calls it a Center button. You get the idea.

Center button

Controller

Figure 3-2: The Nikon multiselector is a good example of a navigation controller.

- *Cancel:* Most times, you press the Menu button to cancel an operation. You may also be able to press the shutter release button halfway to kick yourself out of the menu system.

- *Additional controls:* You may also need to turn other dials or press other buttons to navigate and make selections. Check your camera's documentation to see whether this is the case. For example, some Canon models use the Main Dial to move between tabs in the menu system, and the Nikon D300S has an OK button that's separate from the Control button.

  Sony dSLRs also have a Function (Fn) button. See Figure 3-3, and check out the controller as well. It accesses exposure-related items, such as ISO, white balance, and flash settings when the camera is in Shooting mode, and it accesses review functions when it's in Viewing mode.

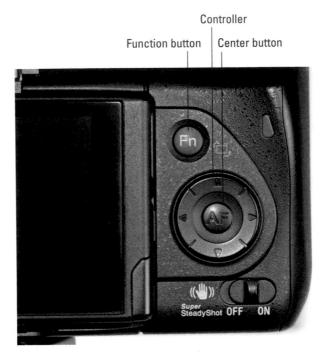

Figure 3-3: The Sony Fn button is quite functional.

Configuring Common Features

The features I describe in this section are common to most digital SLRs. Some, such as the ones that set the date and time, should be set when you turn the camera on for the first time. Others can be set at your leisure, or whenever you know enough about how things work to realize that you want a setting changed from the default.

I grouped each major settings category into a separate heading. Although differences will undoubtedly occur, you usually find many of the same divisions reflected in your camera's menu tab system.

Befriend your manual

I use the menu system from the Nikon D300S to show you examples of different menu types and possible option locations. I can do this because a great deal of similarity occurs across digital SLRs, even those manufactured by different companies. After all, Setup is Setup, whether you're from Canon, Nikon, Olympus, Pentax, Sigma, Sony, or another company.

However, unless you have a D300S, prepare for your menu to look and be organized somewhat differently.

My point in illustrating this chapter with photos of the Nikon D300S menu system is to familiarize you with how menus look and work — not to provide a model-specific tutorial.

Please read your manual carefully for information about *your* particular camera.

Basic setup

You need to set up some basic options to get your camera running. Figure 3-4 shows a full-featured Setup menu from the Nikon D300S. Notice that the icon is a little wrench (or a *spanner,* if you're from Great Britain).

Some options, like the date and time, need to be set only once. You use others, such as formatting the memory card, more frequently. Here are some typical Setup menu options:

Figure 3-4: Setting things up.

✔ **Date and time:** Set the date and time so that all your photos have the correct date and time imprinted in their EXIF data. Some cameras pop up the date and time screen the first time you turn it on.

Notice that you can set the time zone on the D300. Check to see whether you can, too — but remember to change it if you travel.

✔ **Language:** No, your camera can't speak to you (not yet, anyway — although if Apple made a dSLR, it probably would). Specifying the language makes it possible to read all the menus.

✔ **Memory card format:** This option erases all data on the memory card. Some cameras toss only the file structure and don't reinitialize the card (reinitializing is similar to formatting a hard drive on your computer). If this is the case, you may be able to rescue lost files before you overwrite them. (On other cameras, the files truly disappear when you format the cards.)

Be sure to reformat the card on a computer, not on a camera, if you ever sell it or give it away, to protect yourself and your privacy.

I always format my cards in the camera after I download the photos to my computer. This trick produces a clean slate, created by the system that will store my photos.

✓ **File naming and numbering:** This setting determines the scheme the camera uses to name your files. The camera counts every photo you take, from 0001 to 9999, and appends the number to a preset base filename. You can sometimes change to a different base name and alter the camera's behavior when it starts over on the renumbering.

Let image management programs take care of naming files for you. I used to obsess over filenames, but now I ignore them, as long as they work.

✓ **File structure (folders):** Some cameras let you change the way folders are named on the memory card from a standard form (sequential numbering) to a date form (based on the date you take the first photo in the folder).

✓ **LCD brightness and color:** You may have the option to dim or brighten your LCD monitor, such as when you're outdoors and need to better see the monitor. Dim the beast if you're taking photos at night or somewhere in low light where a superbright LCD monitor might be distracting to you or other people. Lowering the brightness of the LCD also decreases battery drain.

You can change the color of some LCDs.

✓ **Cleaning:** In some cases, you can activate the camera's self-cleaning mode — which may include shaking the mirror and automatically cleaning the sensor (or the filters on top of the sensor). In other cases, the mirror shakes and locks up for you to blow dust out or clean the sensor yourself. You may have the option to choose either method from the menu.

Don't confuse Manual cleaning mode with mirror lockup (Nikon names it Mirror Up mode), which delays the photo more than normal after the mirror flips up to reduce camera shake from the mirror movement.

✓ **Auto rotate (camera orientation):** This setting records the camera's orientation when you take the picture and stores the information in the EXIF information. When you review the photo or open it in "smart" software (photo management or editing software that looks at the orientation information in the file to correctly display it), the picture is automatically rotated to its correct orientation.

The auto rotate option prevents you from having to turn the camera every time you review a portrait-oriented photo. It makes the photo smaller-looking, though.

✔ **Video system:** Let the camera know what type of television, VCR, or other video device you might connect it to so that you can review photos.

✔ **Grid:** The grid in the viewfinder or on the LCD monitor is turned on or off. In some cases, you may be able to customize the grid by having more or fewer lines.

> Keep your camera's grid turned on to help keep elements level within the viewfinder and to better frame the shot.

> Some cameras (such as the D300S) have a virtual horizon that acts like a level so that you can keep the camera level. When enabled from the menu system, the horizon is displayed on the LCD monitor

✔ **Auto power off:** Set this option to automatically turn off the power and save batteries if you leave the camera unattended or forget to turn it off.

✔ **Battery information:** On some cameras, you have to identify a battery type. On others, this settings displays only how much battery life remains.

✔ **Revert to default settings:** Having the option to automatically change all menus (or a good percentage of them — see your manual for details) to their factory default settings is helpful because it ensures that you can restore the standard camera setup if you change a setting and cannot later recall its original values. This option frees you to be wildly creative and experiment with your camera and not be afraid that you can never return it to its normal condition.

Basic recording and shooting

Your camera's basic recording and shooting settings control how your digital SLR saves photos, and the settings may contain other photo- and exposure-related items. Figure 3-5 shows the Shooting menu from the D300S. The highlighted icon in the left menu column represents a dSLR. Select this icon (or the ones above and below it) to change menu tabs. The scrollbar on the right side of the menu system tells you where you are — up or down — as you review the individual options within a menu tab. You often have to scroll more than one page of details.

Figure 3-5: Configuring shooting options.

The following important settings affect photo size, quality, and type.

✔ **Image size and quality:** Choosing the size and quality of your pictures is an important part of shooting. Normally, JPEGs are available in three or four sizes (small, medium, large, and possibly extra large) and three qualities (low, medium, and high). Because smaller photos taken at low quality have fewer pixels and are more compressed than high-quality JPEG files, you can fit more photos on your card.

Choose raw or RAW+JPEG options from this menu. Choosing RAW+JPEG normally sets the JPEG size and quality to large and high, respectively. Check to make sure that this is true for you. You may be able to select a lower-quality JPEG, even when shooting raw.

To gain flexibility, try shooting in RAW+JPEG format, a camera setting that stores every photo in both raw and JPEG formats. You can then use the JPEG if it looks good (and can quickly preview it or immediately send or post it) or use the raw photo and process it yourself.

Some cameras separate image size from quality.

This setting in the menu system, if it even exists, varies widely depending on your camera. For example, you access photo quality and size options on the D300S and other Nikon cameras by using the QUAL button, in conjunction with the Main or Sub-command dial. However, because many other cameras put photo quality in their menu systems, this seemed like as good a place as any to discuss it.

✔ **Review time:** Specify the number of seconds a photo appears on the LCD monitor immediately after you shoot.

If you're shooting in Live view, reviewing eliminates your ability to frame and shoot. Similarly, long review times are a hassle if you look at the camera back for exposure information.

If you find the length of the review distracting, decrease the display time or set your camera to continue shooting and not stop to review. When I use my Sony Alpha 300 in Live view mode and want to continue framing and shooting quickly, a photo review always slows me down. Even when I'm using the viewfinder, I use the LCD monitor to review exposure and camera settings when I have the camera mounted on a tripod. When a photo is being displayed on the monitor, the exposure settings and Live view disappear.

✔ **Red-eye control:** Enabling red-eye reduction is sometimes part of the flash menu.

✔ **Color space:** Specify the color profile assigned to JPEGs file. Raw images *do not have* a color profile — it's assigned by the raw processor when you convert it to TIFF or JPEG format.

You should have these two color space options in your menu system to choose from:

- *sRGB:* Ultra compatible but has a smaller color space. It limits the number of colors that can be displayed.

- *Adobe RGB:* Has a larger color space but is less compatible with programs such as Web browsers. Most image editors support this option.

Use AdobeRGB unless you're going directly to the Web with a photo When I save a final file for the Web, I convert the color space to the more compatible sRGB format.

✏ **Picture style:** This option specifies how the camera processes JPEGs from the image data. You normally have Standard, Portrait, Landscape, Vivid, Neutral, and Monochrome choices. Depending on the camera, you may have more or fewer choices.

This setting doesn't affect raw photos. It's like you're providing guidance to the camera about how to convert the raw data to a JPEG.

If you aren't saving raw exposures, *be careful:* When you apply a picture style after the JPEG is saved, you cannot undo the change. Test the settings you like with test photos — not the ones you want to keep.

✏ **Dustoff:** Depending on the camera, this option may be named Image Dust Off Reference Photo or Delete Dust Data or a similar name. Your sensor's dust information (where the little dust bunnies are stuck to the sensor) is recorded by taking a photo of a light, featureless object to enable camera raw software to automatically remove it during processing.

If you use a dust reference photo with your camera's raw software, your mileage may vary. I prefer using the Photoshop Clone Stamp or Spot Healing Brush (or similar tools, depending on my software) to remove obnoxious dust myself. (Chapters 2 and 3 of Book VI describe my manual dust-removal technique.) I can often detect where the automatic dust-removal process tried to cover a dust spot but didn't match the surrounding texture or tone as accurately as a human could have.

I performed an outdoor test with a new reference photo and applied it to a featureless photo of a piece of paper. My Nikon Capture NX 2 found *some* of the dust and removed it.

Some photographers report that automatic sensor cleaning invalidates the reference photo (which is especially irritating to them when they have the camera set to clean the sensor every time it's turned on). It's good practice to take another reference shot every time you clean the sensor. After all, some or all of the original dust is surely gone.

✔ **No card:** This option, which might be named Release Shutter without Card, determines the camera's behavior if it has no memory card. I wonder why any camera will let you take a photo when you're not "locked and loaded," but they do (probably so retailers can demonstrate camera settings without loading a card).

Always leave the No Card setting turned on so that you don't mistakenly believe that you've taken 100 outstanding photos and then find nothing there.

✔ **Dynamic range:** The dynamic range tries to protect you from blowing out highlights and losing details in shadow — not a bad deal, but not a free lunch, either. You may lose detail in certain tonal ranges, depending on what the camera has to do to enhance or protect shadows or highlights. You can do the same thing yourself, and enjoy total control over the process, when you process raw exposures and, to a limited degree, edit JPEGs.

✔ **Noise reduction:** You can toggle two types of noise reduction: high ISO and long shutter speed. The camera automatically processes the photo when you take it according to the type of noise reduction it has and the settings you've chosen.

The noise reduction setting can be frustrating. Every time I shot a thunderstorm, I had to wait a minute to take another one because the camera was performing noise reduction: It takes a "dark image," one with the shutter closed, and subtracts the data in that photo (which is noise) from the photo you just took.

✔ **Auto ISO:** You can give the camera permission to raise the ISO, if necessary, to set the proper exposure.

Use the Auto ISO carefully, or else you'll take ISO 1600 photos when you would rather snap on the flash. Some cameras limit how much ISO can be raised or allow you to set the parameters.

✔ **Aspect ratio (normal/wide):** Some cameras offer to crop photos to a high-def aspect ratio of 16:9 for you. Be wary of this option. You aren't getting more photo — you're getting *less*.

You can always do this yourself in software and decide at that point what to keep and what to cut. If you don't have the time, this option is truly helpful.

✔ **Live view:** The Live view settings, if applicable, control whether and how long to display the grid, autofocus modes, and exposure information.

You may need to turn Live view on and off from the menu. Other cameras have a handy button somewhere on their bodies.

✔ **Multiple exposure:** When you use multiple exposure mode, you can take two or more photos and have the camera "expose" the same frame with each new shot. It's a neat special effect.

✔ **Timer settings:** Sets the self-timer, if you have one, and configures it.

Basic playback

The menu items I describe in this section control how photos are played back, or reviewed. You often have many options to mange. Figure 3-6 shows the D300S Playback menu.

Figure 3-6: Playback options.

✓ **Protect images:** Use this option if you review your photos and want to protect them from accidental deletion (but not from reformatting).

If you're like me, and you *never* delete photos from your card while it's in the camera, this option is somewhat superfluous.

✓ **Rotate:** Automatically rotate photos during playback that were taken vertically (in portrait orientation).

✓ **Erase:** Delete a photo. (Be careful!)

✓ **Print order:** Identify exposures to print on a compatible PictBridge printer and many photo finishing kiosks (and in which order) by setting the Digital Print Order Format (DPOF) options.

The more you look into the print order, the more interesting it is. If you need to print the contents of an entire memory card, it can be a true timesaver. Depending on your camera, you can "imprint" on each photo (print on top of the photo) the shutter speed, aperture, file number, and date the photo was taken.

✓ **Transfer options:** Canon EOS Rebel users can customize photo transfer options when downloading photos from the camera to a computer, such as new images or those you have selected.

✓ **Histogram:** Turn on the histogram (this graph indicates how brightness is distributed between dark and light in the photo) when reviewing a photo on the LCD monitor. This option is helpful in analyzing whether you have the correct exposure.

Other settings

A few settings don't fit easily into other categories. They may be located on their own menu tab on your camera or integrated into another one:

✓ **Movie:** These menu items control movie settings, such as autofocus, movie size, and sound input. If your camera can't shoot movies, you don't have this one.

✔ **Retouch:** Some cameras let you retouch photos on the memory card. You can find those settings on the Retouch menu.

✔ **Shooting profiles:** More advanced cameras let you create, save, and load different shooting profiles with different settings. For example, you may have one optimized for portraits, one for HDR, and another for casual photography with your general-purpose zoom lens.

Custom Settings

A number of other, more advanced menu options are available to most digital SLRs. I describe several general items to acclimatize you to what you might expect. Spend some time reading your manual to receive camera-specific instructions.

Figure 3-7 shows the plethora of custom options in the D300S. Each menu item opens the settings for that submenu. As you scroll the list, you transition seamlessly to the next menu.

Figure 3-7: Lots of custom settings are possible here.

These options are divided (in the case of the D300S) into several categories:

✔ **Autofocus:** This custom setting lets you tweak and customize camera autofocus routines. For example, you can change whether the camera can take a photo when it's out of focus, change the dynamic autofocus area, specify when autofocus activates, and determine whether the autofocus point is illuminated in the viewfinder.

Figure 3-8 shows some of the Nikon D300S Autofocus options. These settings test your knowledge of photography and your camera.

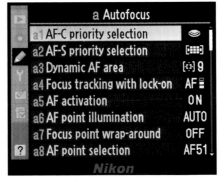

Figure 3-8: You wouldn't think that so many autofocus possibilities would exist.

✔ **Metering/exposure:** These settings can be critical. Often, you set the ISO sensitivity here, in fractions of a stop of exposure (sometimes called *steps*), EV steps for exposure control, fine-tuning exposure compensation, changing the diameter of the center-weighted area when using center-weighted metering, fine-tuning exposure, and more.

You often have the ability to fine-tune the way your camera sets exposure. Take advantage of these advanced settings to customize the way you like to work.

Figure 3-9 shows how to customize exposure and metering in the Nikon D300S.

✔ **Timers/AE lock:** Control timers and AE lock behavior. In this case, you have only four options (labeled c1 through c4 in Figures 3-9 and 3-10). It's one of the smaller submenus.

✔ **Shooting/display:** These extensive settings let you customize shooting and display properties, such as beeping, turning on the viewfinder grid or screen tips, choosing a maximum frame rate or the maximum number of continuous shots, specifying when to reset the file number sequence, setting the exposure delay mode and batter information, and more.

✔ **Bracketing/flash:** This menu contains bracketing and flash settings. Figure 3-12 shows the D300S Bracketing/flash menu.

The AEB, or auto exposure bracketing, feature on most digital SLRs shifts the exposure for a series of shots, enabling you to "bracket" the scene. You can use it for high dynamic range (HDR) photography or in situations where you want a single exposure and aren't sure that the exposure meter is nailing the right settings. In that case, you take several exposures and choose the best one. With HDR, you combine them all and tone map the HDR image.

For more information on HDR photography, consult Book VI, Chapter 4.

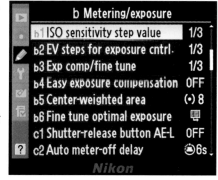

Figure 3-9: These settings enable you to customize metering and exposure.

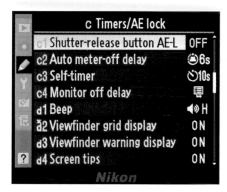

Figure 3-10: Setting timer and AE lock options.

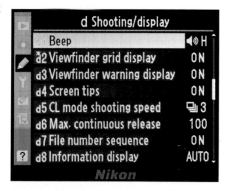

Figure 3-11: This menu helps you customize shooting and display properties.

Controlling your flash is vital in flash photography. Don't neglect these menu options because they intimidate you. Read them carefully and slowly. Don't rush it.

For more information on flash photography, turn to Book IV.

✔ **Controls:** Customize some of your camera's buttons and dials, which is handy at times.

Be kind to other people's cameras. If you customize their controls, "decustomize" them when you're done shooting. Ensure that you know (or that the camera knows) the factory setup and can revert to the original settings if you experiment with a custom control and decide that you don't like it.

Figure 3-13 shows server options to customize the D300S controls.

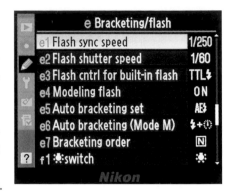

Figure 3-12: Flash and bracketing details.

Figure 3-13: The height of customizability: programming buttons to do what you want.

Chapter 4: Say Cheese: Taking Pictures with Your dSLR

In This Chapter

⟋ **Reviewing your before you-leave-home checklist**

⟋ **Starting out on a good foot**

⟋ **Preparing your camera**

⟋ **Taking pictures**

⟋ **Modifying the checklist**

*I*n many ways, this chapter is the most important one in this book. In it, you put it all together and take photos with your digital SLR camera.

Don't hesitate to flip back and forth among chapters and minibooks to find more details about certain subjects, such as lenses, composition, and HDR. That's the beauty of books in the *For Dummies* series: They're nonsequential reference books.

Fortunately, I'm a nonsequential author.

Checklists are great argument-starters — everyone has an opinion. Feel free to argue and quibble over this chapter. It stimulates your thinking. My purpose isn't to "straitjacket" you into a set of rules you don't want to follow. I give you a sense of what you need to take care of when you're shooting photos. It can be complicated, and there are a lot of things to forget.

I've organized this chapter into four main checklists. Each of these sections is a subset of a larger checklist:

1. **Plan ahead:** Find out what to do to prepare so that when you're out on location, you have what you need.

2. **Set up:** Unpack and prepare to take pictures.

3. **Fine-tune the camera:** Make sure that all your camera settings are dialed in where you want them to be, and then tailor your camera for the scene and purpose at hand.

4. **Take photos:** Get to the nitty-gritty of setting exposure, framing, and shooting photos.

It's about what you want

If you would rather put your digital SLR on autofocus and work in Autoexposure mode, good on ya! Then you can concentrate on content and framing. Much can be said for the "point and shoot" philosophy, even if you fancy yourself an advanced photographer.

If you want to go 100 percent manual, focus with your fingers, and work your camera "old-school" style, that's fantastic. You're in charge, so make it happen.

If you want to split the difference, there's no problem with that method, either. Learn a little bit at a time. Incorporate what you like into your routine and make it your own.

Unless you're taking a photography class and your instructor has certain skills that you're expected to master to pass the test, you don't have to do anything you don't want to.

These scenarios point out the brilliance of digital SLRs. They have something for just about everyone. As you read through this chapter, remember to customize the lists to suit how you want to work with your camera.

Within each section, I created (geek alert) subchecklists that have their own numbering. At times, you can customize the specific order of tasks I recommend to suit the way you want to work. For example, I suggest turning on your camera before removing its lens cap. If you want, you can remove the lens cap before turning on the camera. At other times, the order of steps is quite important. For example, you should compose the photo before pressing the shutter release button.

Step 1: Plan Ahead

To save yourself loads of time and potential frustration when you go out to take photos, make sure that you have all these items before you leave your house:

- **Batteries:** Charge your camera's battery the day or night before you leave. (If you leave charged batteries lying around, they slowly discharge.) I have at least two camera batteries for all my dSLRs. That way, I always have a fresh battery in the bag in addition to the one in my camera. If the in-camera battery is low the day before a big shoot, I recharge it so that I have two fully charged batteries.

- **Memory cards:** Download photos first and then format the card to wipe it clean.

    Formatting erases photos. Make sure that you first download photos *to your computer.*

✓ **Lenses and filters:** Clean lenses and filters before packing them (see Chapter 5 for more information). As long as you don't stick your finger on the glass, you should only need to dust them off when you're on location.

✓ **Sensor:** If necessary, clean your camera's sensor (see Chapter 5 for more information). You may also want to take a dust registration shot.

✓ **Basic camera options:** Make sure that the day and time are correct. Ensure that fundamental options are set, such as the file format you want to use, filenaming conventions, photo quality, auto ISO, and review time.

Some people use a checklist to return all camera settings to their defaults, or to return to a personal default. If that's you, take notes of your favorite settings and return them to their proper position now.

✓ **Camera bag:** Pack and check contents to make sure that you have all the items you need. For me, they're normally a lens cleaning pen and cloth, reading glasses, a remote shutter release, filters, a level, the lenses I want to use, extra memory cards, extra batteries, my cellphone, and WhiBal, my white balance tool. (You use this tool, a type of gray card that you take a photo of, during processing on location to set the black-and-white points in your photos.)

Attach to the camera body the lens you plan to use now. That's one way to minimize the amount of dust and debris that can get into your camera on location. If the lens doesn't fit in your bag, don't put it on the camera. Rather, put a body cover on the camera and carry the lens in another compartment or in a separate carrying case.

I occasionally pack bug spray, kneepads, a level, a pan head for my tripod (I use a ball head predominantly), alternative dSLRs and lenses, and a few compact digital cameras to take comparison shots. (After I load all my tools, I usually need a pack mule.)

Step 2: Set Up

When you have your gear and you're on the scene, follow these steps to prepare yourself to take pictures with your dSLR:

1. **Unpack your camera.**

   Yes, taking photos while your camera is still in the bag is quite difficult.

   Don't unpack everything and spread it around on the ground. Wait until you need something to take it out of the bag.

2. **Attach or swap the lens.**

   Either attach your lens now or swap out the lens you have mounted for the one you want to use.

Don't forget to keep track of the rear lens cap. See Step 4 in this list for pointers on cap tracking.

3. **Power-up your camera (see Figure 4-1).**

4. **Remove the lens cap.**

   Be consistent. Pick a place to store your lens cap when it's unattached, and don't change the location. You don't lose many lens caps this way, and you can more quickly reattach it.

Figure 4-1: Must have pow-ah.

5. **Attach an external flash, if necessary, and turn it on (see Figure 4-2).**

   For the most part, you don't need to complete this step if you're shooting objects such as landscapes or sunsets. For other shots (portraits, still life, casual photography indoors), this step is critically important.

Figure 4-2: External flash. Check!

6. **(Optional) Attach the remote shutter release.**

   Keep the cord out of the way unless it's a wireless remote.

7. **Cross-check and prepare for departure.**

   Make sure your tray tables are stowed and your seat is in the upright and locked position. Then prepare the camera to make exposure decisions, and shoot some pictures.

   Quickly run through this list to make sure that your camera is working and set up properly:

   - *Power:* Make sure that your camera and its flash are turned on.

   - *Physical damage:* If you haven't inspected your camera, lens, and flash for physical damage, do so now.

   - *Battery level:* Quickly note the battery level to make sure you didn't accidentally load a bad battery. Replace it, if necessary.

   - *Exposures remaining:* Look to see whether you're starting out with an empty memory card (like you should be). If not, you might swap out or format the card, if you know that you downloaded the photos.

- *Knobs and buttons:* Make sure that all knobs and switches are set to their default settings (even if they're *your* defaults). For example, my Sony has a Super SteadyShot switch that sometimes gets switched off. I check for it in this step. Other cameras have vibration reduction built into the lens.

- *Lenses:* Speaking of which, check any switches on the lens. Typical switches include manual versus autofocus, focus range, macro, vibration reduction, and others.

Step 3: Fine-Tune the Camera

After all the items you need for a shoot are put together and working, it's time to get down to some serious photography business. (Don't worry: It's fun, too!)

This section of the checklist gets your camera ready to shoot. You're making decisions in light of your location, the environment, your creative goals, and your subject:

To fine-tune your camera and prepare to shoot, follow these steps:

1. **Choose a view.**

   Enter Live view mode or switch out of it to use the optical viewfinder.

   - *Live view:* If you prefer to frame and compose shots using the LCD monitor, switch to Live view now, if possible. You may need to access your camera's menu, press a button, or move a switch. If you have an articulated LCD monitor, swing it out to an appropriate position.

   Not all Live views work the same way. Some, like the Nikon D300S, have tripod and handheld submodes. Each uses a different autofocusing method. In the case of a tripod, the camera uses contrast detection. In Handheld mode, the camera focuses normally with phase detection. Tripod mode is slower but lets you precisely zoom in and focus.

   Not all cameras have Live view.

   Look in your camera's menu system (see Chapter 3 for more information on menus) for Live view settings.

   - *Viewfinder:* In this classic method, using the optical viewfinder is generally the best way to compose and take photos. However, you can't always crane your neck up to or down to see through it. Focusing manually and precisely (or checking the autofocus) is also difficult. In these situations, Live view is a helpful alternative.

Figure 4-3 illustrates the viewfinder on the Nikon D300S. It's quite nice to look through because of its size and brightness.

My Nikon D200 has no Live view. My Sony Alpha 300 does, and I take advantage of it. I find that the best place to use it is indoors, especially when I'm taking pictures of children and events such as birthday parties. Because I have a greater situational awareness of what's

Figure 4-3: Find your view through this thing.

going on around me when my head isn't attached to the camera, I can generally avoid tripping over obstacles. I also get an indication of where to point the camera.

Outdoors, the situation is reversed. I use the viewfinder almost all the time. It doesn't wash out, and I can better concentrate on framing the subject at hand.

2. **Specify the flash operation.**

For more information on setting up and using a pop-up flash, or using a flash, please refer to Book IV. I'll wait for you here.

If you want to use the pop-up flash, pop it up now.

Some cameras pop up the flash automatically when you meter, and the camera needs more light to create the right exposure.

Set the flash type you want to use: for example, slow sync, red-eye reduction, or rear-curtain sync. Use your experience as a guide, or take a few test shots and compare. I've been experimenting with slow sync and loving it.

Don't forget about using flash compensation or controlling the flash's output manually in certain situations.

3. **Set the drive mode.**

Set the drive mode to match the type of shooting you're doing:

- *Single shot:* You take one shot at a time (also known as *single-frame* shooting).

    Use this deliberate mode whenever you want to avoid inadvertently shooting extra pictures because you released the shutter button or the remote too slowly.

- *Low-speed continuous:* In this mode, which is a little easier to control than high-speed continuous, the camera shoots as long as you hold the shutter button down, but it doesn't get quite out of hand. In other words, it shoots continuously but at a fairly leisurely pace. Good when you want to make sure and capture fleeting moments but aren't photographing professional athletes.

- *High-speed continuous:* Faster is better! In this mode, photos fire in rapid succession as long as you hold down the shutter button. To take a single photo (if you're manually bracketing a scene for HDR, for example), be sure to exit this drive mode. I use it when taking photos of my kids in action or when shooting AEB brackets for HDR.

Not all cameras have two continuous shooting modes, and some (Olympus dLSRs, for example) refer to Continuous mode as Sequential mode.

4. **Choose a focus mode.**

   Most people prefer to autofocus, which is fine in many situations. It's reliable and takes the workload and sometimes stress of having to focus off your shoulders. If you need to switch to Manual mode, now is a good time.

   This list describes when to use each focusing mode:

   - *Manual:* Use this mode whenever the autofocus system wants to lock on intervening objects, and you have no time to switch a microscopic focus point in the viewfinder to the proper spot in a rapidly changing scene. Manual focus is also helpful for shooting landscapes and still lifes.

   - *Auto:* Use this mode the rest of the time. Whenever it works, I use Auto.

     Autofocus can have several submodes, generally optimized to shoot either still or moving subjects. Choose one.

     For example, my Nikon D200 has two autofocus modes. In *single-servo AF,* the camera focuses once whenever you press the shutter release button halfway. If I want to refine the focus, I have to do so manually or release the shutter button and press it halfway again to start over.

     In *continuous-servo AF,* the camera focuses continuously whenever you press the shutter release button halfway. Use this mode to track moving subjects because the camera attempts to keep them in focus as long as you have the shutter button pressed halfway.

     (If you see the term *servo,* it refers to the servomechanism, which is a small motor that focuses the lens. Autofocus servo modes, therefore, tell you how the motor will work.)

The Nikon D200 also has four AF-area modes to choose from (yours may vary):

Single-area AF: Select a focus area by using the controls on the back of the camera. It works well for still lifes and landscapes but not in dynamic situations such as sports, other action photography, or children running around.

Dynamic-area AF: You select an area manually, but the camera tracks the subject and adjusts the focus accordingly (similar to locking in on an enemy plane).

Group-dynamic AF: You choose a group of autofocus points rather than a single one. The camera senses whether the subject moves from one focus area to another within a group and changes focus, if necessary.

Dynamic-area AF with closet subject priority: The camera essentially focuses on the object closest to the camera and then tracks the object and adjusts the focus accordingly. (As you can see, at this point the situation can sometimes become complicated.)

Figure 4-4 shows the focus mode selector switch on the D300S. Notably, it has only three modes versus the four I'm used to on my D200. Hmm.

5. **Set the metering mode.**

Your camera should have at least two metering modes, and possibly three or more.

Figure 4-5 shows the meter mode selector thingy on the D300S. It's the dial around the AE-L/AF-L button. The dial controls metering, and the button controls focus (which always trips me up).

This list describes different metering modes:

- *Pattern, matrix, multipattern, or evaluative metering:* The camera uses its metering sensors to indicate where, across the entire scene, the bright and dark spots are located and then adjusts the exposure

Figure 4-4: This mysterious switch changes autofocus modes.

Figure 4-5: Metering modes on the D300S; 3D Matrix II is selected.

appropriately. I recommend using this mode in most situations. The name of this depends on its manufacturer; the D300S, it's 3D color matrix II; the Canon EOS 7D calls it Evaluative metering.

- *Center-weighted:* The camera meters the entire frame, as it does in pattern metering but weighs the center more heavily. It creates a good balance between spot mode (see the following bullet) and equally evaluating the entire scene.

  Use center-weighted mode whenever a subject is backlit, and you want to prevent the bright background from dominating the camera's evaluation of the exposure and from leaving the subject too dark.

- *Spot:* Spot metering mode is a precise way to read a meter from the center (normally) of the frame.

  Use this mode when you want the best exposure possible for the object at the center of the scene and are less concerned about the rest.

  Spot metering mode is also a good way to evaluate the scene yourself. Switch to this mode and then meter (usually, by pressing the shutter halfway) dark and light areas of the scene. Compare exposures to determine the dynamic range.

- *Other:* Canon, in particular, has another mode to choose from — partial metering. It's similar to spot metering except that the spot is bigger.

For more information on metering and exposure, please refer to Book III, Chapter 1.

6. **Set the white balance.**

   When you look at an object that should be white, your brain "corrects" what you see and tells you that it's white. A camera, on the other hand, doesn't know that the white car in the shadows is white, so it dutifully records an off-white car.

   You must tell the camera about the lighting conditions so that it can identify where white is and correct the colors in the photo.

   You have two main options: Leave white balance on its automatic setting or set it to a preset value. Typical presets are described in this list:

   - *Auto:* You let the camera figure out the conditions. This setting works well outdoors and when you're using a flash, but not so well indoors without a flash.

   - *Direct sun:* Use this white balance setting whenever you're outdoors in the sunlight.

   - *Flash:* When you're using flash, choose this setting.

   - *Cloudy:* Use this setting on cloudy days.

   - *Shade:* The Shade setting is used differently from the Cloudy setting.

   - *Tungsten lights:* Use it when you're indoors, working with normal "old-fashioned" light bulbs with a tungsten filament in them.

- *Fluorescent lighting:* You may have a few options for fluorescent lights. Some cameras break this setting into several categories, based on the type of bulb. For example, the Nikon D300S has Sodium-vapor lamps, Warm-white fluorescent, White fluorescent, Cool-white fluorescent, Day white fluorescent, Daylight fluorescent, and High-temp mercury-vapor.

- *Custom/Set temperature:* Set the color temperature manually, in (geekazoid alert) degrees Kelvin.

- *Others:* Depending on the camera, you may even have more settings to select.

Set the white balance based on where your subject is. If that person is in the shade and you're in the sunlight, set the white balance to shade. For landscapes, set it to the overall conditions (sun or cloudy, for example). For mixed lighting, do your best or leave it on Auto.

You can easily correct white balance as you process raw photos, but the process is more destructive with JPEGs.

7. Set the base ISO.

Try to use the lowest ISO you can get away with, to introduce less noise into your photos and to create better results. I usually work at ISO 100 outdoors (depending on the camera; not all begin at ISO 100) and ISO 400 and higher indoors.

Whenever necessary, set your camera to Auto ISO and specify a maximum ISO for your camera.

Figure 4-6 shows the ISO button on the D300S. You have to push it and dial in an ISO by using the main command dial.

8. Specify or check the AEB.

If you're shooting brackets for HDR or exposure blending or you want to shoot exposure brackets to keep the best photo and ditch the rest, set the number of brackets and the exposure difference now.

Figure 4-6: ISO gets its own, big button.

For more information on HDR, please see Book VI, Chapter 4.

9. Choose a shooting mode.

The decision you make now affects the rest of the checklist. If you choose a more automated mode, you don't have to complete certain tasks, such as setting the exposure controls. On the other hand, if you're more inclined to shoot manually, you'll be *required* to perform them. Not all cameras have all the same shooting modes. These are the types of modes you might encounter:

- *Auto:* The camera evaluates the exposure and sets its controls to match it. This mode is easy to use and most often results in good photos.

   The problem with Auto mode is that the camera knows neither your subject nor your creative intentions. For example, do you need a fast shutter speed because your kids arc running around like crazy? Do you want a shallow or deep depth of field for an artistic or practical purpose?

- *Scene mode:* This mode provides guidance to the camera and answers the questions I just asked. I think that scene modes are better than pure auto modes because you can direct the camera to make intelligent decisions based on the situation. The hassle occurs when you need to switch scenes 15 times in 15 minutes, for example.

- *Programmed auto:* Program mode is a blend of automatic and manual modes. The camera sets the aperture and shutter speed for you but leaves the other controls alone.

   Most cameras have either Program Shift or Flexible Program mode, which lets you choose a combination of shutter speed and aperture that will work for the conditions. Use this mode if you have a particular aperture or shutter speed you want to use to achieve a depth of field (for aperture) or to freeze action (for shutter speed).

   This mode is an easy way of trading shutter speed for aperture without having to mess with them separately. You scroll through different combinations that result in the same exposure.

- *Aperture priority:* You set the aperture, and the camera sets the shutter speed. Figure 4-7 shows the command center of the Nikon D300s in Aperture priority mode.

- *Shutter priority:* You set the shutter speed, and the camera sets the aperture.

- *Manual:* In a total manual override, you set everything yourself.

Figure 4-7: Setting the Aperture priority mode.

In all except Manual mode, you don't need to worry about setting the correct exposure yourself. The camera does it for you. If it cannot reach the correct exposure for some reason (if it can't set the shutter speed fast enough or widen the aperture, for example), it might beep at you to get your attention. Some cameras flash the shutter speed or f/stop display.

10. **Set the mirror to delay (the Mirror Lockup or Mirror Up setting), if you want.**

    This setting reduces camera shake caused by mirror motion by introducing a delay between the time the mirror moves up and out of the way and the time the photo is taken. You don't need this feature unless you're using a tripod or another type of support and want the most stable, shake-free shot possible.

    Don't forget to revert to normal mirror operation when you finish. I've used mirror delay and forgotten about it, and then wondered why a delay occurred between the time I pressed the shutter button and when the camera took the photo the next time I went out. After four or five shots, I usually remember that I left the Mirror Delay setting on.

11. **Mount the camera on your tripod — as shown in Figure 4-8 — no later than now (if you're using a tripod).**

Figure 4-8: Stabilizing the camera.

Going with the flow

You don't have to complete a 57-point checklist before you take every photo. After you set up and begun taking photos, the process goes much faster. For example, exposure settings remain fairly stable as long as you don't change subjects and the lighting conditions don't change dramatically. In addition, after you set the ISO, you can forget about it unless you move from outdoors to indoors.

Problem-solving is the task that slows you down. (It's the truth — I was having a lot of trouble one day shooting indoors with some extra lighting, and my shots-per-minute ratio fell through the floor as I tried to figure out what I was doing wrong.) For example, when you review a photo, and the subject is dark but the background is bright, you have to take the time to figure out what to do — and then do it.

Step 4: Take Photos

Are you ready to take photos? I am! Follow these steps:

1. **Frame the photograph.**

   Compose and frame the shot, including setting the correct focal length if you're using a zoom lens or moving to get the right scene if you're using a prime lens.

   When shooting certain types of shots (animals, people, or everyday items), this step takes a moment. When you're setting up a portrait or shooting macros in a studio, it can take a while.

   If your subject is off center, and you need to center it to spot-meter or focus and activate the focus lock, finalize the frame just before taking the photo. In other words, you can't frame and then meter and then take the photo. You have to "preframe" by centering the subject (and if necessary, focus), and *then* meter (and, if necessary, lock in the autoexposure or change exposure controls manually). Then you can frame to the final composition and take the photo.

2. **Preview the depth of field and adjust the aperture (if necessary).**

   This matter is an artistic or practical one. It has nothing to do with exposure at this point. For example, if your subject is posing for a portrait, and you want to isolate the person by using a wide aperture, previewing the depth of field is an important part of the process.

   Over time, you'll discover a handful of favorite apertures and be able to predict what they'll look like without having to preview them.

3. **Prefocus.**

   If I have time, I like to prefocus (my term), whether I'm focusing manually or using autofocus. Prefocusing focuses the subject in the viewfinder or LCD monitor so that I can see what's going on and make framing corrections, if necessary. I find it harder to compose shots that are out of focus.

   Prefocusing also dials in the lens (it will have less work to do when you achieve the final focus) and alerts me to any potential autofocusing problems.

   If necessary, I change focusing modes or focus points if I'm using autofocus.

   If you want, press the Focus Lock button to lock the focus.

4. **Meter.**

   Press the shutter release button halfway. Some cameras have an AF-ON button that focuses and meters. I use it on my D200 all the time to prefocus and meter so that I don't inadvertently take a picture with the shutter button. (I shoot a lot of HDR using AEB. If I inadvertently take a shot, it means that I have to restart the AEB process after aborting the current bracketing sequence.)

If you're using AF lock or AE lock, continue to press the shutter button halfway and press the AE Lock button.

Figure 4-9 is an illustration of the back of my Sony Alpha 300 in Manual shooting mode. I have just metered, and the exposure is +2.0 EV over nominal. If I want to decrease that number, I need to dial in a faster shutter speed, assuming that I want to retain the f/stop and ISO.

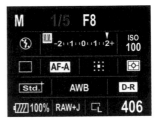

Figure 4-9: The photo will be overexposed with the current settings.

5. **Check the histogram, if possible.**

   Some cameras (I can find only Olympus dSLR models, but you may be able to find more) display a histogram before you take the picture if you're using Live view. Use it to ensure that the exposure looks good and you're not blowing out highlights.

   For more information on histograms, see Chapters 2 and 3 in Book VI.

6. **Check and adjust the exposure if necessary.**

   If you're shooting manually, adjust the exposure by adjusting the shutter speed or aperture or, as a last resort, ISO. (Adjust ISO if it's too low. If it's already high, adjust it as a first resort.) If none of these suggestions works, enable the flash.

7. **Finalize manual focus (if necessary).**

   If you're focusing manually, this is your last chance to get your subject in focus.

   Your camera may be able to help you out, even when you focus manually. For example, Nikon D300S acts like a rangefinder in Manual focus mode as long as the lens has an aperture of f/5.6 or faster. Press the shutter button halfway when focusing to see whether the selected focus point is in focus. (You may have to go back and change the focus point, depending on your subject, or keep it in the middle.) The in-focus indicator in the viewfinder lights up if the focus is good.

8. **Take the photo (see Figure 4-10).**

   Press the shutter button all the way to take the photo.

   Hold the shutter release button if you want to take a bunch of shots (if the drive mode is set to continuous). Likewise, if you're using AEB, hold the button until the brackets are done.

Figure 4-10: Ah, the photo.

9. **(Optional) Review the photo.**

Most of the time, I glance down and look at the shot I just took. (In Figure 4-11, I'm reviewing a photo of my wife while she's painting — and, of course, she's taking the photo of me reviewing her photo.) For initial or test shots, this step is even more important. It lets you evaluate or check the framing, exposure, and focus to ensure that no blurring occurs.

Figure 4-11: Check for focus and exposure — not just content and framing.

The histogram is a good tool to use at this point. Some cameras show you an RGB or luminance histogram and make blown or lost areas blink on the photo.

Checking the histogram helps ensure that the exposure is set so that no highlights are blown and no shadows are clipped. When you take photos of scenes with an extreme range of light and dark, some level of clipping may be unavoidable.

10. **Rinse and repeat.**

Depending on how successful the shot was, you may jump back to a different step in the overall process.

If you have to make dramatic changes to your setup, see the earlier section "Step 2: Set up."

If you're only recomposing or shooting the same basic subject, start again at the beginning of this section.

Mix to Match

Setting up and shooting in a home or professional studio is different from taking a walk with your camera. The situation is more controlled, and shooting is more deliberate. You have lighting and flash gear to work with. (Flash photography and studio lighting gear are discussed in Book IV.)

Similarly, casual interior flash photography is different from setting up a tripod outdoors and shooting the sunset.

Identify the most important elements of your routine and make sure that you know how your camera works, that you can operate all its controls, and that you know which settings you like.

Chapter 5: Handling and Cleaning Your Camera and Gear

In This Chapter

✔ **Handling your dSLR with care**

✔ **Working with memory cards**

✔ **Handling lenses**

✔ **Cleaning without breaking**

✔ **Working in weather**

✔ **Benefitting from tips and tricks**

*G*ood woodworkers know how to handle saws, hammers, screwdrivers, and other tools. Good electricians know how to handle wire, multimeters, lineman's pliers, wire strippers, breakers, wire nuts, and more. I'm dying to go on with more examples (painters, plumbers, machinists, teachers, musicians), but you get the point.

This practical chapter emphasizes working with your digital SLR in the real world. Knowing how to handle your tools is part of the photographer's art and craft.

I just peeked ahead and saw lots of diverse information in this chapter. You can find out how to secure your camera with a strap, hold and shoot with it, work with lenses and memory cards, protect your camera from the elements, clean it, and more.

Handling Your Camera

An important part of being a dSLR photographer is knowing how to handle your camera. You can know the names of all the controls and be able to program the dickens out of the menu, but if you can't hold the camera properly and take pictures, you won't get far. I refer to this issue as "when reality smacks you upside the head."

Looking at objects is one thing. Reading about them is another. Watching them is still another. (Are you growing weary of me yet?) Physically holding the camera in your hands, working the controls, and taking pictures are tangible actions. They're real. You can't emulate them, pretend, or otherwise fake it. You have to do it.

Figuring out how to use your camera involves being exposed to the information, repeating it to lock it into your gray matter, and practicing on your own to create muscle memory of working the camera.

Strapping it up

Using a camera strap is an important step toward safeguarding your investment. I love having one, frankly, more for the feeling of security it gives me than for the physical support.

Put the camera strap over your neck whenever you mount your camera on a tripod or remove it. I learned this trick the day I tripped the tripod release lever and almost dropped my camera. It took a nosedive off the tripod, and I barely caught it. I had a heavy lens on the camera that yanked it right off.

In addition to securing your camera, snazzy straps make the camera easier to hold and carry. You can find as many types of straps as you can find cameras. Three broad categories of straps are listed here:

- ✔ **Standard strap:** The common neck strap that comes with all cameras. Most often, the default strap is a bit cheap and uncomfortable. Its main selling point is advertising for the camera manufacturer (see Figure 5-1). (If they would only pay the wearers for the free marketing!)

Figure 5-1: The Nikon D300S strap.

- ✔ **Better strap:** A wide, cushioned strap that has a quick-release mechanism. I have a couple of this kind. One is shown in Figure 5-2.

- ✔ **Hand strap:** Acts like a strap you see on a video camera. It loops around your hand and secures it to the camera — unlike a neck strap.

Manipulating the controls

A dSLR camera has a ton of buttons and controls. How are you supposed to work them all while you're holding it?

Figure 5-2: One of my OP/TECH USA straps.

Most often, camera manufacturers design their digital SLRs with accessible and usable buttons. It isn't always the easiest task, but it's possible.

I keep between two and six fingers free when I'm holding the camera. Then I can press buttons, turn knobs, and take pictures while supporting the camera with my other fingers.

You'll likely find that you support the camera body with the bottom three fingers and the palm of your right hand. That leaves your thumb and index finger to operate controls on the right side of the camera. Conveniently, you can work the back of the camera with your thumb and the front with your index (or, in a pinch, middle) finger.

My left hand remains free to work the lens, if necessary, and the controls on the left side of the camera. Then they settle down and support the weight of the camera so that my right index finger can take the picture.

At times, you may be more comfortable supporting the entire weight of the camera with your left hand so that you can remove your right hand from the grip and work various dials, buttons, and controls. When you're ready to take the picture, move your right hand back into position on the grip to press the shutter button.

Figure 5-3: Push a button and get a treat.

The following list describes the different controls you have to manipulate:

- ✔ **Buttons:** Push them with a free finger. My wife is shown pushing the Function button in Figure 5-3. The most important button is the shutter release, or shutter, button. Press it firmly and steadily. Don't jab at it, or else you'll shake the camera.

- ✔ **Knobs:** You'll more than likely have to remove a hand from the camera to turn a knob, as shown in Figure 5-4. It shows the Mode dial on my Sony Alpha 300.

- ✔ **Wheels:** Spin with your thumb or other free finger.

Figure 5-4: Knob turning requires a few fingers.

✔ **Other doohickeys:** Your camera has levers and selectors and other controls that you should practice reaching and activating. Figure 5-5 shows my wife sliding the Super SteadyShot button to the Off position. My Nikon D200 has a funky push-down control to slide the drive mode spinner. Working it one-handed is difficult.

Figure 5-5: Sliding with a thumb.

✔ **Lens controls:** If you're comfortable using your left hand, use it to activate lens buttons and switches (which are normally on the left side of the lens as it faces away from you). You have little choice other than to use your left hand to zoom and focus. Your right hand will hold on to the camera, ready to press the shutter release button. Manual focusing takes practice!

Inspecting other odds and ends

Digital SLRs certainly have a lot of parts on them. In addition to operating the main shooting controls, lens, and whatnot, you need to know how to accomplish other, general tasks.

Familiarize yourself with your camera and practice the following actions:

✔ **Open covers:** Every time you remove a memory card, as shown in Figure 5-6, or every time you change batteries, you need to open a cover on your dSLR. You also open it to access other connectors.

Sometimes a cover has a lever you need to operate on the camera back to pop it open. Or, you might slide it toward the back of the camera to unlatch it and then swing it open. Others are basically rubberized covers that pop in and out of the camera body.

Figure 5-6: Carefully remove covers.

Regardless of the type of cover, *be careful not to force it open* and possibly break it. If it's stuck and you just can't seem to open it, check the manual to make sure you're operating the specific cover correctly. If so, try again carefully. If it seems impossible, search for help on the Internet, e-mail the camera manufacturer for advice, seek help from a local camera shop, or consider taking the camera in for servicing.

✔ **Connect cables:** Open the compartment that the connector is in or remove the cover carefully. Align the cable with the connector so that they join together correctly. USB cables have a specific up-and-down orientation. My wife is shown connecting a remote shutter release in Figure 5-7, which consists of a rectangular connector with holes for the three pins you see sticking out of the socket on the camera. This connection also has an orientation. A bump in the socket matches a groove on the plug.

Figure 5-7: Connecting a remote shutter cable.

Do not forcibly insert a cable where it doesn't want to be inserted! If it doesn't go in, pull back and look things over. Make sure that you have the correct cable and the correct connector. See whether you have all parts aligned correctly. If not, twist or turn it so that you do. It becomes more difficult at night or in dimly lit locations. Ideally, you know your camera by touch. If necessary, take a small light with you so that you can see what you're doing.

I rarely connect USB or HDMI cables, but I continually attach my remote shutter release. I also have to contend with flash synch cords, microphone cables, A/V-out lines, and AC power cords.

✔ **Change batteries:** It's simple. Open the cover and pull out the battery. The only glitch is that your camera might have a battery catch to keep it from falling out when the door is open. If yours does, press it in and slide out the battery.

✔ **Attach grips:** Vertical grips are functional, and they look cool and give your camera extra battery power. Attaching one is easy. First, make sure that all your batteries are charged and loaded. Then screw the grip into the tripod socket.

Gripping and Shooting

You'll become a much better shooter if you work on your grip — how you hold the camera — in different situations.

Getting a grip on handheld photography

Handheld photography is fun and rewarding. I love walking around with my camera and looking for cool things to shoot. I feel a sense of freedom that I don't feel when I'm working with a tripod shooting landscapes in HDR or in the studio working on portraits or macro shots.

Mastering your grip pays dividends in your photography. You have a more stable platform to shoot from, you rely less on vibration reduction, and you reclaim a stop or two by minimizing camera shake. All these factors translate into sharper, cleaner photos right out of the box.

Here are some photo-shooting positions to work on:

Figure 5-8: Me, holding the camera normally.

✔ **Standard grip:** With the standard grip, shown in Figure 5-8, use your right hand to grip and support the camera horizontally.

Specifically, your right palm and lower three fingers bear the weight. You need your index finger to shoot the picture. Your thumb has two jobs: Press buttons at first and then settle down to support the camera when you're ready to take a picture.

Don't forget about operating the flash. I use my right hand to operate external flash controls.

Support the lens with your left hand near the mount or where the zoom or focus rings are located. If necessary, transfer the weight of the camera to your right hand so that you can press buttons and pull levers with the left. As you zoom or focus, you see that your left hand needs to be somewhat free. If you hold it palm up, you can rest some of the weight of the camera on your thumb pad.

To help promote good posture and add some stability, lock down your left elbow against your stomach.

Look through the peeper or watch the LCD screen to frame and focus.

✓ **Vertical grip:** Your hands and fingers stay in the same place, but you twist them to hold the camera vertically. If I'm using auto focus and not zooming in and out, I use my left hand to support most of the camera's weight (see Figure 5-9), and my right hand stabilizes the camera vertically and takes the picture.

✓ **Over-the-shoulder grip:** A well-known photographer promotes a grip style where you turn your body and point your shoulder to the subject. Turn your head and rest the camera against your shoulder. Your left hand wraps underneath and across the camera (not in front of the lens) to rest on the right, stabilizing and securing it.

I've tried this technique and can't quite seem to get comfortable with it.

✓ **Kneeling:** Being able to kneel and shoot a picture is important when working without a tripod. Keeling stabilizes the camera and helps you avoid camera shake or blur, as shown in Figure 5-10. (Yes, I'm taking a picture of myself in the mirror in this shot and the preceding two shots.) Hold the camera normally — just kneel at the same time. Rather than bring your left elbow close to your body to stabilize it, as with standing, you may find that resting the camera on your knee is comfortable when kneeling.

✓ **Your eyes:** You can use either eye to look through the view finder. Set the diopter, if necessary, so that you're seeing clearly.

Figure 5-9: Vertical grip.

Figure 5-10: Kneeling to shoot.

When I use my left eye, it squishes my nose against the LCD screen. I'm much more comfortable turning my head and using my right eye.

✔ **Your body:** Maintain good posture. Don't hunch or bend over or else you'll tire easily and possibly hurt your back. Don't hold the camera at arm's length. This position strains your back too. Hold the camera close to you so that it becomes part of your central mass.

Using a support

If you're seeking stability (and, to some degree, safety), invest in a good tripod. Monopods offer less support but are much more mobile. This list describes ways to support a camera other than with your hands:

✔ **Tripod:** I use a tripod all the time (see Figure 5-11). It's good for ya. When taking more formal portraits or landscape shots, nothing works better. It moves the weight of the camera from your hands and neck (remember the strap?) to the tripod.

Aside from giving the camera a stable, jigglefree zone to shoot from, you don't grow as tired on location. Using a tripod frees you and allows you to concentrate more on camera setup and framing and on taking a steady shot.

✔ **Monopod:** It has a single leg that telescopes in and out to the height you want to work at, as shown in Figure 5-12. Most often, you see professional photographers at sporting events using monopods. They stand, sit, or kneel on the sidelines and use the monopod to support the weight of their camera. If they're using bulky, heavy telephoto lenses, they need all the support they can get (in that case, the monopod mounts to the lens).

Figure 5-11: Ready and steady.

The trade-off with monopods is versatility for stability. Walking around with a monopod Is much easier than lugging around a tripod. They're faster to set up and tear down. Setting the exact height you need on one leg versus fiddling around with three is a snap.

But monopods aren't as stable as tripods.

🖛 **Other:** Use a fence, a rock, a vehicle, the ground, or another item if you need to stabilize your camera.

Memory Cards

Treat your memory cards as though they hold the most precious cargo. They do! The main activity in digital SLR photography is taking pictures. The pictures are stored on memory cards. If they go, your pictures go.

Here are some general tips for handling a memory card:

🖛 **Weather:** Don't expose memory cards to the weather. Don't let them get wet. Don't let them fry in the heat. Try to limit their exposure to dust and humidity.

🖛 **Electromagnetism:** Contrary to what you may believe, a flash drive (which a memory card is a subset of) is immune to normal magnetic fields. Notice that I said *normal* magnetic fields: If you run the card through an X-ray or MRI machine (maybe the one in your basement?), you may be in for trouble.

🖛 **Weight:** Memory cards aren't made from titanium. They can be crushed. Don't sit on them, step on them, drive over them, or rest heavy objects on them.

© Lino Mantrotto & Co.

Figure 5-12: The basic monopod.

To insert a memory card into your dSLR, follow these steps:

1. **Power-off the camera.**

   Most cameras suggest strongly that the camera be powered down before swapping out memory cards.

2. **Open the card cover.**

   Depending on your model, you may have to operate a card cover release latch. Other models pull out and swing open.

3. **Orient and align the card properly.**

4. **Insert the card into the slot and press until it's securely in place, as shown in Figure 5-13.**

   An eject button may pop up, indicating that the card is in position.

5. **Close the card cover.**

6. **Power-on the camera.**

7. **Check to see whether exposures register and the card seems to work.**

Figure 5-13: Push the card firmly until it seats.

To remove the card, follow these steps:

1. **Power-off the camera.**

2. **Open the card cover.**

3. **Depending on your camera model, press the eject button once to make the card pop up and press another time to make the card pop out, as shown in Figure 5-14. Or, press in the card gently so that it releases and pops up.**

Figure 5-14: Ejecting the memory card.

4. **Fully remove the card, as shown in Figure 5-15.**

   Cameras that take larger Compact Flash cards (shown in the figure) use a helper device to lift the card far enough from its socket to enable you to grab it. Smaller SD cards pop up when you push down on them.

5. **Insert another card or close the cover.**

Figure 5-15: Pulling out the card.

Working with Lenses

Lenses work with your camera body to take photos. Handling and being able to clean them are fundamentally important tasks. And, you don't learn how to do it from shooting a million shots with a compact digital camera. You have to use a dSLR.

Mounting a lens

Mounting lenses isn't difficult, but it can be a little frightening until you get used to it. I remember being a bit nervous about the camera's insides being open to the world while I made a lens swap. Don't be. Unless you're in a dust storm or outside in the rain with no cover when changing lenses, the camera will survive.

When you're mounting a lens, the keys are to be quick about it without being rushed and to be firm about it without being harsh. Got it?

Here's how to attach a lens to a digital SLR camera:

1. **Turn off the camera.**

   If you forget (I have), it isn't the end of the world. Ideally, you want the power to be off, though.

2. **Remove the rear lens cap from the lens, as shown in Figure 5-16.**

   Place the cap on a table, in your camera bag, or in your pocket for safekeeping. If you're standing up, you need three hands, or two hands and a tripod, or two hands and your camera strap.

Figure 5-16: Take off the rear cap first.

3. **Remove the camera body cap or lens.**

   Most body caps twist off, as shown in Figure 5-17. Some have a locking function. Put away the cap or lens, if necessary.

   See the next section for how-to steps on removing lenses.

   You obviously want to be more careful with a lens than with a small plastic cover. At these times, you can easily drop lenses and damage or break them.

Figure 5-17: Remove the body cap to access the lens mount.

4. **Line up the mounting index on the lens with the one on the camera body, if it exists.**

   Sometimes, it's orange, as shown in Figure 5-18. It can also be white or red or another color.

5. **Press the lens onto the mount.**

   You feel the lens and the camera fit together if they're in proper alignment, as shown in Figure 5-19.

6. **Rotate the lens in the proper direction until it locks and clicks in place, as shown in Figure 5-20.**

   Don't mess with the lens release button as you mount a lens.

   Nikon users rotate the lens counterclockwise, as you're looking at the camera from the front. Others rotate the lens clockwise, which feels more natural to me.

7. **When you're ready, power on the camera and remove the lens cap from the lens.**

   Check and set switches on the lens, such as autofocus or vibration reduction. You're ready to shoot.

Removing a lens

Taking a lens off is just as important as putting one on. Follow these steps:

1. **Turn off the camera.**

2. **Press and hold the lens release button, as shown in Figure 5-21.**

   Hold on to the lens as you do this step. You may hear or feel a click that tells you the lens is no longer locked in place and is free to rotate.

3. **Turn the lens until it releases from the mount.**

   Keep holding the button as you turn the lens. Figure 5-22 shows this process in action.

Figure 5-18: Carefully line up the index marks.

Figure 5-19: Press in the lens.

Figure 5-20: When it clicks, it locks.

Nikon users turn counterclockwise. Other users turn clockwise.

When you've turned the lens far enough, you feel the tension ease up and the lens float free within the mount. You might hear a click or a pop. You should see the mounting index line up from the lens to the camera body.

4. **Pull the lens gently away from the camera body, as shown in Figure 5-23.**

   If you yank out the lens like you don't care, you might damage the sensitive contacts on the lens mount.

5. **Secure the lens.**

   Put the rear lens cap on quickly, and set the lens in a safe place. If that spot is in your camera bag, you're done with it. Otherwise, make sure to pack it away safely after you take care of the camera body.

6. **Replace the body cap or attach another lens.**

   Don't leave the camera open to the elements. Always replace the body cap or mount another lens on the body.

Figure 5-21: Press the button.

Figure 5-22: Turn it the opposite way from when you mounted it.

Figure 5-23: Pull out the lens.

Cleaning

Cleaning your camera and lenses is an important part of the quality-control process. Your equipment will thank you, and you'll take better photos. The camera has lots of different elements to clean, so hang on!

Wiping off the camera body

Most manuals tell you not to use any sort of organic solvent to clean your camera body — no thinner, alcohol, or benzene.

For a normal level of cleaning, wipe the body with a soft cloth. Wet the cloth, if needed. I recently have begun using microfiber cloths for all my cleaning needs. I use the Quickie brand microfiber cloths from Lowe's because they're large, and I use them around the house too. Photo shops such as Adorama and Amazon also sell a number of microfiber products. Check them out. They're easy to use and require no chemicals or cleaners. If something is truly stuck on, wet the cloth with a little water.

Turn off the camera before you clean its body. That way, you can push buttons and turn knobs without throwing off your settings.

If your camera is in *bad* shape, be safe and take it to an authorized service center to see whether someone can help.

Cleaning LCDs

Treat LCDs as you would treat your lenses. Don't use caustic chemicals or abrasive cleaners to clean. You may mar or scratch the surface. In addition, pay special attention to the cloth you use. If it's especially rough (such as an industrial strength paper towel), you might scratch the LCD monitor.

As with my camera bodies, I use microfiber cloths to clean the LCD monitor on the back and any LCD monitors elsewhere on the camera. My wife is shown cleaning the LCD monitor of my Sony Alpha 300 in Figure 5-24.

Figure 5-24: Buffing the LCD.

Getting dust out and off

Every dSLR user must learn to deal with dust. Even weatherized cameras are vulnerable to this problem. Unless you're working in a NASA clean room, you allow dust to enter your camera every time you change lenses.

Dust that shows up in your photos should be obvious: You see big, fuzzy, dark spots. (Shots of the sky are the best places to see them.) You don't see much by looking into the camera when you change lenses unless you have a *loupe,* a special type of magnifying glass. Chapters 2 and 3 in Book VI show an example apiece of removing dust from photos.

Address the problem — don't ignore it. Over time, dust bunnies will start showing up in your photos.

Self-cleaning

Self-cleaning (sensor shaking) is your first line of defense. The camera shakes the dust off the sensor to try to clean it. You don't have to open the camera, blow anything in, or swab anything out. In that respect, it's relatively foolproof.

Many cameras have a self-cleaning mode. For example, the Pentax K-x has a dust removal routine that shakes the CMOS sensor. Some cameras, such as the Sony Alpha 330, integrate self-cleaning with manual blowing. After you activate the menu, the sensor shakes and then the mirror locks up so that you can blow out dust.

Some cameras, such as the Canon EOS 7D, can be set to perform the sensor shake every time you turn on the camera. Others, like the Nikon D700, enable you to choose when the self-cleaning routine activates. For example, the D700 has options to clean at startup or shutdown or both. It can also be turned off entirely.

Most manuals suggest that you place the camera on a flat surface, bottom down.

Blowing dust out

To blow dust out of your camera, follow these steps:

1. **Charge your camera's batteries.**

   Camera manufacturers recommend locking the mirror for manual cleaning with fresh batteries. If you have an AC power adapter, you can use it.

2. **Turn on the camera.**

3. **Navigate to your camera's sensor cleaning menu and activate the manual cleaning mode (regardless of its name — Mirror Lock Up, Mirror Up, or Self Cleaning).**

   Do not select an option to self-clean — you want the mirror raised and out of the way, but you're going to do the blowing yourself. The camera may shake the sensor during this step to throw off dust — that's fine.

4. **Take off the lens or remove the body cap.**

5. **Orient the camera so that the opening faces or is tilted downward.**

   This step makes it easier for the dust to fall out of the camera when you blow it. (I had to take the photo, so we oriented it facing up. Just ignore that.)

6. **Take a blower and squeeze-blow air into the sensor cavity (see Figure 5-25).**

Don't thrust the tip of the blower into the open cavity. It isn't a vacuum cleaner. You get plenty of air movement by hovering the tip even with the lens mount or just outside the camera.

Do not use a canned-air spray blower, or else you may damage your camera. Use a blower that

Figure 5-25: Blow out the dust.

you squeeze with your hand. Do not use a blower brush, either. Touching the sensor with the bristles might damage it.

Give three or four bursts. I don't have a scientifically calibrated recommendation to give you. I give it a couple of shots and then close it up.

Do not dally!

7. **Put the camera back together.**

8. **Power-off the camera.**

9. **Power-on and check the camera to make sure it's working.**

You might even take a few test shots. Stop down to a small aperture and take a photo of the sky or your ceiling, to see whether it has any dust spots. If it does, you can try cleaning the sensor yourself or send in the camera for maintenance.

Manually swabbing or brushing the sensor

Manually swabbing the sensor can be a terrifying experience. (Who would have thought that cleaning a camera could be so frightening?)

I don't think a camera manufacturer out there recommends swabbing or brushing your dSLR sensor manually, but dust is such a problem that people have come up with innovative solutions to try to tackle it on their own. After all, who wants to send in their camera to a service center every time a dust bunny lands on the sensor and won't come off?

Do not open your camera and touch anything inside it unless you're sure of yourself and willing to take the risk.

Never touch the mirror or the pentaprism.

Disclaimers aside, cleaning a sensor isn't impossible. It takes the proper equipment and a steady but gentle hand. Although you have many cleaning technologies and products to choose from (sensor brushes, for example), I use Sensor Swabs with a drop of Eclipse lens cleaner by Photographic Solutions, Inc. I have everything prepared and ready to go (including the mirror) in Figure 5-26.

Figure 5-26: Prepping the materials.

Here's how it works:

1. **Perform automatic sensor shake cleaning.**

   You might as well get as much dust off as possible beforehand.

2. **Follow the checklist for blowing out dust until you get to Step 7.**

   This step also removes as much dust as possible from the camera before you insert the swab in it.

Figure 5-27: Dropping the drops.

3. **Take out a swab and put two drops of Eclipse cleaner on it (see Figure 5-27).**

4. **Firmly wipe the swab across the sensor in one motion, as shown in Figure 5-28.**

   Do not scrub! Don't twirl, press hard, or otherwise try to "sand" off the dust. The cleaner loosens the dust, and the pad picks it up and removes it from your camera. Trust those two items to do their jobs. It's not about elbow grease.

Figure 5-28: Swabbing the deck from left to right.

5. **Turn over the swab and swab back across the sensor in the opposite direction (see Figure 5-29).**

6. **Close your camera.**

7. **Turn it on to see whether it works.**

If dust is still a problem, you should send the camera to an authorized service center for a professional cleaning.

Figure 5-29: Swabbing the other way.

Cleaning lenses

Cleaning lenses is a lot less intimidating than cleaning your camera's sensor. I can relate to cleaning a piece of glass, even if it's small and circular.

I use a microfiber cloth, as mentioned in the earlier section "Wiping off the camera body," and I love it. My wife is shown cleaning a 50mm prime lens in Figure 5-30. Notice that some lenses are set back from the edge quite a bit. Just reach in with your finger and clean.

Figure 5-30: Cleaning and polishing a lens.

I also like my Nikon 7072 Lens Pen Cleaning System. It has a soft brush on one end, shown in Figure 5-31, and a little scrubber on the opposite end. The brush takes care of dust and other debris, and the scrubber squeegees off smudges and fingerprints.

Figure 5-31: Brushing away dust.

The important points are to use a soft, clean cloth or lens cleaning tissue and only approved lens cleaning solutions (or none). Most lens manufacturers recommend against thinners or benzene because of the plastics involved in the lens body.

Be careful using any sort of chemicals on lenses with coatings. In any case, you want to use something very soft on the lens so that you don't scratch it. Always brush or blow debris off first. That way, you won't grind it in with a cloth or scrubber. Then clean the lens from the center outward (if you're using a NIKKOR lens; Canon recommends wiping from the outside in!), using a circular motion ("wax off"). Make sure that all cleaning fluid has been wiped off if you use a lens cleaner.

Dealing with Adverse Weather

It's not always partly sunny and 72 degrees outside with no chance of rain. Sometimes, perfect weather is good. Sometimes, it's bad. If you want to shoot in bad weather (or anything less than ideal conditions), you must know how to protect yourself and your camera under different conditions.

- **Cold:** Working in the cold makes everything more difficult. It can be a literal pain. Plastic and metal get extremely cold and uncomfortable to touch. You can't wear gloves the size of parkas and operate a camera. You can wear thinner gloves, but they can be slippery or ineffective against the cold.

  If you do a lot of cold-weather shooting, check out special gloves designed with silicon "grippies" that make holding the camera easier. Some have finger caps that come off, exposing one or more fingertips to operate the camera with. Some are fingerless.

  When you're working in the cold, plastics become more brittle. Be careful not to drop your camera or lens. In addition, your batteries don't last as long as they do in warm weather.

- **Snow:** Snow is easy to work in as long as you're not wallowing around in it. You're not likely to drown the camera if a little snow gets on it. The main thing you have to deal with is the cold temperatures.

- **Heat:** Don't leave your camera lying around in the sun. It's hot and can melt things or fry whatever it doesn't melt. Not only that, LCD monitors don't like heat (they don't like cold, either) and can discolor.

- **Dust:** You can't do much about dust. Don't open your camera in a dust storm.

- **Rain:** Rain equals water. Water equals bad. Avoid.

  If it's a slow sprinkle, water won't automatically get into your camera. Keep lens changes to a minimum, and if you must change one, seek cover or point the camera downward to protect its insides.

If it's raining even harder, don't go out without a weatherized camera and lens. Even then, I would try to protect it from the elements as much as possible.

Weather sealing is a debatable proposition. Some photographers think that it's more of a marketing gimmick than a practical advantage. Others swear by it. My sense is that additional protection from dust, humidity, and water is better than nothing, but I wouldn't trust it so far as to drop it in a bathtub.

If you must be out in a lot of rain, consider getting an underwater housing and using it on land.

Opteka (www.opteka.com) makes an interesting-looking rain cover. Try it out if you need to be out in the rain. You can also make your own cover, from trash bags and duct tape, to impress everyone!

✔ **Humidity and condensation:** Bad. Your camera has circuits running all around inside it. Don't shoot if your camera or lens have fogged up. It can happen if you walk out from a cool house to the hot temperature outdoors or the reverse. Give the camera and lens some time to adjust to the shooting temperature and let the condensation evaporate.

✔ **Underwater:** Buy a special underwater housing that's certified for use with your camera. They vary greatly in capability and price, so shop around. Some are little more than sturdy plastic bags with room for lenses and access for your fingers. Others look like they were invented by Jacques Cousteau.

Following Good Practices

Here are some good practices to keep in mind as you work with your digital SLR. They apply when you're out shooting and when you're at home, cleaning, learning, practicing, and storing:

✔ **Keep the lids on:** Don't leave your camera lenses or body uncovered. Always make sure that all lens and body caps are in place and secure. This keeps out dust, not to mention creepy-crawlies.

✔ **Keep lenses from rolling:** Lenses are round. If you set one down on its side, it can roll off a table or whatever it is on. Crash!

Resist setting longer lenses on top of tables, even when they're upright. They aren't stable and can be knocked over, leading to rolling, crashing, and crying. Store them in their case, your camera bag, or a locker of some sort.

✔ **Use a comfortable strap:** Get a strap that you like and will use. The more comfortable it is, the more likely you are to keep it on for long periods. It's not only good for your photos (and your back), it's also safer.

✓ **Safeguard memory cards:** Don't leave memory cards in a pile. Put them in protective sleeves or plastic cases. Don't place anything heavy on them.

✓ **Use a camera bag:** Bite the bullet and get a good camera bag, as shown in Figure 5-32. Make sure that it's large enough to carry what you need but small enough not to be too heavy or bulky.

Look for the following characteristics when shopping for a bag:

- *Size:* Most bags let you carry a dSLR body with lens and at least two more. If you need more space, get a bigger bag. If you need less, look for a smaller bag. It is *not* brain surgery.

- *Padding:* Bags with padding protect your gear better. Baby it!

Figure 5-32: Slinging my camera bag on the tripod for show.

- *Strap support:* Test out your back and see whether the strap was made to cut wood or will feel comfortable. Sling bags (my favorite) have good support in their straps.

  I have *two* sling bags — a Tamrac Velocity 8x (www.tamrac.com) for one camera and a Lowepro Slingshot 100 AW (www.lowepro.com) for another.

- *Use:* Ask yourself how you're going to use the bag, and then get the right one for you. You carry a conventional bag over your shoulder or by its handle. You tend to put it down when you shoot. I found myself not picking it back up again and walking over somewhere else, only to have to go back and get it. When I got a sling bag, I found the solution for me. I don't take it off. I sling it over my shoulder and when I need something out of it, I rotate it around front and open it.

✓ **Be sensible when packing your bag:** You don't need to take everything with you. As long as you have your camera and lens, you're set. Having extra batteries and memory cards is preferable and doesn't occupy too much space or weight. Try to narrow the number of lenses you want to use and take only those — not everything in your arsenal.

I've found, quite by surprise, that as I winnowed down my bag, it became easier to use and more practical. I don't have to wade through a bag full of items I don't use to find the one item I need. I have my glasses, remote shutter release, WhiBal (a white balance card) card, lens cloth, extra battery, extra memory card, camera with lens, and one or two other lenses. If I think I'll need a level, I may take it, and a Speedlight.

Book II
Through the Looking Glass

*L*enses are so important to digital SLRs that they deserve their own minibook. They are inseparable subjects, really. That statement is paradoxical because dSLR lenses are interchangeable. You can take them off and put them back on again whenever you want.

My purpose, therefore, is to show you different types of lenses and the sorts of pictures you can take with them. I have divided the Book II topics into four chapters. Each one describes a different lens category (Chapter 4 has two), tells you what makes those lenses unique, and shows you some of the photos I took using those lenses.

Chapter 1 covers the prime lens. It has a fixed focal length and doesn't zoom in or out. The focus of Chapter 2 is the wide-angle lens, which has a wider angle of view than a standard lens. Chapter 3 features general-purpose zoom lenses. They zoom in and out, making them quite versatile. Macro and telephoto lenses are highlighted in Chapter 4. Macros are best used for shooting close photos of near subject. Telephoto lenses, on the other hand, magnify far-away subjects.

I had a blast writing this part of the book. I hope that you have a blast reading it. I'm sure it will make you want to go out and buy some interesting and exciting new lenses for your camera.

Chapter 1: Following the Prime Directive

*P*rime lenses: The term evokes a certain simplicity of purpose, quality, and importance.

Prime: This lens comes first.

Nothing about a prime lens is complicated — it's simply a good lens that doesn't zoom. The key is to find the focal length you prefer in a given situation and then decide whether you can deal with not being able to zoom in and out.

This chapter discusses the prime lens and describes how to tell it apart from other types of lenses. You see several examples of shots from my prime lens collection (plus rentals) so that you can see how it works and what the big deal is all about.

Identifying a Prime Lens

A *prime* lens has a fixed focal length.

A lens with a fixed focal length cannot zoom in or out. Its magnification level is fixed from the day you buy it until your grandkids sell it on eBay. You cannot change it.

This characteristic has significant ramifications for you as a photographer, as you can see throughout this chapter.

Comparing focal lengths

To determine whether a lens is a prime lens, you have to look at its name, though you don't often see the term *prime* or *fixed focal length*. (The focal length is italicized in the next two examples.) If the lens lists a single focal length, such as the AF-S NIKKOR *50mm* f/1.4G, it's a prime. The 50mm lens is fixed at 50mm, whether you put it on a full-frame digital SLR or a cropped-frame.

If the lens lists a range, such as Sony DT *18-70mm* f/3.5-5.6, the lens can zoom and is *not* a prime lens. In this case, the Sony lens begins in wide-angle territory and zooms into the near telephoto area.

Compare Figures 1-1 and 1-2 to see whether you can tell which one was taken using a prime lens. Both figures show the same subject (my son) and the same activity to throw you off.

Figure 1-1: Enjoying life at age 7.

Determining whether a prime lens was used to take a photo (just by looking at the photo) is impossible. Though you can often determine the general focal length of the lens used to take the photo (whether it's a wide-angle lens, standard, or telephoto), the actual focal length used is cloaked in a degree of mystery because the photo might have been cropped.

The photo shown in Figure 1-2 was taken with a 300mm prime telephoto lens. I took the photo shown in Figure 1-1 with an 18-200mm zoom lens at 170mm (which is nothing to sneeze at!).

Figure 1-2: Running the bases.

Determining whether a lens is a prime

I've included examples here to test your knowledge of prime lenses. I'm leaving all the extra letters in the lens names to make you think harder. Look at the name, decide whether it's a prime lens, and then read my description.

✔ **AF-S NIKKOR 50mm f/1.4G**

This is a classic example of a prime lens. Favorite focal lengths for prime lenses are 35mm and 50mm.

✔ **AF-S NIKKOR 300mm f/4D IF-ED**

Technically, a fixed focal-length lens (a prime lens). Its status as a telephoto lens often trumps its "primeness." (You would refer to it not as your "300mm prime lens" but, rather, as your "300mm telephoto lens.")

✔ **Canon EF 85mm f/1.2L II USM**

Another example of a prime lens; marketed as a (Canon-specific) *medium telephoto lens*. A visit to the lens area of the Canon Web site shows its lens offerings in such functional categories as Ultra-Wide Zoom and Standard Zoom.

REMEMBER

If a lens is in a Zoom category on the manufacturer's Web site or lens brochure, it isn't a prime.

✔ **Sony 35mm f/1.4 G-Series wide-angle lens**

Another classic prime focal length. Don't be misled by its designation as a wide-angle lens.

Sony puts fixed focal-length lenses into a separate category on its Web site.

✔ **ZUIKO DIGITAL 25mm f2.8 (Olympus)**

A prime lens; although it certainly has an odd focal length (I have an old, manual-focus NIKKOR lens that is 28mm, one of my favorite focal lengths), it's still a prime lens.

✔ **smc PENTAX DA 50-200mm F4-5.6 ED WR**

It isn't a prime lens; it's a zoom lens. Notice that the focal-length range is 50-200mm.

Let me tell you how you can tell every zoom lens apart from a prime lens. Zoom lenses have a focal length *range,* not a single number. Their focal lengths vary widely. Pentax alone sells zoom lenses that range from 16-50mm, 50-135mm, 60-250mm, 18-55mm, 50-200mm, 10-17mm, 12-24mm, 16-45mm, 17-70mm, and (can I stop yet?) more.

For a list of the manufacturer's Web sites, check out this book's Cheat Sheet online at www.dummies.com. (See the inside front cover for more information about the Cheat Sheet.)

A Prime Comparison

If you frequently use a zoom lens, analyze the focal lengths of your favorite photos. If you consistently gravitate toward a "sweet spot," you've found a great candidate for a prime lens. For example, if most of your photos are at 40mm, you might try a 35mm prime.

You can also set your zoom lens to a specific focal length and experiment with not moving it. See whether you experience any frustration while framing the shot or have any trouble getting the right exposure.

Table 1-1 describes some possible uses of the general prime categories.

Table 1-1	Prime Lens and Cropped-Sensor dSLRs	
Focal Length	*Class*	*Best Use*
Up to 35mm	Wide angle	Interiors needing more than standard coverage; parties and groups of people; outdoors; landscapes.
		(I like to use 28mm on a cropped-sensor dSLR.)
35mm	Standard	Everyday shots of virtually any subject; good overall coverage; not much magnification; for shots of people, take group shots and full body shots unless you get very close.
		The 35mm prime is the equivalent of the ubiquitous 50mm prime of yesteryear. If you want to experience what it felt like to take photos with an old film SLR and a 50mm prime, put a 35mm prime on your cropped-sensor dSLR.
50mm	Standard	Fantastic for close-up portraits when you don't want to get too close to the subject; excels at head-and-shoulder shots; not useful if you want to see what is going on in the room besides the immediate subject — switch to 35mm or lower.
50-100mm	Near Telephoto	85mm is often used for portraits; you can stand a significant distance away from the subject and still take a good-looking head-and-shoulders shot. It's ideal for macro work or anything else you need magnification to capture.
Over 100mm	Telephoto	A lens that's often physically large but still fun and rewarding to work with. Use it to get up close and personal with whatever subject you're shooting.

The following sections lead you on a tour of photos I've taken with several prime lenses so that you can see what some different prime lens focal lengths look like.

I used cameras with a crop factor of 1.5 for all the photos in the following sections. The 35mm equivalent focal length is listed in parentheses.

28mm

(42mm in 35mm equivalent terms on a camera with a crop factor of 1.5)

I have a 28mm manual focus lens from a bygone day, but that fits my modern Nikon D200 body. This focal length, which used to be considered wide-angle, is more of a standard focal length on a cropped-frame body.

Figure 1-3 shows a doorknob. It was catching light coming in the window and reflecting the orange paint we chose for the walls. (The doors were taken off their hinges for painting during a recent renovation.)

Book II
Chapter 1

This is a manual focus lens and I have to pay attention to that. Sometimes I forget and rattle off five or ten photos without thinking about it and none of them is in focus. If you're using a manual focus lens, remember to focus!

In this case, I decided to move in close — you can do it with wide-angle (or near-wide) lenses and still pull off a good shot.

Figure 1-3: Pretty little thing.

Figure 1-4 was taken outdoors. The photo is an odd one, but I think it works. The contrast between the blue sky, white siding and gutter, and shadows is interesting.

In this case, the 28mm focal length gives the photo some space breathing room. When I took this shot, I was close to the house, yet the photo is anything but claustrophobic.

35mm

(53mm in 35mm equivalent terms on a camera with a crop factor of 1.5)

The 35mm lens is an excellent standard prime lens for today's cropped-frame bodies. It's perfect for everyday interior shots of people and events, if you're close to your subject. I often use my 35mm lens for birthday parties and holidays.

Figure 1-5 shows an HDR image of the interior of a local bank. I stood in the middle of the lobby and simply looked up at one end to photograph the brackets. The 35mm focal length was great for the room. It had enough "zoom" for me to stand pretty far back and still see the far wall, but not so much that it cropped out the width of the lobby. This is a very practical lens.

Figure 1-4: No rain today.

Figure 1-5: Tower Bank says hello.

Figure 1-6 shows a casual shot of my three kids playing with their cousins' vehicle. Its battery was low, and my wife was helping them get back to the garage. Our then-2-year-old was just learning how to drive.

The magic of using 35mm on a cropped-frame camera for casual shots is that they have a very natural appearance.

Figure 1-6: My son takes a driving test.

50mm

(75mm in 35mm equivalent terms on a camera with a crop factor of 1.5)

Use a 50mm prime lens for close-ups and portraits when you want to concentrate more on the person than on the activity. The focal length emphasizes a person's face at normal distances. If I want to stand further back, the lens is powerful enough to capture good details.

Figure 1-7 shows my wife at a sporting event. I took the shot from about four seats away, which made it a head-and-shoulders shot. (Keep in mind that you can't zoom in and out using a prime lens. I had to take what I could get or move elsewhere). With a maximum aperture of f/1.4, this 50mm lens is fast. I took this photo at f/4.5 and 1/80 second at ISO 100 at the end of a cloudy day with exposure room to spare.

Figure 1-7: Smile for the camera!

I converted the photo shown in Figure 1-7 to black and white and then used software to convert it to Duotone. (See Book VI, Chapter 6 for more information on color conversion.)

Two of my family's antique cameras are shown in Figure 1-8: an old Kodak and a Zeis Ikon Nettar 515.

For shooting still life (small subject studio-type shots), use 50mm lenses. They have enough zoom to photograph small objects but not so much as to be "macro-esque." This lens also generally produces very high-quality photos — perfect for product shots. (To show-case the foreground camera, I used an aperture to soften the Kodak.)

Figure 1-8: Antique cameras.

**Book II
Chapter 1**

**Following the
Prime Directive**

50mm versus 35mm

The 50mm lens is a classic, but the modern cropped-frame equivalent is *not* another 50mm lens. You're better off shooting with a 35mm prime lens if you want to relive the days when every 35mm film SLR had a 50mm prime lens attached to it.

It makes sense if you think about it:

A 50mm lens on a cropped body is closer to telephoto than wide-angle. You *can* get too close with a 50mm lens. The 35mm and 28mm lenses, on the other hand, generally impart a sense of space in photos. They take photos that feel like you're looking at the subject with your eyes.

105mm

(158mm in 35mm equivalent terms on a camera with a crop factor of 1.5)

In the range of 105mm (a significant increase from 50mm) are mostly macro and telephoto lenses.

The image on the left in Figure 1-9 is a shot taken at 105mm in my backyard with a NIKKOR 105mm macro lens. As a bee harvested pollen off a flower, I went outdoors to photograph her. I moved close to the flower (the lens is a macro, after all), and the 105mm gave me a very close field of view.

Figure 1-9: A flower with a bee, and a bee with a flower.

The image on the right in Figure 1-9 shows the same, basic scene at 210mm (the 316mm equivalent), which is what I was able to produce after mounting a 2x teleconverter to the back of the lens.

The difference is astounding. Rather than the flower having plenty of background, the flower occupies almost the entire frame. The background is minimized at 210mm, and the bee is huge.

I don't mean to imply, however, that 210mm is always better than 105mm. Each focal length serves a purpose. As you can see in the caption, the left image is a flower with a bee, and the right image is a bee with a flower. The subject of each photo is very different from the other.

To give your prime lens more flexibility, use a teleconverter or lens extender. Check to see whether your lens is compatible before buying one, and read the fine print. Teleconverters/extenders may not support autofocus, and you will pay a "light penalty" when using one. In other words, the teleconverter will darken the scene by one or more stops, which limits the overall exposure envelope.

300mm

(450mm in 35mm equivalent terms on a camera with a crop factor of 1.5)

The 300mm focal length is powerful, but not *the* most powerful one you can use. It's telephoto, but not supertelephoto. I found this focal length easy to use, which surprised me.

After loading my camera, a few lenses, and one of my sons, into our van, we headed to our family's storage unit. Partway there, we saw a huge crane in action at a hospital and agreed to take some shots on our way back home.

The image on the left in Figure 1-10 shows the crane at 300mm. We were a good distance from it, which is a testament to how powerful a 300mm lens is on a cropped-frame. The crane was set up near the center of the hospital's main building, and we were well positioned in the parking lot.

Figure 1-10: A big crane in action.

You can clearly see the crane operator crossing his legs and the details of the crane. Two benefits of using this lens are not having to fight *lens creep* (when a lens won't stay at the same focal length and wants to subtly zoom in or out, especially when you're not holding the camera straight and level) and not having to make focal length decisions. I put the lens on the camera and started shooting. Whenever I needed to get closer or further away, I just walked.

When I put the 2x teleconverter on the lens, it turned into a 600mm (or 900mm equivalent) super-telephoto monster — jaw-dropping coolness.

I took the shot in the right in Figure 1-10 with the teleconverter attached. It shows the (easily discernable) operator of the crane leaning forward in his cab. You can tell he's bald or clean shaven, is wearing sunglasses, and has blue jeans and a dark blue T-shirt on.

I raised the ISO to 800 for all telephoto shots, to keep the shutter speed high, and I shot with a handheld, if you can believe it. The photos are quite clear, and a little time spent using noise reduction software helped clean them up.

Knowing Why You Should Bother with a Prime Lens

Okay, if you can take the same shots with zoom lenses simply dialed into the focal lengths that I describe earlier in this chapter, why should you bother with primes? Well, as with all lenses, prime lenses have both strengths and weaknesses, and both factors help determine whether prime lenses are the right fit for you.

The following list describes some weaknesses of the prime lens:

- **Flexibility:** A 50mm prime is a 50mm prime. It can't be another lens, so you have to live with the lens' limitations. If you're shooting indoors during a birthday party and can't take the right shots, for example, you have to change lenses.

  The wider the angle, the less trouble I get into (generally) by using my prime lenses. For example, when I put on the 50mm for event photography at home, I tend to take only head shots because that's all I can shoot successfully without leaving the room. Putting on the 35mm provides breathing room.

  Teleconverters add flexibility. Check to see whether your lens has a compatible model. Lenses are available in different magnifications.

- **Lens lugging:** If you want options, you have to carry extra lenses. You can easily pack three or four prime lenses to cover the same focal length range as with a standard zoom lens.

  As your accessories bag becomes heavier, you'll more frequently root through it. More lenses means more to clean, too.

✔ **The switch factor:** Switching lenses takes time, and the process can quickly turn into a major hassle: Stop what you're doing, open your bag, remove the lens from your camera, secure the lens in the bag, take out the new lens and put it on, and return to shooting. (I find this task hard to do with only two hands, which is all I have, and I hate interrupting the action.)

To combat the challenges described in the last two bullets in the list, find a favorite prime lens and try not to switch.

On the other hand, prime lenses have several strengths. Consider them when you're considering buying a prime:

✔ **Sharpness:** Prime lenses are generally sharper than zoom (general purpose or otherwise) lenses. Primes aren't universally sharp at all apertures — in other words, even prime lenses have "sweet spots" and softer zones — but are recognized for their relatively high quality.

✔ **Cost:** Depending on the focal length, prime lenses can cost less than a standard or telephoto zoom lens. You can now buy the best Nikon standard prime lens (the 50mm f/1.4G) for less than $500. The Nikon 70-200mm f/2.8G costs more than $2,000!

The cost benefit decreases as you buy more primes to make up for the limited focal length range. However, you can spread out purchases to make it easier on your bank account.

✔ **Single-mindedness:** Prime lenses force you to focus as a photographer. As the lens recedes into the background of your consciousness, it becomes less of a distraction. You can then think more about composition and exposure than about zooming in and out all the time.

✔ **Speed:** Prime lenses tend to have smaller f/numbers. When a lens has a small f/number (at or under f/2.8), it's called a *fast* lens because the wide aperture lets in more light and allows you to use faster shutter speeds and lower ISO numbers.

The Nikon 50mm f/1.4G, for example, has the widest aperture on any auto focus NIKKOR lens now available. The next closest primes are f/1.8 and then f/2 and f/2.8.

✔ **The absence of lens creep:** Because a prime lens doesn't move in and out, you can hold it in any angle and the lens stays stable. The focal length *cannot change,* so you don't have to worry about lens creep.

This problem can occur on heavy zoom lenses, especially on the less expensive end of the scale. These zoom lenses aren't as solidly built as more expensive zoom lenses and may have trouble staying at their assigned focal length.

Chapter 2: Casting a Wide-Angle Net

In This Chapter

✏ **Defining wide-angle**

✏ **Shooting with wide-angle lenses**

✏ **Going overboard with fisheyes**

✏ **Handling wide-angle distortion**

*N*ot getting fixated on your camera's zoom capability is difficult. It's sort of an arms race: 50mm is fine at first. Then it's not. You need something more. You try 70mm, and then creep toward 85mm, and then 100mm, and then 200mm.

You know, life isn't all about how large you can magnify something in your shots. There's room for the other end of the focal length spectrum too. I want to use this chapter to entice you to try it out.

The wide-angle lens need not be intimidating. It's just as easy to use as any other type of lens. It isn't more expensive. It isn't necessarily heavier than a standard zoom, prime, or telephoto lens.

But wide-angle lenses and the photos you take with them *are* different. You have to deal with it. Cope with it. Embrace it. You shoot subjects differently when you use a wide-angle lens. You can't rely on superduper zoom levels to wow an audience. You have to work at choosing subjects and framing shots to take advantage of a minimal zoom level and a maximum field of view.

Sounds like fun!

Wide-Angle Whatzit

Most photographers have kit lenses with a focal length range of 18mm or so to 55mm, 70mm, or even 85mm. If you've shot on the low end of that range, you've shot wide-angle.

Wide-angle lenses have focal lengths well below those of standard lenses. On cropped-frame cameras, any focal length at or below 24mm is considered good wide-angle territory. On a full-frame camera, 35mm is still considered wide-angle, but it falls into the standard lens category on a cropped-frame dSLR.

Figure 2-1 is a product shot of a typical wide-angle zoom, the Sigma 12-24mm F4.5-5.6 EX DG ASP HSM. This lens hits the sweet spot for full-frame wide angle lenses.

A cropped-frame camera increases the effective focal length of a lens by its crop factor, which means that a 12-24mm lens designed for use on a full-frame dSLR doesn't have the same field of view when you put it on a cropped-frame body. For cropped cameras, the 10-20mm range — technically, ultra wide-angle — creates the same basic photos.

©Sigma Corp.

Figure 2-1: A classic Sigma wide-angle lens.

Table 2-1 lists wide-angle lenses by focal length for cropped-frame dSLRs.

Table 2-1	Cropped-frame Wide-Angle Angles		
General Focal Length	*Wide Angle Class*	*Field of View (with 1.5 Crop Factor)*	*Notes*
8mm to 17mm	Fisheye	As much as 180 degrees	Massive distortion but useful
10mm to 15mm	Ultra-wide angle	110 degrees (at 10mm)	Packs an ultra wide-angle punch; distortion possibly more of a problem when you need the coverage
15mm to 24mm	Wide angle	70 degrees (at 20mm)	Considered the normal wide angle range, with lots of useful wide angle zooms and wide angle primes; distortion less of a problem, depending on lens
28mm to 35mm	Depends on sensor size	44 degrees (at 35mm)	Good wide angle lenses (especially 35mm) on full-frame bodies; narrower field of view on widely used cropped-frames

I discuss fisheye lenses later in this chapter. A fisheye lens has a greater field of view than even an ultra wide-angle lens does — as much as 180 degrees.

The AF DX Fisheye-NIKKOR 10.5mm f/2.8G ED is shown in Figure 2-2, in the center of the photo, between the Nikon D300S camera and the old NIKKOR 28mm prime.

The lens is much smaller than I had imagined. My Sigma 10-20mm F4-5.6 is just behind it, to the left.

Figure 2-2: A gorgeous fisheye lens in the center.

Wide-Angle Fever: Catch It!

You can easily become infected with love for wide-angle lenses. They're fun to use for shooting photos.

A wide-angle lens is more versatile than you might think. It excels at shooting sweeping landscapes, of course, but can also reward you with great-looking shots of other interesting subjects, including interiors.

I shot all photos in this section with my Sigma 10-20mm F4-5.6 on a cropped-sensor body (either the Nikon D200 or Sony Alpha 300). (If you're wondering why I have the same lens in two mounts, it's because I love the lens and want to be able to take photos with it no matter what camera body I am using at the time. Most people don't need two digital SLRs from two different manufacturers. As an author, I value the lessons I learn from each camera and pass them on to you.)

Looking at landscapes

There's no better tool for shooting landscape shots than a digital SLR with a wide-angle lens.

When I shot the photo shown in Figure 2-3, the sun was setting over a river. I bracketed the scene for HDR, but for this figure decided to use a single exposure, to emphasize the silhouettes. I set the lens to 10mm for this shot, which captures a wide area of the river, clouds and sky, and tree line.

Distortion, a common problem with wide-angle lenses, is less obvious when you're shooting landscapes (like the one shown in the figure).

Figure 2-3: Blue-and-gold sunset shot with a wide-angle lens.

Figure 2-4 shows a completely different type of landscape. This more intimate shot looks down a road at a cemetery. The trees on either side restrict your vision, as opposed to the "wide-open-ness" of the last shot.

The trees show a bit more distortion in this shot. You'll find that anything close to the camera will do that. If it bothers you, try removing lens and perspective distortion in software. It rarely bothers me.

You want to know the truly odd part? I took both shots at 10mm.

I converted this scene to black and white; then I tinted it ever-so-slightly to emphasize the shades and tones in the trees.

Capturing interiors

Believe it or not, a wide-angle lens is indispensable when shooting indoors, especially in a small location. If you plan to shoot photos for realtors, invest in a quality wide-angle lens.

Figure 2-5 is a tone-mapped HDR (for more information on tone mapping, flip to Book VI, Chapter 4) image of a set of stairs leading from the top of a parking garage. Shooting with a wide-angle lens enabled me to capture the width of the stairs. A normal focal length lens would have made this example impossible to shoot. You don't always have room to back up when you're indoors!

Figure 2-4: A paradoxically intimate wide-angle landscape.

You point the camera down to make all vertical lines in the photo lean out, or away from the center of the photo. When you point the camera up, vertical lines converge above the frame. These physics concepts are important to remember when you're framing. Sometimes, your audience members won't mind vertical lines not being vertical, but if the photo makes them feel like falling over, they will.

Wide-angle lenses can be incredibly practical. Figure 2-6 is a shot in the kitchen of a house that my family viewed. (We renovated our house while I wrote this book.) The lens can show most of the room — just ignore the decor. Taking this shot is *impossible* without a wide-angle lens.

Figure 2-5: Stairwell in HDR at 10mm.

Choose your digital SLR with a wide-angle lens (or, better, an ultra-wide one) over your compact camera for tasks such as house shopping. When you review the photos, you can look at *whole rooms* (Figure 2-6 was taken at 10mm) instead of only corners. This way, you can more easily plan where to put your stuff and how you want to decorate it or how to tear it out and replace everything.

Figure 2-6: Inspecting a kitchen.

Getting those buildings

Wide-angle lenses are useful for photographing buildings.

If you want to see an entire *building* in your shot, use a wide-angle lens. If you want to see a specific feature of the building, take out your zoom or telephoto lens.

Figure 2-7 shows a wide-angle shot of the hospital in my hometown, where my oldest son was born. We returned a few years later and showed him the hospital while we were there. I took the shot as we were leaving.

You would expect to see some distortion in the shot I took at 10mm, or possibly perspective problems, but this photo proves that you can shoot conventional-looking photos using a wide-angle lens.

Figure 2-7: Wide-angle shots can look delightfully normal at times.

The key to keeping things looking natural is to keep the camera level with the ground and mask the outer edges of the photo with natural objects that hide the distortion.

Figure 2-8 shows the courthouse in my town. I was standing close to it as I took this photo. One advantage or working with a wide-angle lens is that you can stand close to a building and see quite a bit of it at one time.

When I processed the photo (taken at 16mm), the sky in the upper-right corner didn't look right. It wasn't blown out (overexposed), but it looked like it was. I did the best I could in raw and then applied an artistic filter to the photo in Photoshop. The result looks like an illustration.

Figure 2-8: An artistic courthouse.

Odds and ends

Wide-angle lenses can help you photograph subjects that you might not believe are suitable for an expanded field of view.

I took the photo shown in Figure 2-9 of a John Deere 863B Series II Elevated Scraper parked in its depot. The focal length was 10mm. You would think that, at 10mm, a vehicle would be small and the landscape would be huge.

Think again.

The key to using a wide-angle lens to shoot vehicles is to get up close and personal to your subject. You can't stand 20 feet away and expect to fill a wide-angle frame with a vehicle. You have to be within 5 feet or so, depending on the size of the subject. In this case, I set up my tripod about 3 feet away.

Figure 2-9: Big scraper, sitting idle.

On the other hand, you can take photos of smaller items too. Figure 2-10 shows an emergency call box located on top of the parking garage that the stairs led to earlier (refer to Figure 2-5).

It isn't tiny, but it isn't as large as a huge construction vehicle, either. To get the shot, I set up my tripod close to the box and oriented the camera vertically. Afterward, I corrected a bit of distortion in software and added a cross-processed look. That brought out the texture in the concrete wall and the electrical boxes.

At a focal length of 20mm, the lens acts more like a conventional wide-angle lens. Experiment with different focal lengths and try to make the best use of the lens with the subject.

Figure 2-10: A nonstandard, wide-angle shot.

Using Fisheye Lenses

On the extreme end of the wide-angle spectrum are fisheye lenses. Just like their wide-angle relatives, they're incredibly fun to use. The (roughly) 180-degree diagonal field of view puts a whole new twist on taking unique photos.

I shot the following photos with the Nikon AF DX Fisheye-Nikkor 10.5mm f/2.8G ED lens.

Figure 2-11 shows an interesting take on a flower as shown through the fisheye lens. I was close to it when I took the photo.

Unlike a macro lens, which zooms in so closely that it omits all else from the frame, a fisheye lens *includes* everything else.

Figure 2-11: Coming in for a landing.

You see the interesting zoom effect where the stems and flowers surrounding the center of the photo appear to be coming out at you because I corrected the fisheye distortion in the Nikon Capture NX 2. On many photos, I leave in the fisheye effect, but in this photo, taking it out made the photo even more interesting. Blurring the other flowers made the center flower more prominent.

Decisions you make in software programs can dramatically affect your photos.

Not everything has to be done outdoors. I took the photo shown in Figure 2-12 in the same kitchen as the one shown earlier (in Figure 2-6). Because of the fisheye lens, you can see everything in the kitchen, out into the hallway, and into the room beyond. The perspective is fascinating. The door behind the refrigerator is visible, as are the lights on the ceiling and most of the floor. (The only thing not in the shot seems to be me.)

REMEMBER

Figure 2-12 shows a practical use of a fisheye lens. As with wide-angle lenses, you can use fisheye lenses indoors to take photos of entire rooms. With a fisheye lens, you get not only the two or three walls you're pointing at but also all four walls in the same shot. Looking at rooms within a home (or elsewhere) then becomes much more effective.

Figure 2-12: Kitchen v1.5.

If you're wondering whether fisheye lenses work as well with people as they do with objects, the answer is

Yes.

Figure 2-13 is a charming photo of my daughter, taken with a fisheye lens. All four of my kids were jumping around and generally hamming it up to help me get some interesting fisheye shots. Figure 2-13 captured a moment of calm. (Everyone else — the rest of the kids and my wife — are hiding directly behind me in the photo.)

Figure 2-13: Grace, with her big blue eyes.

My daughter is quite close to the camera, but that doesn't stop you from being able to see the entire room. (I love that about fisheye lenses.) I took out the fisheye distortion from this photo, which made her head look less distorted. Unlike Figure 2-11, the rest of the room wasn't affected by this process.

The photo shown in Figure 2-14, proves that you can "go crazy" with people and fisheye lenses. After struggling with ways to help my kids look interesting, I remembered an earlier idea.

At the end of *Flash Gordon* (1980), one of my favorite offbeat movies, Flash jumps up victoriously toward the camera. This funny moment is a wonderful way to end the film. My idea was for the kids to jump up. I would take their photo, just like Flash.

Figure 2-14: Jumping Ben Flash.

Dealing with distortion

If you're a serious architecture photographer, you might want to remove as much lens distortion as possible. If you're shooting general landscapes and other subjects, distortion is often less noticeable and not seen as such a drawback. I generally leave it in and don't worry about it, except in the most egregious situations.

You can try taking out distortion by using the Photoshop (or Elements) Remove Camera Distortion filter or, depending on your raw convertor, as you develop the raw exposure. I cover the former topic in Chapter 3 of Book VI.

It worked, mostly. A few photos looked like they could close the movie, but keeping my kids from blurring was difficult. I wasn't using a flash at first.

Rather than raise the ISO all the way to 1,638,400 to create a faster shutter speed, I decided to try out a speedlight. The result was a cool photo not even close to what I had envisioned but nonetheless compelling.

Sometimes, you have to roll with the punches.

This shot is framed vertically so that you can see the difference in a conventional fisheye shot. The distortion seems to be lessened. Some vignetting occurs, which I purposely made more pronounced. I also darkened the background more than it was originally.

Wide-Angle Tips

Consider the tips in this section as you use wide-angle lenses. And, don't let my list of Things That Can Go Wrong scare you away from using wide-angle lenses — even the wide-angle region of your zoom lens.

- ✔ **Watch your feet:** If you're not careful, you can capture yourself or your tripod or other unintended objects in the frame.

- ✔ **Be careful:** If you happen to be walking while looking in the viewfinder (not a great idea, but sometimes it happens), pay attention to where you're going.

- ✔ **Watch the horizon:** Wide-angle shots make you pay a heavy penalty for poor composition and framing because so much more scenery appears in the shot. Don't be a slave to the rule of thirds, but don't bisect the frame with the horizon unless you intend to. And, try not to intend to do it often.

- ✓ **Level:** A crooked horizon can be distracting unless it's a purposeful design element of the photo. If you can't eyeball it, use a level.

- ✓ **Background:** Backgrounds are more important in wide-angle photography because more of them appear in each frame. This element is frustrating because sometimes it seems like an ugly background lurks around every corner. Watch for light, power, and phone poles and wires, people, and vehicles.

- ✓ **Vignetting:** Wide-angle lenses vignette quite often. Their corners are darker than their centers. You can correct this problem in software, but I sometimes use vignetting purposely, to make the photo look interesting.

- ✓ **Distortion:** Wide-angle lenses tend to distort more than normal lenses. Also, you can more easily point the camera at odd angles and introduce perspective problems. Pay attention to perspective when setting up. Correct either problem by using software.

- ✓ **Chromatic aberration:** I've run into more chromatic aberration problems with wide-angle lenses as compared to standard prime lenses and normal zoom lenses. You can try correcting this problem with software, but I've never been particularly happy with the results. Most often, it happens when I'm trying to shoot into the sunset.

- ✓ **Ease up:** If you have a lens with particularly bad distortion and vignetting, try easing up on the focal length. See whether a sweet spot shows off the lens best. If not, consider returning it to the store for a different wide-angle lens.

- ✓ **Auto focusing:** Using auto focus to target a specific feature in your scene may not work, even if you place the object under an auto focus point. This is a problem of scale if the object of interest is small: The background overpowers it, and the camera doesn't lock onto what you want. Switch to manual focus.

- ✓ **People indoors:** I find that photographing a room full of people (for example, sitting in a circle and opening Christmas presents) with an ultra-wide-angle lens brings out excessive camera distortion and perspective problems. It feels like the people are too small and the room is too large. Vignetting can also be a problem. These problems don't seem as severe when photographing single subjects.

Book II
Chapter 2

Casting a Wide-
Angle Net

Chapter 3: Focusing on Versatility

*T*he first dSLR lens I owned was a kit lens from Sony — the DT 18-70mm f/3.5-5.6 — and it came with my Alpha 300. The lens has been discontinued, but I still have every photo I've ever taken with it (and still use it).

Is my Sony lens the sharpest one available? No. It's not the best model ever made either, nor is it all that rugged or indestructible. In fact, it's pretty average.

That's not the whole story though. My inexpensive Sony zoom lens is versatile, takes good pictures, and fits my needs. I learned a lot from using it.

This chapter describes lenses that are just like my Sony 18-70mm, with its focus on versatility. This single lens is capable of wide-angle shots, standard photography, and moderate macro or telephoto work.

That sounds like a deal!

What Makes a Swiss Army Lens?

A Swiss army knife, noted for its versatility, has a screwdriver, a toothpick, a magnifying glass, a wine bottle opener, and, of course, knife blades. That list sounds like it has everything you would ever need for a nice wine-and-cheese picnic in the Alps.

But I digress. (Is it possible to digress before I even make a point?)

A *standard zoom* lens, also known as a *multipurpose zoom, zoom, normal zoom,* or *general-purpose zoom* lens, is designed to be, above all else, versatile. Table 3-1 organizes several types of zoom lenses into classes.

Table 3-1	Cropped dSLR Zoom Ranges	
Class	*Sample Focal Length*	*What It Does*
Wide-angle zoom	10-20mm	Takes wide-angle shots; has no true "normal" focal length. An example is my Sigma 10-20mm, used for interiors and landscapes. You trade some versatility for better wide-angle characteristics.
Normal zoom	18-70mm	Serves as an excellent everyday lens. This versatile lens has good wide-angle capability (18-24mm) and zooms into low telephoto range (50-70mm) on cropped-frame dSLRs.
Telephoto zoom	70-200mm	May provide good wide-angle coverage. For example, the NIKKOR 18-200mm lens takes excellent wide-angle and telephoto shots — and everything in between. The feature that differentiates these lenses from the rest is its telephoto end; 200mm is far more effective at reaching out than 70-85mm.
Super telephoto zoom	200-400mm	Serves in place of a pure telephoto lens. You trade overall versatility for telephoto versatility — helpful because changing a telephoto lens can be a hassle.

This chapter primarily describes normal or standard zoom lenses. I use my wide-angle zoom lens (10-20mm) in Chapter 2 of this minibook. For this chapter, I'm using two lenses: 18-70mm (on a Sony Alpha 300) and 18-200mm (with a Nikon D200).

The Zoom Lens, Pro and Con

As you might imagine, zoom lenses have pros and cons. Not everyone likes them. Some people love them.

Here are some areas where you can benefit from using a zoom lens:

- **Versatility:** A general-purpose zoom lens is the king of versatility, whether it's wide-angle or zoomed in, or somewhere in between.

- **Weight:** Carrying around one lens is a lot easier than carrying three or four prime lenses. One weighs less and takes up less space. You don't need an extra-large camera bag in which to carry all your equipment.

✓ **Cost:** A manufacturer may offer several tiers of zoom lenses, but entry-level general-purpose zoom lenses are generally reasonably priced. You get a lot of versatility for not a lot of money. When you decide to upgrade, you can always find something more expensive.

✓ **Economies of scale:** Manufacturers build and sell a lot of zoom lenses. This translates into a good selection. Large manufacturers may have three or four or more viable zoom lenses, each with different focal length ranges, strengths, and weaknesses.

REMEMBER

You can probably find exactly the lens you need without having to look too far.

Here are some potential disadvantages of using a zoom lens:

✓ **Quality:** Some people resist buying entry-level, general-purpose zoom lenses. Objectively, these lenses don't have the same quality as lenses that sell for $1,000 or more. If you're a novice or don't have much to spend, an average-quality lens is better than no lens at all.

✓ **Cost:** As you move up the quality scale, zoom lenses can become quite pricey. And, who can stop at one lens, even if it's a good zoom? Not me.

✓ **Weight:** Some zoom lenses are quite heavy, especially compared to primes. Although a handful of primes may weigh collectively more, you can't put them on the camera all at the same time.

Varsity Versatility

In this section, I show you some of the versatility of the zoom lens.

I reviewed my photo library and chose the following four completely different photo shoots, to mirror what you might do with your zoom lens:

✓ **Photo walkabout:** We all take walks with our cameras in hand. Take a zoom lens with you the next time you're out, so that you can photograph large and small subjects.

✓ **Birthday party:** Birthday parties are a challenge to photograph. Having a zoom lens gives you the flexibility to go with the flow.

✓ **Sports activity:** You need more zoom than normal if you're heading out to practice or a ballgame. If you want shots that include more than the athlete, don't neglect wide-angle focal lengths.

✓ **Street festival:** Street photography is all about people. When you use your zoom lens, you have the flexibility of moving in close or standing farther back.

I used my Sony Alpha 300 and its kit lens (DT 18-70mm f/3.5-5.6) to create all photos in this chapter except for the ones taken at baseball practice. For those, I used a Nikon D300S with an AF-S DX NIKKOR 18-200mm f/3.5-5.6G ED VR II lens. The latter proved quite useful in helping me reach out and get some good telephoto shots.

Table 3-2 categorizes the figures in this chapter by focal length and briefly describes each photo, to give you some context.

Table 3-2			Focal Lengths
Figure	*Focal Length (mm)*	*35mm equivalent (mm)* *	*Notes*
3-1	18	27	Wide-angle shot of the road ahead
3-2	35	53	Standard shot of an interesting tree stump
3-3	45	68	Looking up at leaves from a distance
3-4	70	105	Close-up of flowers
3-5	18	27	Wide-angle shot of partiers around a table blowing out candles
3-6	35	53	Standard portrait of my daughter wondering about her present
3-7	50	75	Close-up of my daughter kissing her doll
3-8	60	90	Close-up of my son plugging his ears
3-9	18	27	Wide-angle shot of team practice
3-10	29	44	Standard shot of bats
3-11	70	105	Throwing and catching from a distance
	120	180	Zooming in to isolate my son and his teammate
3-12	200	300	Telephoto of my son from a distance
3-13	18	27	Close-up, wide-angle portrait
3-14	35	53	Standard close-up but with a background distraction
	18	27	Way too many bystanders
	40	60	Zooming in crops out distractions
3-15	55	83	Portrait from a distance
3-16	60	90	Telephoto portrait getting head and shoulders

* 35mm equivalent was calculated using a crop factor of 1.5. Your mileage may vary.

Going on a photo walkabout

Zoom lenses are fun to take on photo excursions. They give you the flexibility to zoom in for close-ups and zoom out for landscapes regardless of whether you stay on or off the trail. You have much more flexibility when framing than if you walk around shooting with a prime lens.

You may not always be able to find a good spot to take photos. Having a zoom lens means that you can get those shots and many others without a hassle.

I took the wide-angle shot in Figure 3-1 while looking down the road. The point of the photo is to see the trees on both sides of the road. After I zoomed out as much as possible, I was able to capture the scene. (Score one for wide-angle.)

Figure 3-1: Wide-angle perspective of the scenery.

As I walked, I saw other interesting things. They didn't all scream "wide-angle!" In fact, I needed to zoom in for most of the others. Figure 3-2 shows a 35mm shot of a tree stump that someone converted into an attractive display of a house number. To avoid walking on the lawn, I zoomed in a little to capture the scene.

This shot is standard: It's neither wide-angle nor super close-up. This focal length is natural, and being able to quickly zoom to this range as you're walking is helpful.

I took the photo in Figure 3-3 to show off some dogwood blooms. I had to stand below them and zoom in because the tree was fairly tall.

Using a general purpose zoom lens isn't rocket science. You walk around, point your camera at things you see, zoom to frame the shot you want, and then snap the picture. Having a zoom lens gives you the ability to flexibly frame subjects at different distances, whether they're trees, stumps, or roads.

Figure 3-4 shows a close-up of some red and purple flowers amid their green leaves. Shots like this one show off the telephoto end of a zoom lens. I was standing quite close to the flowers and wanted them to dominate the photo.

For a comparison, refer to Figure 3-1. Both photos were taken with the *same lens*. (Let that statement sink in for a minute.) Even using a standard zoom lens, you can move from sweeping wide-angle to extreme close-ups.

Figure 3-2: Americana at 35mm.

Figure 3-3: Dogwood in bloom.

You do a bit of zooming with your feet on walks because subjects vary widely with respect to size. Standard zoom lenses generally work well. They have wide-angle capability to photograph the landscape as a whole yet you can zoom in on flowers or other singular subjects.

Figure 3-4: Zooming in on flowers.

Having fun at parties

Standard zoom lenses are useful for events and parties. They prevent you from having to carry around your camera bag and change lenses every few minutes because the action keeps changing, and they prevent you from repeatedly shooting the same photo because you're "stuck" on a focal length. (I've been there.)

Figures 3-5 through 3-8 show you what I mean. Our immediate family celebrates six birthdays per year, which gives me lot of opportunities to experiment with different lenses, focal lengths, and distances.

Figure 3-5 shows my kids blowing out candles during my daughter's third birthday party. A shot like this one *must* be taken with a wide-angle lens. I didn't have enough room to back away and use a standard or telephoto lens. A 35mm prime would have come *close*, but having the extra field of view in a crowded room is priceless.

Room dynamics continually change. Zoom lenses enable you to adapt to the situation and take the right photograph for the moment. Figure 3-6 illustrates this point well. As my daughter sat on the couch surrounded by her presents and her siblings and other partygoers, I zoomed in to block them out because I wanted to show her shaking her present.

Figure 3-5: Blowing out candles is a wide-angle event.

Fortunately, I wasn't using a prime lens that had too much zoom (my 50mm prime would have been too close). By the same token, I wasn't shooting with a wide-angle lens, either, which would have meant I couldn't "crop out" the other partygoers.

Figure 3-6: What's in there?

Some moments are fleeting and magical. Figure 3-7 shows an example. My daughter had just opened a present and happily puckered up to show her excitement. I quickly framed the scene and snapped a close-up of the action.

Advantage: zoom.

Figure 3-7: Puckering up.

In Figure 3-8, the last photo in this group, I stood on the opposite side of the table from one of my sons and sang "Happy Birthday" along with everyone else. I dialed in a near telephoto focal length (60mm) and captured the memorable image of him sticking his fingers in his ears. (I guess our singing bothered him!)

You don't need a super zoom to shoot party photos. You'll appreciate having a lens that has a wide-angle focal length of 18 to 20mm and zooms to between 50 and 70mm. If you're standing farther away, you might be able to get by with a lens that zooms to 85mm, but in rooms of normal size, 85mm is often too strong.

Photographing sports and action

If your kids or someone else you know plays sports, having a good zoom lens is important. Take it to practice and games to photograph the action on and off the field (or court or diamond or whatever).

Figure 3-8: Apparently, not a fan of certain songs.

Your camera needs more zoom than a standard zoom offers during these types of activities because you tend to be farther away from the action. Look for a lens with more than 100mm at the telephoto end, though having a good wide-angle capability is helpful for taking context shots of the field and your surroundings. The 18-200mm zoom lens I'm using to write this section is perfect: It has the same wide-angle capability as my 18-70mm.

Figure 3-9 shows a wide-angle shot of my kids practicing throwing and catching. A coach stands nearby, to teach. I'm standing just behind home plate. Because I was at practice, I wandered around more than I would during a game.

This wide-angle shot shows off everything that's happening. It has the field, the players, the trees, and the sky.

As I walked around, I tried to take photos of other interesting items. Figure 3-10 shows where bats are hung on hooks mounted to a board and then mounted on a fence. I took this photo at 35mm and was standing close (but the photo is not too close and not too wide).

The image on the left in Figure 3-11 shows a closer shot of my son and his teammate throwing the ball to each other. The element that separates this photo from others is its feeling of space. Despite being at 70mm, it has a wide-angle feel to it. You can see the dugout in the background, people watching, and the scenery beyond the field. This would be as close as my 18-70mm could get. It would be nice to have more, which is why I was using an 18-200mm.

Figure 3-9: Wide-angle shot captures the field of dreams.

In the image on the right in Figure 3-11, I zoomed to 120mm. The result is a completely different shot of exactly the same subjects doing the same thing. The shot is closer and more focused, and although you can see the background, it has less of an impact on the photo. The photo has the feel of a shot taken at 35mm, which demonstrates the importance of using the telephoto end of the lens in certain situations. It does, however, exhibit some *telephoto effect*. At longer focal lengths, distances between objects appear more compressed than photos taken from the same perspective but with smaller focal lengths.

The shot shown in Figure 3-12 is another one that looks more like it was taken with a standard lens rather than a telephoto. My son was near second base, and I was close to the dugout along the first base line (according to

Figure 3-10: Bats in the belfry.

the EXIF data, I was 15 meters away). I shot the photo at 200mm, which is perfect for nearby sideline shots like this. It shows the action, but because I'm relatively far away, it still has some "breathing" room.

Figure 3-11: The telephoto effect in action.

As you can see, sports and action photography requires more zoom level than a standard zoom lens has, but you can use wide-angle focal lengths too. If you can't (or don't want to) get an 18-200mm or similar lens, look for the Canon 70-200mm line or a 70-300mm lens. Not all of them are super expensive. For example, the Canon EF 75-300mm f/4-5.6 III lists for only $199.99.

Figure 3-12: Close-up shot from across the field.

Traveling light

Historically, street photographers attached 50mm lenses to their cameras and never changed them again. These folks could make do with a single focal length for years. Having a zoom is helpful, however, when you're walking around and want to frame people with some variety.

In Figure 3-13, a woman is hammering a copper bowl. I took this shot at a wide angle — 18mm. I stood close to the woman so that she would be large enough to see without occupying the entire photo. Framing people "loosely" — so that you can see their surroundings — is an effective way to shoot portraits (although in this case I could have isolated her from the

Figure 3-13: Getting up close but getting a lot of scenery.

background better and waited for the guy bending over in the background to move). Using the wide-angle area of your zoom lens makes it possible.

I shot the first photo shown in Figure 3-14 at 35mm. It feels a little closer to 50mm than a standard 35mm shot because I was standing next to the gentleman as I shot the photo. The zoom lens gave me the flexibility to widen the shot to include his head and shoulders (and the lady to the left, unfortunately).Compare the 35mm with an 18mm and 40mm shot of the same subject. At 18mm, there is quite a bit of background distraction. I like the shot at 35mm (the lower-left image), but it too has someone straggling by. I turned the camera vertically and zoomed in to 40mm to isolate the subject from the background and get the best shot.

Figure 3-14: Three photos of the same subject with different focal lengths.

Figure 3-15 show an example of focal length role reversal. This photo looks more like it was shot at 35mm than 55mm, but I stood far enough away to avoid crowding the subject. I zoomed in to 55mm and took the shot as though it were a 35mm portrait.

Having a zoom lens gave me the flexibility to choose just how to frame the scene. I didn't have to move closer or farther away — I simply gave the lens a twist and took the shot.

Figure 3-16 shows another portrait, taken at 60mm from a normal distance. Had I been closer (or zoomed all the way to 70mm) in this typical head-and shoulders-shot, I would have cropped out the shoulders and lost the background.

As you can see, street photography is about people, including lots of variety and changing situations. Sometimes you're close to a subject, and sometimes you're farther away. Having a zoom lens gives you the flexibility to frame the shots you want, no matter where you are.

Figure 3-15: Zooming in on someone.

Figure 3-16: Using zoom for a close-up.

Chapter 4: Going to the Extremes

*I*f you like being different, this chapter is for you.

Most photographers own a kit lens or have upgraded to a better general-purpose zoom. Many have prime lenses. Quite a few, especially landscape and interior photographers, have wide and ultra-wide-angle lenses. A few have macro lenses, and a few still have true telephoto lenses. Both macro and telephoto lenses excel at making things appear big.

The manner in which you use them tends to be completely different.

A macro lens tries to focus on what it sees on the camera's sensor without changing its size. In other words, it doesn't (ideally) magnify or reduce. It translates. For this reason, you work at close distances with macro lenses.

A telephoto lens, on the other hand, uses its long focal length to magnify small or distant objects, like a telescope. You can be hundreds of feet away from your subject, and the telephoto lens enlarges it in your viewfinder.

Both types of lenses are fun to work with and can create stunning photos.

Doing the Macro–Micro Tango

If you're interested in shooting close-up, you're in the right half of the right chapter. Pull up a chair *real close* and have a listen. Macro photography is somewhat specialized — you can't just slap a kit lens on your camera, zoom in close to your subject, snap the photo, and call it a macro. (Many people do, but the resulting photo is not technically a true macro shot.)

To see how macro photography differs from a standard close-up, have a look at these characteristics:

✓ **Distance:** Macro photography requires getting close to your subject. Depending on the lens you're using, you can position yourself a foot away from your subject (and possibly even closer). True macro lenses have the ability to focus on objects much closer than standard zoom or prime lenses.

In Figure 4-1, I've positioned myself close to my wife's wedding and engagement rings. Because I'm so close and also because of the lens' magnification, the rings look huge. With a standard or telephoto lens, you rely more on the focal length to magnify.

Figure 4-1: Get close with a macro lens.

✓ **Reproduction ratio:** Macro lenses focus objects on the sensor closer to their actual size than non-macro lenses. This is called the *reproduction ratio*. Because one-to-one ratios aren't impossible, if a marble is a half-inch in diameter in real life, it's the same size on the sensor.

Figure 4-2 shows the marble in question. The macro lens was able to reproduce the marble on the sensor at or near the same size it is in real life. It's like putting it on a copying machine.

Contrast the reproduction ratio of a macro with your favorite wide-angle lens. The wide-angle pulls in vast amounts of scenery and squeezes it onto a tiny (all things considered) sensor. In that

Figure 4-2: Big, blue marble.

case, the lens micro-miniaturizes what is in the frame as it focuses it on the sensor.

✓ **Specialized lens:** True macro photography relies on special *macro* lenses. (Nikon calls them micro lenses.) They're constructed to be able to focus at very close ranges and have reproduction ratios that are as large as possible.

Despite what you might think, focal length has nothing to do with whether a lens is considered macro. You can find macro primes with focal lengths beginning at 35mm and 50mm and "topping out" around

100mm. Sigma has a line of zoom macro lenses that tend to start in the teens, such as the 17-70mm F2.8-4.5 DC Macro, and may have focal lengths at the upper end of 300mm, such as the 28-300mm F3.5-6.3 DG Macro.

I'm using the AF-S VR Micro-Nikkor 105mm f/2.8G IF-ED lens to write this chapter. This lens is also compatible with the Nikon 2x teleconverter (AF-S Teleconverter TC-20E III), which converts the lens into a 210mm macro monster.

✏ **Cool factor:** Macro photos tend to evoke "oohs" and "aahs" from people because they give us a vantage point we don't see normally. Small bugs become huge. Hidden details become visible. The mundane can become magical. You can even literally see the hair on a fly's backside.

Backyard macro-que

You don't have to set up in a studio to shoot macros. To shoot photos for this section, I walked around in my backyard with a Nikon D300S and the 105mm macro lens. You do, however, have some issues to consider:

✏ **Tripod shooting is nice but inflexible:** I found out when I set up my camera on its tripod and zeroed in on a flower, all the bugs chose the other flowers to land on. Hmm. After waiting for a few minutes, I ditched the tripod and began stalking bugs on foot.

If you're patient in the right situation (for example, you have a bird feeder within close range that birds visit regularly), you can set up your camera on a tripod and pretend that you're on safari in Africa.

✏ **The camera gets heavy:** After I abandoned the tripod, the camera felt fine in my hands. By the end of the day, however, it felt heavy, and the D300S is a heavy camera to begin with. The macro lens was big and beefy, and when I added the heavy metal teleconverter, it got heavier.

The heaviness isn't a big deal in normal photography, but when shooting macros, you're focusing on such tiny items that any camera movement can knock you out of the focal plane. Keeping elements steady is difficult, even with fast shutter speeds and vibration reduction turned on.

✏ **Focusing can be difficult:** Add in camera weight, a very shallow depth of field, and bugs that don't stay still for long, focusing was hard to keep up with. (No matter the aperture, I was so close to my subjects that the depth of field was always very small.)

I tried using auto focus in the beginning, but the camera kept focusing on the wrong part of the plant, bee, or fly. Switching to manual focus was an improvement, but I had to continue to fine-tune the focus.

For example, in Figure 4-3, I nailed the focus on the fly's back and flower. The problem is that his head and tail are out of focus. Part of the problem is depth of field, but the other part (which is sizeable) is the speed at which you have to focus manually because bugs fly and crawl at insanely fast speeds.

Figure 4-3: Focus problems ruin this photo of a fly.

✔ **Bugs are speedy:** If you're shooting bugs, you have to handle movement. One bee I tracked moved diligently from flower to flower to flower. (That's what bees do.) Every time it landed, I had to locate the bee again, position myself and the camera, and then frame, refocus, and shoot before she buzzed away.

In the frame shown in Figure 4-4, I showed up a little late. The bee had already collected the pollen and was on its way to another flower when I snapped this photo.

Figure 4-4: Buzzing away.

If you're shooting either inanimate or slow-moving objects, tracking, framing, and focusing gets easier.

✐ **Shutter speed needs maximized:** On the whole, I tried to keep the shutter speed at a high level. The bugs and flowers were moving, which made a fast shutter critical for clear, sharp photos. To get the speed I wanted, I raised the ISO and enabled vibration reduction. (I used an external speedlight toward the evening hours.)

✐ **Aperture is critical:** At first I opened the camera, but then realized that the depth of field was too shallow for me. Because I couldn't keep my subjects in focus, I stooped to try to deepen the depth of field.

However, on a different rainy day, I experimented with depth of field effects. Figure 4-5 shows rain droplets on the leaf of a plant. The depth of field is incredibly narrow, but was done purposely. As a result, the resulting photo is much more interesting.

Figure 4-5: Depth of field is about four water droplets deep.

✐ **Having a flash is helpful:** One evening, I went out with my teleconverter and an SB-600 Speedlight. The speedlight let me lower the ISO and maintain the shutter speed. I had no problem with the lens casting a shadow.

Figure 4-6 shows one of my best shots with this lens. The image of the fly is sharp, clear, colorful, and in focus. Everything seemed to work right for this photo. If you look carefully, you can see my reflection in the fly's body segments. The brighter spots are from the flash.

Figure 4-6: That is one hairy-bottomed fly!

✔ **The wind is a factor:** Outdoors, the wind blows and flowers blow with it. Setting up a shot and ensuring that it's in focus, only to have the wind blow the flower out of the frame, is frustrating.

✔ **You don't always need to be microscopically close:** I took the photo shown in Figure 4-7 of a rusty grating. I'm close to the subject, but the photo isn't one that you would think was shot by an electron microscope.

Figure 4-7: Mix it up!

✏ **Feel free to zoom in by using software:** Even though you've taken the shot with a macro lens, no law says you can't zoom in when you process the photo in software.

In Figure 4-8, you can see that another fly landed on a paver in the garden. As I leaned over to take a picture and moved closer to refocus and shoot, I wanted to avoid rushing and scaring away the fly. I shot several clear-looking photos, which cried out to be magnified in Photoshop.

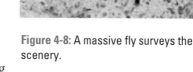

Figure 4-8: A massive fly surveys the scenery.

✏ **It's fun:** Despite the challenge, backyard macro shooting is fun. I felt great satisfaction at being able to get superclose shots of amazing subjects. Even *I* "oohed" and "aahed."

Figure 4-9 shows a Japanese beetle on a plant. You can see where it was (or they were) eating. I sat down, thankful to have a bug that moved at a more leisurely pace and wasn't flitting to and fro. (It looks like it's scaling Everest.)

Figure 4-9: Because it's there.

Going to the Extremes

Shooting macros in the basement

Shooting indoors is a world all its own. There, you routinely set up your camera on a tripod and shoot carefully framed subjects at very close ranges. You don't have to worry about the sun, the wind, flying bugs, or a camera that grows heavier with every photo you take.

In addition to choosing interesting subjects, the challenges are mainly lighting and depth of field.

✏ **No flash:** You can shoot macros in a studio without using a flash. The character of the lighting is different than with a flash. You have to be content with slower shutter speeds or higher ISOs.

✏ **Pop-up flash:** Don't even bother unless you have a very short macro lens. The 105mm I was using was long, and I used the lens hood. I have this problem with many of my normal non-macro lenses, so it didn't surprise me. The problem is, the longer the lens and the shorter the distance to the subject, the more distance you need to move the flash away from the camera to keep the lens from casting a huge shadow over everything. Pop-up flashes won't work in these cases because the lens is always getting in the way.

✐ **External flash:** Seriously consider investing in an external flash, or speedlight. When you mount it on your camera's hot shoe, the flash can clear the lens in most situations.

Ideally, you want to be able to mount the flash off-camera using a sync cord. (Wireless is even better.) You can then creatively design the photo and the flash away from the lens. When you're working at very close ranges, it can mean the difference between lighting your subject or not.

You can also get a *ring light,* specifically designed to light close subjects unobtrusively.

✐ **More complicated lighting setups:** Because your goal is to shed light on your subject, having more gear enables you to be as flexible as possible. The possibilities that arise from using extra gear are endless. You have more options to create different lighting setups and effects.

The downside to using more flashes and lighting is that you must buy a lot more gear, have the space necessary to set up a studio, and become a flash expert.

The upside is that you can patiently work your craft and *design* the photos you want to shoot — an amazing feat when it works out. Figure 4-10 shows a bunch of breath mints I dumped and then photographed by using an external speedlight as a strobe and two continuous lights mounted on stands, pointing down at the table. I wanted a lot of light!

Figure 4-10: Designing with breath mints.

Where to go from here

I can't possibly show you all the ins and outs of macro photography in half a chapter. I hope you can see what's possible, though, when you use these fantastically cool lenses.

The deeper you get into macro photography, the more you'll discover different equipment and techniques such as using bellows, single lens reversal, teleconverters (extension tubes), reversing lenses, advanced flash techniques, and more.

Tele- (Oh, My Word!) Photo

A telephoto lens pulls in detail from far away and brings it directly into your camera. Chances are good that the first thing that pops into your mind when you see a huge telephoto lens is "Holy cow!" Your second reaction is most likely "How much did it cost!?"

Telephoto lenses are expensive. Most of them cost more than a thousand dollars, and many more cost well beyond that. Using one isn't a task for the timid.

The telephoto lens is irreplaceable, however. A digital zoom, popular on compact digital cameras and an option in software, can take you only so far. Without detail, you're only magnifying mush.

Moon shot face-off

In this section, I describe the difference between a true telephoto lens and a high-quality zoom lens. (And, I want to take advantage of having rented two awesome lenses for this part of the book.) The contenders are both from Nikon. On one side is the AF-S NIKKOR 300mm f/4D IF-ED. (Check out Figure 4-11 to see it on a Nikon D300S.) This modest telephoto lens has a lot of power for a reasonable (all things considered) price of just under $1,500.

Figure 4-11: An impressive but semi-affordable telephoto lens.

To augment this lens, I rented the AF-S Teleconverter TC-20E III lens. It optically doubles the focal length of the lens it's attached to (2x), but at the price of a few f/stops of light-gathering capability. (In other words, the effective aperture of the lens is reduced by two full stops due to the increased focal length.) I had 600mm of cropped focal length and 900mm of 35mm effective focal length at my fingertips.

On the other side of this face-off is the AF-S DX NIKKOR 18-200mm f/3.5-5.6G ED VR II — a *good* lens. For about $800, it includes vibration reduction and good speed, and it's ultra versatile.

Beginning with the zoom lens, I show you a progression of moon shots with various focal lengths, as shown in Figure 4-12.

From 18mm through 70mm, the moon looks like a dot that grows to a blob. No details are visible. Only after I reached 135mm (remember that I'm using a Nikon D200, which has a crop factor of 1.5 — convert that number to your situation to compare apples to apples) did the resolving power of the lens start to pick0 up detail on the moon (which, to be fair to the lens, is quite good).

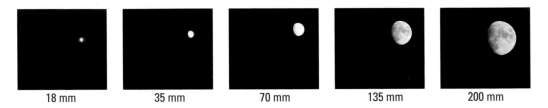

18 mm	35 mm	70 mm	135 mm	200 mm

Figure 4-12: Shooting the moon with an impressive zoom lens.

Most general-purpose kit lenses "top out" at between 70 and 85mm. If that's the lens you're using, you see the blob.

The difference between 135 and 200mm is large. At 200mm, more details are visible and you get a sense of the smaller craters and structures. The contrast is better, too.

This list describes how the moon looked at each focal length:

- ✔ **18mm:** The moon is a fuzzy dot, with lots of wide-angle black sky.
- ✔ **35mm:** The moon has lost its fuzz and has resolved into a disc. It has no discernable features.
- ✔ **70mm:** The moon looks better at 70mm than 35mm, but not by much. The featureless blob of a disc is growing larger.
- ✔ **135mm:** The moon looks like the moon! You can see details, but they're small.
- ✔ **200mm:** All things considered, this photo isn't bad. It could be magnified, but the details wouldn't be as sharp.

At 300mm, as shown in Figure 4-13, the moon starts to fill the frame. (In nerdspeak, the moon is about one-fifth the height of this frame.) The level of detail is impressive. The photo looks nice and sharp with good contrast. In other words, a viewer doesn't have much to complain about. The photo has plenty of detail to be magnified in software.

I added the 2x teleconverter, and it blew my socks off. Figure 4-14 shows the result. The moon filled the frame much more impressively than it did at 300mm. Rather than remain one-fifth of the height of the frame, the moon grew to become one-third the total height of the frame. The photo has clear details. It's sharp and has contrast, and it has a very low noise level.

Figure 4-13: True telephoto.

Figure 4-14: Wow — the moon just keeps getting better!

LensRentals.com

I rented the macro and telephoto lenses I used in writing this chapter, plus several other pieces of gear, from www.lensrentals.com. The site's employees were polite, professional, timely, and trustworthy, and the list of available gear is impressive. The site offers flexible plans based on the amount of time you rent items and whether you purchase insurance. (I highly recommend it.) Give a few weeks' notice, to ensure that the gear you want is in stock. Do your best not to break anything, and return all items on time, or else you'll pay extra. The system is clear and easy to understand.

Try out that 300mm lens you've always dreamed of having. Rent it for a week to see whether it's one that you want to budget for. If you've never tried out a macro lens or if you need a better zoom lens for a wedding, just rent one. You can rent a camera body that's different from yours and an all-purpose zoom lens to check out the "competition." If you have a Nikon, for example, rent a Canon. Or, if you have a Canon, rent a Sony.

Using a telephoto lens turns the result into more than just a casual shot of the moon.

If you need the length, most likely for a professional project or client, you can find 400mm, 500mm, and 600mm lenses — and even more. These *super telephoto* lenses cost between $5,000 and $30,000.

Everyday shooting

Although telephoto lenses are larger than normal lenses (the focal length has to come from *somewhere*), you can carry them around and use them in everyday life. I did.

The series of shots in this section show my kids at a baseball game.

The outstanding factor in owning a telephoto lens is that you can be positioned far away from the action and still feel like you're right in the middle of it. (That last sentence brought to you by Mr. Obvious.) The shot shown in Figure 4-15 gives the impression that I stood between home plate and the dugout entrance, but the metadata says that I stood about 30 meters (98 feet) away.

Figure 4-15: Summer baseball fun.

Technically, *metadata* is called EXIF data. Each photo you take has extra information the camera writes into the file with the picture, such as when it was taken, the focal length you were using, and other odds and ends. Access this information through your photo organizers or editor.

I chose a position all the way across the infield, beyond the other dugout — a safe spot for the lens and a little less conspicuous one for me.

You've probably noticed professional photographers at professional sporting venues shooting professional athletes in action. Well, you can too, in a manner of speaking. For example, Figure 4-16 shows my son in the process of hitting the ball while his eyes are locked on it. The telephoto lens is your ticket to success for this type of action.

Figure 4-16: Swing, batter!

Anticipate the action and be ready to shoot it. Learn to feel the action and set up your camera for high-speed, continuous shooting. Let the camera roll through a few shots so that you can be sure to get a good one of action in action!

After the baseball game, I had my son and daughter run the bases so that I could take more shots. Figure 4-17 shows Grace running, from home plate to first base, for all she's worth. And I was 20 meters (more than 65 feet) away!

This photo shows off a nice *bokeh* (the out of focus area in the photo), created by the shallow depth of field. When the bokeh looks really good, it has a creamy appearance. This is caused by shooting with a large aperture. In this case, I was at f/4.

Figure 4-17: Running to first base.

Overall, the photo looks like it could be in a professional sports magazine: The colors are good, the focus is sharp, and the bokeh is creamy. This is a nice lens to have!

Macro with telephoto

If you like, you can take close-up shots of small subjects with a telephoto lens, even in your studio. When in the studio, telephoto lenses almost act like macros because they magnify the subject so much. The problem is that you have to stand a good distance from your subject because telephoto lenses can't focus on very close objects. In addition, camera shake and the practical matters of framing and focusing contribute to the hassle.

Macro

Telephoto

I set up the 300mm f/4 in my basement and took the shot shown in Figure 4-18 so that you can see how it compares with a macro of the same subject.

The two photos are different because I was able to set up the camera much closer when using the macro lens. I had to move back with the telephoto, which made the angle appear flatter. In both cases, the rear of the fire truck starts to become soft and out of focus.

Figure 4-18: Macro versus telephoto face-off.

The macro lens is probably a better choice, but it's a close call. The macro lens, which was easier to work with, is the definite winner in terms of practicality.

Book III
Hey, Your Exposure's Showing

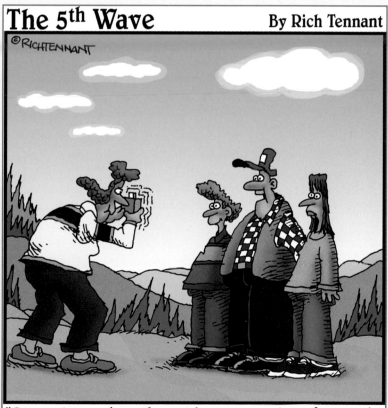

The 5th Wave   By Rich Tennant

©RICHTENNANT

"Remember, when the subject comes into focus, the camera makes a beep. But that's annoying, so I set it on vibrate."

*E*xposure. Yee-ouch. It's a tough topic, and I have five chapters that talk about it. Not just one — five!

If you want to put your camera in Auto mode and not worry about trying to figure out the right exposure and set your camera's controls to achieve it, go ahead. I used to. In fact, that's how I started out. Scenes and other creative shooting modes are also a great way to let the camera handle the work of deciding how bright a scene is and how to set the camera to take the best picture.

If only it worked all the time! It doesn't.

You know, you're much smarter than a camera. Your brain has more computing power than any machine I've ever run across, not to mention your additional creativity, intuition, experience, and wisdom. When I learned more about how to use the camera to evaluate exposure and venture away from full Auto mode, my photos began to look *much* better.

Chapter 1: Strategizing Exposure

In This Chapter

- ✏ **Exposure**
- ✏ **Meter reading**
- ✏ **Trading units of exposure**
- ✏ **Picture-taking**
- ✏ **Exposure tricks**
- ✏ **The light meter**

Exposure isn't complicated.

The problem is that you can become so overwhelmed by everything else going on that exposure is the last thing you think about. You're busy working the controls of your digital SLR, framing the subject, and trying to keep the right distance and focus, and at the same time trying not to trip and break your neck. Exposure becomes a distant priority. You put things on autopilot and let the camera handle it. You press the shutter button and hope for the best.

It doesn't have to be that way.

You can quickly learn enough about exposure to start integrating it into your photography and start taking better pictures. Then you'll soon be telling your camera who's the boss.

So That's What Exposure Is!

Simply put, *exposure* is the amount of light that enters the camera when you take a photograph.

I told you it wasn't complicated.

Understanding exposure is one thing. Being able to control it (which is why I'm here to help you) is another.

Going over under and over

In the days when film cameras ruled the earth, light came into an SLR and interacted with the film inside. If you let too much light in for too long, you *overexposed* the film. The resulting photo was too light and looked washed out. If you didn't let enough light in the camera, the photo was too dark. That's called *underexposed*.

Figure 1-1 shows the two horns of the under- versus overexposure dilemma — literally! Notice that the first shot has no detail in the shadows whereas the second shot has no detail in the sky.

Figure 1-1: Exposure problems cause under- and overexposed photos.

Either way, you lose important details. And, either way, the exposure is off.

So what's the solution?

Controlling how much light gets into the camera is a critical step to shooting a good picture. Too much or too little light and the photo suffers. You have to complete two important process to get your photos to turn out right:

✔ **Metering:** Calculate the best exposure first. This information comes from metering, discussed later in this chapter. In a nutshell, the camera senses the amount of light in the scene and knows whether the conditions are bright or dark or in between.

✔ **Adapting:** After you know the proper exposure for the photo, you can set the camera's controls to let the right amount of light inside the camera.

Regulating light

The whole point of photography is to take a photograph, and your camera is designed to control the amount of light that enters it. When you think of it that way, your camera is a machine that allows you to regulate the amount of light that enters it.

Figure 1-2: The aperture is the hole in the middle of the lens.

Light enters a camera through the opening in the lens known as the *aperture,* as shown in Figure 1-2. You can make the aperture larger or smaller. Larger apertures let in more light, and smaller apertures let in less light.

The camera turns the light on and off by controlling the shutter, which is normally locked tight to keep light from reaching the sensor. The length of time that the shutter is open is the *shutter speed.* Figure 1-3 shows the back of the shutter on my old Nikon FE2 SLR. A digital SLR has shutters, too, but you can't open the back of the camera to take a picture of them. (You have to push the mirror up and out of the way from the front.)

Figure 1-3: Shutters shut out light.

The element that triggers this process is the *shutter button,* shown in Figure 1-4 and also known as the *shutter release button.*

Figure 1-4: Press here for your photos.

Here's a sequential look at what happens:

1. You press the shutter button.

2. The camera's mirror flips up, and the shutter opens for the length of time indicated by the shutter speed. Shutter speed is all about time. Slower shutter speeds let in more light; faster shutter speeds let in less light.

3. Light enters the camera through the lens aperture. Aperture is all about area. The wider the aperture, the more light that gets in during a given exposure time. The smaller the aperture, the less light that gets in.

4. Light strikes the sensor. The sensor collects light during the exposure in individual photo sites. Each photo site is like a glass being filled with water.

When a glass fills to the brim, it overflows, as shown in Figure 1-5. You don't get to keep that information, though. Sites that overflow can cause blooming, which is when other photo sites pick up light that wasn't meant for them.

The sensor's sensitivity to light is its *ISO*. A low ISO is good for bright light. A high ISO is often necessary for shooting in dim light.

For now, ignore ISO and assume that it's constant.

Figure 1-5: I'd say this glass is half full.

5. The shutter closes when the shutter speed time duration is over, ending the photograph. At this point, the analog capacitors that collected the photons send their data through the analog-to-digital converter and the image is saved to file.

You probably already knew all of this, but perhaps not in terms of controlling light.

Metering Madness

Metering refers to the camera sensing how much light is in the scene. The camera uses this information to calculate the proper exposure for the photograph you're taking. You can control how the camera senses light by switching metering modes. This may affect the exposure the camera suggests because every metering mode has unique characteristics. The long and the short of it is that by switching metering modes, you can come to different exposure conclusions given the same lighting conditions.

This list describes the main metering modes and what they do:

- **Pattern:** Camera manufacturers call their scene-based metering modes by different names: 3D color matrix metering II (Nikon), evaluative metering (Canon), digital ESP metering (Olympus), and multi segment metering (Pentax and Sony).

The camera divides the scene into a bunch of smaller areas that form a pattern, as shown in Figure 1-6. Each area is evaluated separately in terms of brightness. Some cameras perform more sophisticated analysis and look up precalculated exposure "answers" in tables stored in the camera's memory. Tables may consider distance and color and areas of focus.

Metering zones come into play in a camera's list of specifications. A lot happens behind the scenes, much of it super-secret and proprietary, but the more zones on the list, the more the scene is broken apart and each area evaluated discretely.

Although Pattern mode is best to use for most scenes, using it isn't foolproof.

- **Center-weighted:** This mode meters the entire frame but gives more weight to elements it measures in the center than around the edges. Though the weighting ratio varies, it's in the range of 70 percent center to 30 percent edges. Figure 1-7 shows what happens. I've darkened the edges to illustrate that they're given less consideration than the center.

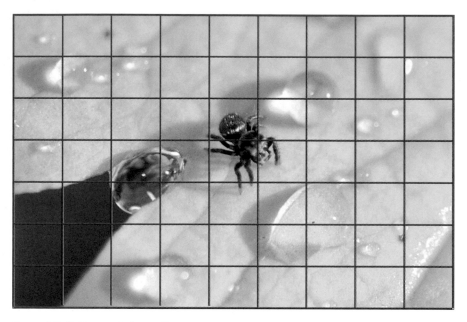

Figure 1-6: Pattern metering pattern.

Quite often, you can create outstanding results with center-weighted metering. Use it for portraits so that your subjects dominate exposure analysis — not the background behind them.

Figure 1-7: Center-weighted metering gives the center more emphasis.

✓ **Spot:** Spot metering measures light in a narrow circle and ignores everything else, as shown in Figure 1-8. This feature is useful if you want to ensure that a specific point in your frame is used to calculate the exposure. Photographers use spot metering frequently to meter a bright area, to keep it from being overexposed.

Figure 1-8: Spot metering is quite targeted.

I recently used Spot mode to shoot the moon because 3D Color Matrix II (this is Nikon's term for pattern metering) couldn't calculate the correct exposure: It overexposed the moon. Figure 1-9 shows a comparison.

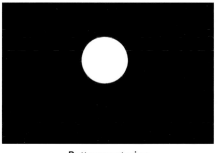

Pattern metering

Spot metering

Figure 1-9: Different metering approaches sometimes produce different results.

Setting Exposure and Swapping Exposure Values (EV)

Exposure Value (EV) is the currency of exposure. To be able to understand it, you have to know what goes into it. The following list describes the camera controls that allow you to change the exposure:

✔ **F-number:** Each f/stop halves or doubles the amount of light going through the lens because it halves or doubles the open area. For example, there's 1 stop between f/8 and f/5.6 and 1 stop between f/5.6 and f/4.

An f-number doesn't double or halve like shutter speed and ISO do. The *aperture area* is what doubles or halves.

✔ **Shutter speed:** Each stop of shutter speed halves or doubles the amount of light that reaches the camera because the stops are half or double the current value. For example, there's 1 stop between 1/125 and 1/250 second and 1 stop between 1/250 and 1/500 second.

✔ **ISO:** Each stop of ISO doubles or halves the sensor's sensitivity to light. So, ISO 200 is +1.0 EV (1 stop) compared to ISO 100.

Can you see why this concept is powerful?

Each stop has the same effect on exposure, whether it comes from shutter speed, aperture, or ISO. You can swap one for another to get to the exposure you need.

Say you choose to shoot at f/8 and ISO 100. You set the shutter speed to 1/125 second and meter. The meter says you're 1.0 EV underexposed. You need an additional stop of light. You can get it from any one of these three places:

✔ **Aperture:** You can lower the aperture to f/5.6 and keep the same ISO and shutter speed.

✔ **Shutter speed:** You can lengthen the shutter speed to 1/80 second and keep the same f-number and ISO.

✔ **ISO:** You can raise the ISO to ISO 200 and keep the same aperture and shutter speed.

Which elements you set first and which ones you change is entirely up to you. With that much freedom, you need some guidelines. Here are some suggested steps to set exposure manually:

1. **Decide what you want to limit first.**

   Each one of the three exposure elements has a side effect:

   • *Aperture:* Aperture's side effect is depth of field. Wider apertures have a shallower depth of field.

   • *Shutter speed:* Shutter speed's side effect is blurring. Slower shutter speeds can blur moving objects and risk camera shake when shooting from a handheld.

   • *ISO:* ISO's side effect is noise. A higher ISO introduces more noise into your photos.

I make a decision about what effect I'm seeking or what's important for the shot.

- *Aperture:* When shooting landscapes, I tend to put aperture at f/8, f/11, or higher. When shooting portraits or still subjects, I switch to f/5.6 or lower. This gives me an exposure region to operate in.

TIP

Set the aperture to provide the depth of field you want. Landscapes benefit from a greater depth of field, which keeps near and far objects in the scene in focus. Portraits, on the other hand, look better with a shallow depth of field, which separates the subject from the background and puts the attention on them.

- *Shutter speed:* I'm normally not concerned about shutter speed unless I'm shooting handheld shots, action shots, or portraits. Then I either keep tabs on the shutter speed or switch to Shutter priority and use 1/60 second for handheld, 1/250 second for casual shots of people, or 1/500 second for action.

TIP

The key is to set the shutter speed high enough to avoid camera shake or subject blurring caused by movement.

- *ISO:* This setting is the one I most resist changing. I set it to ISO 100 when I'm shooting outdoors and to ISO 200 to ISO 400 for most indoor situations, even with a flash. Under very low-light conditions, when I can't use a flash or when I need a fast shutter speed and can't open the aperture any more, I raise it higher. Note your camera's specific characteristics. Some dSLRs have a minimum ISO below 100 (for example, ISO 50), and others have a minimum ISO above 100 (for example, ISO 200).

2. **Lock down one or two elements.**

   After you decide which side effect is most important (limiting blur, limiting noise, or limiting depth of field), lock down the elements that create that particular side effect.

   For me, it tends to be ISO and aperture or ISO and shutter speed.

   For example, I set the ISO to ISO 100 and aperture to f/8 when shooting landscapes and then take a look at what the shutter speed must be in order to get a good exposure. If I'm using a tripod and the subject isn't moving, I can ignore blurring problems. When shooting indoors, I often set the ISO higher, firmly set the shutter speed to avoid blurring, and float the aperture.

   How you do this depends on the exposure mode you choose to work in. If you want total control of all the exposure elements, choose Manual mode and sequentially work through the elements. If you want to lock a single element down, such as the aperture, choose Aperture priority mode. Likewise, choose Shutter Priority mode if you want to select a specific shutter speed and have the camera choose the appropriate aperture (and possibly ISO).

**Book III
Chapter 1**

**Strategizing
Exposure**

3. **Float the other elements to get the right exposure.**

   Move into position whatever elements aren't critical to your creative goals to take the shot. If you don't care about noise, for example, it might be ISO. If you don't care about depth of field, you may set aperture last.

4. **Make adjustments, if necessary.**

   At this point, if you realize that your exposure solution won't work — you can't set the right shutter speed to avoid blurring or you're concerned about too high an ISO, go back to Step 2 and reset your priorities. You may have to live with more noise, or a smaller depth of field.

   Shutter speed is generally the least forgiving exposure element if you're on the boundary of camera blur and subject movement, both between 1/30 and 1/250 second. If you need to move from 1/4000 down to 1/500 second, that's not as much of a problem.

Pulling Out the Stops

You've got more controls at your disposal than simply aperture, shutter speed, and ISO. Aside from using flash, you can take a meter reading and lock it in (AE lock), bracket exposures (manually or using AEB), or use exposure compensation (EC). All are valid responses to fine-tuning the exposure.

AE lock

Use AE-Lock when you use center-weighted or spot metering modes if your subject is off-center and you want a good reading from the subject. You should be in an auto or semi-auto shooting mode for AE lock to make sense. Manual mode is like the ultimate AE lock — no exposure controls change between metering and shooting unless you change them.

Here's how to lock in Auto Exposure:

1. **Select Spot or Center-Weighted Metering.**

   Pattern modes don't work because they evaluate the entire scene.

2. **Center the subject or center it under an autofocus point.**

   This choice depends on the camera.

3. **Press the shutter button halfway down and hold it to autofocus.**

   Some cameras lock both focus and exposure with a half-push of the shutter button.

4. Press the AE lock button, as shown in Figure 1-10.

This is where it feels like you have too much to do with too few fingers. You have to hold the camera with the help of your right palm and fingers, operate the shutter button with your index finger, press the AE lock button with your thumb, and possibly rotate a dial or two in between.

AE lock

Figure 1-10: Press the AE lock and hold with an extra finger.

5. While holding down both buttons, recompose the shot.

6. Take the picture.

To lock in the exposure for more shots, continue to hold the AE lock button down. You can also note the shutter speed and aperture, switch to manual mode, and dial in those values yourself.

Exposure bracketing

Exposure bracketing used to have nothing to do with high dynamic range (HDR) photography. Now HDR photographers routinely use the digital SLR's auto exposure bracketing (AEB) feature to automatically take under- and overexposed photos, combine them, and tone map them in their HDR software. AEB is also used for exposure blending, also known as exposure fusion.

You can use AEB for its original and intended purpose: to take enough photos exposed differently enough that one of them is bound to be exactly the one you want.

It seems imprecise in this modern, digital age, but sometimes taking more exposure bracketed is the best you can do. If you can't get the perfect exposure with one shot, bracket the daylights out of it. You can choose the best one later.

For more information on bracketing (within the context of HDR), see Book VI, Chapter 4. The mechanics of using AEB are the same whether or not you're shooting HDR. In this case you don't have to mess with HDR, which means that you can use AEB handheld and not worry so much about moving the camera around.

Exposure compensation (EC)

Sometimes, despite your best efforts to meter and shoot a scene correctly, the picture isn't exposed correctly.

Welcome to another edition of When Reality Strikes.

You see, setting the right metering mode, adjusting the exposure, and taking the picture all happen independently of shooting the actual picture. Is it what you want? Does it look right? The answer to those questions can be given only *by your brain*.

You have to look at a photo and subjectively evaluate it. If the camera is underexposing photos by about a third of a stop, you should correct that issue now rather than wait until you're working in software. Thankfully, an easy-to-use tool helps you do it: exposure compensation.

Here's how it works. When you review your photos and see that they're all under- or over-exposed, dial exposure compensation in the direction you want the pictures to go, as shown in Figure 1-11. If you want more light, boost EC. If you want less light, reduce EC.

Figure 1-11: Exposure Compensation moves the exposure up or down.

Most cameras give you at least two stops of correction to work with. Some have as many as five! If you have to take that route, I suggest that you reevaluate your metering and see what's happening to make the photos so far out of whack.

Using an External Light Meter

Cameras have a fatal flaw concerning metering: They all measure reflected light. That's helpful for metering and shooting distant objects or scenes such as landscapes, but not so good for portraits and smaller studies.

The problem with spot (reflected) metering is that *not everything reflects the same amount of light*. Go figure. For this reason, spot meters assume that everything reflects light as an 18 percent gray card would. It's a debatable proposition.

Another type of metering is available only in an external light meter. It measures *incident* light, which is how much light is shining in the scene.

Those light meters have a dome or disk (most often a creamy white color) that either "bubbles out" from the meter's body, as shown in Figure 1-12 for a shot of my light meter, or lets light pass through. The meters measure the actual light in the scene, not how much is reflecting off objects.

Figure 1-12: Behold, the L-758DR.

That's why when you photograph a light object on a white background, the camera reacts to the reflected light and underexposes the photo (it thinks there's too much light). A light meter, on the other hand, measures the light as it falls on the scene, which is a better method of getting an accurate exposure reading.

Figure 1-13 shows an example of this happening. (Just so you know, neither photo has been retouched other than removing some dust.)

Figure 1-13: Comparing baseballs.

I took the first shot of this baseball with my Sony Alpha 300 and kit lens (18-70mm zoom). I used in-camera spot metering to try to get the brightness of the baseball and not the background. The camera overreacted to the light and suggested 1/8 second at f/11. (I was using ISO 400 and didn't use a flash.) You can see that the photo is clearly too dark.

I metered the scene with my Sekonic L-758DR, and it suggested a much longer exposure — 1/2 second at f/11 and ISO 400. That might not sound like a lot, but 1/2 second is two stops more than the camera's reading of 1/8 second.

I was skeptical because I didn't want to blow anything out. However, when I took the shot and reviewed it, it was perfect. You can see from the photo that the scene is much lighter but not blown out.

You don't need a light meter to tell you that the first shot is too dark, and you don't need a light meter to tell you to increase the exposure. You can review the first photo and either input some exposure correction or adjust the shutter speed for the next shot. A digital SLR gives you the tools you need to make adjustments on the fly if you take the time to use them. But it's nice to cut to the chase and be able to dial in settings that are spot-on from the get-go. Roger that?

Chapter 2: Setting Aperture

In This Chapter

✔ **Understanding aperture**

✔ **Discovering depth of field**

✔ **Setting the aperture**

✔ **A practical aperture guide**

*O*f the three main tools to control exposure, the aperture is the most creative.

By setting a wide aperture, you not only increase the amount of light that enters the camera but also limit the depth of field — the area that looks like it's in focus. The area out of focus looks blurry. (It's the bokeh, which I describe later in this chapter.)

Photos with limited depth of field work well for portraits, actions shots, macros, and still lifes. Conversely, if you're interested in maximizing the depth of field, you reduce the size of the aperture. It's similar to squinting when you want to sharpen the scene you see. Photos with extended depth of fields work well for landscapes, cityscapes, and product-type shots.

Any way you slice it (everyone has their own creative path), setting the aperture is more than just an exposure decision. This chapter is designed so that you can start making those decisions on your own as fast as possible.

You Have a Hole in Your Lens!

Did you know that your lens has a hole in it (see Figure 2-1)? In fact, every lens has one.

Don't panic: It's the *aperture,* and it's supposed to be there. It lets light pass through the lens and into the camera. If it weren't for the aperture, you would have a useless block of metal, glass, and polycarbonate plastic.

Figure 2-1: Don't return it to the store — it's supposed to have that hole.

An aperture can be large, small, fixed, or variable.

The F/stops here, buddy

One weird aspect of photography is that you hear apertures and f/numbers (or f/stops) thrown around as though they refer to the same item, but they don't. Even *I* do it.

The *aperture* is the opening in the lens that lets light through.

An *f-stop* (or *f-number*) describes the relationship between a lens' focal length and its aperture diameter. Because that relationship is inversely proportional, when one goes up, the other goes down, and vice versa.

Figure 2-2 shows a lens moving through a progression of f/numbers. The smallest f-number but the largest aperture is f/2.0. The largest f-number but the smallest aperture is f/16.

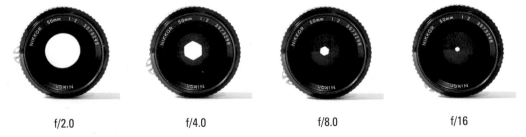

f/2.0   f/4.0   f/8.0   f/16

Figure 2-2: Visible evidence of an inverse relationship between aperture and f/numbers.

For a given focal length, therefore, a large aperture has a smaller f-number, whereas a small aperture has a larger f-number.

This topic can be confusing because smaller f/numbers refer to larger apertures. For example, f/1.4 is a *larger aperture* than f/8, even though the f-number is smaller.

You might wonder why you would need to know about f-numbers. The answer is that they give you the means to compare apples with apples. At different focal lengths, the same aperture size has different exposure effects. It's just the way it is. If you were to set the aperture of your zoom lens to 6.25mm and the focal length to 24mm, the exposure would be a certain value. If you zoomed in to 85mm while keeping the aperture the same size, you would change the exposure. Being able to set the aperture so that it doesn't change the exposure every time you zoom in or out simply makes sense.

F-numbers tell you something about exposure. f/8 means something, whether you zoom out to 24mm or zoom in to 75mm.

I show you how that aperture size changes with focal length when the f-number remains the same.

In plain(ish) language, the diameter of a lens' aperture is equal to the focal length divided by the f-number. Suppose that you have a zoom lens with a focal length range of 35-70mm. (It's the lens shown in Figure 2-3.) Set the f-number to f/3.5, and then set the focal length to 35mm. Note the size of the aperture. Now set the focal length to 70mm. Note the size of the aperture. Are they the same or different?

35mm   50mm   70mm

Figure 2-3: The size changes as the focal length increases, but the f-number (f/3.5) stays the same.

Fast lenses

Lenses with small f/numbers are known as *fast* lenses because you can take photos in low-light conditions or use faster shutter speeds and lower ISOs.

These lenses cost more, but if you need the low-light capability, they can be worth the price.

They're different. At 35mm, the lens' aperture size at f/3.5 is 10mm. You get this result by dividing 35mm (the focal length) by 3.5 (the f-number).

At 70mm, the lens' aperture size at f/3.5 is 20mm — divide 70mm (the focal length) by 3.5 (the f-number).

At both focal lengths, the f-number is the same, which means that the effect of aperture on exposure is the same, even though the physical aperture size is different. At 70mm, the aperture size is double that of 35mm. This concept makes sense because 70mm is twice the focal length of 35mm (meaning light has to travel twice as far through the lens to the sensor).

Whew! Take a breather.

You use f-numbers in exposure, not as an absolute measure of the aperture size.

Hitting a moving target

As usual, some lens characteristics weren't run past the Division of Common Sense or the Bureau of Aperture Management. When a lens name lists a single aperture, that doesn't mean that it's the only sized aperture it has.

For example, the AF-S NIKKOR 50mm f/1.4G, shown in Figure 2-4, has an aperture in its name: f/1.4G. (The *G* indicates that the lens has no aperture ring, which means that you have to control aperture from the camera.) The name isn't indicating, however, that the lens can have only one aperture — f/1.4. It's simply the widest aperture possible on that lens.

Because a prime lens can't be zoomed in or out, the maximum aperture is *constant*, or *fixed*.

Figure 2-4: My handy 50mm f/1.4G prime with constant maximum aperture.

When you look at a zoom lens, you will see one of two cases: a fixed aperture or a variable aperture. Fixed apertures behave the same as in the 50mm example I just described.

The Canon EF 24-70mm f/2.8L USM lists a single aperture, just like the Nikon 50mm prime. You can access f/2.8 no matter where you are in the lens' focal length. That solution is ideal, but you'll pay a lot more for this lens ($1,449 list) than those with similar focal lengths and variable apertures. (The Canon EF-S 17-85mm f4-5.6 IS USM lists for $599.99.)

On the other hand, the Canon EF-S 18-200mm f/3.5-5.6 IS, shown in Figure 2-5, lists two apertures. What gives? It means that the maximum aperture changes and depends on the focal length of the zoom lens. You're given the two extremes: At 18mm, the maximum aperture is f/3.5, and at 200mm, the maximum aperture is f/5.6.

© Canon Corp.

Figure 2-5: The Canon zoom lens with variable maximum aperture.

Using a lens like this one makes exposure decisions more difficult, but not impossible. I run into similar situations all the time. If I'm working toward the maximum aperture and then zoom in on a subject, the aperture changes, which can be disconcerting if you're working in manual mode. In Aperture priority, the camera handles it by changing shutter speed (and as a last resort, ISO) to make up the difference.

You have three situations to contend with when you're trying to decipher a lens name:

✐ **Fixed maximum aperture prime lens:** An example is the AF-S NIKKOR 50mm f/1.4G. Although you can make it smaller (moving to f/8, for example), the maximum possible aperture in this case is f/1.4. It never changes.

✐ **Fixed maximum aperture zoom lens:** An example is the Canon EF 24-70mm f/2.8L USM. Although it's a zoom lens, it works just like the prime example. The maximum aperture is f/2.8 and that doesn't change, no matter what the focal length is.

✔ **Variable maximum aperture zoom lens:** An example is the Canon EF-S 18-200mm f/3.5-5.6 IS. This common lens tend to be more inexpensive than fixed aperture lenses. Its maximum aperture changes, depending on the focal length. At 18mm, the maximum f/number is f/3.5; at 200mm, it's f/5.6.

Visualizing Depth of Field

Each of the three primary exposure controls (aperture, shutter speed, and ISO) has a side effect.

The aperture's side effect is depth of field.

The side effect of the side effect is the bokeh.

Understanding depth of field

The *depth of field* concept is easy to understand: It's the area in front of and behind where you've focused that looks sharp and in focus. It's a funny concept when you think of it. You can't focus the lens at more than one distance, yet the area you perceive to be in focus has depth.

Figure 2-6 illustrates this concept with a shot taken at f/5.6. Both blue cars on the end are out of focus. The green car and the truck on the boundary of the depth of field aren't as badly out of focus as are the cars farther out. The yellowish-orange car in the middle is in focus. The point of focus is directly in the middle of the yellow car. You can see the near and far limits of acceptable sharpness. Everything within them is in the depth of field.

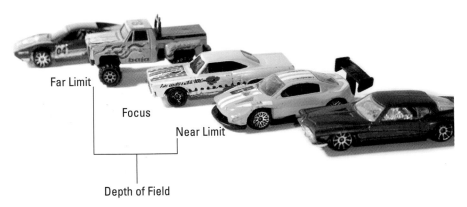

Figure 2-6: Illustrating depth of field.

As you can see, it truly matters where you focus and which f-number you choose. Depth of field also depends on the focal length of your lens (shorter focal lengths give greater depths) and your distance to the subject (the closer you are, the shallower the depth of field).

These statements makes sense. Why do you think it's necessary to focus in the first place?

Sometimes, the depth of field is extremely small; sometimes, it's extremely large. Which one it is depends on several factors (discussed later), one of which is the f-number you're using to shoot (which incorporates focal length and aperture size). The other factors are your camera (and its circle of confusion, which is defined later) and the distance to the subject.

Here's the minimum amount of information that you need to know.

Keeping all factors constant (focal length, camera, and distance), smaller f-numbers result in shallow depths of field. Larger f-numbers result in deeper depths of field. So, if you're shooting at f/1.4 the depth of field is shallower than when you're shooting at f/11.

Figure 2-7 shows a progression from f/1.4 to f/2.8, f/5.6, and f/11. I focused in the middle of the scene, along a line that runs near the M for Monday on the calendar. Pay attention to the depth of field as the f-numbers increase. (Remember that the aperture is decreasing.) It grows larger, and you can read much more.

**Book III
Chapter 2**

Setting Aperture

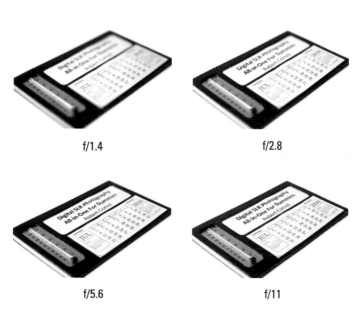

f/1.4   f/2.8

f/5.6   f/11

Figure 2-7: You can read more of the calendar as the depth of field increases.

The depth of field isn't circular. The center is a line that runs straight across the photo and extends to both sides.

If you know this, you can select f-stops to dictate the depth of field. Most often, a landscape photographer wants a deep depth of field so that the entire scene looks sharp and clear. On the other hand, a portrait photographer likes a shallow depth of field because, while the subject is in focus, the background is nicely blurred.

Although photographers tend to focus (ha) primarily on aperture and its effect on depth of field, several other factors determine how large or how small it is. They are

- **Circle of confusion:** You see this factor in online depth-of-field calculators. Find the circle of confusion that matches your camera and plug it into the depth-of-field equation. That's the least you need to know.

   If you want a fuller but still nontechnical explanation of what the circle of confusion is, here you go: The circle of confusion is the largest spot on your camera's sensor that you perceive as a point and not a spot. In other words, you'll think that the spot (and anything smaller) is perfectly in focus even when it's actually a fuzzy blob. Common values for digital SLRs range from 0.015 to 0.03mm.

- **Distance to subject:** Focusing on nearby objects results in shallow depths of field. Focusing on faraway objects yields deeper depths of field.

- **F-number:** Smaller f-numbers result in shallow depths of field. Larger f-numbers result in deeper depths of field.

- **Focal length:** Telephoto focal lengths result in shallow depths of field. Wide-angle focal lengths result in deeper depths of field.

If you want the maximum depth of field, focus your lens at the *hyperfocal* distance. This is the distance at which halfway to the subject and everything beyond is in focus. For example, if I wanted to get the maximum depth of field out of my Nikon D200 and NIKKOR 28mm lens (say I am out shooting landscapes), I should focus at the hyperfocal distance (providing there isn't a specific subject I want to focus on that is nearer). In this case, if the aperture is set to f/8, the hyperfocal distance is 15.2 feet.

DOFmaster (`www.dofmaster.com`) has online and downloadable depth-of-field calculators that will tell you how large your depth of field is as well as show you the hyperfocal distance for your situation.

Meet the bokehs

And now, for the side effect of the side effect.

When you set the aperture, you dial in an f-number, which helps determine the depth of field. Inside the depth of field, you see objects in focus.

What lies outside the depth of field is blur — or bokeh, in Japanese. The term *bokeh* has been in use for only about the past ten years. However, saying "bokeh" is more convenient than saying "the blurry area that isn't in focus."

Another characteristic of bokeh is its look. Some lenses create pleasing bokehs, and other lenses have harsh and unsightly bokehs. The good ones cost more, of course.

Photos with shallow depths of field have larger bokehs. (It's nice to have a lens that creates an acceptably pleasing bokeh.) If you want to minimize the bokeh, stop down (or reduce the focal length of the lens you're using, or increase the distance between you and the subject) to deepen the depth of field. Figure 2-8 shows a telephoto shot of my son Jacob running the bases. The lens I used (Nikon 300mm f/4) has good characteristics and has nicely blurred out the onlookers and fence.

Figure 2-8: Notice the nice, creamy bokeh — the sign of a good lens.

**Book III
Chapter 2**

Setting Aperture

Photos with deeper depths of field may have no bokeh. Landscape photos, for example, generally remain in focus from a distance reasonably close to the camera to infinity. Figure 2-9 shows Jacob again — this time, batting. In this case, I used a lens-and-aperture combination that created a deep depth of field and no bokeh to speak of. My son, the bench, the coach, and even the trees are essentially in focus.

Figure 2-9: A wider aperture and shorter focal length creates no bokeh in this shot.

Swampland for sale

The problem with high-quality "fast" lenses and shallow depths of field is that you may end up with too much of a good thing.

When I brought home my 50mm f/1.4G lens. I immediately opened it wide and started taking photos of my kids and my wife, objects lying on the table, and other items. The problem was that the depth of field was *so shallow* that the photos were effectively useless. Figure 2-10 shows what can happen when you use a wide aperture and don't pay attention to the autofocus setting. The camera is focused on my son's hand, and everything else is out of focus. The reason he's out of focus is that the depth of field is too shallow at the aperture I was using (f/2.5) and distance (a few feet) to overcome the autofocus problem. The funny thing is that his thumb is in pretty good focus, but the toy he's holding and his arm aren't.

There's not much point in having one eye in focus and the other eye blurred, unless you're seeking a specific shot to emphasize limited focus.

The aperture has a practical point: You may not always be shooting at the maximum aperture for your lens — if for no other reason than you need a deeper depth of field and can't change the focal length or distance enough to get it. At that point, you have to suck it up and stop down (meaning make the aperture smaller by raising the f/number).

Another factor (aside from exposure and depth of field) to consider when choosing an aperture is lens sharpness. Not all lenses are equally sharp at all apertures. Most, in fact, are a little "soft" (seemingly a tad out of focus) at their widest apertures. Likewise, diffraction is a problem at the smallest apertures (above f/22). *Diffraction* happens when light rays are bent as they reach around the edges of the aperture, which makes it impossible to focus them together, again resulting in softness, or fuzziness.

Figure 2-10: The thumb — but nothing else — is in decent focus.`

Figure 2-11 shows a progression from f/5.6 to f/8, f/16, f/22, f/32, and f/36. At f/5.6, the foreground vehicle is nice and sharp. Everything else is out of focus in a nice bokeh. If you move to f/8, the cars in the background sharpen quite a bit but are still blurred. The next two f-stops, f/16 and f/22, continue the trend. Beyond f/22, the effects are barely discernable. After toggling the files on my computer, I think I can discern some diffraction at f/32, but I definitely see it at f/36. The vehicle seats are noticeably blurrier when magnified to 100 percent.

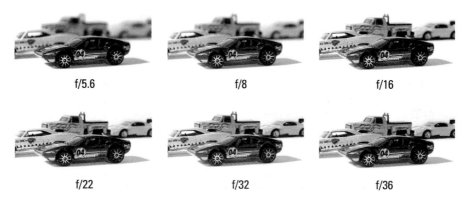

| f/5.6 | f/8 | f/16 |

| f/22 | f/32 | f/36 |

Figure 2-11: Moving from f/5.6 to f/36.

You'll drive yourself crazy if you try to remember all these numbers, definitions, and settings. Instead, try to remember these two main points:

✔ **Too wide is often too wide:** Opening the lens wide may result in a wildly impractical depth of field. It may also move you out of the sweet spot of the lens. The former problem is caused by physics; the latter is related to the optical quality of the lens.

Don't buy a lens with a maximum aperture of f/1.4 and expect to shoot at the widest aperture (f/1.4) often.

I feel your pain. It's a killer to invest in an awesome, very fast lens and never use the widest aperture. Don't despair: You haven't wasted your money. Having those extra f-stops means that you're still likely to capture sharper photos at wider apertures than by using a lens that isn't as fast. It also means that the sweet spot is at or below the spot where the other lens bottoms out.

✔ **Too small is often too small:** Set the f-number higher than f/22, and you're likely to start seeing the results of diffraction in your photos. If your lens can be set to f/32, f/45, or smaller, take some test shots and compare sharpness. Besides, for applications such as portraits and general photograph, you can't isolate the subject from the background effectively at f/22.

Managing the Aperture

You can set the aperture in one of two ways:

✔ **Aperture ring:** Some lenses have an aperture ring (see Figure 2-12). Turn it to set the aperture.

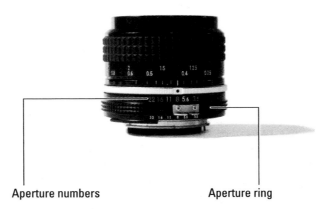

Aperture numbers   Aperture ring

Figure 2-12: This lens has an old-school aperture ring.

✔ **In-camera:** Other lenses (this is the trend) do *not* have aperture rings, as shown in Figure 2-13. You have to set the aperture in-camera by selecting the correct shooting mode and then setting the aperture.

You can directly set the aperture in these shooting modes:

✔ **Manual:** You set the aperture along with everything else.

✔ **Aperture priority:** Set the aperture you want in this semiautomatic mode, and the camera sets the shutter speed and sometimes the ISO to arrive at the right exposure.

Figure 2-13: This new lens has no aperture ring.

Use this mode if you aren't into full-manual shooting but want control over the depth of field.

✔ **Program shift:** You can indirectly set the aperture by choosing a program that uses the aperture and shutter speed combination you want; also known as Flexible Program mode.

✔ **Scenes:** You aren't setting the aperture when you select a scene, but if you pay attention, you can see what's happening.

When you understand why certain scenes have certain apertures, you can start setting them yourself.

Shooting with Different Apertures

Experimenting with different apertures is fun and rewarding. I encourage you to play with settings on your own to see which ones are your favorites. In the meantime, here are some of my thoughts on different aperture ranges:

✔ **f/4 and "faster" apertures:** Shooting with a large aperture can sometimes be difficult. You may think that because you have a "super-light-catching lens," you don't need a high ISO or flash, but the tradeoff is a limited depth of field.

However, the effect of using a wide aperture, as shown in Figure 2-14, is often very nice. If you're very close, you have to catch someone looking at you straight-on to be able to put his face in focus when shooting wide open. However, if you're back a bit, as with this figure, a wide aperture is easier to shoot with. Jake, my son, looks well-focused and nicely isolated from the background.

Figure 2-14: My son hitting the ball at f/1.8.

Figure 2-15 shows the effects of a minimal depth of field outside. The photo was shot with a manual focus 28mm lens.

If you use autofocus in situations where the focal point isn't in the middle of the frame, you should select an autofocus point or prefocus on the foreground and then press AF Lock to lock in the focus, recompose, and shoot.

✔ **f/5.6 to f/11:** The sweet spot — I shoot a lot of photos in this range.

f/5.6 is a useful indoor and outdoor aperture, regardless of whether or not you have a "normal" or "fast" lens. It gives you a good bokeh from the limited depth of field (see Figure 2-16). The closer you are to the subject, the smaller the depth of field. In this case, I am sitting right across the picnic table from Ben.

Figure 2-15: A simple hedge with a nice bokeh at f/3.5.

A useful all-around setting for outdoor shots is f/8. It has a good depth of field and is normally a sharp aperture for most lenses. I shoot most of my HDR brackets at f/8.

Figure 2-17 shows a helicopter on its pad at a hospital. I took the shot with a telephoto lens, so the photo doesn't act like a normal shot at f/8.

Longer focal lengths have that effect. I was at 100 feet, which means the calculated depth of field for my camera (Nikon D200) and focal length (300mm) is just under 11 feet. If I were using a 100mm lens, the depth of field would have been over *127 feet*.

I use f/11 if I'm outdoors and it's too bright for f/8. Using f/11 gives you a slightly better depth of field. You can use this setting indoors, in a studio (for product-type shots or stills), if you want.

✓ **f/16 and "slower" apertures:** Use smaller apertures if you're in great lighting (outdoors, toward the sun, inside with good flash or studio lighting) or you don't care about raising ISO or extending shutter speed.

Indoors, shooting using these f-numbers gives you a much better depth of field when shooting small, tabletop subjects. Figure 2-18 shows the cars I shot for this chapter, taken at f/22. The depth of field is good, even at this range. The drawback is that you have to pump up the ambient light, use a flash, or raise the ISO. (This was shot at ISO 400 with extra light and flash.)

I used the same aperture outside to take photos of a Japanese beetle invading our backyard, as shown in Figure 2-19. I wanted a reasonable depth of field to capture the entire beetle. Remember, when you are shooting close to the subject, depth of field is always less, and at this close range, f/22 is still very limited. I shot this at 1/400 second to freeze the action of the moving beetle and raised the ISO to 1600 to counteract the very small aperture and fast shutter speed.

Figure 2-16: Picnic at the park at f/5.6.

Figure 2-17: Helicopter at f/8.

Figure 2-18: Small subjects at f/22.

On the other hand, small apertures enable you to shoot with slower shutter speeds in bright light, as I did in Figure 2-20. I was on a bridge, photographing scenery, when a bike rider approached. I quickly dialed in a long shutter speed to capture the effect of him blurring past and stopped down to f/22 so that I wouldn't blow out the sky.

Figure 2-19: Close subject at f/22.

Figure 2-20: Rider on the bridge at f/22.

Chapter 3: Go, Shutter Speed, Go!

In This Chapter

- ✔ **Opening and closing the shutter**
- ✔ **Translating speeds**
- ✔ **Catching the blur**
- ✔ **Managing the shutter**
- ✔ **Dealing with slowpokes**

*O*f all the chapters on exposure, the concept of shutter speed is the easiest to explain and understand. Some of the terminology can be quirky, but you'll get the hang of it.

The harder part is getting shutter speed to work. It isn't something you can fake or easily fix in software. If you're too slow, you blur the scene.

This chapter talks about shutter speed and how it fits into exposure, and then it describes how shutter speeds work with various activities and how to manage shutter speed.

This chapter is an exciting one.

Don't Shudder at the Shutter

The shutter speed isn't like the aperture, which involves having to understand f/stops, which get smaller when the aperture gets larger and get larger when the aperture gets smaller.

Shutter speed isn't like ISO, which began life describing film speed but has been pressed into service nowadays to describe a digital sensor's sensitivity to light. It's the same concept, though rather clunky.

The shutter speed tells you how long the shutter stays open and allows light to expose the sensor in your digital SLR.

Figure 3-1 shows the shutter of my Nikon D200 (proving that digital SLRs have shutters). The shutter is a bit tricky to photograph. It normally hides behind the mirror, which means you don't see it when you remove the lens.

The shutter opens when you enter mirror lockup mode to clean the camera, so you don't see it then, either.

Figure 3-1: The hidden digital SLR shutter.

To photograph the shutter with the mirror out of the way, I put the D200 in mirror delay mode and then put remote shutter release cables on both cameras. When I took a photo with the D200, the mirror locked up, but the shutter didn't open because of the delay. I quickly pressed the button on my Sony Alpha 300 to capture it at the perfect time. I was also holding a remote flash in my other hand (that makes three, if you're counting) and aimed the flash into the inside of the D200 body.

Unless you rely on Scenes to tell the camera the type of subject you are shooting (that gives it an indication of how fast the shutter speed needs to be), your challenge is to be able to predict which shutter speeds are appropriate in various situations. With experience, knowing which shutter speed will work in a certain situation becomes easy.

Reading the Speed

Reading the shutter speed is fun for the whole family. You'll have hours of enjoyment as you decode shutter speeds in a fast-paced game of strategy and mayhem.

To be able to reliably read shutter speeds, you should know about a few twists that sometimes make it confusing to interpret and understand them:

- **Fractional:** Shutter speeds less than a second in length are most often displayed as fractions of a second. For example, 1/20 equals 1/20 of a second.

  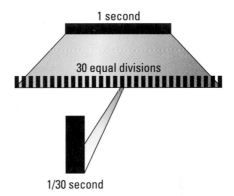

  Figure 3-2: The fractional number 1/30 second is one of 30 equal parts of a second.

  If that thought scares you, just think of it this way: If you divide a second into 30 equal parts, 1/30 is one of the 30, as shown in Figure 3-2. Likewise, 1/30th of a second (fractions are sometimes written as 1/30th) is one part of a second divided into 30 equal parts.

  Most shutter speeds are somewhere between 1/30 and 1/1000 second.

Fractional shutter speeds sometimes show up as the bottom number of the fraction without the top. For example, you might see 1/20 second displayed as 20. Yes, it's confusing, and it happens often in viewfinders where space is at a premium. In this case, you have to know what to expect. If you don't see a quotation mark (stay with me), assume what you're seeing is a fractional shutter speed.

In other words, you can differentiate 1/2 second from 2 seconds by knowing that 2 seconds usually has an *s* (sometimes displayed as sec.) or an inches mark after it, like this: 2". If it's a fraction of a second but is displayed in this format, it looks like 0"25, which is the same thing as 1/25 second.

- **Decimal:** When some cameras near 1 second, they start to flake out and go decimal on you. You then have to know that 0.5" means one-half second (1/2), not 1/5 of a second (see Figure 3-3).

$$0.5 = 1/2 = 0"5$$
$$1/2.5 = 10/25$$

Figure 3-3: Decimal seconds confuse everything.

Seeing 1/2.5 can be confusing. Is it a fraction or a decimal? Both. It represents 1/2.5, or four-tenths of a second. When you see a number like this one, it's sometimes easier to move the decimal point one place to the right for both numbers. (Mathematically, you're multiplying both numbers by 10.) This example results in 10/25 second (see Figure 3-3).

Book III Chapter 3

Go, Shutter Speed, Go!

↳ **Seconds:** The most common technique to display seconds is to insert an inches mark after the number. For example, 4 seconds is shown as 4". Two and a half seconds is 2.5", as shown in Figure 3-4.

$$2.5'' = 2\text{-}1/2$$

Figure 3-4: Converting seconds to seconds.

↳ **The mysterious bulb (B):** One shutter speed (technically not a speed in and of itself, but a shutter speed mode) is different from the rest. It's *bulb,* and it's undefined. You determine its length by pressing the shutter button as long as you want it to remain open.

Press and hold the shutter button to open the shutter. Release the shutter button to close the shutter and end the exposure.

I seriously recommend that you buy a locking-remote shutter release cord if you're going to use bulb much. It can save your finger.

The term *bulb* comes from the way old camera shutters were operated. Photographers squeezed a pneumatic bulb to open the shutter and released it to close it.

Full-stop shutter speeds from 1 second to 1/4000 second are shown in Table 3-1:

Table 3-1	Full-Stop Shutter Speeds
Fractional	*Also Shown As*
1	1"
1/2	.5"
1/4	.25"
1/8	8
1/15	15
1/30	30
1/60	60
1/120	120
1/250	250
1/500	500
1/1000	1000
1/2000	2000
1/4000	4000

Taming the Blur

Shutter speed is just like other exposure elements: It has a *side effect,* or an issue you need to consider when choosing the precise setting. The aperture side effect is depth of field. The ISO side effect is noise.

Setting the scene

The shutter speed side effect is blur. There are two types of blur and one type of anti-blur:

- **Camera shake:** Shaking is caused by motion on your part — such as a long shutter speed, instability in your grip, or stabbing the shutter button like it's the last button you'll ever press.

  In Figure 3-5, I'm photographing my daughter, Grace, with a few teddy bears. The shutter speed was too long for me to hold still (1 second), which results in a ton of camera shake.

Figure 3-5: Shake, rattle, and roll.

Faster shutter speeds overcome camera shake, as do tripods and monopods and vibration reduction. Work the exposure so that you can set a faster shutter speed. Relax and take it easy. Work on a stable, steady, grip.

- **Subject blur:** This type of blur occurs when your subject is moving too fast for the shutter speed to freeze. The subject blurs across the sensor. The only way to avoid this effect is to ratchet up to a faster shutter speed.

Figure 3-6 shows a photo of one of my kids playing on "the blue chair." I'm steady, and the shutter speed is at 1/20 second — not that fast, but adequate to illustrate this point. He's the one causing most of the blurring in this photo, not me.

Figure 3-6: Playing on the furniture.

✐ **Motion freeze:** Freezing a moving object in time is the opposite of blurring. Motion freeze is different from just taking a picture where people aren't blurry. It's capturing a ball in the air or a car on the road or a person running. Figure 3-7 shows a photo of my son that I took at 1/640 second. He's well frozen in mid-gallop.

Figure 3-7: Running the bases.

Considering focal length

Focal length matters because you're zeroing in on a smaller area. Whatever is in your frame can jiggle, jostle, move, or otherwise jerk around much more and cause blurring.

Go outdoors and watch some traffic. Take your digital SLR and a zoom lens. Go wide-angle first, and then try to focus on a moving object. Follow it by *panning* (focusing on a moving object and moving the camera to track it until you take the photo) and taking a photo.

Now zoom in and try it again. Tracking a moving subject and taking the photo is much more difficult when you're zoomed in! You have to move the camera much more to keep the subject centered. That's the point: You need a higher shutter speed to compensate for your extra motion.

The traditional rule for shutter speed and focal length is that the shutter speed (technically, the denominator of the shutter speed fraction) should be faster than the focal length. For example, if you're shooting at 70mm, aim for a shutter speed of 1/80 (using a partial stop shutter speed) or faster. Likewise, if you're using a wide-angle lens at 24mm, you can probably hold a shake-free photo at 1/30 second.

Vibration reduction features may let you eke out between one and three additional stops, meaning if you're shooting at 1/30 second without VR, you may be able to shoot a hand-held, blur-free photo at 1/15 or 1/8 second.

Things that go fast

It strikes me that a good way to practically show you how fast objects move and whether or not a particular shutter speed is fast enough to photograph them without blurring is to convert the object's overall speed into the number of millimeters (my apologies to fans of the inch) it moves in 1/500 second. If the object (say, a car moving at 40 miles per hour) moves several millimeters in that time, you can expect blurring, depending on how close you are zoomed in.

The results of compiling my spreadsheet are eye-opening. Table 3-2 shows you those results.

Table 3-2		Millimeters Traveled per Given Shutter Speed						
Subject	*mph*	*1/125*	*1/250*	*1/500*	*1/1000*	*1/2000*	*1/4000*	*1/8000*
Walk	3	10.53	5.26	2.63	1.32	0.66	0.33	0.16
Jog	6	21.05	10.53	5.26	2.63	1.32	0.66	0.33

(continued)

Table 3-2 (continued)

Subject	mph	1/125	1/250	1/500	1/1000	1/2000	1/4000	1/8000
Sprint	25	88.89	44.44	22.22	11.11	5.56	2.78	1.39
Drive	40	140.34	70.17	35.09	17.54	8.77	4.39	2.19
Play MLB fastball	100	350.86	175.43	87.71	43.86	21.93	10.96	5.48
NASCAR	180	631.55	315.77	157.89	78.94	39.47	19.74	9.87
Fly a plane	300	1052.58	526.29	263.14	131.57	65.79	32.89	16.45

This table shows why action photography puts a strain on shutter speed. Take a look at the slowest subject: someone walking at 3 miles per hour. If your shutter speed is set to 1/125 second, that person can move over 10mm. That's about half an inch, which doesn't seem like a lot but can still cause blurring if you're zoomed or close enough to them.

Double the shutter speed, and the walker moves half as much during the photo, or a bit over 5mm. That's not bad, but if you want to reduce subject movement to a millimeter, you have to shoot for 1/2000 second.

Not every photo taken of any subject will blur, even if the subject is moving as fast as Table 3-2 suggests. If someone is moving across your field of view, you can pan with that person as you shoot, which will keep them from blurring as much as the background. Likewise, if someone is coming at you or moving away from you, it's a matter of nailing the focus. You don't need the same shutter speed in that case, either.

People moving around indoors may not be moving at 3 mph all the time. You might catch someone in a moment of relative rest. Not only that, but every time a moving object changes direction, you can time your shot where their relative motion is fairly small.

Managing Shutter Speed

Shutter speed is one of those concepts that people like to put on autopilot and leave alone. This is the number one mistake inexperienced photographers make. They assume the camera knows what shutter speeds to use when in Auto mode. The problem is that it doesn't. It will use a shutter speed to get the right exposure, but it ignores whether or not you're photographing something that's moving. Aside from using Scenes (which I endorse over using full Auto exposure mode for this very reason), the only way for the camera to set the right shutter speed for the subject is if you do it.

If you want to control the shutter speed yourself, you have to get into a shooting mode that lets you fiddle with it. The two best modes for this task are

- **Shutter priority:** The quintessential mode for the shutter speed aficionado. Set your camera to Shutter priority mode and then set the shutter speed yourself. Your camera meters the scene and then adjusts the aperture and possibly ISO (if you're in Auto ISO mode) to set the proper exposure.

  It's a simple yet effective process.

- **Manual:** It's a bit harder to juggle shutter speed in Manual mode, but you can do it. Enter Manual shooting mode and then set the shutter speed based on the conditions and your estimate of how fast you need to be. Meter, and then bring aperture and ISO in line to reach the right exposure. Take a shot and review it. If you need a faster speed (you see blurring), set it and then readjust aperture and ISO.

  You can set aperture or ISO first if you want, but because this chapter talks about shutter speed, I figure you're looking to set that variable first. Refer to Chapter 1 in this minibook for tips on working the whole equation.

See Table 3-3 for recommended shutter speeds.

Book III Chapter 3

Go, Shutter Speed, Go!

Table 3-3	Recommended Shutter Speeds*	
Situation	**As Slow As**	**Notes**
Handheld (no support)	1/60	If you're steady, you may be able to use 1/30 or 1/15 second.
Handheld (supported)	1/15	Depends on your ability to support or stabilize the camera against an object to hold it steady.
Tripod or monopod (action)	1/250 and higher	Depends on the action, but you can freeze some as slow as 1/250; if in doubt, go faster.
Tripod (scenic)	Can be virtually anything	Depends on the lighting and movement in the scene (clouds or vegetation, for example); tripod offers stable support, so camera shake isn't a problem.

(continued)

Table 3-3 *(continued)*

Situation	As Slow As	Notes
Monopod (scenic)	Can be virtually anything	Depends on the lighting, movement in the scene, and your ability to stabilize a monopod; shutter speeds can be slower than handheld but probably not as good as tripod.
Fireworks	Bulb	Hold the shutter open for one or more bursts; experiment with closing the shutter at different points during a burst to see the possible effects.
Lightning	Bulb	Depending on ambient lighting, you may be able to hold the shutter open a long time while you wait for lightning to strike; if not, end the exposure and start a new one.
Dusk	Seconds	Depends on the light and movement in the scene.
Night	Seconds to Bulb	Depends on the light and movement in the scene, but several seconds isn't unreasonable.
Fast action	1/500 and higher	Some types of action (motor sports) require extremely high shutter speeds; other types of action require less.
Casual photography	1/125 to 1/250	Freezes the images of people who aren't running around; prevents camera shake.
Portraits (handheld)	1/60	Ensure that subjects remain still and say "cheese."
Typical flash	1/250	You're limited in most cases to minimum and maximum flash sync speeds.
Crisp	1/250	If in doubt, set the shutter speed reasonably high, or higher, to produce a nice, crisp-looking photo; camera shake (even if it's barely noticeable) can soften the photo, which may not be as discernable as blur but reduces the resolution.

* This table assumes a standard focal length between 35 and 85mm. Shorter focal lengths (wide-angle) are easier to stabilize, so you may be able to use a slower shutter speed. Longer focal lengths (between 85mm and up to telephoto) are harder to stabilize, and you may need faster shutter speeds to prevent blur and shake.

Working with exposure

Getting the right shutter speed is tough sometimes unless you're using a flash.

The three tables in this section show you how to shoot at a faster shutter speed by compensating with ISO and aperture.

All the following tables work the same way. Table 3-4 deals with trading aperture for shutter speed, and Table 3-5 involves trading ISO for shutter speed. Table 3-6 shows how much the shutter speed can change when you change both ISO and aperture.

This is a problem-solving exercise. The numbers you see here will differ from photo to photo. The point is to get you to think of how to get faster shutter speeds. How can you? By "trading" aperture and ISO for shutter speed.

Start at the top line. It represents a potential situation where you're initially at 1/15 second shutter speed, f/8, and ISO 100, and realize you need a faster shutter speed. What do you do? Open up your lens. For every stop you open it, you get to double your shutter speed. The exposure will stay the same. If you need to get to 1/250 second, for example, open your aperture (if possible) to f/2.

Table 3-4	Trading Aperture for Shutter Speed
Shutter Speed	*Aperture*
1/15	f/8
1/30	f/5.6
1/60	f/4
1/125	f/2.8
1/250	f/2
1/500	f/1.4

If you can't or don't want to trade aperture, try ISO. You'll probably get more out of ISO than aperture unless you start at f/22 and can change to f/2.8 (6 stops). To move from 1/15 second at ISO 100 (assuming a constant aperture, whose value doesn't matter for this table) to 1/25 second, for example, you would have to raise ISO to 1600. It isn't ideal, but if you can get the shot, it works.

Table 3-5	Trading ISO for Shutter Speed
Shutter Speed	*ISO*
1/15	100
1/30	200
1/60	400
1/125	800
1/250	1600
1/500	3200
1/1000	6400

If you can trade aperture and ISO together, you can get from 1/15 second to 1/250 second by changing the aperture from f/8 to f/4 and raising the ISO from 100 to 400. That's a reasonable amount.

Table 3-6	Double Dealing for Shutter Speed	
Shutter Speed	*Aperture*	*ISO*
1/15	f/8	100
1/60	f/5.6	200
1/250	f/4	400
1/1000	f/2.8	800
1/4000	f/2	1600

As long as the numbers add up in the end, you can change aperture and ISO by different amounts. For example, if you need a faster shutter speed by six stops, you can get there by trading any combination of ISO and aperture, as long as the change in ISO and aperture adds up to six stops. (Don't forget to change the shutter speed too.)

Testing Theory and Reality

I recently took photos in my driveway of my boys riding their bikes, scooters, and skateboards so that I could perform some practical shutter speed tests.

Figures 3-8 through 3-11 show a progression of shutter speeds from 1/30 to 1/4000 second. I was standing, holding the camera with no other support. I set the ISO initially to 100 but later enabled Auto ISO with an upper limit of ISO 1600. I didn't use a flash. I was in Shutter priority shooting mode. I used a 35mm lens on my Nikon D200.

Figure 3-8 was taken at 1/30 second. I panned to get one son somewhat in focus, but both he and the background are blurry.

Figure 3-8: The lower limit of handheld stability in this case is 1/30 second.

I took the photo in Figure 3-9 at 1/60 second. It's better than 1/30, but if you look at the front of the bike and its rear wheel, you can see a lot of motion blur going on.

Figure 3-10 shows my 1/125 shot. The photos are progressively getting sharper. My son looks clear, especially in his face. Notice the wheels and his moving hand. They aren't frozen yet.

Figure 3-11 shows my son Sam, taken at 1/250 second (Image A). At this speed, he's mostly frozen. The scooter wheel looks good, and he's fairly sharp.

Believe it or not, much of the time, auto focus was more of a problem than camera shake or blur. As the kids moved toward me, the camera had trouble locking on to them fast enough to take the picture at the moment I wanted because it was getting late and the light wasn't particularly strong. I was in "Dynamic area AF with closest subject priority" autofocus mode, which should have picked them up and tracked them. I considered changing to Single-area AF or one of the other modes, but didn't want to lock myself into using a specific autofocus area or group. I repeated the test with an external flash and had much better success.

Figure 3-9: Moving out of camera shake territory but still blurry at 1/60 second.

I took the photo in Image B at 1/500. Sam is running alongside his scooter. That's a good indication of what 1/500 can stop. His right foot is frozen in the air.

I use 1/500 for many indoor shots where people are moving around. After all, although they may not be perfectly still, no one is riding a bike around the living room.

At 1/1000 (see Image C), my son Ben looks like he's balancing the bike and not even moving. The spokes on his wheel are frozen.

At this point, getting a good exposure is more challenging because the fast shutter speed starts pushing other exposure elements to their limits. The aperture was wide open at f/1.8, and the ISO was starting to increase (ISO 220).

Image D shows the 1/2000 photo of Ben. He's clear and is riding hands-free. The photo has depth-of-field issues that aren't related to camera shake or subject blur because of the very wide aperture.

At this point, when you're taking photos of kids, continuing to shoot with faster shutter speeds becomes less effective.

Figure 3-10: A shutter speed of 1/125 sec. does a good job except in fast-moving areas.

Image E shows the last photo in the sequence. I took this shot of Ben at 1/4000 second although I didn't need to. You can see little, if any, difference between 1/1000 and 1/4000 second. (Maybe you could see it if he were riding a rocket cycle, but not casually circling the driveway.) To get the exposure, the camera boosted the ISO to 1250 and the aperture was open to f/1.8, the maximum setting the lens had to offer.

If you're taking photos of different subjects, you may see a different break-point where the photos stop blurring and start looking quite clear. You also reach a point where exposure becomes a real challenge. If I weren't using a fast lens (f/1.8 for the 35mm), ISO would have had to jump higher, sooner.

Book III
Chapter 3

Go, Shutter
Speed, Go!

A. 1/250   B. 1/500   C.1/1000

D. 1/2000   E.1/4000

Figure 3-11: Performing practical shutter speed tests.

Using Slow Shutter Speeds

I hate to be the one to tell you, but slow shutter speeds aren't that interesting. The trouble is that telling them apart from your average, everyday, shaky or blurry photo is difficult.

Some exceptions are described in this list:

✔ **Subject blur:** Occurs when an object moves across your field of view and imprints enough information on the sensor to be a discernable blur. Sometimes, events move so fast that they just don't register.

Figure 3-12 shows all four of our kids starting a race. They clearly are blurring. You can best see Grace and Sam. Ben is moving directly toward me and shows up fairly well. Jake is the blurriest.

Figure 3-12: Ready, set, *go!*

✔ **Background blur:** Occurs when you pan to photograph a moving object. The effect can be interesting, as shown in Figure 3-13. Jake is sitting on his bike saddle and has his feet up, off the pedals. I panned with him to shoot the photo, and the result was a blurry background — a nice-looking effect.

✔ **Flash:** Slow shutter speeds get more interesting when you use flash, especially a repeating flash and slow sync (rear curtain, which is explained in Book III, Chapter 1).

In Figure 3-14, you can see a shot where I enabled the repeating flash and threw some dice onto a black background. The dice don't blur. It's sort of a quintuple exposure — very cool. What happened is that

Figure 3-13: Having a helmet on makes tricks safer to perform.

in the darkened room, the only light came from the flash, which acted like a shutter taking multiple exposures. Each burst lasted in the area of 1/1000 second.

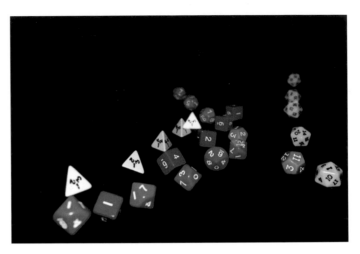

Figure 3-14: Single long exposure, multiple flashes.

Chapter 4: Hi-Ho, Hi-Ho, Choosing an ISO

In This Chapter

✔ **All about ISO**

✔ **Looking at the ISO effect on exposure**

✔ **Keeping a rein on ISO**

✔ **Comparing ISOs**

*I*SO is a subject that can get lost in the mix. It's not as exciting as shutter speed, not as interesting as aperture, and not as "big picture" as exposure.

ISO is one of the three main exposure controls on your camera. ISO has to do with the sensitivity of the camera's sensor. Shutter speed is a mechanical function that moves the shutter out of the way of the sensor for a set amount of time. Aperture refers to the opening in the lens which lets more or less light in, depending on its size.

Although you may not think about raising ISO to get the right exposure until after you've already tried using aperture and shutter speed, you should know how to use it. Sometimes, it's the only way to expose the photo properly.

The Holy Grail of Photography

In days of yore, when film cameras ruled the earth, ISO (sometimes referred to as ASA, but that's another story) was a measure of *film speed* — the speed at which the emulsion chemically reacted to light. Film that was more sensitive to light was considered fast, and film that was less sensitive was considered slow.

Although modern digital SLRs use no film, ISO is still an important part of photography. The term *ISO* is now (within the context of digital photography) a measure of the sensor's sensitivity to light, which can be changed on the fly.

As you can imagine, having a sensor with *varying* sensitivity to light is stupendously beneficial. Before, you had to shoot an entire roll of film before you could switch to a film with a different ISO. You can change ISO in digital SLRs on the fly — from picture to picture, if you want. You can react to changing lighting conditions or move in a different exposure direction at the drop of a hat.

Every exposure control has two effects: one on exposure and one not related to exposure. The effect of raising ISO is *noise* (small artifacts in the photo generated by the camera and sensor), which causes the photo to look grainy when magnified on screen or printed at larger sizes.

Digital camera sensors collect and even generate noise. At low ISOs, the noise is essentially invisible. It's below the human ability to perceive, so it isn't a big deal.

The problem is that as you raise the ISO, you turn up noise as you raise the sensor's sensitivity to light. (I'm simplifying this explanation dramatically.) Think of the ISO knob on your camera as a noise inducer. So the Holy Grail of digital camera design is increasingly higher ISOs with acceptable levels of noise.

Frankly, ISO performance is one area where dSLRs kick the pants off of digital compact cameras — even expensive ones. Digital SLRs have larger, more noise-free sensors that are capable of operating at much higher ISOs than their smaller counterparts.

How sensitive to light a sensor can be without being too noisy depends on your specific digital SLR. As technology advances, efforts to raise ISO and the battle against noise continue — sometimes with counterintuitive results. As you raise the megapixel count on a sensor without increasing its size, you raise the noise level. In other words, if you had two cropped frame (APS-C) cameras with identical sensor sizes, the camera that stuffed more pixels into the same area would probably have a poorer high-ISO performance.

ISO and Exposure

Every stop of ISO equals a stop of exposure (1.0 EV).

Raising ISO from 100 to 200 doubles the light-catching power of the sensor.

By the same token, lowering the ISO from 400 to 200 halves it.

ISO works just like shutter speed and f/stops — only the numbers are different.

Table 4-1 shows ISOs from 100 to 6400 in whole stops.

Table 4-1	ISOs from Low to High in Whole Stops
ISO	**Notes**
100	Most often the lowest native ISO on your camera; best noise performance; needs bright light
200	Used by some cameras as the lowest setting; excellent noise performance; requires bright light
400	The most common indoor ISO setting; used on cloudy days; can be noisy; much better performance from high-end cameras
800	Rarely used outdoors unless it's cloudy or during evening hours; indoor ISO in low-light conditions; noisy in entry-level cameras
1600	Starting to see noise in most cameras even when the photo is unmagnified; use when necessary
3200	Creates a good deal of noise in most cameras; use when you have no other choice
6400	Use when you have to get the shot and the noise doesn't matter

I finish this section with sort of a random list of ISO factoids:

✔ Not all cameras start at ISO 100. For example, the Pentax K-x has an ISO range from 200 to 6400.

✔ Not all cameras end at the same spot, either. For example, the Nikon D3000 has an ISO range from 200 to 3200.

The fine print in the D3000 manual states that you can set the ISO approximately one step below ISO 200 (the equivalent of ISO 100) or one step above ISO 3200 (the equivalent of ISO 6400).

✔ Some cameras use numbers to identify ISO from beginning to end. Some don't, and they rely on ISO expansion. For example, the Canon EOS 5D MkII has L, H1, and H2 ISO settings, which are the equivalent of ISO 50, 12,800, and 25,600, respectively.

Just so you know, some Nikon dSLRs also use identifiers other than numbers for high ISOs, but doesn't call it ISO expansion.

Managing ISO

Digital SLRs let you manage ISO just like the other exposure controls. Use it to reach the exposure you want.

I generally try to keep my ISO setting as low as possible, and I resist raising ISO unless I have no other choice. This strategy ensures that I shoot the least noisy photos possible. But, when you have to raise ISO, you have to raise it. It makes no sense not to take a shot just to prevent raising the ISO. After all, a grainy, noisy photo is much better than no photo.

Keeping ISO low

The $64,000 question is this: How can you keep ISO as low as possible?

You have all the tools of exposure, and then some:

- **Shutter speed:** Lower the shutter speed to let in more light. Every stop of shutter speed that you can slow down saves you a stop of ISO. For example, rather than raise ISO from 400 to 800, try lowering the shutter speed from 1/250 to 1/125 second.

- **Aperture:** Enlarge the lens' aperture (lower the f-number) to let in more light. Every full f/stop of aperture saves you a stop of ISO that you would otherwise have to raise. For example, rather than raise the ISO to 400 from 200, change the f/stop to f/5.6 from f/8.

- **Image stabilization:** This feature helps you lower shutter speeds and prevents blurring from camera shake by one or more stops, depending on the camera and lens and on the effectiveness of the particular jitter-reducing system. For every stop you can lower the shutter speed without shaking, you save yourself a stop of ISO.

- **Tripod or monopod**: If you can, mount your digital SLR on a tripod or monopod to free you from camera shake and give you more reliable, shake-free access to slower shutter speeds, depending on the subject.

  A tripod or monopod is one reason that I can use ISO 100 for virtually all my HDR shots. The tripod lets me use much longer shutter speeds than if I were shooting handheld.

- **Flash:** Using a flash changes the game quite a bit. Raise ISO if you need to extend flash range.

- **Reflectors:** If you've ever seen a movie set, you've probably seen members of the production crew holding large light reflectors and pointing them at the actors and actresses. These reflectors bounce light onto the subjects being filmed, making them lighter and easier to see.

Photographers use reflectors as well. You can use them to balance light and brighten a scene.

✔ **The outdoors during the day:** You can't always do this, but I throw in this option to encourage you to be creative. If you would rather take a photo outdoors in nice daylight than indoors, you don't have to raise the ISO as much, if at all.

✔ **Other lighting:** If you're indoors, open the drapes and turn on the lights. All the light you can bring into the room helps lower the necessity of raising ISO.

✔ **The ISO Automatic setting:** If you have the option, take your ISO off the Auto setting. Then you have to make the ISO decisions. The good news is that the camera doesn't raise the ISO when you don't want it to. You have to compensate by other means.

✔ **Limit Auto ISO:** Set your camera's Auto ISO settings to a range you're comfortable with. If it's between ISO 100 and 400, make it so. If you're comfortable going to ISO 1600, then by all means set the high end of your Auto ISO range there.

✔ **Invest in fast lenses:** If you find that you're shooting indoors a lot, ditch your slow lens and get one with a lower f-number. If you're shopping for zoom lenses, try finding one you like (and can afford) that has the same performance throughout the focal length range.

For example, if you're using the Canon EF-S 17-85mm f/4-5.6 IS USM, consider moving to the Canon EF-S 17-55mm f/2.8 IS USM or EF 24-70mm f/2.8L USM. If you can't afford a new Canon lens of this caliber, look for a used lens or one from a third-party lens manufacturer (Sigma or Tamron, for example).

✔ **Get a newer and better camera:** This step may seem dramatic, but when you look at the price of a single expensive zoom lens (the Canon EF 24-70mm f/2.8L USM lists for $1,449), you can almost get a Canon EOS 7D instead for near the same price ($1,699).

Configuring ISO

The good news is that you have to worry about only two ISO modes:

✔ **Auto:** In Auto ISO mode, the camera raises or lowers ISO to reach the proper exposure. Ideally, it raises ISO as a last resort (that's what the Nikon D300S says in its manual), after trying to get the exposure with aperture and shutter speed.

Figure 4-1 shows the Auto ISO menu on my Sony digital SLR.

If your camera is in manual shooting mode, Auto ISO does nothing because you've told the camera to let me handle exposure.

And now, some caveats:

Most cameras limit the ISO range when in Auto ISO mode. In other words, the entire ISO range of the camera *isn't available* in Auto ISO mode. You may or may not be able to expand or contract the range. If you need more ISO, swap out of Auto ISO mode and switch to manual.

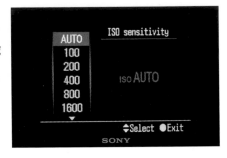

Figure 4-1: ISO is on Auto, Captain.

Some cameras, such as the Nikon D3000, let you change the maximum ISO sensitivity available in Auto ISO mode in conjunction with a minimum shutter speed. The minimum shutter speed is the trigger that the camera uses to raise ISO. You can set the minimum shutter speed to be faster or slower, depending on your ability to hold the camera steady, whether or not you use image stabilization, and other factors. The camera lowers the shutter speed below the minimum only if it can't raise ISO enough to get the necessary exposure.

Some cameras, such as the Canon EOS Rebel T2i, let you set only the maximum ISO.

Some cameras don't allow you to enable Auto ISO if you're in manual mode. You're on your own.

Some cameras round ISO to the nearest full stop (100, 200, or 400, for example) when displaying the setting in the viewfinder or on the LCD screen. When you review the photo, you see the exact ISO.

When I'm photographing birthday parties and events indoors, I sometimes switch to Shutter priority shooting mode and enable Auto ISO. This strategy puts a premium on allowing an adequate amount of light into the camera while keeping shutter speeds high enough to avoid blurring everyone. I set my Auto ISO to around ISO 800 — any more than that on my D200, and the noise starts showing. If these settings don't work, I may drag out the flash or give in and raise the maximum ISO possible in Auto ISO mode.

✔ **Manual:** Manual ISO mode takes the camera out of the ISO loop. You have to set it yourself.

Setting manual ISO is easy: Press the ISO button (or its equivalent), and dial in the ISO you want. You may be able to set ISO in whole stops, half stops, or even by thirds of a stop. Check your camera's menu system to see what your options are.

Figure 4-2 shows the ISO menu on my Sony being set to ISO 100.

Some cameras prevent you from setting ISO manually in certain shooting modes. For example, the Sony Alpha 300 fixes ISO to Auto when you're in Auto or Scene Selection shooting mode.

I use manual ISO mode whenever I can. It ensures that I'm on top of ISO and that it isn't changing from one extreme to another. This consideration may be an important one if you want all photos from the same photo shoot (such as taking pictures of your cat in the living room) to have the same noise characteristics.

Figure 4-2: Manual override engaged and ISO set to 100.

Following ISO guidelines

My best ISO advice boils down to this: Keep ISO as low as you can to take the shots you need. If you need to raise it, do so. If you can lower it, do so.

Having said that, there are times when you have to raise ISO to be able to expose the photo adequately. Table 4-2 lists some general ISO pointers by situation.

Table 4-2		ISO Guidelines
Situation	*ISO*	*Notes*
Bright daylight	200 and lower	ISO should be as low as possible; very low noise; in addition to noise, higher ISOs can push shutter speeds too fast if you're in a bright environment.
Cloudy day	200-800	You may need an ISO boost to keep shutter speeds fast; in general, try to keep ISO as low as possible; minimal to moderate noise; consider using flash.
Bright interior with daylight	400-800	Start at 400 and see what happens; you may be able to tweak downward, but you may also need to raise it; watch the aperture and depth of field.
Lit interior but no outside light	800 and higher	Depending on the strength of the lighting, you may need quite a bit of ISO; potential for a lot of noise.

(continued)

Book III
Chapter 4

Hi-Ho, Hi-Ho,
Choosing an ISO

Table 4-2 *(continued)*		
Situation	*ISO*	*Notes*
Dusk	800 and higher	ISO depends on the shutter speed you want; fast speeds may require high ISOs.
Dark interior	1600 and higher	These situations never have as much light as you might believe, because your eyes and brain adjust to the conditions.
Night (fast shutter)	1600 and higher	This one depends on other light sources, such as moonlight and streetlights, and on how fast you're trying to shoot.
Night (slow shutter)	100	Set for your convenience; if you're taking long exposures, higher ISOs make them shorter; if you don't need them shorter, don't worry about it.
Fireworks	100 or lower	ISO doesn't matter in this case because you should be shooting in Bulb mode and the fireworks are bright.
Lightning	100 or lower	See the preceding Fireworks bullet; the problem here is waiting for a flash of lighting — you can overexpose the scene if you raise ISO too high.

Shooting with Different ISOs

First, I took the photos in this section with my cameras and lenses. They're not set to, nor do they represent, the Universal Objective ISO Noise Level Standard.

In other words, each camera is different. Some cameras have better ISO performance than mine do, for example, and some have worse, and some might even have the same.

Technologies are continually being improved. Newer cameras will therefore have different capabilities and noise levels. In addition, entry-level digital SLRs will have worse noise performance at the same ISO levels than more expensive, professional dSLRs. There's little point in comparing a Canon EOS Rebel XS to a Nikon D3X. They're in totally different leagues. Compare the Rebel XS against the Sony Alpha 290 or 390.

Changing technology doesn't invalidate the following information as long as you use it to learn how to compare ISO performance between different cameras within the same basic class. The general principles you should learn are summed up in the following list:

✏ **Exposure:** Using lower ISO renders your camera less sensitive to light, which may be exactly what you want. A higher ISO means your camera is more sensitive to light. Use these ISOs when you need them.

✏ **Noise:** Lower ISOs capture and create lower noise than higher ISOs. ISO 400 and lower should be relatively noise-free in most dSLRs. Your camera may be better or worse than this, though. My Nikon D200 has low noise levels from ISO 100 to 400, some at ISO 800, and then becomes dramatically worse. The newer D300S outperforms this, as shown in the following section.

On the other hand, my Nikon D200 is better than my Sony Alpha 300, which is an entry-level dSLR.

Comparing moons and moons

While photographing the moon one night, I conducted an ISO test. The moon appears in each frame so you can compare crops of darkness and moonlight for each ISO I tested.

Figure 4-3 shows a sequence from my Nikon D200 and NIKKOR 300mm f/4 telephoto lens. I had the 2x teleconverter on the lens, extending the focal length to 600mm. The shutter speed varied, so I got a constant exposure. My camera was in Aperture priority mode, and I was shooting at f/8. These photos are unsmoothed and unsharpened.

Can you discern the onset of noise? If you compare the images carefully, you might be able to see some, beginning at ISO 1600. Noise is present below ISO 1600, but not very much. There's more noise at ISO 3200, but it still doesn't look too bad to the naked eye. You might not even recognize it as noise if it weren't being discussed in a chapter about ISO and noise. Notice that you can't see any noise in the night sky. It's quite clear, even to ISO 3200.

Noise increases with ISO, but sometimes it doesn't matter. Sometimes it does matter: It may be there, even though you can't see it at first. You may only detect it when you process a photo heavily or if you try to print it out at a very large size.

Figure 4-4 shows the noise when I use Levels to crank up the brightness in Photoshop. The artifacts are accentuated. From ISO 100 to ISO 800, the D200 clearly performs well. At ISO 1600, you can start to see noise in the sky. Remember, though, that I have accentuated the noise by using software.

Although ISO 1600 is bearable in this example, ISO 3200 is where the noise hits the fan. Though the effect is much larger here than in the unprocessed photo, the point is to show you that it's there.

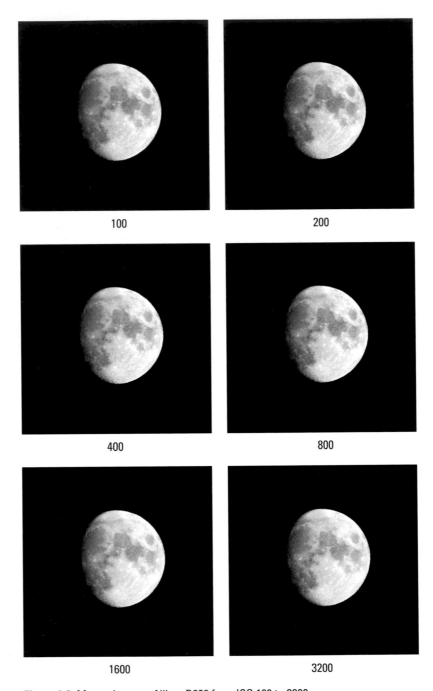

100 200

400 800

1600 3200

Figure 4-3: Moon shot on a Nikon D200 from ISO 100 to 3200.

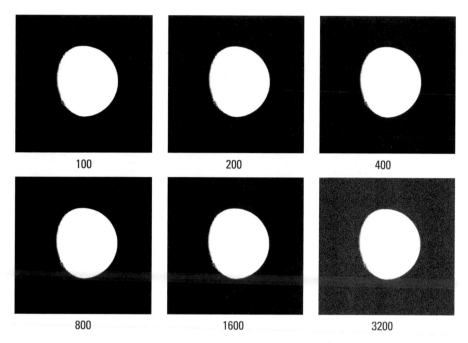

100 200 400

800 1600 3200

Figure 4-4: Noise levels elevated for comparison.

Figure 4-5 shows you a side-by-side comparison of ISO 100 and ISO 3200. Both are unretouched photos. If you look in the darker areas of the moon, you can see lots of noise at ISO 3200. At ISO 100, the photo is clearer and sharper and has better contrast and is more noise-free. When in doubt, keep the ISO down.

100 3200

Figure 4-5: Side-by-side comparison of ISO 100 versus 3200 (Nikon D200).

Technology advances. Figure 4-6 compares the Nikon D200 with the Nikon D300. At ISO 1600, the D200 performs well, but the D300S is outstanding. It's at least a few ISO stops better. The normal-looking photo is much clearer, sharper, and more noise-free than the D200. When you look at the enhanced version, you can't detect any noise. It performs as well as ISO 200 or so on the D200.

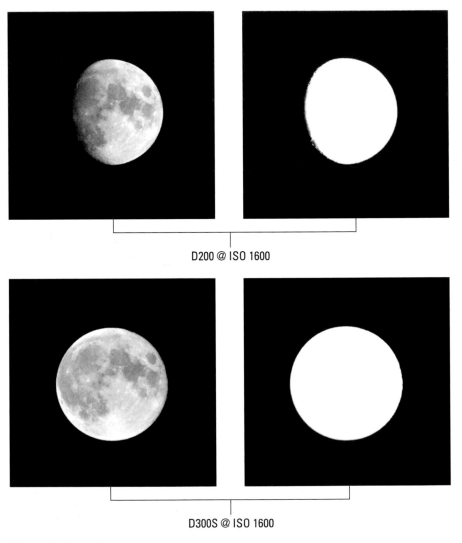

D200 @ ISO 1600

D300S @ ISO 1600

Figure 4-6: Comparing cameras.

You can perform tests on your camera to evaluate its noise performance and determine where your limits are.

Entry-level cameras have poorer noise performance than what I've shown you in this chapter, and more advanced and newer cameras have better performance.

Shooting indoors

When you're taking photos indoors at night, don't expect to be able to raise ISO enough to take anything other than fairly noisy pictures — unless you have studio-style lighting in your living room. The only practical option is to use a flash. The following steps describe what I call the "ISO Death Spiral":

1. **The Scene:** You're taking photos indoors and you don't want to use a flash. It's dark outdoors.

   Figure 4-7 shows a room we're renovating in our house. I took this shot at night. The room is well lit, but the sun is down and provides no help. When you walk in, you wouldn't think that the camera would have so much trouble with exposure — but it does.

Figure 4-7: Open areas are excellent places to shoot photos.

2. **The Equipment:** If you have a fast lens, you can open it all the way to f/1.4 and enter Aperture priority mode. I used f/8 for my test image because I wanted to photograph my guitar at close range and have more than a microscopic depth of field. I conducted a test at f/1.4 and f/2.8 and found little appreciable difference to the scenario, meaning that I still had to pull out the flash.

3. **The Crunch:** When you start metering, you'll realize that you can't possibly take a blur-free photo because the shutter speed the camera suggests at these settings (f/8, ISO 100, Aperture priority mode) is too long for stable hand-held photography.

   Figure 4-8 shows the conundrum — 1 second exposure time, f/8, and ISO 100. I can't possibly hold the camera still.

Figure 4-8: Blurry at the required shutter speed.

4. **Reality hits:** You have to start raising ISO because shutter speed needs to be faster. You can't or don't want to increase the size of the aperture. You have nothing else to trade with, short of bringing in the Klieg lights.

   Figure 4-9 shows why you have to raise ISO. I set the shutter speed to 1/60 second but kept ISO and aperture constant. It's way too dark.

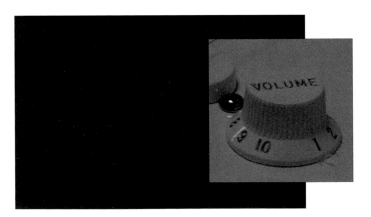

Figure 4-9: Too dark at a reasonable shutter speed.

5. **Reality bites:** You reach ISO 3200 and realize that you cannot take the picture without a flash.

   Figure 4-10 shows the result at 1/30 second, f/8, and ISO 3200. You can see a lot of noise in the guitar.

Figure 4-10: ISO equals noise.

Figure 4-10 is a little fuzzy because of the slow shutter speed and the fact that I was holding the camera by hand.

Figure 4-11 shows the result of a faster shutter speed — fast enough for me to hold without shaking (1/125 second) — another underexposed (but sharper) photo.

If you're shooting somewhere that you can't use a flash (such as at the zoo in front of a lion's face), continue raising ISO and hope for the best. You may be able to minimize noise by using software or in-camera noise processing. One possibility is to convert the photo to black-and-white and refer to the noise as "film grain."

6. **Pull out:** You scale ISO between ISO 100 and ISO 400 and use either the pop-up or an external speedlight.

7. **Add practicality:** If your aperture is wide open, you might need to make it smaller (raise the f/number, also called *stopping down*) to get more depth of field and sharpness. I decided to use f/8 because I wanted a reasonable depth of field in this photo.

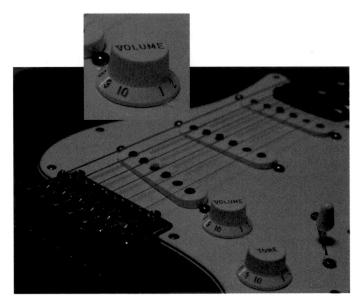

Figure 4-11: Faster shutter speed results in an underexposed photo.

Figure 4-12 shows the last photo in this example. I set up my SB-600 Speedlight for remote wireless operation and put it to the side, a couple of feet away from the guitar so that it would shine from the side.

My solution was to shoot at 1/80 second, f/8, and ISO 400 with the flash. Using it enabled me to keep a reasonable aperture (remember that depth of field decreases dramatically when you're close to the subject) and shutter speed (1/80 is on the low end of handheld territory, but it looks stable). I still had to use ISO 400. The exposure looks good, and I'm happy with the photo.

Raising ISO doesn't always solve all your problems. In a seemingly well-lit room, for example, I couldn't raise ISO high enough to get a good shutter speed for a handheld photo at the aperture I wanted to shoot at. I ended up using a flash *and* raising ISO.

The funny thing about noise

Noise tends to show up differently in different photos. Figure 4-13 shows a telephoto shot of a large construction crane. I shot this one at ISO 800 to get a fast shutter speed (1/4000 second). The operator is clearly visible. Some noise is present, but it's confined to the darker regions of the photo and the glass on the crane. The noise, in this case, is apparent when you zoom in but doesn't matter at normal magnifications.

Figure 4-12: In this case, the flash was necessary.

Figure 4-13: This noise is hard to see.

Figure 4-14 shows a much closer shot taken at a higher ISO (3200). Though the noise is much more visible, it adds to the aesthetics of the photo. When that happens (your artistic antennae have to be up to recognize it), don't try to eliminate all traces of noise in the photo. You may remove some, or none, and let the photo stand on its own.

Converting a photo to black and white (see Figure 4-15) increases the visibility of the noise. It *still* works. In this case, the noise looks like film grain and contributes to the photo.

Figure 4-14: This noise adds to the character of the photo.

Don't let noise scare you. Try to keep a tight rein on it, but realize that there are times when you can ignore it or make it work for you.

Figure 4-15: This noise is even better.

Chapter 5: Fabulous Filters

*I*n the digital world, everything seems to be computerized, gadgetized, electronicized, microminiaturized, and replaced by software. Or it's getting there.

Filters, on the other hand — and I'm not talking about software effects in Photoshop — are *real*. Using an optical filter instead of a software filter is like the difference between watching a Jackie Chan movie that doesn't rely on computer generated (CG) stunts and effects and a computer animation. You don't get CG in a Jackie Chan movie. You get the actual actor. You can hold a filter in your hand and bang it on a table, if you want. (I wouldn't advise it.) Filters clink in your camera bag. Someone made them. They're smooth and pretty to look at. They have weight.

The trouble is, standing in front of a large filter display in a camera shop (or going online and browsing page after page of filters) can be highly intimidating. Questions course through your gray matter. What are these gizmos? How do they work? What do I get? Which ones are best for me? Should I bother? I hope to answer these questions in this chapter about fabulous filters.

A Cram Course on Filters

Answer time. If you've used Photoshop, Photoshop Elements, Lightroom, Aperture, PaintShop Photo Pro, Picasa, iPhoto, Capture One — you get the idea — you have the digital equivalent of physical filters built into your program.

If you're familiar with filters in image editing software, you can easily move from the virtual thing to the real thing.

Filter facts

In the digital world, *filters* (or *effects* or *styles*) and general photo adjustments change the color or exposure of a photo. In the real world, physical filters do the same thing and can be applied for many reasons (organized generally into problem solving and artistic categories), as described in this list:

- **Balance exposure:** Certain filters (ND grad) help you tame a bright sky, tone down the sun, or brighten darker areas in the foreground. Others (ND) darken or change the entire scene equally.

  I took the photos shown in Figure 5-1 — both are unretouched — to show what a neutral density (ND) filter does. (You can find a fuller definition later in the chapter, but for now, all you have to know is that ND filters make a scene darker.) The first shot was taken without a filter. I was shooting toward the west during a bright afternoon, and the sky and clouds were bright. In the second photo, I put on an ND filter to darken the scene and change some of the tone. The telling factor is that the shutter speed moved from 1/320 second (without filter) to 1/90 second (with filter). Less light was coming in, and the camera made up the exposure by slowing down the shutter. If you're having trouble with too much light, ND filters are the answer.

No filter   ND filter

Figure 5-1: Using an ND filter to tone down the glare of the sun.

- **Contrast enhancement:** Circular polarized filters boost contrast to make a photo pop more.

- **Color cast removal:** Colored filters can take out red reflections when you're shooting toward evening hours, and make it look like a mid-afternoon shot with late-in-the-day shadows.

- **Glare removal:** If you had a digital polarizer filter, you could remove glare from reflected light in software. The problem is that it doesn't exist. This is one area where optical filters perform a chore that software can't.

Figure 5-2 shows an example of removing glare with an actual filter. The first shot is the same as in Figure 5-1. The second has a circular polarizer filter turned to block out reflections off the water. (Circular polarizer filters work with the autofocus and through-the-lens metering systems of digital SLRs because they create circularly polarized light, which can make it through the camera, while linear polarizer filters do not.) You can see on the left side of the photo that the reflections have been successfully rejected. The contrast and tone in the water are better.

No filter

Circular polarizer filter

Figure 5-2: The circular polarizer filter is circularly polarizing.

Book III
Chapter 5

Fabulous Filters

Popular uses for filters include

- ✓ **Sepia tone:** Turn a normal-looking photo into an aged antique.
- ✓ **Add a colored tint:** Turn the sky purple and the water orange.
- ✓ **Skin tones:** Warm up skin tones and give your subjects tans.
- ✓ **Create special effects:** Soften focus, add a radial zoom, add haze, mask out areas, add lens reflections, stars, and more.

The key to moving from using digital to physical (also called optical) filters is correlating the tasks you perform using software with a physical filter that does the same thing. For example, you might realize that you're always fighting overexposed skies and underexposed landscapes. Rather than fix that problem in software, match your need (balancing exposure) with the filter that will solve the problem or give you the creativity you want (ND graduated, or ND grad). Table 5-1, which appears at the end of the chapter, helps you determine which filter to use for what purpose.

Looking at the way filters work

You use filters by affixing them on the outside of a lens so that they're in front of your camera's sensor. Light from the outside world passes through them on its way to be measured by the sensor — simple stuff.

What the filter does to the light depends on the type of filter.

Surely you've worn pairs of sunglasses. They are ND filters. Those "shades" (that's a big hint as to their purpose) protect your eyes but still let some light through. In photographic terms, they reduce exposure.

Sunglasses are also made with gradients. These types of sunglasses work like an ND grad filter. They darken the sky but let you see the lay of the land without alteration. Those expensive polarized sunglasses eliminate glare and reflections, just like polarizing filters do. In those old BluBlocker sunglasses commercials, the lenses are amber colored and filter out blue light (see Figure 5-3). They don't shade your eyes by making everything look darker: They target specific wavelengths of light and remove them. (You can also get them polarized.)

©*BluBlocker Corp.*

Figure 5-3: I *still* want a pair of these.

The pros and cons of using filters

I'm brutally honest in this section: Filters are useful, and using them brings you many benefits, but you have equally compelling reasons not to use them.

Here are some pros:

- **Quality:** You have to find a balance between degrading a photo by making light pass through more "stuff" to get to the camera's sensor while acknowledging that software can't perfectly emulate a quality filter interacting with actual light. Many question the benefit of putting a $20 filter in front of a $1,500 lens and the affect it has on reducing the optical quality of the lens.

- **Physicality:** Filters are real, not emulated. Someone didn't have to program it to get the effect *reasonably close* in software. It's the filter being emulated. In other words, an ND grad filter cannot fail to emulate itself. Having said that, there may be quality differences between filters and brands of filters that affect how well they perform.

- **Time:** You should always try to shoot the best photo you can with your camera and not rely so much on software to fix exposure or color problems. You then spend less time developing (also called processing) raw exposures and editing them.

✔ **Exposure control:** If you have a camera whose fastest shutter speed is 1/4000 second and you can't stop down (make the aperture smaller) or lower ISO, the right ND filter can, in effect, give you three additional stops of exposure control. In this scenario, that's similar to having a maximum shutter speed of 1/32000 second. (Or, if you prefer, it's like moving from ISO 100 to ISO 12.5.)

✔ **Creativity:** Add color, mists, stars, frames, and soft focus, and convert temperatures and more with filters. It's like having a Hollywood special effects division supporting your photo shoot.

And, here are some areas in which the cons (or disadvantages, not to be confused with convicts), unfortunately, show up:

✔ **Convenience:** You have to carry filters around and they take up precious space in your camera bag. Software filters are much lighter by comparison.

✔ **Fragility:** Optical filters (unlike their software counterpart) break. Buying an expensive one and then breaking it is heartbreaking.

✔ **Cleanliness:** Filters can get smudged and dirty. Fingers are a filter's worst enemy.

✔ **Durability:** Filters can scratch, which can't be good.

✔ **Cost:** Filters cost money, which always seems to be in short supply. You're limited in the number of filters you can buy, the number of lenses you can support with filters, and the number of times you can replace or upgrade them. With programs like Photoshop, you buy it once, and the filters work on every photo.

✔ **Interoperability:** Different lens sizes need different filters.

✔ **Time:** Setting up and swapping out filters takes time and effort.

✔ **The X-factor:** You have one chance of getting it right. In software, you can try out a lot of different filters and effects with the same photo until you're happy with the result.

Weigh the pros and cons to see what's right for you. You don't have to go out and buy everything at once. Start out with one or two different filters and see what you think. Having a circular polarizer filter to block annoying reflections is a good first choice if you shoot a lot of landscapes with water, buildings with glass sides and windows, or portraits of people who wear glasses. If you shoot indoors, or shoot mostly portraits, you will benefit from filters that correct white balance.

Using filters with digital SLRs

Using filters is easy enough. You spend a few moments setting up and getting going, but when you get the hang of it, the decision of which filter to use becomes second nature and you get faster setting it up. Remember to clean your filters at home before setting out on your shoot.

1. **Evaluate the scene and choose a filter.**

   Over time, this choice becomes almost automatic. If you go out during the golden hour (the hour before sunset or after sunrise) and shoot landscapes into the sun (see Figure 5-4), you know that either an ND filter or an ND grad filter works well.

Figure 5-4: Bright sun requires an ND filter or ND grad. I will use the ND grad.

   If you shoot portraits and like warm skin tones (and you don't use reflectors or gels for that task), you might choose a warming filter almost all the time.

   If you're experimenting, try something different. Choose a filter first and dedicate your shoot to exploring its potential.

   Most people agree that using more than two (three at the most) filters at the same time degrades image quality. Every pane of glass, resin, or polyester is another layer between your expensive glass and the sensor. I tell you more about filter types later in this chapter.

2. **Slide or screw in the filter.**

   Depending on the filter system you use, either screw your precleaned filter to the end of your lens or slide it in the holder. More on the different filter systems later.

3. **Meter and adjust exposure.**

   Digital SLRs use *through the lens (TTL)* metering, which means that anything mounted on the lens is automatically compensated for when your camera meters the scene. You shouldn't have to manually adjust the exposure, therefore, even with a filter mounted.

   For graduated filters, the center of the scene should be properly exposed, even with the filter in place. If you're using spot metering, you may see better results from pre-metering and then mounting the filter. Read your filter's documentation to see whether it provides specific metering instructions. Experiment and take test shots to fine-tune the exposure.

   In the past (or now, if you're using a camera without TTL metering), photographers had to manually account for the way every filter affected exposure. They even had a name for it: Filter Factor.

4. **Take the photo.**

5. **Review it and evaluate.**

   If you're using a filter with an evenly distributed effect, such as an ND filter, examine the entire photo and evaluate whether it has the correct exposure or effect. For an ND or color grad, check to see that the filter is lined up properly with the horizon and that no halos appear around buildings or objects near the horizon.

   In this example (see Figure 5-5), to show you how the gradient looks when it's out of whack, I intentionally skewed the horizon line of the filter so that it covers the right side of the photo.

   For color filters, check the hue. For polarized filters, check for glare.

Figure 5-5: This thing isn't lined up right.

6. **Correct and start over or continue on course.**

Figure 5-6 shows the completed, correct photo. The ND grad filter has darkened the sky but left the far tree line and water alone. That's what an ND grad does best — selectively control exposure.

Figure 5-6: An ND grad filter, successfully applied.

Thinking outside the box

Filters expand the shooting envelope of your camera, but if you don't think outside the digital box, you can't take advantage of them.

This just happened to me at a recent family gathering.

I had my 50mm f/1.4 lens and wanted to open the aperture up to limit the depth of field for some nice portraits. When I did, I overexposed everything. The problem was the flash. I was using the pop-up flash (didn't take my external speedlight) to provide fill flash (see Book IV for more information on flashes), and the fastest flash sync speed possible with the pop-up flash and my camera was 1/250 second. That wasn't fast enough to limit the exposure for the bright conditions. I didn't have my filters with me either — oops — so I had to live with a smaller aperture and deeper depth of field.

Had I remembered to put an ND filter in my camera bag, I could have put it on the lens, opened the aperture a few stops, and the filter would have compensated by lowering the exposure back down to normal.

Filter Systems

Filters come in two main flavors: circular filters that screw onto the lens and rectangular filters that slide into a frame mounted on the lens. Both have their pros and cons.

Circular (screw-in)

Circular filters are quite popular and easy to work with. Figure 5-7 shows a circular Sigma UV filter.

I suppose that the terms *circular* and *screw-in* are redundant. Can you even turn a square or triangular screw?

Figure 5-7: Trust me — there's glass in the ring.

Circular filters have two primary characteristics:

- ✓ **Circular filter and frame:** A glass (some filters are made from other materials) interior mounted in a (mostly) metal frame.

- ✓ **Screw-in:** Circular filters screw into the front end of dSLR lenses. Be careful not to cross-thread it when mounting. You might ruin the filter or, worse, strip the threads on your lens.

    Take your time and, if necessary, back out the filter by turning it counterclockwise until you feel it correct itself and get back on track.

    If your hands are slippery and can't grip the filter, get a gripper from a kitchen store and use it for better traction as you grip the edges of the filter.

Each lens has its own front filter diameter, measured in millimeters. Be sure to check the documentation that came with your lens so that you know which size to buy.

It positively stinks when every one of the lenses you use often takes a different filter size. I have three prime lenses that I use with my Nikon D200, and I have one ultra wide-angle. The 28mm manual focus and 35mm prime both take 52mm filters. The 50mm lens takes a 58mm filter. My Sigma 10-20mm F4-5.6 takes a 77mm filter. Yeah.

The other filter type, described in the following section, addresses this problem nicely.

Rectangular frame slide-in

Another main filter type relies on a frame mounted to the lens that allows rectangular filters to slide in and out. The beauty of this system is that as long as you have the right adaptor or coupling ring, you can use the same filters on lenses of many different sizes.

Here's a description of the primary components:

- ✓ **Adapter or coupler:** This piece screws into the filter ring on your lens and has fittings to slide on the filter holder and make a secure attachment. Simply buy the correct adapter for each of your lenses, and you're ready to rock.

    Read the documentation to ensure that this type of filter system is compatible with the lenses you want to use it with. Most normal dSLR lenses work fine. You may have to buy a different system for use with wide-angle lenses.

Figure 5-8: Screw in the adapter like it's a filter.

    Figure 5-8 shows the Cokin adapter (at www.cokin.com) screwed onto my 35mm lens.

- ✓ **Filter holder:** This element, shown in the top image of Figure 5-9, holds one or more filters. The holder slides onto the adapter. Filters slide into the holder rather than screw onto the lens, which makes changing them extremely easy. It also makes the filters compatible with many different lenses. Notice in the figure that there's room for three filters in this particular adapter.

- ✓ **Rectangular filter:** The reason for the entire setup is the filter. It's larger than a screw-in filter and is rectangular. Most rectangular filters don't have frames around them, so be careful when handling them. You can buy filter wallets, sleeves, and boxes for storage.

    Figure 5-10 shows the entire setup, complete with an extra filter leaning against the lens.

Figure 5-9: A filter holder (top) and what it looks like on the lens.

Figure 5-10: This rectangular ND grad filter is ready for action, with backup standing by.

All in all, this system is ingenious if you have several lenses that take different filter sizes. Having a rectangular filter holder makes a robust filter library more cost-effective. However, the size of the mount with filters is bigger and bulkier than the traditional circular screw-in variety.

Filter Types

This section has information on several different filter types. Browse through them to see what excites you. Think about the photos you normally shoot as you consider whether a particular filter type is right for you.

The sheer number of filters and filter types can be overwhelming, and getting this all straight in your mind can take some time. Come back and review the different filter types in this section if you need to. I summarized them in Table 5-1, at the end of this chapter.

In each case, I tried to compare the filter I'm describing to a pair of glasses or sunglasses that do the same thing. When you realize how similar they are, it takes away a lot of the confusion surrounding filters.

Protective

Using a protective filter is similar to wearing shop glasses. You don't do it because it's pretty — you do it to protect your eyes.

A protective filter is simply clear, optical-quality glass meant to protect the lens. You can leave it on your lens all the time and as long as the filter is clean, the photo shouldn't be affected. The filter essentially serves as a clear lens cover.

You might think that putting a filter on your lens that does nothing is a scam, like buying a box of air, but it isn't a bad idea. When a clear protective filter is in place, you don't have to constantly clean your lens. You clean the filter, which prevents the lens (and its irreplaceable coating) from accidentally being scratched.

Circular polarized

Polarized filters act like a good pair of polarized sunglasses: They filter out distracting reflections and glare.

The details of this type of filter are somewhat technical, so you have to pay attention.

Natural light is unpolarized. After it hits an object and bounces off, it becomes polarized. The energy rotating around the reflected light "ray" becomes organized and directional, which makes it susceptible to filters.

When you rotate a polarized filter, you line up the filter with the more organized reflections *to block them out.* Most of the direct, natural light passes through the filter because its energy isn't limited to a single direction.

That's why you rotate polarized filters, and that's why they work to reject *reflected* light more than direct light.

The circular part has to do with the characteristics of the light as it leaves the filter. After filtering out linearly polarized light (reflection), a circular polarizer filter imparts a circular twist to the light, which makes it compatible with autofocus sensors behind partially reflective modern digital SLR mirrors.

Ultraviolet (UV)

Sunglasses with UV protection are preferable for your eyes because they block a lot of haze. If your eyes are exposed to too much UV radiation for too long, you can damage them.

Ditto for UV filters: They specialize in blocking ultraviolet light, which causes blue haze when shooting around water, into the air, or into the distance. (Think of the phrase *purple mountains majesty* in the hymn *America the Beautiful.*)

REMEMBER

UV filters are not the same as polarized filters. Although you can find both types of filters in quality sunglasses, they perform different functions. There's some debate as to whether digital cameras respond to UV filters, as most manufacturers build UV and IR protection into their sensors. In addition, many lenses are coated to reject UV wavelengths. There's no doubt UV filters work at blocking UV light, but if the lens and the camera can do as good a job, you may not need the filter.

Neutral density (ND)

Neutral density (ND) filters act like normal sunglasses: They darken. ND filters come in different strengths; some darken a lot, and some darken only a little.

Figure 5-11 shows an ND filter that's basically dark shaded glass.

ND graduated (ND grad)

ND grad filters resemble cool-looking aviator sunglasses with a gradient. They're darker at the top to tone down light from the sky, and they're clear toward the bottom so that you can see your instruments.

©The Tiffen Company

Figure 5-11: I wear my sunglasses at night. (If you remember the pop song, feel free to set this caption to music.)

TIP

In photography, ND grads help darken the sky so that you can set longer exposure times for the land.

Figure 5-12 shows two types of ND grads: circular and rectangular.

Circular

Rectangular

Figure 5-12: ND grads, any way you slice them.

**Book III
Chapter 5**

Fabulous Filters

Color filter

Look through these "rose-colored glasses" to change the color of the scene. Figure 5-13 shows a pleasant-looking blue filter. I include cooling and warming filters in this color category. Think of them as white balance correction on the front end of your lens. Figure 5-14 shows a warming filter.

©The Tiffen Company

Figure 5-13: The "Avatar" filter, if you want to turn things blue.

Color grad filter

A color grad filter combines elements of both color and ND grad filters. Imagine an ND grad filter that isn't gray, but in color. A color grad filter is shown in Figure 5-15.

Other filters

A ton of filter types are available, in addition to the ones I describe earlier. If you catch the "filter bug," visit a store in person or online and check them out. Download a brochure to see before-and-after photos for each type of filter. Here are some details on a few other types of filters:

©The Tiffen Company

Figure 5-14: This filter is named 85B — look for it in the Photoshop filters.

- ✓ **In-camera filters:** Many digital SLRs offer in-camera filter processing (sometimes called filters or art filters — the Olympus E-620 is a good example). These filters are just like the software filters you find in programs like Photoshop.

- ✓ **Black-and-white filters:** Used in black and white film photography to enhance contrast and bring out certain (which ones depend on the filter color) tones. They work under the same principles programs like Photoshop do when you convert a color photo to black and white in Photoshop. Use this type of filter in color digital photography and experiment with color effects.

- ✓ **Infrared filters:** Infrared (IR) filters are like X-ray goggles. Use an infrared filter to filter out all except infrared light, turning your photos into surreal works of art. That's the good news. The bad news is that new digital cameras,

©The Tiffen Company

Figure 5-15: Warm the sky or land and leave the other elements alone.

including dSLRs, are engineered to filter out infrared light and reduce their sensitivity to it. This defeats the purpose of putting an infrared filter on your lens.

If you're curious, you can experiment with an IR filter by mounting your camera on a tripod, using long exposure times, and raising ISO through the roof. Your lens/dSLR combination may make IR photography impractical, however.

As an alternative, the folks at Life Pixel Infrared (`www.lifepixel.com`) will convert your camera so it can shoot hand-held IR photos (much like standard photography). They take your camera apart and replace the filter that covers the sensor. If you feel up to the do-it-yourself challenge, they also have conversion kits.

✔ **Creative filters (stars, mist, or haze, for example):** Use these filters to exercise your creativity. The sky is the limit. (If you ever saw Elton John in his heyday, you know what glasses to compare these filters to.)

In Table 5-1, I listed the most practical filters for dSLR photographers. You can experiment with plenty more. Have fun!

Table 5-1	Filter Types	
Type	*What It Does*	*Notes*
Protective	Protects your lens	Used as a clear lens cap and works well.
Circular polarized	Filters out light reflections	Controls reflections, eliminates glare, and enhances contrast.
Ultraviolet (UV)	Filters out UV light	Reduces glare.
Neutral density (ND)	Darkens a scene	Available in different strengths; used to decrease shutter speeds.
ND graduated (ND grad)	Darkens the sky while leaving the ground alone	A practical filter for landscape photographers.
Color filters	Corrects colors or effects	Think of white balance.
Color grad filters	Corrects color for half the photo, like an ND grad filter darkens	Color-corrects landscapes.

Book IV
Lighting Strikes

1 used to detest flash photography. In fact, I'll let you in on a little secret: Not until I began writing this minibook did I begin to seriously apply myself to the topic. I quickly found out how much fun it is.

I hope you have the same experience.

I've broken down the subject into three chapters to give you a good overview of flash.

Chapter 1 discusses basic information about flash — the pros, the cons, the challenges, the settings.

The second chapter of this minibook covers using a hot shoe flash in more detail. I review names (it gets confusing), take you on an extensive tour of my hot shoe flash, discuss the controls and getting the flash connected to your camera. I cover using it in wireless mode, and I finish with several practical techniques.

Chapter 3 evaluates a number of different types of lighting gear — items you might want to look at if you're interested in becoming even more serious about flash and lighting.

Chapter 1: Flash Fundamentals

*F*lash. Ah, flash. Yup — Flash.

Our family had Kodak Instamatic cameras when I was a kid. I remember using flashcubes when we took pictures indoors. I was fascinated by the cubes, mostly because of the way the bulb in each side of the cube was destroyed (and the sound it made) after it went off. I also thought it was neat that they rotated when you wound the film for the next exposure.

Digital SLRs act nothing like that, but flash photography is no less fascinating. Gone are flashcubes and other cumbersome disposable bulbs. They've been replaced by supercharged pop-up flashes that can be used, reused, and reused some more. You can also mount larger external flashes on your camera's hot shoe. These units are more powerful and flexible than an in-camera flash. Along the way, the process of taking flash pictures has become more complicated. You don't just pop in a bulb and shoot. You have many more options and many more opportunities.

This chapter focuses on flash in general, understanding some of its settings, and using your pop-up flash. The pop-up flash is helpful because it comes with your camera (unless you're sporting a more than $5,000 camera from Canon, Nikon, or Sony). You don't have to buy a flash or feed it batteries. You just have to pop it up to start using it.

What could be simpler?

Shining a Light on Flash

Your pop-up flash is your entree into flash photography. Start using it now so that when you're ready to progress to a more sophisticated and expensive hot shoe flash unit, you can hit the ground running.

The problem is that flash photography can be difficult to master. Many things can go wrong and some of the settings can be confusing. In the end, I hope that you're encouraged to try. You'll shoot better pictures if you operate your flash effectively.

Why bother with Flash?

Flash solves exposure problems and helps you shoot the photos you want. That's it, in a nutshell. Specifically, flash helps in these areas:

- ✔ **Exposure:** One of the most important reasons to use a flash is that you often need it to properly expose your subject. In other words, you've reached the end of your "exposure rope" and can use some help.

  For example, say the aperture is as wide as it can go (or you want it to go), you refuse to continue raising ISO and adding noise to the picture, and you can't continue dropping the shutter speed without creating conditions for camera shake or subject blur.

  This situation happens indoors much quicker than it does outdoors, but it happens outdoors, too.

  The solution? Flash a bright light on the subject to make up for the lack of natural or ambient manmade light. This means you can set shutter speed fast enough to avoid camera shake and lower the ISO to relatively noise-free levels.

  Figure 1-1 shows this type of situation. Our family was having a birthday party, and I was taking photos. One of my sons was hamming it up, and I took this shot. We were indoors — notoriously hard to expose, especially with a window in the background. The exposure answer was either to raise the ISO through the roof or use the pop-up flash. I chose the flash, in combination with ISO 400, f/8, and 1/60 second.

- ✔ **Balance:** Another reason to use flash is to balance the lighting in a scene between the foreground and background.

  We've all taken casual snapshots or portraits of people indoors and had to contend with windows behind them. If you don't intervene by taking control of the exposure (or spot metering the dark subjects), the windows look great in the photo but the people end up looking too dark. They've been underexposed because the camera kept the bright areas of the photo from being blown out (when highlights are so bright they become a featureless white). In other words, the camera correctly exposed the bright areas, which underexposed everything else.

Figure 1-1: Acting flashy for the flash.

The problem is that if you compensate by changing metering modes, use exposure compensation, or manually set the exposure to brighten your subject, the very event that the camera tried to avoid takes place: blown-out highlights!

Balance problems happen outdoors as well, when the camera decides to keep from blowing out the sky and leaves your loved one in shadow. The solution is to use the flash to illuminate the subject so that you can balance the exposure between the foreground and background.

Figure 1-2 shows two examples. Each one has a light balance problem. In the first one, Anne and Sam are in shadow and the background is brightly lit. Problem! In the second photo, Jake is lit brightly from one side, creating harsh shadows on his face. Problem! Had I used the flash in either instance, the exposure balance between foreground and background (or from side to side) would have been much better.

Dark subjects

Shadows on face

Figure 1-2: Balance problems in both photos.

✔ **Control:** Flash gives you a degree of control over lighting and exposure that you don't have when you rely solely on ambient light.

Figure 1-3 shows a photo of a flower arrangement I took with an off-camera flash mounted on a light stand with a shoot-through umbrella (I cover all these techniques in this minibook). I was able to take my time, set the light in different places, and control the situation. I chose the angles, the distance, and the exposure.

✔ **Creativity:** Finally, you can be creative with flash. That includes your pop-up flash, external flash units, and studio strobes (another word for flash) and continuous lights.

I opened the door this afternoon and took some photos of a thunderstorm. Figure 1-4 shows the results. In the first photo, I didn't use the flash. Bor-ing. In the second photo, I let 'er rip. Exciting!

Figure 1-3: Lighting in a studio setting means control.

Figure 1-4: Flash creates an interesting take on the rain.

I took both shots with autofocus on my NIKKOR 35mm f/1.8G lens. I set the camera to Aperture priority mode, f/8, and had the ISO set to 1600. For the photo without the flash, the shutter speed was 1/40 second.

Being a downer on flash

Some definite challenges exist, however, in using a flash. Flash isn't a bad thing — it's just that it's difficult to master and, when done poorly, difficult to appreciate. Some of the pitfalls are described in this list:

✔ **You have another 50 things to remember:** Hey, what's another 50 things to remember? Well, another 50 things to remember.

Don't get bogged down by all the new things you have to remember. If you apply yourself and tackle one aspect of flash at a time, you can get the hang of it quickly.

✔ **Flash is sometimes harsh:** It's a product of distance, most often. When you're three feet in front of someone's face, the lighting can be harsh and unforgiving.

That's why there's such a thing as bounce flash and diffusers.

Figure 1-5 shows an example of when the flash "goes rogue" and looks too harsh. It could have been a beautiful photo of my daughter, Grace, but her image is totally washed out. It's like blowing out highlights when taking photos outdoors of the sky: You don't get them back.

Figure 1-5: Blinded by the light!

✔ **You often shoot dark backgrounds:** The face of a person being photographed in a room often appears nice and bright but the background is dark. If you don't mind that effect, it can work — and even hide a messy or an unappealing background. However, I have grown tired of it.

Figure 1-6 shows a photo I took of my son in a large room. He's well lit, but nothing else is.

Figure 1-6: Large rooms are problems.

To combat this problem in your photos, raise the ISO or use slow sync, if possible.

✔ **The pop-up flash sucks batteries:** The good news is that a pop-up flash doesn't require additional batteries. The bad news is that it sucks the life from your camera's internal battery. Pop-up flashes are less powerful than external flash units, so the drain they put on your battery isn't as severe; although you will have a shorter battery life if you use flash a lot.

✔ **Conspicuous-ness-ity:** When you fire off a strobe at an event or activity, you're conspicuous. You stand out like a well-lit thumb. At times, indoors and out, you don't want to be the center of attention.

✔ **"The Cringe":** At a certain age, all my kids seem to have become experts at "flash blocking" (though they eventually grow out of it). Whenever I approach them with my camera and flash, they throw an arm over their eyes.

Figure 1-7 shows Anne, my wife, having fun with Sam, one of my sons. He had begun covering his eyes a lot, so she had him cover hers and she covered his.

Figure 1-7: Duck and cover!

✔ **Lens shadows:** Pop-up flashes don't work well with large or long lenses and large lens hoods. For example, I can't use the pop-up flash on either of my dSLRs with my Sigma 10-20mm ultra wide-angle lens. The pop-up flash isn't high enough to shoot over the lens without the lens casting a shadow that ruins the photo.

Figure 1-8 shows an example of a photo where I wasn't doing much right. I had the wrong lens on for the flash, and it was far too bright (an aperture of f/4.5 and my closeness to her contributed to this, along with the camera's thinking that it had to light up a dark room because I was using pattern metering). The lens shadow is what I want you to notice in this photo. Know which lenses you can use with your pop-up flash, or which focal lengths are safe to use with your zoom lens.

Making it work for you

Getting the most benefit from using flash has a lot to do with how you react to the challenges of using it.

The battery monster

An external flash unit normally uses two to four AA batteries, and if you use it continually, you have to keep feeding it batteries to make it happy.

I've tried rechargeable batteries, but to tell you the truth, they always run out at inopportune moments and then I have to wait to recharge them. To be fair, you can buy quick-charging batteries, so if you're working in a studio situation or at home, you may be able to wait. The other solution is to have multiple sets charged or charging at all times. The problem, though, is keeping track of which batteries have been changed, which haven't, and how long it's been since they've been charged. Their charges seem to dissipate faster than single-use batteries when you're not using them.

It's enough to make your head swim.

A rechargeable battery *does not* have an infinite life. After a certain number of charges, it either doesn't recharge or discharges very quickly.

I've recently switched to plain old single-use batteries, and I'm happier. Check to see whether a battery recycling center is located near you.

I'm not against the use of rechargeable batteries, by the way. I love having them for my cameras, but they aren't your garden-variety AA or AAA types. It's just having them in an external flash unit that frustrates me.

Figure 1-8: So many things are wrong.

Here are some simple solutions to try:

- **Knowledge:** The more knowledge you have about flash, the better. Let your gray matter soak it up.

- **Practice:** Knowledge combined with practical experience is an unbeatable combination.

For example, knowing that your pop-up flash can be set to repeating mode is one thing. Experimenting with it enough that you develop a feel for it — including the good points and bad points — is another.

You don't have to become the end-all, be-all Master of Flash. You just have to know how to work your gear to create the photos you want. Start practicing in the situations you shoot in the most.

✔ **Flash compensation:** Flash compensation is a simple yet effective solution to many flash problems. Flash not bright enough? Turn it up. Flash too bright? Turn it down. More on flash compensation later in this chapter.

Those are a few simple solutions. Here are some more advanced solutions to make the flash work for you:

✔ **External (hot shoe) flash:** Buying an external flash unit that mounts in your camera's hot shoe is the first step into the larger world of lighting. It opens a number of creative possibilities, such as off-camera lighting, and can solve common flash problems.

The downside to having an external flash unit (Canon calls it a Speedlite, and Nikon calls it a Speedlight) is that it costs more than you think it should, eats batteries, and adds size and weight to your camera.

Most camera manufacturers offer two or three external flash units in a range of prices and capabilities (see Book VIII for more information on the flash lineups of dSLR manufacturers).

Speedlights are covered in Chapter 2 of this minibook, including flash bouncing, diffusers and snoots, and taking the flash off the camera.

✔ **Studio lighting:** If you want the ultimate level of control, set up in a studio. Use external flash units, more powerful strobes, or continuous lighting, backgrounds, umbrellas, and more.

I cover the gear in Chapter 3 of this minibook and some of the technologies in Chapter 2.

Exposure and Flash

Note that when using any kind of flash, you're talking about metering and exposing two light sources: ambient (room or exterior) and flash. Both contribute to the equation.

When you leave the camera and flash on Auto mode (TTL), the camera does a good job of figuring out how strong to flash, given your camera's ISO, aperture, shutter speed, and sometimes (critically) distance.

If you don't plan to mess with manual flash modes, stop reading and skip to the next section.

When your flash is in manual mode (you may have to dig in your camera's menu to switch between TTL and manual flash modes for your pop-up flash; external units have mode buttons on them to change to manual mode), you have to juggle all these factors yourself. The weird part is that your control over the situation is muddled by different techniques that step all over each other.

When you're in manual flash mode, the flash isn't being told what to do and fires at full strength every time you take a picture. You have other ways to control the flash besides intensity, though. This list gives you directions for how to balance flash in the scene and get the right exposure:

- **To tweak flash range (ISO):** Increase ISO to increase flash range.

- **To tweak flash range (Distance):** Move closer or farther away.

- **To change flash intensity (Flash):** Lower or raise the flash intensity from the in-camera flash strength menu (pop-up) or LCD screen (external).

- **To change flash intensity (Distance):** Move closer or farther away.

- **To change flash intensity (Aperture):** Increase or decrease the aperture to diminish the flash effect on the exposure (given constant settings elsewhere).

- **To alter the background exposure:** Slow shutter speed to increase exposure of the background.

The first five items in this list involve getting the exposure right on the main subject. With that, you're primarily concerned with how strong the flash is and whether it can reach as far as you need it to.

You have only one way to alter the exposure on the background, assuming the subject is metered correctly: shutter speed. The other alternatives involve bringing in additional lights specifically for that purpose (which is a valid technique).

When working with flash, distance to the subject is an important factor. Light from the flash diminishes in intensity according to the inverse-square law. In other words, light doesn't fall off in proportion to distance, but rather in proportion to the inverse square of the distance. For example, an object twice as far away would be lit a quarter as strongly.

ISO increases the camera's sensitivity to light and extends the flash's range. If you find that you need more distance, increase the ISO if you're shooting in manual flash mode. If you're in TTL, forget it. The camera compensates downward and takes away what you just added.

Aperture has an effect on flash as well. Larger apertures let more light in, but if you're in TTL mode, it's already taken into account and the flash strength modified so that you don't blow anything out.

Unless you're a glutton for punishment, stay in TTL mode. It's worth it. Tweak the flash by distancing yourself appropriately, using flash compensation, ISO, aperture, and choosing an appropriate shutter speed to avoid blur and to light your background the way you want.

Choosing Flash Settings

Every digital SLR has some basic flash settings you should be aware of. Finding out how to set your flash is, in fact, an important part of using it effectively:

✔ **Disabling flash:** Sometimes, you don't want the flash to pop up and go off. At other times — if you're at an event that discourages or prohibits flash photography — you can't let the flash accidentally go off. The best way to prevent it is to disable the flash.

Some cameras have a setting on a mode dial that you can turn to disable the flash (the Canon EOS Rebel series). Some, like Sony, let you turn off the flash from the flash menu, accessible from the Function button. Other cameras, especially midlevel and high-end dSLRs, don't go off unless you pop up the flash.

✔ **Auto:** For many cameras, putting the flash in Auto mode turns over control to the flash. If it senses poor light, the pop-up flash pops and fires.

Some cameras require that you pop the flash yourself.

Your camera may have specific shooting modes that enable or limit auto flash. The more manual modes you're in, the less automatically the flash generally behaves. If you're in full auto shooting or scene mode, you may not be able to change how the flash works. Please check the manual.

✔ **Fill flash:** On some cameras, this setting makes the flash fire whether it's needed or not. Use it whenever your subjects are backlit and you're using pattern or center-weighted average metering. Even if you use spot metering, you stand a better change of not blowing out highlights if you use a flash.

Figure 1-9 shows my wife in our kitchen, reading a magazine and working on a computer. I took the first photo without a flash for comparison. It's good, but the outside is washed out. I used the pop-up flash as a fill flash for the second photo. In this instance, using fill flash lights the room and balances the outside light.

No flash   Fill flash

Figure 1-9: Pretending to work.

Try using fill flash outdoors. Though it seems counterintuitive, it helps keep faces out of shadow. Watch your exposure, though. You may have to enable high speed sync (covered in this section).

✔ **Red-eye reduction:** Use this mode to force the flash to try to prevent people from displaying red-eye in photos.

Experiment with more advanced settings and use them in the proper situations. Try the following settings on for size, if your camera supports them:

✔ **FE lock:** Not a setting as much as a technique. Use FE lock as you would use autofocus lock (AF lock). Meter on a subject you want off-centered, press the FE lock button (wherever yours is), and then recompose. The flash exposure (or FE) is locked until you release the button — even after taking multiple shots.

✔ **Slow sync:** Slows the shutter speed so that the background is exposed in low-light conditions, and then the flash fires and ends the exposure. The result is a brighter background.

The brighter background doesn't come from the flash, but rather from the extended shutter time. The foreground looks good too. Slow sync works well indoors if you're shooting casual shots or portraits. You can also take some great shots with movement in the background and a clear subject.

Try this tip for indoor photography: Pay attention to shutter speed and blur. If you don't want blur, try switching out of Slow Sync mode or use a tripod. I show you an example in Chapter 2 of this minibook.

✏ **Rear-curtain sync (or 2nd curtain sync):** Rear-curtain sync sets the flash to fire just before the exposure ends, as opposed to when it begins (normal, front curtain, or 1st curtain).

Figure 1-10 shows front-curtain versus rear-curtain flash.

Front curtain flash | Rear curtain flash

Figure 1-10: Late-night flash experiments.

I led my wife, Anne, out to our driveway one night with my Nikon D200 and an old 28mm manual focus lens. I used the pop-up flash and experimented with long shutter speeds with her moving the flashlight around.

It took some trial and error, but I ended up using a 5-second exposure at f/5.6. I left the ISO on 100, which best showed the light from the flashlight.

I had Anne walk toward me during the exposure, making a pattern on the driveway with the flashlight.

In the first photo, I used normal (front curtain, or 1st curtain) flash. It flashes as soon as the shutter opens and then does nothing. You can see that Anne appears at the end of our driveway but that the light from the flashlight travels toward me. The flash froze her where she started, and then she became, for all intents and purposes, invisible. The light from the flash was picked up by the sensor as she walked toward me. Very cool!

In the second photo, I used rear-curtain (or 2nd curtain) flash. In that case, the flash waits to go off until the exposure is just about over. You can see the difference in the photo. The flash caught her at her closest approach to me, but the trail of the flash is also visible.

✔ **High-Speed Sync (HSS):** This mode enables the camera to use the external flash capability to sync up with much faster shutter speeds than the built-in pop-up unit. In other words, you're more than likely limited from 1/160 to 1/250 second with your pop-up (sync speeds vary, depending on your camera). With an external unit and HSS, you could go much faster.

The flash emits a series of low-powered strobes that pulse throughout the exposure. This means that the flash is on for the duration of the exposure, as opposed to being fired after the front curtain or before the 2nd curtain during normal-speed, flash-sync shots.

I used to think high-speed sync was for freezing motion at very high shutter speeds. That's wrong. High-speed sync is no better at that (often worse) than a normal flash. High-speed sync excels at limiting exposure on a bright day when you want to use fill flash.

Figure 1-11 shows this very practical purpose in action. For both shots I used my NIKKOR 50mm f/1.4G lens. In Aperture priority mode, I set the f-stop to f/1.4 and the ISO to 100. For the first photo, the pop-up flash provided fill-flash. The shutter speed automatically rose to 1/250 second, which is the maximum flash sync speed on my Nikon D200. The photo is completely overexposed; ruined. For the second shot, I put my SB-600 external flash on the camera and enabled high-speed sync. The shutter speed automatically rose to 1/2000 second to compensate for the wide-open aperture, bright conditions, and fill flash. The exposure? Fantastic.

Don't use high-speed sync thinking you're entering some sort of super slow-mo, action-freezing mode. You're not. High-speed sync enables you to use fill flash outside on a bright day (or in a studio with bright lights) with a wide-open lens. This is an especially effective technique when shooting portraits, as Figure 1-11 shows.

Figure 1-11: Using high-speed sync on a bright day to limit exposure for fill flash.

✔ **Repeating:** Repeating flashes break up what the camera would shoot as one flash into smaller, "miniature" flashes spread out over time. You can create some good special effects this way. Figure 1-12 shows what happens. I threw some colorful dice on the table and triggered the pop-up in repeating flash mode. It caught the dice as they rolled away from me.

Figure 1-12: Special effects with a repeating flash.

Oddly enough, this mode is available only on my Nikon D200 in-camera pop-up flash. When I put a Speedlight on, I can't use it.

✔ **Wireless (or Commander):** If possible, set up the camera to become a wireless master. You may be able to enable a single option (Sony cameras are good at it), or you may have to dig into some menus (Nikon). *Note:* Not all cameras can be a wireless master.

I have a few wireless flash examples in Chapter 2 of this minibook.

✔ **Manual:** In manual mode, you set the flash intensity yourself. TTL (and variants thereof) isn't available.

✔ **TTL:** You may have the option of setting your built-in flash to TTL mode (rather than off or in Commander mode) and make it the default setting.

Flash sync speeds

I had been using my first digital SLR for some time before I realized that using the pop-up flash limited the maximum shutter speed I could set. This speed (the maximum shutter speed possible while using a flash) is the *sync speed*, or *flash sync speed.*

Why this is an issue is a little technical. You have to know how shutters and shutter curtains work. Shutter curtains are like moving horizontal blinds. During an exposure, the front curtain races down, uncovering the sensor. At the right time, the rear curtain follows and covers the sensor back up. The time distance between when the front curtain uncovers and the rear curtain covers the sensor is the shutter speed.

At slow shutter speeds, the entire sensor is uncovered at some point during the exposure. In other words, the front curtain made it all the way to the bottom before the rear curtain started down to cover the sensor. The flash can fire at any point during this time and be synced. When it fires after the first curtain clears, it's the *front,* or *1st curtain, flash.* (Most likely, it's not called anything special because this is the default flash mode.) When the flash fires just before the rear curtain follows and covers the sensor, it's called *rear,* or *2nd curtain, sync.*

At higher shutter speeds, the curtains are closer, reducing the amount of time between when the 1st and 2nd curtains start across the sensor. The curtains are travelling so close together that at no point during the exposure is the sensor fully exposed. This is why, even though flash durations are much faster than shutter speeds (the Nikon SB-600 Speedlight has a flash duration range from 1/900 to 1/25000 second), flashes have a problem syncing with fast shutter speeds. It's not the flash's fault but the shutter's.

Your manual might explicitly identify your camera's sync speed for you (look for XSync, X-Sync, Flash Sync, or Xnumber, for the sync speed under Shutter or Flash in the specifications). If not, it's easy to find yourself. Here's how:

Set your dSLR to Shutter priority and pop up the flash. It's a good idea to be in Auto or Fill flash mode. Dial in the fastest shutter speed you can. My Sony Alpha 300 won't let me go past 1/160 second with the pop-up flash in Fill flash mode. On my Nikon D200, the maximum shutter speed is 1/250 second.

The long and the short of it is that if you need a faster shutter speed to limit exposure in bright conditions (you don't want to change to a smaller aperture or you're there, the ISO is as low as it can go, and you don't have an ND filter), you're stuck unless you use high-speed sync.

Using a Pop-Up Flash

Using a pop-up flash is technically quite easy. This section is devoted to showing you.

To enable and use auto flash, follow these steps:

1. **Look on your menu to see whether flash is enabled.**

   It should say Auto or TTL or something similar.

2. **Check your camera manual to see in which shooting modes auto flash is supported.**

   Some cameras turn off auto flash whenever you enter manual mode.

3. **Enter an appropriate and compatible shooting mode.**

   Let the camera handle some or all aspects of exposure. Enter Auto Exposure mode, select a scene, use Programmed Auto, or enter a priority mode (Shutter Speed or Aperture) to accomplish this.

   When using manual mode, I set my aperture and ISO first and then set the shutter speed within the camera's flash sync speed. I set the shutter speed fast enough so the camera shake is minimized when taking the photo (faster than 1/30 second). Looking at the exposure index isn't going to give you much help. Normally, it tells you when you're under or overexposed, or right on the money. If you're above or below, you adjust one or more exposure controls. Because the flash is going to handle the adjustment, you can set the shutter speed to whatever you want, as long as your flash is in Auto mode.

4. **Take and review photos.**

   The flash should pop up and fire whenever necessary.

5. **Use flash compensation, if necessary.**

   If the flash is too bright, turn it up with flash compensation or lower your ISO (if possible, given the shooting mode you're in). If the scene is too dark, make sure you're metering correctly and turn up the flash or ISO.

TTL madness

When you read about flashes, metering, and exposure, the term *TTL,* which stands for *through the lens,* continually pops up.

One defining characteristic of SLRs, and now digital SLRs, is the single lens reflex mirror. This architecture enables the camera to be focused, light to be metered, depth of field to be previewed, distance information to be collected, and certain flash-metering functions to be accomplished by looking through the lens of the camera. The lens focuses light on the sensor during the exposure.

Flash throws around TTL like it was going out of style. Fundamentally, TTL means the flash strength and its effect on exposure is metered through the lens. Digital SLRs send a pre-flash a split second before the main flash to measure the light intensity. The main flash strength is calculated and used for the best exposure.

Manufacturers seem to continue adding letters and numbers to TTL. These proprietary schemes fit within their metering and flash systems. Canon has E-TTL and E-TTL II. Nikon uses i-TTL. Sony uses ADI (Advanced Distance Integration) as its acronym. Some use P-TTL.

To pop the pop-up flash and force a fill-flash or manual flash, follow these steps:

1. **Remove from the hot shoe any accessories that might interfere with the pop-up flash.**

   In other words, if you have an external flash, a level, or a cup holder stuck in your hot shoe, take it out so that you don't damage the flash.

2. **Find the pop-up flash button.**

   It should be on the left front side of the camera body, within easy reach of the index finger on your left hand.

3. **Press the button to pop the flash.**

   Figure 1-13 shows a pop-up flash, in all its glory.

To force the pop-up flash to fire (for fill flash), follow these steps:

1. **Pop the flash.**

2. **Press the shutter button halfway.**

   Wait for the flash-ready indication.

3. **Press the shutter button all the way down to take the photo.**

4. **Review the photo and check the strength of the flash.**

5. **Make the necessary adjustments to the flash or exposure.**

Figure 1-13: The pop-up flash has been popped.

To stow the pop-up flash, press it down gently until it clicks. It locks in place.

Using Flash Compensation

Flash compensation is a quick and easy way to adjust the strength of the flash without having to be in manual flash mode. It's just like exposure compensation, which enables you to fine-tune the camera's exposure without messing directly with aperture, shutter speed, or ISO. Flash compensation tweaks the strength of the flash without having to manually adjust it — or change the exposure of the scene.

Suppose that you're photographing someone in the living room and the flash appears too strong — your subject is washed out. Rather than try to recalibrate the exposure (which might be on automatic, anyway), use flash compensation to dial down the strength of the flash and *compensate*. Get it?

On the other hand, if your subject looks too dark, try increasing flash compensation.

You can also try increasing the camera's ISO setting, to extend the flash range, as mentioned earlier.

Chapter 2: Of Speedlights and Speedlites

In This Chapter

- ✔ **Naming names**
- ✔ **The first commandment**
- ✔ **Working the flash**
- ✔ **Connecting your flash to devices**
- ✔ **Speedlite soiree**

To immediately and effectively produce better results in your flash photography, go out and buy an external flash unit.

I'll wait.

As good as pop-up flashes are (they're certainly better than nothing), they have a number of inherent limitations. They can't be taken off-camera. They can't be bounced or swiveled. Putting a diffuser on one isn't easy. They don't go well with umbrellas, soft boxes, or snoots. You get the idea.

As soon as you buy an external flash, you're in the running for many or all of these enhanced lighting capabilities.

This chapter describes how to take your external flash, Speedlight or Speedlite, hot shoe flash — whatever you have — and find out how to make it work for you.

What's in a Name?

Flash terminology is a bit confusing. An *external flash* is a flash you can mount on your camera's hot shoe. Because *external flash unit* is a boring name, though, I've included the Nikon Speedlight and Canon Speedlite flashes in the title of this chapter — it's catchy and fairly recognizable.

Table 2-1 shows the disparity in how companies name their external flashes.

Table 2-1	Representative Flash Names	
Company	*Name*	*Example*
Canon	Speedlite	Speedlite 430EX II
Nikon	Speedlight	Speedlight SB-600
Olympus	Flash	FL-36R Flash
Pentax	Electronic Flash Unit	AF360FGZ
Sony	Flash, flash unit, external flash	HVL-F42AM Flash for DSLR Cameras
Others	Various	Vivitar 285HV Auto Professional Flash

Know Thy Flash

You've plunked down some cash for your Speedlight, so I recommend getting to know it as well as you know your camera, even if you don't need every option, bell, whistle, doodad, or whatchamacallit your particular flash offers. That includes knowing how to integrate it with camera and shoot with it.

Figure 2-1 shows a typical midrange flash from Nikon — the SB-600. It is a great example of mid-level flashes today and supports many advanced features. The notable exception is not having a PC sync terminal and the lack of wireless master capability (it can be used as a wireless slave, however). The latter (master or commander mode) is what typically differentiates high-end flashes from the rest.

This list describes the parts of the flash and how to use them:

Figure 2-1: Midrange practicality and affordability.

✔ **Flash head:** The part that holds the flash. It may rotate up to bounce or swivel from side to side. Some units lock (see the release button), and others sort of snap into place or move under resistance.

Not all flashes bounce or swivel. Some heads (entry-level models, normally) sit on top of the body and point straight ahead.

✔ **Flash:** Where the light comes out. Don't look directly into the flash when the unit flashes. Keep the flash clean and dust-free.

The flash is arguably the most important part of the unit. Pay attention to where it's pointing. Small differences in positioning can make big differences in photos.

Snap or push Sto-Fen-type diffusers directly on the end of the flash. Other accessories, such as small soft boxes, also fit over the end of the head.

Some accessories rely on hook-and-loop fasteners. Wrap the loop around the head and fix it securely to itself. The piece with the hook part attaches to it.

✔ **Built-in wide-angle adapter:** A handy aspect of the SB-600 but not available for every unit. The wide-flash adapter is conveniently built into the head so that you always have it with you, as shown in Figure 2-2. The adapter slides out and drops over the flash, directing the light from the flash into a wider-than-normal pattern. In this case, the angle matches the field of view of a 14mm lens.

Figure 2-2: Pulling out the wide-angle adapter to flip it down over the flash.

Flip the wide-angle adapter down over the flash when using a wide-angle lens. When you put the adapter down, the flash may automatically set itself to that focal length. If not, set the proper zoom on the flash. When you finish, lift up the adapter and slide it back in.

Many flashes have adapters, but some aren't built in. If that's the case with your flash, the flash case should have a place to store it. Snap it on the flash head to use it. Pop it off when you're done.

✔ **Tilt/swivel release button:** On the unit shown in Figure 2-3, you have to push a tilt or swivel release button to unlock the flash head. When it's unlocked, you can change the bounce and swivel angles. It pops back out when you release it, locking the head in that position.

If your unit has a locking button, *do not forget* about it and try to force the head — you might break it.

✔ **Tilt index:** These marks are built into the head and show you the tilt angle of the head. Knowing the angle helps you duplicate setups.

Most units show the bounce angle (the angle you have tilted the flash head) on the flash head. If you see 75, you're bouncing at 75 degrees. If you see 75 and 60, you're at 60 degrees.

This list describes the body of the flash unit:

 ✔ **Body:** Contains the guts of the flash — the controls, batteries, and mounting foot. Whereas the flash flashes, the body controls, supports, and stabilizes.

 ✔ **Swivel index:** A series of marks on the body that indicate how far from center the head has been swiveled. Frankly, the indicators on my camera are so small and hard to read — in raised black plastic on black plastic — that they're fairly useless. You can see them (maybe) in Figure 2-4.

Swiveling is useful when you take pictures in portrait orientation and want to bounce the flash upwards. Tilting the flash doesn't work — you have to swivel the flash to point it toward the ceiling. You may also find it helpful to swivel the flash to bounce light off a reflector or neutral colored wall when you are holding the camera normally.

 ✔ **Battery compartment cover:** The plastic piece covering the area where the batteries are stored. To open the battery compartment, press the cover and slide it toward the bottom of the unit to release the catch. The cover (which can fit

Figure 2-3: Push here for coolness and power.

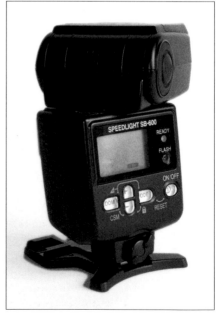

Figure 2-4: Look — it swivels.

tightly) opens to reveal the batteries. Be sure to slide down the cover completely and exert the force necessary to open it.

Sometimes, it feels as though the force I'm applying might break the cover. I have yet to do so, but I am careful not to use undue force each time I open the cover.

✓ **Battery compartment:** The area where your camera's batteries are stored. Four AA batteries seem to be the standard for larger flash units. Smaller, entry-level models may have only two. (See Figure 2-5.)

Pay special attention to battery orientation. When the battery orientation marks are inside the compartment and not on the door, you may not be able to see them easily.

✓ **Ready light:** A light on the side of the flash (or sometimes on both sides), indicating that the unit is ready to fire when in Wireless mode.

The ready lights blink and the unit beeps in Wireless mode. Look and listen to the number and length of the blinks and beeps and decode the meaning with a table in the product manual. The flash may be

Figure 2-5: Insert batteries in the battery compartment.

working properly, or it may be telling you something is wrong (such as not flashing brightly enough to reach the set exposure).

✓ **AF-assist illuminator:** A feature that helps the camera autofocus when the lighting is too dim for the camera's normal autofocus sensor to work. You can usually set the parameters of this function in the camera's menu system.

An illuminator mounted on an external flash unit (when it's mounted on the hot shoe) disables the camera's built-in illuminator or takes priority over it.

When the flash is mounted off-camera, this feature (on the flash, your camera still has its internal AF-assist mechanism if it has one) is unavailable unless you're using a cord that supports the AF-illuminator function.

✓ **Light sensor:** Senses wireless IR pulses from the master/commander or camera's pop-up flash in master mode and allows it to be used as a wireless remote. Pay attention to the direction the sensor faces and be sure not to block it.

✓ **Mounting foot:** A metal (on this model; some are plastic) plate that slides into the camera's hot shoe, as shown in Figure 2-6; one of the more critical parts of an external flash. Make sure that the foot is clean and isn't bent.

Most cameras use a standard *hot shoe,* a metal guide that sits on top of the camera. Sony has a different type of connection than the other manufacturers (see Book I, Chapter 4, Figure 4-2 for a look at the hot shoe on my Sony Alpha 300), but it serves the same purpose.

✔ **Hot shoe contacts:** Electrical contacts, shown in Figure 2-6, that connect the camera to the flash. Electrical signals communicate exposure, autofocus, shutter release, distance, and other information. The number and placement of contacts differs from brand to brand.

Don't try to place a flash unit on an incompatible camera. You can short out the flash or the camera.

Figure 2-6: No touchy.

Protect the contacts from touching metal with electrical tape when mounting the flash on an external light stand with a shoe adapter. The only item that needs to be secured is the mounting foot. The contacts (unless you're using a hot shoe adapter) are irrelevant when securing the flash in place. This is why I use the mini stands that come with my flashes to mount them on stands; you get built-in protection.

✔ **Lock:** A flash may use a locking lever or ring to secure the flash on top of the hot shoe. Turn or slide the lever one way to lock the flash. Turn or slide the lever the other way to release the flash. A flash may also click into place.

For example, my Sony flash clicks whenever I mount it on the hot shoe. (I don't need to flip a lever.) When I want to remove the flash, I press and hold a button on the side of the flash.

On the other hand, my Nikon SB-600 has to be locked down by using the lever. I came close to dropping the unit several times while switching over to the Nikon as my main dSLR because I kept forgetting to lock it down. I wasn't used to having to lock the flash down (my Sony just clicks in place) and it took a series of close calls to scare me into remembering.

✔ **Controls:** Most flashes have several buttons and controls on the back of their bases (the bottom of the flash, not where the mounting foot is). Look for these controls:

- *Jog wheel:* Used for navigation or selecting options.

- *Mode:* Changes the flash mode.

- *Power:* Turns the unit on and off.

- *Test:* Emits a test flash.

- *Up and down indicators:* Used for navigation or changing options.

- *Wireless:* Lets your camera go wireless.

- *Zoom:* Zooms the flash in and out to match the focal length of the lens. Normally, zoom works by scrolling a list of focal lengths. You should not need to zoom the flash to the correct focal length in Auto mode.

Other controls: There may be a high-speed sync button, flash level button, or light buttons to illuminate the LCD screen, for example.

🗸 **LCD panel:** A top-of-the-line, "super duper" flash has a large LCD screen, shown in Figure 2-7, that shows you all the details of how your flash is set up and which mode it's in so that you can easily see at a glance what's going on.

🗸 **Other indicators:** The back of the flash always seems to have room for another light or indicator. The SB-600 has a ready light. My older Sony flash has a number of LEDs that light up, as shown in Figure 2-8, telling you which mode the camera is in. This particular model has no LCD. The newer, midrange model has a backlit informational panel but still no LCD screen.

Many external flashes come with a few accessories. They're more important than you might think. Some examples are described in this list:

🗸 **Mini stand:** Some flashes come with a mini stand (if yours doesn't, you may be able to buy one), also known as a *flash stand* or *Speedlight stand.* You mount the flash on this small, plastic stand, as shown in Figure 2-9.

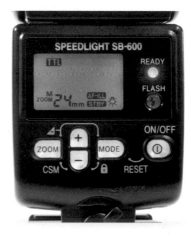

Figure 2-7: The backlit LCD panel in action.

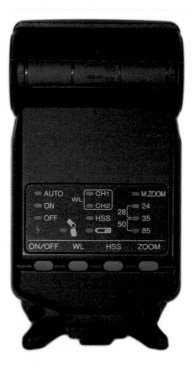

Figure 2-8: A different type of control setup.

**Book IV
Chapter 2**

**Of Speedlights
and Speedlites**

The stand is useful for taking the flash off-camera (if it's wireless-capable) and putting it on a table or on the floor.

In addition, its light stand socket underneath gives you an easy way to mount the flash on a larger light stand.

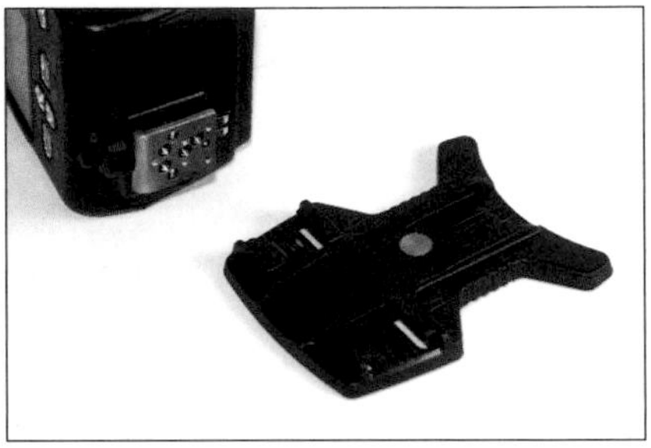

Case: Flash cases are useful. They protect the flash and hold small accessories. My Sony flash case holds the stand and wide-flash adapter. Some cases even have room for a flash diffuser.

Wide-angle adapter: Buy this adapter if your flash has no built-in adapter. Don't lose the adapter — keep it in the case unless you need it.

Figure 2-9: The stand, standing by.

Diffuser: Some flashes come with a diffuser, or you can buy one that's officially approved to fit your flash head.

Gel or filter: Look for colored gel filters to add ambiance to a scene or use them for color correction.

Adapter, bracket, cord, coupler: The number of ways you can connect your flash to other gear is dizzying. Look for all these pieces of equipment to get connected.

Operating Speedlight Controls

This section briefly describes the types of things you can do with the physical Speedlight controls:

Mode: Most speedlights have several shooting modes. Use the Mode button to switch between them. For example, pressing Mode on the SB-600 toggles between i-TTL Automatic Balanced Fill Flash, Standard i-TTL flash, and Manual flash.

Zoom: Pressing Zoom cycles through the flash head's zoom settings. The settings, in millimeters, should match the focal length of your lens, or at least come close if they're midway. The Nikon SB-600 settings are

- 24mm
- 28mm
- 35mm
- 50mm
- 70mm
- 85mm

✔ **Increment/decrement button or dials:** You may have a flash that enables you to increase or decrease setting values (like zoom focal lengths) or scroll through options (like turning Wireless mode on or off). If so, the increment/decrement buttons or dials are what you use to adjust the values.

✔ **Other controls:** As mentioned in an earlier section, some flashes have other controls and indicators that aren't listed here. Some are single-use, such as the Wireless button on Sony flashes, and some serve multiple purposes.

✔ **Two-button controls:** Some flashes require you to press and hold two buttons simultaneously in order to access certain settings and information. For example, on the SB-600, press these combinations of buttons:

- *Zoom+Mode:* Recalls the last underexposure value

- *Mode+Power:* Resets the flash

- *Mode+Decrement:* Locks the buttons

- *Zoom+Decrement:* Switches to custom settings

✔ **Navigating:** Look at your camera manual to see how to navigate menu choices and options. Some buttons switch options; some buttons change the value of the option you're currently looking at.

For example, when I press Zoom+Decrement and hold for a few seconds on my SB-600, the flash enters Custom Settings mode. Only one option at a time is shown on the LCD (for example, Wireless mode).

I have to scroll the options by pressing the Increment (marked with a plus) or Decrement (marked with a minus) buttons. When I find the option I want to change, I press Zoom or Mode to toggle the option. For example, to turn Wireless mode on or off, I scroll until the Wireless mode shows on screen. I can see the current setting on the screen. I then press Zoom or Mode to change the setting. When I'm done, I press the Zoom and Decrement buttons again and hold to save the setting. (I can also press the power button briefly to save the setting and redisplay the main LCD screen.)

Consult your flash manual for detailed instructions on how to operate your flash. Then you can get an idea of what's possible for a midlevel flash.

Making Physical Connections

This practical reference section details some of the connections you need to make with your flash.

Regardless of the type of flash you have, treat it with care. Don't force it onto a hot shoe if it seems to be sticking. Be careful when you thread items into the stand or adapter. Keep the two parts you're connecting level with each other so that you don't cross threads and strip them.

Connecting an external flash to your camera

Connecting a flash is easy though sometimes cumbersome. The more you practice, the more normal making the connection feels. Use a camera strap or tripod for additional support, and follow these steps to connect an external flash to your camera.

1. **Turn off the flash and your camera.**

   Don't rush. You don't want to short out any features.

2. **Hold the camera in one hand and the flash in another.**

   Keep the camera strap around your neck for support.

   You may have to experiment until you find the most comfortable method for you.

   I like to hold the camera with my right hand on the grip and work the flash with my left hand.

3. **Bring the flash in line with the hot shoe and slide it in.**

   Line up the mounting foot with the camera's hot shoe. This process takes place mostly by feel. Then slide the flash straight onto the shoe.

   I use my left hand to slide the flash onto the hot shoe until it clicks into place and then use my left thumb to flip the locking lever and lock the flash in place.

   (Alternatively, support the camera with your left hand. Your palm works well if you hold it underneath and partially grip the lens. Then use your right hand to hold and slide the flash onto the hot shoe.)

4. **Lock down the flash, if necessary.**

   Don't forget this step! Figure 2-10 shows the flash attached to the camera. Don't swing it around and bang it on stuff. You can take out the hot shoe if you're not careful.

5. **Turn on the camera and flash.**

6. **Make any necessary settings or adjustments.**

   You're ready to rock!

Figure 2-10: Locked on and ready to rumble.

Removing the flash from your camera

Removing the flash from your camera is the reverse of putting it on. Follow these steps:

1. **Turn off the camera and flash.**

2. **Grip the camera.**

   I hold the camera by its grip using my right hand. Your mileage may vary.

   Using a strap helps immensely, as does a tripod.

3. **While supporting the flash, release it.**

   This step may involve turning a ring, moving a lever, or pushing a button. I can flip my lever on my Nikon flash with my left thumb and support the flash body with the other fingers and palm of my left hand.

   Keep one hand on the flash at this point so that it doesn't drop out.

   On my Sony, I use my right thumb to press the release button while cradling the flash in my right palm.

4. **Slide the flash out of the shoe.**

   Slide it straight back. Don't twist it, or else it binds in the rails.

5. **Secure the flash without banging the camera on anything.**

   A camera swings around when it's attached to a strap. If you bend over to put away the flash, it swings away from you and bonks itself on whatever is in front of you.

Putting on a diffuser

Putting on a diffuser is as easy as putting on a diffuser. Make sure to buy one that's compatible with your flash unit, and pop it on the end of the flash head. Push it in a bit so that it fits securely and doesn't fall off the first time you take a step.

Figure 2-11 shows a diffuser on a Speedlight on a stand on a background on a table.

Attaching a reflector

LumiQuest (www.lumiquest.com) and other companies make external flash products that attach with the old

Figure 2-11: Diffusers for the modest flash.

hook-and-loop strap. Wrap the strap around the flash head and secure the strap to itself. Then attach the reflector to the strap where the hooks and loops meet.

The downside to this setup, shown in Figure 2-12, is that you have to ensure enough headroom to use it and not come across like a superflash freak.

Mounting a small soft box

Different soft boxes may have different parts and pieces, but they shouldn't differ dramatically from what I will show you here.

First, you have to assemble the soft box. Mine, from Interfit (www.interfitphotographic.com), consists of a flex mount stuck to the end of my flash unit and the soft box. Figure 2-13 shows all the components.

The soft box has an outer shell that's expanded by plastic "tent supports." A translucent white front slips onto the outer shell after it's complete.

After the box is built, just slip the flex mount over the end of the flash. If the fit is tight, slip your hand inside the white front to push on the inside of the mount. Figure 2-14 shows the complete assembly, mounted on the flash head.

Figure 2-12: Flash products seem to keep getting taller.

Figure 2-13: Some assembly is required.

Mounting your flash on a light stand

This section tells you how to mount your flash to a mini stand and then gives you a few pointers.

To mount the flash, follow these steps:

1. **Make sure that the flash is turned off.**

2. **Connect the mini stand to the flash.**

If the stand isn't attached to anything (such as a light stand), I hold the flash body in my right or left hand and slide the mini stand onto the mounting foot.

If the mini stand is already mounted on a light stand, I use my right hand, but rather than slide the mini stand, I slide the flash.

3. **Lock down the flash, if necessary.**

A mini stand is the easiest adapter for mounting a flash to a light stand.

You need an adapter because the bottom of your flash has no tripod socket on it. The light stand needs for an item, such as an adapter, to screw into it and thus mount the flash.

Figure 2-14: It looks more impressive in person.

To mount the mini stand to the light stand, screw it on.

Using an umbrella adapter

An umbrella adapter can be difficult to work with. It rarely comes with instructions, and mounting it upside down and backward is an easy mistake to make.

My Manfrotto adapter (www.manfrotto.com), shown in Figure 2-15, is a solid performer. I use a mini stand to mount the flash to the adapter, and the adapter screws directly into the larger light stand.

When you put an umbrella in the adapter, it should look like the one shown in Figure 2-16.

This list describes some umbrella adapter items you need to know about if you intend to use this type of setup:

Figure 2-15: Now, that's cool.

✓ **Cold shoe:** If an adapter has a cold shoe on it, you can forego the mini stand and mount the flash directly to the adapter.

If you use the cold shoe, protect the mounting foot and contacts on your flash. If you ever want to remount the flash on the camera, don't over tighten the locking bolt and deform the foot.

✔ **Coupling adapter (stud):** You usually have options to fit brass parts of differing sizes into the adapter, to fit the screw post of the light stand and your mini stand. If your screw post doesn't fit, swap it out.

✔ **Right side up:** Mount the umbrella adapter on the light stand so that the hole the umbrella rod fits into is on the upper piece. You should be able to rotate that part up and down, with the umbrella pointing to the same place as the flash.

✔ **Umbrella:** Unfurl the umbrella, lock it open, and insert it into the hole in the upper part of the adapter. Turn the locking screw to lock in the adapter.

✔ **Versatility:** If you want a flash mount that's easier to position than a standard light stand setup, don't mount the umbrella.

Figure 2-16: A good-looking, shoot-through umbrella setup.

Using Different Speedlight Techniques

A Speedlight is useful and a lot of fun. I show you in this section a few effects that are possible to create using just *one* external flash. The more you add, the more creative you can be. You can use many more techniques than I can show you in this section, which is a testament to their versatility.

Using a balanced fill flash

A flash is a useful device to have, even when you don't think you need one. For example, I recently photographed my wife outdoors in reasonably bright light. Because she was under an umbrella, she was in partial shade.

Her face ended up being in shadow — despite the bright light — so the solution was to use my Speedlight as a fill flash. The flash had no diffuser on it.

Figure 2-17 shows the difference between using ambient light and the flash.

Bouncing and diffusing the flash

In the examples in this section, I first bounced and diffused the flash. Then I took three shots of my wife. The Speedlight was on the camera for all three shots.

No flash   Fill light flash

Figure 2-17: Using a flash for fill light.

The first shot in Figure 2-18 is undiffused and the flash was aimed straight at her. The photo is well lit and clear, and its white balance is good, yet the problem is that my wife is casting lots of shadows.

Normal flash   Diffused flash   Bounced flash

Figure 2-18: Flashing, diffusing, bouncing.

For the second shot, I stuck my Sto-Fen diffuser on the flash but didn't bounce. This trick softened the light and made the shadows less prominent while still lighting the scene (which is exactly what it's supposed to do). In the third shot, I removed the diffuser and swiveled the flash up to bounce it off the ceiling.

The last shot is the most natural-looking photo. It has no harsh shadows, and the subject is well lit. If you look at the wall behind her in all three photos, the bounce flash brings down light from the top. The shine on the pan shows where the light is coming from and makes it look more interesting. The only thing missing is a little catch light in her eyes to add sparkle. I could have added (or enhanced) this in processing, but I wanted to preserve the original photo for you to see. Another option would have been for me to use another off-camera flash to gently flash from behind and to the left of me toward her face. Or I could have used an umbrella, as I do in the next example!

Using an umbrella

For the examples in this section, I set up my shoot-through umbrella. I then took a lot of pictures in our kitchen to give you a sense of using flash in a practical, everyday setting.

I placed the umbrella and flash to my left, opposite the window, and pointed it toward my wife's face. The result is a charming photo (see Figure 2-19). The light from outdoors contributes to it. You see no blown-out areas, which is always tough to avoid when you show a window in an interior photo. My wife looks great. The flash is more powerful than the outdoor light, which casts a slight shadow on her face toward the window, but the photo looks very good.

Figure 2-19: Balancing and diffusing light with a shoot-through umbrella.

One advantage of moving the flash off the camera is that the lighting looks natural.

Having fun with shadows

Working with a flash doesn't always involve removing shadows. In fact, you can have a lot of fun with shadows.

In the examples in this section, I took some shadowy pictures of a Godzilla figure in front of a blue background. I'm giving you three different looks at it in Figure 2-20.

The first one shows the big guy well lit and without shadow. The photo looks nice but not interesting. The second photo shows what Godzilla looks like with the light to the right, shining directly at it. (I used a snoot to strengthen the light so that it casts sharper shadows.) The third look is from the top, making the shadow discernable and *part of the photo.*

Diffused shadows

Shadow to the left

Shadow behind

Figure 2-20: Godzilla on the attack.

Going wireless

If you use a wireless flash, you don't need cables, which run around all over the place. In some cases, you have no choice, such as when interference occurs or the distance or angles limit reception. However, if you're using flashes (as I have) that have no PC sync cords, you have to buy specialized shoe-to-shoe cables to connect all the pieces. (Headache!) Go wireless whenever you can.

If your camera and flash are compatible (both my dSLRs have compatible flashes), setting up a wireless shoot is *easy.* I make a change on the flash to enable it to receive commands, and then I change the behavior of the on-camera pop-up flash to send the right signals. Four button-presses later, I'm in business!

The main advantage of using an off-camera flash, as you can see from the photo in Figure 2-21, is that you can come at the subject from different angles with light. You can light the subject and background, enhance or eliminate shadows, and do all sorts of other things — with *one* flash.

Using a snoot

A *snoot* helps you direct light more powerfully at your subject or the background, by preventing it from being dispersed. The photo shown in Figure 2-22 shows a prism I shined the flash at in order to

Figure 2-21: Sitting pretty.

see what would happen. The effect looked cool, so I added my homemade snoot (see the image on the left). The result was concentrated reflections from the prism.

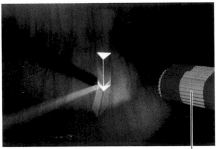 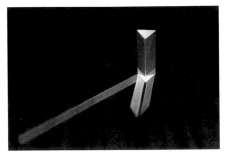

Snoot   Final photo

Figure 2-22: Don't turn up your nose at snoots.

Using Slow Sync mode

Figure 2-23 shows a series of three photos. My model (my wife, Anne) stood at the bottom of our stairway while I took the shots. The Speedlight was on the camera, and I didn't use a diffuser.

No flash   Normal flash   Slow sync flash

Figure 2-23: Comparing Slow Sync flash with no flash and normal flash.

The first photo was taken with no flash. Anne is in the dark, as are the stairs. A bright area is behind her. The second photo shows a normal flash. It's bright on the stairwell and directly on Anne. I wouldn't discard this photo, but I know that I can take better ones.

The third photo shows what Slow Sync mode can do for you. I had to raise the ISO to 800 to be able to hold steady. (I then went back and took all three shots at ISO 800, to make them consistent.) If you're shooting hand-held, you may have to widen the aperture or raise the ISO (like I did) to be able to shoot at a reasonably fast shutter speed, even indoors. Another solution would be to use a tripod.

Anne is bright but not overly so. The stairs look natural and not overblown. The area behind her is a bit brighter than the standard flash shot, but it is not unacceptable.

Chapter 3: The Lighting Gear Chapter

In This Chapter

✔ **Items that strobe**

✔ **Items that help the items that strobe**

✔ **Items that control the items that strobe**

✔ **Bigger items**

✔ **The minimum number of items you need**

*L*ighting encompasses many types of gear, which is why gear deserves its own chapter. Lighting gear can seem complicated to use, costs money, and takes a certain amount of effort to collect, put together, and learn how to use effectively.

Studio-type lighting has everything to do with digital SLR photography, yet it's a completely separate discipline. Lighting and the lighting gear to light what needs lit right belong to a whole 'nother world.

If you're interested in moving beyond the basics of flash photography with a pop-up flash, this chapter is for you. Whether that interest is piqued now or later doesn't matter.

I'm a huge proponent of learning about topics by finding out the items you use to do the things you want. If you don't know which gizmos are out there, how can you find out how to use them?

My purpose in this chapter isn't to provide in-depth steps on how to use every piece of equipment I list here. I want to open your eyes to some of the products that are available when you move beyond an in-camera flash. I can't review every possible piece of lighting equipment, but I've narrowed my list to the ones you might reasonably want to experiment with and use as you discover the larger lighting world.

Despite this limitation, I've thrown in a lot of how-to talk in the process of telling you what sorts of things are out there.

Flashes

Let me start with the obvious topic: the flash. Although you may be setting up a more complicated lighting ensemble, you always have the option to revert to your camera's flash (if it has one) or an optional hot shoe flash. This list describes the various types of flash that are available:

Figure 3-1: The pop-up flash on my Nikon D200.

✒ **Pop-up flash:** The basic flash. All except high-end digital SLRs come equipped with pop-up flashes, as shown in Figure 3-1. They're with you wherever you go, so you can't forget them. You don't have to plug them in or replace their batteries. Cool.

Some cameras have pop-up flashes that pop up pretty high. The higher the flash, the better view it has over the lens.

Downsides to the pop-up flash are limited control, no bounce or swivel capability, and attachments that can be hard to attach.

✒ **Hot shoe flash unit:** Ranges from entry-level models that give you a bit more power, control, and flexibility than the pop-up flash (but not too much) to high-end, professional-level flash units that can become the master units of multiflash wireless setups.

Hot shoe flashes (also called Speedlite, Speedlight, or external flash units) are more powerful and flexible than pop-up flashes. If you're serious about flash photography, invest in an external flash, pronto.

Figure 3-2 shows the back of a Nikon SB-600 midlevel flash mounted on a Nikon D200. You see the same thing when you're shooting and working the controls. The flash adds bulk to the top of the camera.

- **Ring flash:** A specialized type of flash unit designed to mount on your camera and shoot around the lens. It's best suited to macro or close-subject photography.

- **Slave unit:** A dedicated external flash that is triggered by another flash (either external or a built-in pop-up), called a master or commander. (Some slave units can be mounted on your camera's hot shoe and act like a traditional speedlight.)

Figure 3-2: The back of my SB-600 Speedlight.

Flash Accessories

You can customize and tweak your flash, both in-camera and hot shoe units, with several different types of accessories. They're practical and economical:

- **Diffuser:** A flash diffuser softens the light emitted by the flash, eliminating (ideally) harsh shadows on your subjects. Diffusers come in a couple of varieties:

  - *Hard plastic:* Made from translucent plastic and fits over the front end of the flash. When the flash fires, the light has to travel through the diffuser, which softens and spreads it.

    Sto-fen makes the most well-known (and most popular) flash diffuser. You can see mine in Figure 3-3. It's just a little plastic cover, but it works.

TIP

    Check to see whether the brand you like comes in different colors. Sto-fen also has diffusers in green (for fluorescent lighting) and gold (to warm subjects).

Figure 3-3: My Sto-Fen Omni Bounce.

- *Soft box:* Fits on the flash head; tiny cousin of large, studio soft box. It works the same way: The flash lights up the front panel of the soft box, diffusing and softening it.

  Figure 3-4 shows the small soft box I use on my external flashes. It slips over the end of the flash and extends some distance in front. I don't normally use it when the flash is mounted on the camera, because the box dips down a little. Mounted on a stand or sitting on a table, it's ideal.

  A soft box can be taken apart and folded for storage. Additionally, a soft box spreads light more than a hard plastic diffuser does.

Figure 3-4: Small soft boxes are useful.

✔ **Bounce diffuser/reflector:** Although you can find several types and brands of flash bouncers, LumiQuest is the most notable.

  This product bounces, reflects, and diffuses light from your flash, all at the same time. It attaches to the front of your flash, which you aim upward (your flash must be able to point up), and has the shape of a fan. Light from the flash hits the surface of the bouncer and is reflected toward the subject. In the process, it's softened.

  Figure 3-5 shows my Pocket Bouncer. Notice that you rotate the flash head straight up and let the bouncer do the bouncing. Though it's effective, you can see that it occupies lots of space at the top of your camera.

Figure 3-5: Bouncing light with a LumiQuest Pocket Bouncer.

You can buy metallic reflectors to change the character of the light, and units that bounce only a percentage of the flash (such as an 80/20 bouncer, shown in Figure 3-6).

✔ **Snoot:** Have you ever watched an old *Star Trek* episode where Captain Kirk sits in the captain's chair and his eyes are brightly lit but the rest of his face isn't?

They created that effect with a *snoot,* a tube or rectangle that you put on the end of the flash to control the directionality of the light. The snoot keeps the flash tightly focused on the subject. The longer the snoot, the more directional the lighting. The shorter the snoot, the more you allow it to expand.

I make my own snoots out of cardboard and painter's tape, as shown in Figure 3-7. You can use whatever works.

✔ **Filter:** Filters color the light of the flash, to either correct it or be creative. You can buy filters that stick on the flash, colored diffusers, and colored reflectors.

These flash accessories are essentially scaled-down versions of actual studio lighting gear.

Figure 3-6: You have lots of cool options.

Figure 3-7: A homemade snoot, if I ever saw one.

Remote Flash Unit Controllers

After you get the hang of using an external flash mounted to your camera's hot shoe, try taking it to the next level, by using it as a remote flash unit.

To move the hot shoe flash off the camera, you must have a way to trigger the remote flash unit. Because this chapter talks about gear (Chapters 1 and 2 of this minibook cover flash fundamentals and wireless external flash), I discuss remote-unit triggering technologies. Depending on your camera model and flash, you might be able to choose among one or more of these methods:

- **Wireless IR or Optical Pulse:** Most midlevel and advanced flash units sold by camera manufacturers now support wireless infrared (IR) or optical pulse (pulse) connectivity. Technically, wireless IR and wireless pulse are different (one sends out infrared pulses and the other sends out visible flashes of light to communicate between master and slave units), but practically speaking, they act the same. Check the manual of your camera and external flash to make sure they use the same method because wireless IR and pulse are not compatible with each other.

  Using either system is as easy as eating cake, and you don't have to buy anything extra to get it to work.

  1. Set up your flash on a light stand or a small flash stand. (These accessories are sometimes supplied with your flash unit.)

  2. Configure your camera and flash to Wireless mode.

  3. Ensure that they're on the same group and channel.

  Both types of wireless units are limited in terms of how far and at what angle you can place them from the camera. Read your manual to see suggested placement. Most often, the range is an arc extending to the front of the camera.

  If you plan to use more than one flash unit, be sure that your flash unit can serve as a master.

- **Wireless radio:** Third-party manufacturers such as PocketWizard (see Figure 3-8) use radio frequencies to connect the camera with an external flash. You have to mount a transmitter on your camera's hot shoe and a receiver to your flash unit.

(C) LPA Design

Figure 3-8: The PocketWizard is "all that."

When the hot shoe receives the "flash" command, the radio transmitter sends a signal to the receiver, which then triggers the remote flash.

Radio systems can support multiple flash units as long as you have enough receivers. Wireless radio systems can get really expensive the more flashes you have to control. Radio has a longer range and better placement options (it doesn't have to be in front of the transmitter) than IR.

(C) Wein Products, Inc.

Figure 3-9: Nifty little things.

✔ **Wireless optical slave:** This wireless option relies on a slave unit sensing the flash from a master (or another flash) unit and then triggering the flash it's attached to. Figure 3-9 shows a little one that plugs into a sync terminal.

✔ **Sync cord:** The ultimate solution to connecting your camera to an external flash is to wire them together using sync cords, as shown in Figure 3-10.

Not all flash units have sync cord sockets. For example, you have to buy the most expensive Nikon unit, the SB-900, to get a sync terminal (or PC terminal). Neither the SB-400 (the budget model) nor the SB-600 (the mid-level flash) has one.

(C) Sakar Inc.

Figure 3-10: Buy one of these only if you can connect on both ends.

✔ **Off-camera shoe cord:** This type of cord, shown in Figure 3-11, is a workaround for not having a sync cord terminal on your flash. Although technically not a sync cord, it serves the same purpose. You attach one end to the camera's hot shoe and the other end to the flash's mounting foot. Presto — they're connected.

Off-camera shoe cords are typically much shorter than sync cords and require you to make more hot shoe connections.

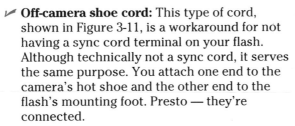

Figure 3-11: These cords are more flexible.

Book IV Chapter 3

The Lighting Gear Chapter

Studio Lighting Gear

Don't be put off by the title of this section. When I say *studio,* it doesn't mean that you have to buy a swanky loft in Manhattan where you cater to your rich clientele.

A swanky loft in Manhattan is nice, but you can also use your basement, an empty room, or the garage or set yourself up on location.

The following list describes the studio gear you're most likely to want and purchase. I put things in a general order of importance, starting with studio lighting. This doesn't mean I think you should run out and buy any one piece of gear over another. (You might start out with some stands and a nice background.) The list is simply a way for me to present information.

✔ **Strobe:** A *strobe,* shown in Figure 3-12, is a light that flashes. Simple, isn't it? *Strobe* is just a word, you see. Like causality. You can call a flash unit a strobe because it is one.

Studio strobes are bigger and more powerful than camera flash units. You have the option to plug most of the strobes into the wall and run them from AC power — no batteries required.

You'll run across the term *monolight* when you're shopping for strobes. It's a large flash (it *strobes* or flashes rather than stays on) housed in a casing that normally contains a fan, some controls, and a power supply.

(C) 2009 FJ Westcott Company

Figure 3-12: A strobe is a big flash.

Flash heads are monolights with external power packs. Rather than plug the head into the wall, you plug it into the power pack. You plug the power pack into the wall. By separating the flash from the power, you can scale them to suit your operation. Many power packs can power more than one flash head. Recycle time is generally faster than on moonlights, and lighting strength is greater.

- **Continuous lights:** Continuous lights stay on all the time. You just plug them in, set them up, turn them on, and leave them alone unless you need to adjust their power level. They require no sync cords or other triggers, which makes them simple.

- **Lighting accessories:** You can stick a lot of things on a light. Among other items, *barn doors* are flaps that direct the light, *snoots* focus the light, and *diffusers* soften and diffuse light.

- **Umbrella:** An umbrella looks just like an umbrella because (wait for it) it's an umbrella! It opens and closes exactly like an umbrella. It's used to diffuse and reflect light. Umbrellas come in two varieties:

  - *Shoot-through:* This type is easy to visualize: You place a flash, strobe, or continuous light behind and within the umbrella and point it where you want it to shine. The flash shoots through the translucent material, which softens and spreads the light.

(C) 2009 FJ Westcott Company

Figure 3-13: Shoot through this umbrella to light it up.

    In this capacity, an umbrella, as shown in Figure 3-13, works like a soft box. The main difference between them is that soft boxes truly constrain the light. They block it from coming outside the box except through the front. An umbrella lets light spill out from the sides and back (called *spill light*), illuminating the room as well as the umbrella.

    Shoot-through umbrellas aren't *see-through*. The light from the flash or strobe makes the entire umbrella light up.

  - *Bounce:* You can't shoot through these umbrellas (see Figure 3-14). Rather, you point them *away* from your subject, and the light reflects off the interior and bounces back toward the subject. The outside surface is opaque and, normally, black. The interior can be white, silver, or gold. Silver is more efficient at bouncing and is therefore brighter than white. Gold warms the photo.

(C) 2009 FJ Westcott Company

Figure 3-14: These umbrellas bounce light back on your subject.

    Some bounce umbrellas can be converted to shoot through by removing their outer covers.

- **Soft box:** Soft boxes are soft, and they are boxes. (It makes sense to me.) Studio-style soft boxes, shown in Figure 3-15, are much bigger than the one you put on a flash unit, as described in the section on flashes in this chapter. You can buy soft boxes in varying sizes.

(C) 2009 FJ Westcott Company

Figure 3-15: You need a good light to power this baby.

Think of a soft box as sort of a lampshade. The analogy isn't perfect, but bear with me for a minute. My family bought some cheap torch lamps a while ago from a home depot store, and every time I look at them, I think of soft boxes. The shade is a translucent plastic that softens the light from the bulb and spreads it. Rather than see a harsh light bulb staring at you, you see a pleasingly well-lit white shade.

Soft boxes (and umbrellas, though this is the soft box bullet) distribute light from a flash or continuous light over a large area in front of the light. That's the soft part.

The box part keeps light from spilling over the sides and out the back. It's completely cool.

- **Diffuser:** A diffuser is an item you shine a light through to diffuse it. Basically, it acts like an umbrella or a soft box (both diffuse), but isn't.

- **Reflector:** A reflector reflects light. Some are large and some are small. Put a flash on one side of the subject and a reflector on the other, and the reflector bounces light from the flash back into the subject, balancing the light.

Figure 3-16 shows my reflector sitting on a dresser. It's collapsible, which makes it easy to store and carry. When I'm on the scene, it pops open for the model to hold or for me to put on a stand.

- **Snoot:** You can put a large snoot on a strobe or continuous light just like you can put it on a flash unit. It works the same way.

Figure 3-16: Reflectors work better than you think they should.

✔ **Gel:** Gel is a fancy name for a colored filter. Use it to throw colored light on walls or backgrounds or your subject. You can also use gels more subtly, and to correct lighting colors.

✔ **Light stand:** Lights need stands. Some heads (the part that flashes or shines) come with a stand, but you can also buy them separately. Some stands are big and beefy. Some are flimsy.

Make sure to buy a stand rated for the weight you need.

You can buy stands for your small flash units. To mount the flash, buy a light stand adapter (many double as umbrella adaptors) or screw your miniature flash stand to the large stand and clip your flash into the shoe mount of the mini stand.

Light stands can be used to hold reflectors, soft boxes, strobes, umbrellas, diffusers — you name it.

If you buy self-contained units (lights with soft boxes on stands with the right adapters), you have less to worry about. If you buy a la carte, you should ensure that everything will fit together.

✔ **Sync cords:** I mentioned the sync cord earlier in this chapter, in the context of connecting an external flash. It also connects other lighting gear.

✔ **Wireless connectivity:** You can use the same technology to trigger professional strobes as you do to trigger off-camera flashes.

Bigger studio setups benefit from wireless systems. Many people use some form of the PocketWizard.

✔ **Background and stand:** Backgrounds come in many sizes and a few materials. The most popular material is hand-painted muslin. You can also find paper backgrounds.

Don't forget that you have to hang up a stand somehow. Stands specifically devoted to backgrounds are available because backgrounds can become quite heavy.

Figure 3-17 shows a swatch from a muslin background and a large stand. These stands occupy lots of room — essentially one end of a room!

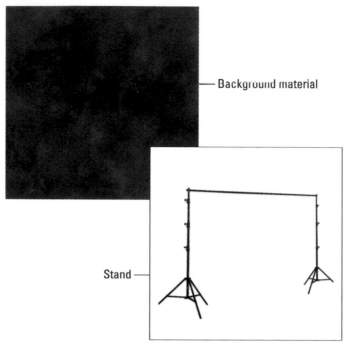

Background material

Stand

(C) 2009 FJ Westcott Company

Figure 3-17: Backgrounds and stands go well together.

✔ **Lighting kits:** Lots of cool kits are out there (see Figure 3-18) that combine stands, strobes, umbrellas, and soft boxes into one, often portable, collection. I'm a big fan of kits. You know that everything in it works together and that you don't need to mix and match. A kit is a helpful way to start getting serious with serious lighting.

 The list of accessories I've given you isn't all-encompassing. All you need to do is go online or to a lighting and photography store to see what I mean. You can find adapters for your adapter's adapter, if you need one.

(C) Adorama Camera, Inc.

Figure 3-18: This kit from Adorama is good-looking.

The Least You Need

In addition to a pop-up flash, what other items do you need in order to boost your ability to light a scene? It depends on what you're doing.

This section is about the *minimum* you can work with, beyond your camera and pop-up flash. You can do things better with more, of course.

For casual photography, you don't need many items:

- **External flash (also known as a Speedlight or Speedlite):** Find one that bounces. You can do much more with it. Swivel is good, but not as necessary.
- **Diffuser:** Get a plastic diffuser right away. It softens the light and is easy to pop on and off.

For tabletop photography, I suggest this type of setup:

- **Background:** You don't need expensive, hand-painted muslin backgrounds for table work. You can squeak by with plastic or paper or another inexpensive DIY solution.
- **External flash (also known as Speedlight or Speedlite):** Ideally, you want a couple of light sources for this type of photography, or one large source with a large soft box.
- **Diffuser:** If you use a flash, look for a small soft box attachment to soften the light.
- **Reflector:** You might end up with a white cardboard box or another, more sophisticated item. The purpose is to balance the light and remove shadows.
- **Kit:** If you buy a tabletop photography kit, you might be able to get everything at once for quite a reasonable price — or a not-so-reasonable price.

For portrait work, you can start with this minimalist setup:

- **External flash (also known as Speedlight or Speedlite):** You can mount your flash on your camera and use bounce when you're indoors or use a diffuser outdoors. You can do a lot with just this device.
- **Diffuser:** Get a pop-on diffuser, such as the one Sto-Fen makes, and drop it in your bag. When you can't bounce, you use this gizmo to soften the light.

Having a few more items can be helpful:

- **Background and stand:** More useful indoors than out, a good background helps out portrait photography quite a bit. It separates the subject from the room, which can be plain or messy or whatever.

- **Umbrella with stand and adapter:** This stand is worth buying. An umbrella, stand, and umbrella adapter that you can slide the umbrella through and mount your flash on doesn't cost much and gives you a large source of soft light. Buy one for every flash you have, unless you're aiming for larger lights and soft boxes or kits.

- **Kit:** Look for lighting kits. For a few hundred dollars, you can find strobes, stands, umbrellas, or soft boxes all in a single transportable package.

 Plan ahead when you buy an external flash. If you buy into your dSLR's wireless capability, if it has it, you can save *lots* of money and effort when you decide that you want to mount your flash off-camera. Connectivity comprises most of the hassle, and you'll have that problem solved.

Book V
Composing Great Shots

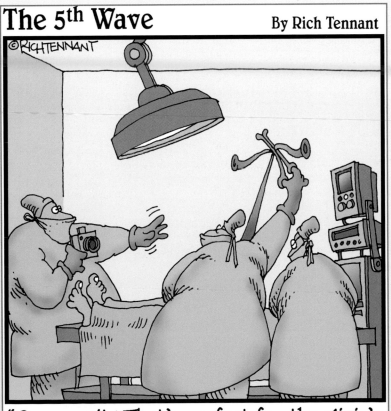

The 5th Wave By Rich Tennant

©RICHTENNANT

"Ooo — wait! That's perfect for the clinic's home page. Just stretch it out a little further...little more..."

𝐵ook V takes a step back from discussing technology and camera-specific information to describe setting up and framing photographs that look good.

I approach this topic in two ways.

Chapter 1 talks about framing a scene — placing subjects in the frame, finding the right vantage point, and specifying the proportion, distance, angle, height, and focus. It's fun! If you want to put your camera in Auto mode to concentrate on this subject, go right ahead. It helps not to have to worry about exposure and the right settings while you're looking to frame the best shot.

The second chapter in Book V covers design, which is different from framing. When you *frame,* elements of the photo remain the same, but the picture changes. When you *design,* the framing may remain the same, but the elements that make up the photo (a barn, tree, clouds, people, or shadows, for example) are different. Photos that are designed well have the right mix of elements, framed properly.

Chapter 1: Taming the Frame

In This Chapter

- ▸ **Locking onto framing**
- ▸ **Shooting low**
- ▸ **Orienting the camera**
- ▸ **Shooting off-angle**
- ▸ **Changing the focus**
- ▸ **Looking at different perspectives**
- ▸ **Framing creatively**
- ▸ **Remembering the foreground**
- ▸ **Integrating variables**

*L*ike many photographers, I've given serious thought to the differences between photos that *work* and photos that don't. I have found that proper framing makes a *huge* positive difference. Photos look much better.

Poor framing can make an interesting subject seem uninteresting. Blah. You can see this type of photo later in this chapter. Photos with good framing, on the other hand, leap off the page at you. I show you some of those, too.

To unlock the secret of "taming the frame" (it might surprise you), you study your photos and compare them to others. As you progress, you copy the techniques you like and paste them into your repertoire — voilà!

This isn't a conventional framing chapter, in which I laboriously lecture you about following framing rules and composing shots. (I was planning that strategy, but you lucked out when I decided to go another route.) Rather, after discussing some preliminary technical issues, I take you on a tour of a dozen scenes to show you what works and what doesn't. (I can do that because I take several badly composed shots for every good one I create.)

Framing 101

A *frame* is simply a basic rectangle. It doesn't matter whether its proportions are 3:2, the most common dSLR sensor width-to-height ratio, or 4:3, on any Olympus model or another dSLR that uses a four thirds sensor.

Figure 1-1 shows a rectangular frame superimposed on a photo. Your job is to fit whatever elements you can into that rectangle, to make it interesting.

Figure 1-1: Fitting the world into a rectangular hole.

You can use built-in grid lines in the viewfinder or LCD monitor to help line up a scene. Sometimes the lines can be turned off or reconfigured. For example, the two grids on the Canon EOS Rebel T2i (550D) appear on the LCD whenever the camera is in Live view. Grid 1 displays a standard tic-tac-toe board. Grid 2 displays a much finer grid, with 24 regions rather than 9.

TIP

An advantage of using a grid is being able to align or balance objects in the scene against each other and the "empty" space, and, to some degree, level the elements in a photo, as shown in Figure 1-2.

Some camera models, such as the Sony Alpha 900, have no grid per se in the viewfinder. Instead, their other marks help you divvy up the scene. The grids on other camera models, such as the Nikon D5000 or Canon EOS 7D, show up in the viewfinder and you can turn them on or off — very cool.

Figure 1-2: Grid lines help you frame and compose shots.

Using the viewfinder

The *viewfinder* sets apart dSLRs from other camera types. When you look into the viewfinder, you see (ideally, all, but most dSLRs have 95–98 percent coverage) what the camera sensor will see when you take the picture.

It's a shame that the viewfinder is falling out of use among many photographers. This list describes two reasons for its decreasing use:

- **Us:** Photographers, who like to use the LCD monitor to frame shots, become comfortable using this type of monitor on other, less capable cameras and then naturally want to continue using it on their dSLRs. In addition, when your camera has a good autofocus system, you're less likely to need the viewfinder.

  You have to consider the comfort factor as well. People like seeing a scene onscreen. Framing a shot and working with the camera feels less intimidating to many people when they use the LCD monitor.

- **Them:** Camera manufacturers are complicit in the decline of the viewfinder. Viewfinder coverage has moved from being a utilitarian necessity to a tool used to identify different camera levels and prices — which, of course, has nothing to do with anything.

I encourage you to use your camera's viewfinder whenever possible. Some camera models have large, bright viewfinders that make looking through them a joyful experience. A viewfinder often has a greater magnification factor than others in its class. Seek out these models and look through them if you can handle a demo model in a store. Most viewfinders offer a way — the *diopter adjustment control* — to change the focus if you need vision correction.

If you don't have Live view, you have no choice, of course. In that case, you have to master using the viewfinder to become a better photographer using the gear you have.

Going with Live view

Live view is helpful — just not in every situation.

When I'm working in the sun, I can't use Live view because its LCD monitor washes out (even when I brighten it or shade it). The viewfinder seems to focus my attention on the scene at hand, which forces me to concentrate more than when I'm looking at an LCD monitor. Another Live view downside is its lack of stability (especially when shooting moving targets) — stabilizing the camera is difficult because I can't lock it against my noggin. Oh, and it eats batteries faster than the viewfinder does.

This section describes Live view, though, so let me give its features some proper respect in this list:

- **Comfort:** I can hold the camera away from my face and not be glued to an eyepiece, such as when taking photos while wearing glasses. I wear reading glasses when I have to look at the camera but invariably take them off to look in the viewfinder. When using Live view, I can concentrate on a single object — the LCD monitor.

- **Mobility and safety:** Walking around is easier because I have peripheral vision — I'm less likely to step in front of a bus or fall into a hole.

- **Familiarity:** Let's face it — compact digital cameras have turned the use of Live view with an LCD monitor into photography standard operating procedure (SOP). Many people learn about photography by using one of the less expensive, user friendly cameras, and they want the same experience when they make the jump to dSLR. (I did.)

- **Difficult shots made easier:** I can take shots in Live view that I can't take when I have to look into the viewfinder, especially when working with an articulated LCD monitor that rotates or tilts (such as my older Sony Alpha 300).

Not all Live view implementations are the same. Older camera models tend to have limited versions of Live view (when they even have it), so don't automatically think you can point and shoot as though you were holding an inexpensive compact digital camera. Read the manual or research Live view specifically if it's important to you and you're making a new purchase.

For example, the Nikon D700 has two Live view options. The default is Handheld, which acts the way you think it should. Tripod mode, on the other hand, is suited only to studio situations where you need precise focus. Then you zoom in using the LCD monitor, and the camera uses a contrast-detect autofocus, which takes longer. Another example is the Canon EOS 50D, where Live view shooting isn't available in all shooting modes.

Understanding coverage

If you must have a viewfinder that sports 100 percent coverage of a scene (you may even need that in an LCD), you know it and you buy cameras that have it. For the rest of us, that some cameras do and some don't can be confusing.

From a marketing perspective, cameras that offer more coverage are generally priced higher than those that don't. Most often, 100 percent coverage is limited to the high or ultrahigh end of a manufacturer's range of dSLRs. We're told by many photographers that cameras without 100 percent coverage aren't up to snuff.

Despite my belief that all photographers should have cameras with 100 percent viewfinders (read the earlier section "Using the viewfinder" to find out why I think that not having them is hurting photography), many don't, and that situation is unlikely to change soon.

Although having less than 100 percent coverage is not ideal, it's not that much of a difference. Pretend that the photo shown in Figure 1-3 reflects 100 percent coverage. Adding the red overlay shows you what you would see if you were looking into a 95 percent viewfinder. For this 10MP image, you lose a band of approximately 100 pixels surrounding the photo.

Figure 1-3: Ninety-five percent versus 100 percent coverage.

When you see the true size difference between 95 and 100 percent coverage, you realize that it isn't much, so don't sweat it. If you need 100 percent coverage, you know it, and that small border around your photos becomes critical. If you don't need the coverage, don't lose any sleep over it. (When you start seeing 75 percent viewfinders, then you can start worrying.)

To follow the time-honored framing technique known as the *rule of thirds,* you mentally divide the frame into nine equivalent sections using two vertical and two horizontal lines (such as on a tic-tac-toe grid) and place interesting items along a resulting line or intersection. Try not to bisect a photo with important features such as the horizon line or people's eyes. Photos look funny when they're too evenly divided into halves. Generally, they look much better when objects and space are divided according to thirds. But, like all rules, the rule of thirds is meant to be broken when necessary.

Taking a Knee

Most people tend to take photos standing up. When you look at their photos, they're all the same. The objects are all seen from the same height. The horizon is in the same place in the photo frame. It helps to vary the height from which you take your photos. Take some standing up. Take others from a crouch. To get even lower, get down on one knee and look up at the scene.

I shot the first example at a local festival, while browsing the exhibits with my dSLR and taking photos. The homemade popcorn booth was fun and tasty (but super hot) — old school style over an open flame.

Notice in the first photo, shown in Figure 1-4, that the scene is divided evenly. In this classic example of breaking the rule of thirds, the photo suffers. The grass, bushes, and the trees take up the same amount of space in the photo as the foreground (in other words, they have the same weight) because I wasn't considering the rule of thirds. Additionally, my subjects are all bunched in the middle. It was simply the wrong moment to take the photo.

Figure 1-4: An interesting subject taken standing up.

I knelt for the next shot, shown in Figure 1-5, for a much better result. The foreground is shortened yet has a lot of action in it. The green trees in the background are nice and large, taking up two-thirds of the frame. The popcorn poppers are evenly spaced out as they work, with nice color, action, and framing.

Aside from the timing, *I* changed. I simply knelt down to reframe the shot and it worked.

Figure 1-5: That's more like it!

Portrait versus Landscape

An important decision you must make when framing is whether to hold the camera normally, in *landscape* orientation, or vertically, in *portrait* orientation.

Quite often, the subject you shoot determines the orientation you must use, but I go beyond that limitation and show you two shots of the same scene, in which both orientations work, but with different effects.

Figure 1-6 shows a courtyard with flowering trees at a local middle school. I was shooting panoramas with my Nikon D200 that day and thought it would make a good location. I took this photo with the camera oriented normally. You can see that I generally followed the rule of thirds, or at least practiced good framing and kept the elements from being too centered.

Framing versus design

I used the following two concepts to help me decide what chapter to put these examples in:

- ✔ **Framing:** If the elements of the photo basically stayed the same but I changed what I was doing, that photo was a good example of framing, which I discuss in this chapter.

- ✔ **Design:** If I essentially took the same photo, but the elements changed, that photo went

into the design chapter (Chapter 2 of this minibook).

Lots of crossover takes place between framing and design. Also, I don't show you poorly framed photos as examples of good design, and I try not to show you badly designed photos as examples of good framing.

Figure 1-6: Landscape orientation imparts width.

In this case, the horizontal width of the frame extends the view to include other trees to the left and right, as well as the walkway and school in the background. The photo creates the effect of *width*.

Figure 1-7 shows the same scene in portrait orientation. You should notice immediately that the feeling of width is gone, replaced by *depth:* Your eyes focus on the tree in front, but are then pulled deeper into the photo as you notice the tree to the left and the dark entrance to the school near the center of the photo.

These photos have nearly identical elements. The difference between them is framing, which in turn causes you to experience different sensations as you look at the photos.

Figure 1-7: Portrait orientation imparts depth.

A Few Feet of Difference

Figure 1-8 shows a crazy-looking structure, which is shiny, metallic, and has contrasting shapes as part of its design. The bushes in front and the trees behind add green to the photo, and the sky adds a lot of character, too. (It's gorgeous!)

Figure 1-8: Timing and location suffer.

Except for framing this structure badly, I'm facing it head-on, which removes the feeling of angularity. Additionally, the sun disappeared behind a cloud when I took the shot, leaving the foreground in shadow.

Figure 1-9 shows the difference a few feet can make. In this case, I walked around so that I could take the photo at more of an angle to the piece. This strategy, plus throwing in the sun for good measure, made all the difference in the world.

Don't run out and take only one photo of a subject. Circle it until you find the right spot. The right photo might be the first one you take, but it might not be, either.

Figure 1-9: I moved a few feet and waited for the sun.

Focusing in Front

In this section, I show you an example of the difference between landscape and portrait orientations and, more importantly, how focus affects framing.

Figure 1-10 shows a conventional shot of an unconventional subject: Johnny Appleseed's grave. (People still debate whether his body is in the grave.) This pleasant setting is complete with wrought iron fencing, bushes, a path in the distance, and lots of trees in the background.

Figure 1-10: A completely ordinary setting.

REMEMBER

If the setting shown in the figure is so nice, why doesn't it work? The answer is that it's ordinary. Anyone could have walked up and taken this shot.

Don't be ordinary.

Figure 1-11 shows a different perspective. Rather than try to fit the entire grave site into the frame, I focused on the near corner of the fence and ignored the gravestone. It's almost an afterthought, yet your eyes are continuously drawn to it. Mission accomplished.

Using Different Vantage Points

The example in this section shows a more extreme change in vantage point.

Figure 1-11: An unusual focal point makes the whole thing interesting.

I was shooting HDR photos (to find out about High Dynamic Range photography, jump over to Book VI, Chapter 4) in the sanctuary of a local church when I took the one shown in Figure 1-12.

The first photo is a straight shot down the aisle to the stage, featuring good framing and presentation. The photo proves that symmetry sometimes works and that the rule of thirds doesn't need to be universally applied.

After taking the more conventional set of shots, I decided to move to the balcony and take some from its uppermost corner. The resulting shot shows off the depth and space of the room. In the second frame, you perceive the enormity of the interior.

Reframing

You can often reframe, or *recompose,* a shot in software after the fact.

Don't let that knowledge keep you from taking good photos in the first place.

Though you can reframe more easily when space appears around your central subject, I have found that when I'm timid and back away from a subject, my photos suffer. When I lose the timidity and zoom in, I'm more successful at taking great-looking photos.

Figure 1-12: The framing difference lets you create unique shots.

(By the way, I used my Sigma 10-20mm f/4.0-5.6 ultra wide-angle lens set to 10mm in both shots. The different perspective makes it an interesting comparison because the shot taken from the balcony seems much wider.)

Unconventional Framing

Figure 1-13 shows a photo of my daughter inside a vehicle used to tear out my driveway. The shot doesn't look terrible for a quick casual portrait, but it certainly won't win any awards.

Figure 1-14 shows a different approach to framing the shot. I walked around the side and shot through the cage. My daughter cooperated by making a fantastic expression, and the result is a photo that's far better-looking than the first.

Figure 1-13: A casual photo.

When what you're doing isn't working, change something.

Making the Foreground Interesting

Figure 1-14: Now, *that's* interesting.

Speaking of the driveway (and I do, in the preceding section), Figure 1-15 shows two photos of workers pouring and leveling concrete for mine. Nothing is stupendously wrong in the first photo. The concrete is interesting because its plain gray color contrasts with all other elements in the photo.

Figure 1-15: Foreground objects often add interest.

For the second shot, I crouched in front to show off the form (the frame that makes the concrete hold a certain shape) and the steel stakes that anchor the form to the ground. This is necessary so the weight of the concrete pressing out doesn't change the form's shape. Although both photos work well, the one with the interesting foreground is better.

A foreground appears in every shot. In this case, I had to change what I was doing to make the foreground interesting.

Integrating Other Elements

Figure 1-16 shows a series of shots I took while walking around a monument in a cemetery. The elements are the same in every photo of this sequence. They include the monument, trees, blue sky, white clouds, and various bushes in the foreground or off to the side.

Figure 1-16: The same elements, shown from different angles.

The best shot is the one that most attractively integrates all elements. In my opinion, the second and third photos look better than the others, and the third one is the best. Figure 1-17 shows a larger shot of it.

Figure 1-17: The photo with the best balance.

Compared to other photos, the framing is better in Figure 1-17. The distance is just right, the trees are nicely balanced against the monument, the sky shows up well, the clouds are attractive, and the bushes don't distract from the rest of the scene.

I took the shot shown in Figure 1-17 at a slight angle off the monument, which is one reason it looks good. That the horizon isn't in the middle of the photo helps, and the structure occupies the middle two-thirds of the frame.

Changing Angles

Figure 1-18 shows three photos I took from different points on a walking bridge over a stream.

Figure 1-18: Investigate scenes to analyze framing options.

One huge challenge that a photographer faces is how to make a subject being photographed *interesting*.

I often spend a few hours photographing a scene from different angles and then analyze the photos at home to find out what makes that scene tick, such as number of elements, symmetry, angularity, texture, colors, depth, or mood. Also, I consider factors such as time of day and positioning (kneeling or standing).

Study your photos and learn from them. Apply whatever lessons you can to your next shoot.

In this case, a vast difference exists in the look of the bridge from the side (bottom right), face front (top right), and within (left). In the top-right shot, the bridge is the clear subject. The lower-right shot focuses more on the destination while the bridge plays a supporting role. In the left shot, the bridge framework artistically cuts across the scenic water below and the sky above.

Stepping Up versus Back

This section shows you the difference between stepping up and shortening the frame versus stepping back and putting more into it.

I took the first photo shown in Figure 1-19 from within a park pavilion. I'm looking out at the playground in the distance. Most of the photo consists of a dark structure, which focuses your attention even more on the color and brightness in the distance.

Figure 1-19: Think in three dimensions.

I stepped back a good distance to take the second photo. It's the same pavilion, and the photos were taken on the same day — in fact, within a few minutes of each other.

The second photo replaces the monotone structure with detail and color. It "opens up" the photo and makes it feel expansive rather than tunnel-like.

Which one is better? In this case, it depends. They both have unique qualities, brought about by different framing decisions.

Finding a Unique Perspective

Figure 1-20 shows a general kitchen scene of four children eating macaroni and cheese. This photo generally has nothing to brag about, which is why I'm contrasting it with another one.

Figure 1-20: Eggs ordinaire.

Figure 1-21 shows a different perspective of the same scene. After crouching to make my line of sight even with the tray of eggs, I took the photo while my son bent his head to playfully look at me. It's a cute shot, and it's framed much better than the preceding one.

Figure 1-21: A better egg-sample.

In Figure 1-21, Jacob has too much space to his left and right, and the power outlet on the wall is unattractive. The third version of this scene, shown in Figure 1-22, indicates what you can do by using software to correct framing and composition problems.

Evaluating background

Make background evaluation a conscious part of your shooting routine. When you set up a shot, your attention is most often focused on your subject, not on guarding against an ugly, cluttered background. People can also walk blindly into the middle of your shots, so look out for them ahead of time.

You can see that I cropped out extra space to create a completely different (and better-looking) photo that has no distractions. Despite the boring white wall in the background, the eggs look good, and Jake appears larger.

Walking Around

Figure 1-23 shows another example of circling the subject to find a good angle. The first frame shows a side shot; the second shows the tank pointing away; the third is from the front but not head-on.

When you're shooting pictures of vehicles and people, angles are quite important. When a person or a vehicle is pointing, facing, or moving away from you, the photo is much less interesting. They look much better from the front, so when you get a chance, frame them this way.

Figure 1-22: A much improved view.

Figure 1-23: Concentrate on where the subject is pointing.

Chapter 2: Deconstructing Design

In This Chapter

- Catching the train
- Using the moon
- Following paths
- Looking at eyes
- Taking care with steps and railings
- Designing with light
- Creating a well-balanced scene

After you develop a sense of how to frame a scene, as described in Chapter 1 of this minibook, you can move to the design phase.

Design chapters in other books tend to be organized around somewhat esoteric design principles, such as color, lines, curves, shapes, light, and timing. I have chosen a different path.

Who sets out to take photos of lines or circles? Not many people, most likely. Most people set out to take photos of *things* or *scenes*, independently of whether they have circles or squares in them. Those design elements are important, and I discuss them in the examples in this chapter, but I want you to think of design as a whole as you frame a scene. Then regardless of whether the scene is furry, fluffy, or smooth, you're good to go.

The answer to what constitutes good design is surprisingly simple: A well-designed photo is nice to look at. You know it when you see it. It grabs you, in part, because it has interesting elements arranged pleasingly.

The challenge is being able to move from knowing good design when you see it to incorporating it into your photos.

My approach in this chapter is to pepper you (again, possibly) with examples. I want to show you what you can do with design and show you side-by-side comparisons of how well-designed photos differ from those that aren't.

Distinguishing between good framing and design is often difficult, but I include a few examples to show where the difference is clear. In essence, those scenes have different elements — sometimes good, sometimes bad — that change, whereas I remain relatively constant.

In other cases, I simply show you a well framed photo that is also well-designed. I point out in the main text what I think makes the design work.

Training Yourself to Spot Good Design

I took the series of shots shown in Figure 2-1 on a moving train as it circled a lake at the zoo. As you can see, the train is relatively empty toward the back.

The framing stays relatively constant throughout the series, but the first two exposures don't have the right mix of elements. In the first photo, the train is too straight — it has no element of mystery. In the second photo, the train has a nice curve to it and the light is decent, but the photo is nothing special.

Only when you compare the second photo to the third do you see how much better it can be. The third one, with all elements in place, is the clear winner: The train curves, the light is fantastic, and shadows add to the photo's overall contrast.

The following list describes how specific design elements improve the third photo:

Figure 2-1: Shots from the zoo train.

✔ **Light:** The lighting is good and shines brightly on the bench seats, grass, and trees, which sets apart the third frame. Notice that the light is coming from the side, not from overhead, which makes photos look nice.

✔ **Darkness:** Equally important is the darkness level. Pay attention to the shadows from the tree to the left, the canopy of the train, and on the two seats in front. Had I taken this photo at noon, the tree shadow wouldn't be cast in the same way.

✔ **Color:** Notice the appearance of the nice-looking orange, red, and green colors. Orange, in particular, plays an important role in this photo.

✔ **Texture:** Compare the smooth canopy and seating with the vegetation.

✔ **Lines:** The curve of the train track is important in this photo.

✔ **Shapes or areas:** The canopy balances the seats and prevents the trees from overpowering the photo, in sort of a mirror image of the seats.

✔ **Timing:** The timing had to have been just right, of course, as the train curved around the bend and obscured the people behind me.

✔ **Depth and width:** The train forms a tunnel that emphasizes depth, which continues into the open background.

✔ **Subject:** The subject is cool and different, though you have to wonder what the shot would look like if the train were crowded with people. (I have a feeling I got the better shot.)

Elements change, as do the conditions. When all elements contribute to a photo, your photos truly shine.

Shooting for the Moon

I took the landscape shot shown in Figure 2-2 at dusk as the moon was rising. I was looking east, away from the setting sun. The most striking element of this photo, aside from the moon, is its balance: The field, trees, sky, and houses in the background all seem balanced against each other, whether you're looking at them in terms of color or space.

Several design elements contribute to this photo:

✔ **Light:** Subdued lighting helps the moon stand out. I emphasized the highlights on the grass to make this effect more visible.

✔ **Darkness:** The trees in the background form a dark line, separating the foreground from the sky, which helps you identify the different areas of the photo — even with a quick glance.

✔ **Color:** Notice the wonderful fall colors: green, yellow, and orange, and a deep blue sky.

✔ **Texture:** Compare the smooth sky versus the grass and trees.

Figure 2-2: Good moon rising.

- ✔ **Lines:** You feel as though you're looking at the earth's curvature in this photo, which is another important element of the photo. (The lens is the likely reason, though it might also be my magnificent photography skills.)

- ✔ **Shapes or areas:** The sky is broken up by a single cloud and the moon. The light road cuts across the photo, dividing the scene into two distinct regions.

- ✔ **Timing:** You wouldn't think that timing is important for a photo such as this one, but it is. Even though I had time to set up my tripod and think about my strategy, I still had to be in the right place at the right time to shoot the outstanding combination of the light and the moon.

- ✔ **Depth or width:** The feeling of width dominates this photo, made possible by the lack of *anything* in the foreground and the uninterrupted road running from one side to the other.

- ✔ **Subject:** The moon (a key design element) converts a nice-looking landscape shot into a more interesting photo.

Taking the Path Less Traveled

The photos shown in Figure 2-3 are the same, but the second one is fully processed (including the brackets and some distortion correction) as HDR. (It's decidedly artistic, but then again, I can be, too.)

Figure 2-3: HDR can emphasize design elements.

Returning gear

The wide-angle lens I was frustrated with was the Tokina 11-16mm f/2.8 AT-X. I hadn't heard anything bad about it before I bought it. In fact, I read rave reviews.

However, I never liked the photos I took with it. I tried using distortion correction to fix things, but was never satisfied. I was able to compare it head-to-head with my Sigma 10-20mm F/4-5.6, and the Sigma always won.

This doesn't mean the Tokina stinks. It could have had a bad lens. What it meant was that the lens wasn't for me. I was on a deadline and needed something I could rely on, so I returned the Tokina and stayed with the Sigma.

I'm a firm believer that if something doesn't work for you, return it. It doesn't matter if no one else has a problem with it. If you do, that's enough.

I walked into a park near sunset with my Nikon D200 and a new wide-angle lens that I disliked and have since returned. The level of distortion made me queasy, whereas I never feel that way when using my Sigma 10-20mm F4.5-5.6.

I took this series of shots first, looking east, away from the sunset (which was hidden from me behind trees, anyway).

You can see that I was able to bring out a number of artistic design elements by using HDR. The framing between the standard exposure and the tone-mapped HDR image, of course, is the same.

Several design elements that make the HDR image work better than the traditional photo are:

- **Light:** A beautiful, bright blue sky is in the distance, along with bright green grass and highlights on the railing to the left, the park bench, and the leaves. Without the brighter areas on and behind the clouds, these elements wouldn't stand out as much. Light is important to this photo.

- **Darkness:** HDR emphasizes contrast and detail, so areas of darkness are vital. In this case, the clouds and trees and the railing as it recedes are nice and dark.

- **Color:** Ah, color. HDR can bring out color from an otherwise dreary scene. In this case, the purple path, yellow leaves, green grass, blue sky, and white clouds were all "boosted."

- **Texture:** The texture of this photo is important but probably overshadowed somewhat by its color. Rough textures abound in the concrete, bricks, grass, and trees and even the clouds. This effect adds greatly to the local contrast, which HDR takes advantage of.

✓ **Lines:** The curved path, which takes your eyes on a journey from front to back, is a strong element of this scene, giving it context and purpose.

✓ **Shapes and areas:** The path shown in the photo has width and depth. It consists of not just a few lines here and there — it has substance. The other areas are equally important because they balance out the path. The trees to the right form a boundary, and the park to the left and the sky beyond open up the scene and give it "breathing room." You see space.

✓ **Timing:** I took this photo during the evening *golden hour,* the last hour or so before sunset. (Another golden hour takes place in the hour after sunrise.) The sun is setting, and its light strikes objects more from the side than from the top. Shadows, which aren't evident in this photo, are longer and deeper. The light seems more magical and not as harsh.

✓ **Depth and width:** This landscape photo has depth, provided by the strong path receding into the distance. Notice that the width of the path, which comprises the foreground, constrains the photo and holds your eyes to the path until you're looking more at the background.

✓ **Subject:** The path is the reason I took the photo, but the other elements are also important. The bench to the right looks nice, as does the railing to the left. The clouds seem moody, and even the yellow leaves on the path add to the design.

Although you may want to focus on a single, simple object, consider other aspects of a scene, too.

Capturing Attention

The photos shown in Figure 2-4 are of my daughter, who was busily nursing her new Christmas toy when I walked over with my camera. Though the first shot is ordinary, the second one is much better. The difference: her eyes.

These design elements contribute to the second photo:

✓ **Light:** The flash isn't so strong that it "washes out" my daughter in the photo, which is always a danger when you move physically close to your subject. If it's a problem, use a bounce flash or a diffuser.

✓ **Darkness:** I like to move close to people to shoot their portraits, which minimizes the background. In interior shots such as this one, in a normally lit room, the background stays dark.

Figure 2-4: Pay attention to where people are looking.

⚬ **Color:** Bright colors contribute to the design of the photo in the form of my daughter's lime-colored shirt and bright pink pony.

Kids and bright colors go well together in a photo. The combination makes it feel happier.

⚬ **Texture:** Kids normally have smooth skin, which imparts a feeling of youth and beauty. Don't expect to see craggy, bearded kids with rough skin, unless they're dressed up for Halloween.

⚬ **Lines:** The lines in this photo are what you would expect to see in a close portrait.

⚬ **Shapes and areas:** My daughter is clearly separated from the background, which I accomplished by using a wide aperture (f/1.4) and moving in close. The depth of field narrows, given a constant aperture, the closer you are to your subject.

⚬ **Timing:** Catching my daughter looking up was an unscripted moment that I had to be ready to shoot instantly. Be patient: Kids, like all people, move around. You can't always pose them, so you have to let them move naturally. The same goes for pets and animals.

⚬ **Depth and width:** The background is nicely blurred out, separating the subject and imparting a sense of depth.

Blurring the background is almost a necessity when shooting casual portraits, especially in homes. It reduces the effect that furniture and other distracting objects can have on a photo.

⚬ **Subject:** The key element — the reason to take this photo — is the slight smile that my daughter is wearing while looking up.

Kneel, crouch, or sit so that you're photographing children's faces, not the tops of their heads. This is a key element for photos of kids.

Framing versus design

I used these two rules to help me decide in which chapter to add these examples:

✔ **Design:** If I essentially took the same photo but its elements changed, that photo was more about design than framing (this chapter).

✔ **Framing:** If the photo elements remained the same but I changed tasks, that photo is a good example of framing. See Chapter 1 in this minibook.

A great deal of crossover occurs, of course. I don't show you a poorly framed photo as an example of good design, and I try not to show you a badly designed photo as an example of good framing.

Stepping into Design

I took the shot shown in Figure 2-5 of some steps at a local park. Steps — how could *steps* possibly be interesting? Believe it or not, steps often make great photos, especially when they have unique shapes or railings, such as the one shown in the figure. The combination of curved steps and railings, straight lines and railings, and trees and sky make this photo interesting (as far as steps go, anyway). Look for elements such as these as you explore your area in search of interesting subjects.

Several design elements contribute to this photo:

Figure 2-5: Linear elements set steps apart from other subjects.

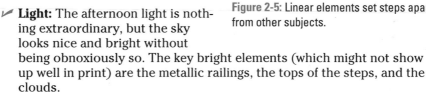

✔ **Light:** The afternoon light is nothing extraordinary, but the sky looks nice and bright without being obnoxiously so. The key bright elements (which might not show up well in print) are the metallic railings, the tops of the steps, and the clouds.

✔ **Darkness:** The shadows in the trees and the steps provide contrast. The lines on the steps divide the steps into discrete chunks. (That's a good thing.)

- ✔ **Color:** The photo is separated into blue, green, and neutral color areas. What do you think? I wish it included some red, orange, or yellow colors, but you can't control everything.

- ✔ **Texture:** Compare the manmade concrete and metallic railings against the natural trees and smooth sky.

- ✔ **Lines:** Let your eyes linger over the curved lines of the steps and the curved ends of the railings, and then compare them with the straight lines in the concrete sidewalk, lampposts, and railing to the right.

- ✔ **Shapes and areas:** The sky balances out the gray concrete. Too little sky, or too much sky, would throw the balance out of whack.

- ✔ **Timing:** Timing isn't an issue in the photo. Because I shot this one on a tripod, I had time to set it up. All I needed to do was ensure that no one walked into the scene. Had I shot more toward the evening hours, I might have gotten to show some pink, red, or golden reflections off the clouds.

- ✔ **Depth and width:** Your eyes are led up the steps and to the right.

- ✔ **Subject:** The angle of the photo invites you to climb the steps with your eyes. Shooting the right angle is imperative: If I had shot this photo more directly, you would be unable to see the curve, and the hand rails would have had a different effect on the photo.

Letting the Light Guide You

In this section, I show you the difference that a few moments can make in the lighting of a photo. I took the two shots shown in Figure 2-6 inside a pavilion at a local park.

Figure 2-6: When lighting strikes.

In the first frame, the interior looks nice but somewhat boring. The landscape beyond is brighter and more colorful.

The only difference in the second frame is that the sun began shining through the pavilion during the golden hour (this shot would be impossible to take at midday), creating bright streaks of light and casting cool shadows.

Notice how much more interesting the photo is. Both photos are framed identically. The difference between them is that I was able to capture the elements as they changed — and you can, too.

Several design elements contribute to the second photo:

- ✔ **Light:** Bright, golden hour sunlight streams from over my left shoulder to the right, creating bright areas on the floor and tables. The exterior is nicely lit, which provides good contrast.

- ✔ **Darkness:** Along with streaming sunlight, shadows make this photo more interesting to look at.

- ✔ **Color:** The exterior forms a narrow green strip that runs across the photo. (Nice!) The tabletops are wood, and everything else is muted.

- ✔ **Texture:** Compare the smooth ceiling and floor with the rougher wood picnic tables and natural foliage in the background. The second photo shows more variation than the first (brought out by the light), which is why it looks better.

- ✔ **Lines:** Wow! The photo has *lots* of lines, which is what I was aiming for when I took the photo and which certainly are important.

    However, I've come to see the lines in this photo in a supporting role now. To me, the light, shadows, and color from the trees are the most compelling aspects.

    The vertical columns and table supports break up the lines leading to the horizon.

- ✔ **Shapes and areas:** The photo has well-defined areas: ceiling, central floor, which leads your eyes to the distant opening, picnic tables, and the outside. The photo is complicated (and interesting) but not busy.

- ✔ **Timing:** I took the photo during the evening golden hour, which made possible the shadows. A man sitting to the far left end is eating dinner. Otherwise, the pavilion is empty.

- ✔ **Depth and width:** Depth is accentuated by the central open space on the floor that leads your eyes to the opening at the far end of the pavilion (the way this effect works is cool!) complemented by the tables.

- ✔ **Subject:** A simple park pavilion is sort of boring when you think about it. Good design is what makes it interesting.

Implementing Good Design

Figure 2-7 shows the same pavilion as in the example in the earlier section "Letting the Light Guide You," shot from the outside and looking back at the sunset. I shot this one using a tripod and, in fact, bracketed (shooting multiple photos at different exposures) the scene. Rather than process it as a High Dynamic Range image in this example, I used the –2.0 EV bracket to prevent the sun from completely "blowing out" the sky and converted the x to black-and-white. You can see the color photo in the first frame for comparison.

For information on High Dynamic Range photography, see Book VI, Chapter 4. To read more about converting color photos to black and white (and the differences between how Photoshop and Photoshop Elements handles these conversions), check out Book VI, Chapter 6.

Figure 2-7: Shooting in black-and-white emphasizes the design of this photo.

This shot transfixes me. It isn't perfectly executed technically, but since when does art have to be? It features a great deal of balance, texture, and details and a good mix of light and dark.

Converting a photo to black-and-white is a design decision. Being able to darken the sky and alter the tone of grass, for example, can make a structure stand out even more.

Several design elements contribute to the final black-and-white photo:

- **Light:** The sun captivates your attention but isn't the focus of this photo. The sky is blown out a bit, but that is sometimes the price you pay for shooting toward the sun. I'm using a darker exposure to mitigate the effect. In the end, the brightness is a key part of the design. Thankfully, the clouds and some darker areas save it from being a uniform white blob.

- **Darkness:** Focus on the tree line in the background as well as inside the pavilion. In addition, the dark sky makes for great contrast.

- **Color:** Black-and-white rules. It's a whole 'nother world, in which tone and contrast can be emphasized. I converted this photo using Photoshop because it gives me much more control over the process than Photoshop Elements does.

- **Texture:** The building looks nice and smooth, which contrasts with the grass and trees. The sky looks "lumpy," which makes it interesting.

- **Lines:** Notice the fence to the left and the path leading from the pavilion. Notice also the line between the trees and the grass. The columns provide a vertical element.

- **Shapes or areas:** Focus on the pavilion. It sits on top of the rise and occupies the middle region of the photo.

To make your photos seem more natural, keep them a little off-center (this is the rule of thirds in action, as explained in Chapter 1 of this minibook). You usually don't want to bash your audience over the head with your design.

- **Timing:** The evening golden hour is priceless. Of course, this photo is in black and white, so you don't see the golden hues. In this case, it's more about the angle of the sun hitting the pavilion and casting a long shadow toward the camera.

Light and time matter. I had a major breakthrough when I decided to shoot some during the golden hour. I had resisted going out at that time of day. And I was dissatisfied with my photos. When I started shooting during the golden hour, I was much happier with the results. My reluctance to take light and time into account had definitely diminished the quality of my earlier photos.

- **Depth or width:** The pavilion and trees impart width and space.

- **Subject:** The design of the pavilion is plain but somehow interesting. The pavilion has enough different elements — the curves on top and the two windows, in addition to the columns and path — to be eye-catching.

Notice again that I shot at an angle in this photo.

Getting into the Action

I'm literally putting myself in the action in Figure 2-8. Sometimes you have no better choice than to step right into it. The key is to pull off the obvious (in this case, looking down the road while in it) without letting your audience become too cynical about the perspective you've chosen.

Figure 2-8: Only the first photo is middle of the road.

In this example, the setup was completed accidentally: I had almost carried my camera, mounted on a tripod, across the street, when I realized, "I have to shoot this!" I hurried back to the middle of the intersection, set up my camera and tweaked a setting or two, and then shot five bracketed photos for HDR (see Book VI, Chapter 4) — not bad! I remember thinking, "You've got time," as cars began growing larger in the distance. Thankfully, I did.

Several design elements contribute to this HDR photo:

- ✔ **Light:** A sunny day illuminates the sky nicely (obviously, not during the golden hour, but still in the late afternoon). The lightness of the clouds and the lines on the street make quite an impression.

- ✔ **Darkness:** The roadbed and tree line on both sides of the street are dark and funnel your vision into the distance.

- ✔ **Color:** The blue sky and green trees give life to this photo.

- ✔ **Texture:** Texture isn't the main feature of this photo, though the puffy clouds contrast nicely with the smooth sky. You can always count on vegetation to be reasonably "rough."

- ✔ **Lines:** Key elements of the photo are the white lines on the road and the lines that stand out in the retaining walls.

- ✔ **Shapes or areas:** Strong elements are visible in the photo. The street is a large triangular area that points upward. The sky mirrors it, and the trees and walls form their own triangles. Everything points to the far horizon.

- ✔ **Timing:** I almost forgot — I took this shot on my birthday in 2009 (good timing, indeed).

  Clearly, the traffic had to be far enough away for me to take the shots and remain alive. If I were shooting only one exposure, I could have finished in 1/500 of a second. The brackets took a bit longer, even with auto exposure bracketing (AEB).

✔ **Depth or width:** My interesting landscape-oriented shot features the effect of both depth and width. The road, with four lanes, is clearly wide. You also experience a great sense of depth because nothing appears in the center of the road until you reach far into the background.

✔ **Subject:** Though you might believe that the road is the subject in the example, it's just a whole lot of nothingness, bounded by shapes (which makes it interesting).

If you're interested, the road is a four-lane, one-way street leading to downtown Fort Wayne, Indiana from the north. (I'm looking directly at the oncoming traffic.) I had driven on this road a thousand times and never thought of it as photogenic until I took these photos. I love that about photography.

When you evaluate the risks of taking certain photos, leave yourself a good margin of error. Shooting in the middle of a street into oncoming traffic, for example (as I did for the discussion in this section) definitely carries with it a degree of danger. If you perceive trouble, abandon your position and return to safety.

Letting the Light Shine

In this section, I show you the difference (only by *example*, not as a universal truth) in designing with a flash versus natural light, as shown in Figure 2-9.

Figure 2-9: Working with natural light.

Remain flexible and open-minded as you design your photos. Note, however, that I am *not* saying not to use a flash, and I'm not implying that using one looks bad in every circumstance.

Now that my disclaimer is out of the way, I'll move on to some photo examples.

The first frame shows my daughter sitting at the kitchen table and looking oddly at me. The flash lit her and the background well — no trouble there. I especially like her eyes in this photo,

The primary difference in the second frame is that I didn't use a flash and the light from the window is shining on her from the side, creating gorgeous light and dark areas.

Parts of the right side of this photo are technically on the verge of being blown out, and the left side is in dark shadow. You can miss out on photos like this one if you buy into the philosophy that mistakes are never supposed to happen, or that uneven lighting ruins photos. Sometimes the "magic" present in the moment overrules technical considerations.

Several design elements contribute to the second photo:

- **Light:** The key to this photo is strong, natural sunlight on the right side. The bright areas of my daughter's face and the curtain contrast with the shadows. That the sun is shining from the side creates an effect that's dramatically different from using a flash from directly in front. (I was using the pop-up flash and it doesn't bounce.) Sunshine like this from the side is similar to off-camera studio lighting, in fact.

- **Darkness:** The photo has a nice range of shadows and darkness. You need darkness to balance light, in most cases.

- **Color:** Though the color in the photo doesn't overwhelm you, it's extremely important. Small areas of color brighten the frame, such as my daughter's eyes, lips, and shirt and the stripes on the curtain. Her hair and skin color anchor the photo with a natural look.

- **Texture:** Though texture isn't the key design element in this photo, you can see when you're photographing people who have hair that it can catch light and add texture to a photo. Skin is also important. In this case, my daughter's skin is smooth.

- **Lines:** The curtain almost subconsciously provides two interesting linear elements: vertical folds and horizontal stripes, which offset her round head.

- **Shapes and areas:** Framing is important when shooting casual portraits. Rather than center the photo on my daughter, I moved her off to the side, by about a third. The shadow and darker regions of her hair occupy about a third of the frame; her face, another third; and the curtain, a little more than a third.

  With experience, you'll see interesting elements, such as the light patches on her face and nose, which add to this portrait.

✔ **Timing:** A casual portrait taken on the spur of the moment is all about timing. The frustrating part is that you cannot control it. To be able to catch some "keeper" moments, you just have to stay ready to shoot.

✔ **Depth and width:** The example has no depth because of the close background, but it isn't a problem. The human eye gravitates to people's faces in close-up portraits such as this one.

✔ **Subject:** What can I say — my daughter is gorgeous and photogenic.

The paradox is that people don't have to be gorgeous to make a photo interesting. If you, as the photographer, succeed in capturing some truth about them — for example, their personality, charm, grit, anger, frustration, or youth — you succeed.

Capturing the Perfect Moment

In the set of photos shown in Figure 2-10, the <ahem> focus is on timing — catching the perfect moment that happens to also have a great-looking design element.

Figure 2-10: Hefting some holiday booty makes a perfect moment.

In the first frame, my kids are hefting their new toy over their heads and squealing with pleasure. It's not a bad photo, but the timing is off.

The second frame is different, though. The kids have hoisted their booty overhead, and everyone's arms (including the one who can't even reach the box) are upraised. Even their mother gets into the act.

Several design elements contribute to the second photo:

- **Light:** The flash is nothing unusual but is somewhat weak.

- **Darkness:** The dark background (which is fine for a photo such as this one) helps separate the foreground from the background.

- **Color:** Brown is the primary color because of the paneling, but one child's shirt provides a flash of color.

- **Texture:** The texture shown in the example isn't a focal point. Note the smooth arms, the kids' hair, and the paneling.

- **Lines:** All lines are vertical, except for the box.

- **Shapes or areas:** When you see the photo in this example, you immediately notice the key element — everyone's upraised arms, holding or reaching for the present.

- **Timing:** To capture fleeting moments in time like this, you either have to have impeccable timing or be in the act of shooting. For action shots, it can help to take your drive setting (also called release) off single shot and let 'er rip with low or high-speed continuous.

- **Depth or width:** The arms in the photo impart a sense of depth *and* width. You can hardly pick out a spot in the photo — from front to back or from side to side — that doesn't have someone's arm reaching up.

- **Subject:** The kids and the gift are important, but the special elements of this photo are everyone's arms in action.

Bubbles, Camera, Action!

Something is always going on, and I hope you're catching it.

You can often reduce the essence of a photo to a single word or phrase, which gives you, for the most part, an indication of the main design element. You can see what the main design element is in the series of photos shown in Figure 2-11.

Bubbles (and lips, although it takes a while to consciously realize it) are the focus of these photos. In the example shown in Figure 2-10, the focus is arms, and in Figure 2-9, it's light.

The fact that a photo may have a "main" design element doesn't mean nothing else is going on. It means that you're seeing the element that's most central to the photo. The more you practice identifying this element, the more you can see it in your viewfinder or on the LCD screen as you take a photo.

When you have all the right elements, shooting a successful photo is simply a matter of arranging or capturing them *just right.* Sometimes it happens by plan, and sometimes not. Either way — be there!

Several design elements contribute to the third photo in the example:

- ✔ **Light:** Notice the nice late afternoon sun. Anne's face is lit from the side (or the front), not from overhead, which can be a problem earlier in the day.

    The more I look at the light, the more I like it.

- ✔ **Darkness:** Notice the shadows to the left, behind the bubbles, and on Anne's hand and face. They provide balance and contrast. You rarely want to take a photo with no shadows in it.

- ✔ **Color:** Color is an important element in this photo.

    The shirt inadvertently matches the green of the bubble blower. The blue handle adds color, as do skin and her lovely lips. The most important thing is that the background is a grayish white — it

Figure 2-11: Blowing bubbles.

    steps out of the way and lets you focus on Anne and the bubble machine. If it were a bright color, it would compete for primacy.

- ✔ **Texture:** Compare the smooth bubbles with the interesting bubble blower, and my wife's lips and skin.

- ✔ **Lines:** The lines on the siding of the house behind my wife are easy to miss, but they bring your eyes back to the center of the photo (accidentally but helpfully).

- ✔ **Shapes and areas:** I centered the bubble machine, but the photo is generally divided into thirds: bubbles, blower, and face.

- ✔ **Timing:** I had to get this one just right — plenty of bubbles and a good time of day.

  ✓ **Depth and width:** Close-up photos such as this one don't hit you over the head with width but create a good sense of space from left to right. In this photo, the bubbles have room to fly.

  ✓ **Subject:** My wife is mostly unidentifiable in this photo.

  The element that makes this frame much better than the others is that her chin and lips are perfectly framed in the top corner. Paradoxically, having more of her in the photo isn't as effective. Her lips play a more prominent role, which is appropriate, considering that she is blowing bubbles!

When you decide whether to keep a photo (from several of the same scene and subject), evaluate whether it was the photo you initially envisioned, but be flexible.

Move in close enough for the photo to have a visual impact.

In the example, had I been halfway across the yard, I would have diluted all the successful design elements of this photo. I was using a 50mm lens (which, on a 1.5x cropped-frame camera is a good portrait lens), but even then I got close to the action — so close that I cropped out most of my wife's face! That made it possible for me, however, to see that her lips were an important part of the photo.

Book VI

"Spiffifying" Photos in Software

*T*aking pictures with a digital SLR camera is the first step in a larger process. Developing (or processing or postprocessing) and editing the photos is another, equally important, discipline.

Because Book VI has so much information in it, I've separated it into six chapters. The thrust of this minibook is to show you the different elements of photo editing and other types of software to make your photos the best they can be.

You'll find out about photo management, archiving, workflow, processing raw photos, editing photos by fixing brightness, contrast, color, noise, sharpness, distortion, having fun with High Dynamic Range (HDR) photography, shooting and creating panoramas, and converting photos to black and white or colorizing them.

Whew!

Chapter 1: Blue-Collar Photo Management

In This Chapter

- Getting into the workflow
- Taking your first photos
- Downloading photos
- Managing your collection
- Processing good photos
- Making necessary edits
- Publishing your best photos
- Archiving all your photos

*P*hoto management — yikes.

You probably bought a dSLR camera in order to *take* pictures, not to manage them. (I did.) I realized early on, though, that hundreds of photos quickly turn into thousands of photos and thousands multiply into tens of thousands. Photos are like rabbits, I tell ya!

At some point, you have to get serious and start laying down the law of photo management, which is the subject of this chapter. I show you which software to use and how to keep track of your photos and establish a big-picture workflow.

Getting a Workflow

Workflow is a hot topic among digital SLR photographers because they do more than simply toss photos from their cameras into their computers. This type of photographer performs tasks such as *develop* raw exposures, which are analogous to frames of film, by manipulating a camera's raw digital photo (using lots of subjectivity) to convert it into a standard image file such as TIFF, JPEG, or Photoshop.

Workflow in this context describes the way you move through the process of getting your photos from Point A to Point B: Your workflow contains the steps, from start to finish, that guide you along the path from shooting photos to archiving them for long-term storage.

Take pictures, process pictures, publish pictures — I help you develop this sort of workflow in this chapter, to help link the other chapters in this minibook.

Workflow is a huge topic of debate, and the more detailed the workflow, the more people love debating it, Favorite topics include whether you should sharpen before you reduce noise or whether you should adjust brightness and contrast before you correct color. No universal workflow exists — all are based, in part, on opinion.

The following general workflow is a good one to start with:

1. **Take photos:** The file starts here. You have, of course, already made decisions that will affect your workflow, such as which camera to buy, which format to shoot in (JPEG versus raw; or both), and which software to invest in.

2. **Download photos:** Move photos from your camera to the computer, and include the initial backup.

3. **Manage:** You organize, sort, rate, geotag, filter, delete, and add keywords to your photos.

4. **Raw-process:** Develop the photos that you think are worth spending time on. If you work only with JPEGs, you can process them in applications such as Lightroom or use a photo editor, though you don't have the same flexibility (settings such as white balance and exposure are harder to fix with JPEGs) as you would if you were starting with raw photos.

5. **Edit:** Edit when necessary. Some photos need more work than is possible with conventional raw processors, especially HDR and panorama photos.

6. **Publish:** The entire point of the workflow is to create materials worth publishing, such as a JPEG to place on your Web page or Flickr Photostream or a high-quality TIFF file to print.

7. **Archive:** Save your work for long-term storage.

You can tailor this workflow example to suit your needs. In fact, you'll do a lot of tailoring, depending on several factors:

✔ **Other people:** Do you have to fit into a process created by other people? Is it collaborative? Do others need to view or approve you work? Are you doing the approving?

✔ **Time:** How much time do you have? Do you want to spend a lot of time per photo or as little as possible?

✔ **Photos:** How many photos do you take? Does your workflow have to be able to handle tens of photos a week or thousands?

✔ **Hardware:** Do you have the camera and computer hardware to manage your workflow and run the software? Do you need mobility, power, or volume?

✔ **Software:** Which software programs are you using? Which software are you willing to purchase? Is it current? Can it handle raw files from your dSLR?

✔ **Priorities:** In the end, deciding which workflow steps to follow and which steps to ignore is based on evaluating priorities. Are you seeking speed, quality, or compatibility — or another quality?

The rest of this chapter walks you through each step of a "macro" workflow.

**Book VI
Chapter 1**

**Blue-Collar Photo
Management**

Taking Photos

Step one: Do it. Have fun doing it. I don't describe taking photos in depth in this chapter because that's what much of this book talks about.

In addition to perusing the other minibooks on photography, lenses, exposure, and composition, don't forget to check out Chapters 5 and 6 of this minibook.

Downloading Photos

I love coming back from a photo shoot and downloading (you can call it *transferring,* if you want) my photos to the computer. Sure, I've seen the thumbnails on the camera's LCD monitor, but seeing them on a large screen for the first time is like opening presents on my birthday.

First, you have two ways to connect:

✔ **In-camera digital terminal:** All dSLRs can now connect to your computer via an interface cable connected to a digital data terminal. The technology of choice for digital transfer is now USB. Look for the USB miniport on your camera, inside a covered area. It's often in the same vicinity as the memory card, as shown in Figure 1-1. (On my Nikon D200, it's on the opposite side.)

Figure 1-1: The USB port on my Sony Alpha 300.

 The problem with this method is that the camera has to be hooked up and turned on in order to make the transfer. This process consumes battery power, which may be miniscule, but I try to preserve it whenever possible. It also places the camera at risk by having to place it somewhere on a table near your computer with a cord that could become snagged or tripped over.

✔ **External card reader:** With an external card reader, you purchase a compatible reader and connect it to your computer (again, most often with a USB cable), as shown in Figure 1-2. When you're ready to transfer photos, simply pop the memory card out of your camera (or your bag, if you have more than one) and into the card reader to start the process.

© SanDisk Corporation

Figure 1-2: A SanDisk reader with disks.

I've seen Wi-Fi memory cards on the market from Eye-Fi and SanDisk and other manufacturers that eliminate the need to connect the camera to your computer with a cord or remove the memory card and insert it into an external card reader. You must first configure the card to access the wireless networks of your choice (you may need a password and username) and then select the computer and folders in which to download. Then photos are automatically downloaded to the computer based on the criteria you select. Ensure that your camera is compatible before purchasing a Wi-fi memory card.

After you decide on a connection type, you also need to choose a download method.

✏ **Automatic:** You can use a small program that automatically downloads the photos to the location you choose. These programs often run in the background. They're ready to bounce into action the moment they sense the presence of a camera or card reader with a memory card in it that's connected to your computer when you're trying to transfer photos. The programs normally have options you can set that control where the photos are saved, the folder name, and whether to erase the photos from the card when you're done. I may be in the minority, but I can't stand these automated applications.

Similarly, you can choose to import photos by selecting a program when you insert a disk into an external card reader or connect your camera to the computer, as shown in Figure 1-3.

Figure 1-3: Choosing an auto import option.

✏ **Manual:** An alternative method is to do it yourself. Either drag the folder from the card reader to your drive and rename it or create folders for photos using your operating system and then select the photos and drag them to the appropriate folder.

I'm a hands-on kind of guy. I like to create folders and drag files myself. I organize my photos by camera and then by the date I downloaded them. I like to complete this process myself in Windows Explorer so that I can transfer and back up the photos immediately.

Managing Your Photos

I've split this section into three parts. One, which is quite short, discusses manual management: Don't do it. The next section consists of a software review. You should be aware of which software is available and know what each one can do. Although I can't describe single applications in depth, I give you enough information to establish a general starting point as you try to decide where to spend your time and money. Knowing what you need and having a list of candidates that may fulfill those needs is half the battle.

Manual management

If you like to start fires by rubbing two sticks together or you like to catch fish with your bare hands, this solution is right up your alley. File under R for ridiculous.

Photo management software

You have a lot of choices, ranging in focus from pure media managers, such as Adobe Bridge, to applications that focus more intently on raw photo workflow and development, such as Capture One. Also, plenty of photo editors have basic image management tools built right in, such as Photoshop Elements.

Adobe Bridge is one of the best (Adobe devotees would say the only) pure media managers. It's big, credible, versatile, well supported, and backed by a powerful company. Bridge is truly a bridge. It links your photos to your other applications in a way that lets you manage thousands of them seamlessly. You can create and manage collections, edit metadata, rotate photos, apply different camera raw settings, and more from within Bridge, but you call on other applications to complete most development and editing tasks.

You don't buy Bridge by itself. It comes bundled with standalone Creative Suite software and Adobe-bundled Creative Suite editions. Notably, Photoshop Elements for Windows isn't supplied with Bridge (the Mac version does include Bridge). It has its own, internal organizer.

The applications in the following list focus on raw photo processing and workflow. All have robust photo-management features as well. These applications are accessible to photo enthusiasts but also have features and capabilities that appeal to professionals.

✓ **Adobe Photoshop Lightroom:** This fantastic application (Mac/Windows) is designed for photographers, not for graphic artists. Compatible with a digital photography workflow, it has just about everything you need in order to import, manage, develop, and publish raw or JPEG photos. Figure 1-4 shows the Library tab. (Look at all those cool photo-management tools.) From this tab, you organize, sift, sort, and select. Lightroom lists for $299 new or $99 if you're upgrading from an earlier version.

Figure 1-4: Taking a peek at the Adobe Lightroom library.

One thing that Lightroom doesn't do is compete with Photoshop in terms of photo editing. Expect to be able to fix dust, turn photos into black-and-white, process raw exposures, and sort, tag (add keywords to), and manage photo collections. Lightroom doesn't natively have features such as layers, masks, and color modes.

In Lightroom, which is structured around catalogs, you create catalogs in which to organize photos. You can have a single massive, all-inclusive catalog or choose to use catalogs based on different cameras, projects, or years.

When you import photos into an open catalog, they show up as thumbnails in the Library tab, where you manage them. You can view, sort, filter, rate, delete, search for, compare, create, and assign keywords, quickly develop photos, and edit metadata. You can also export photos in a number of different formats. I cover the Lightroom raw processing features (you can use them for JPEGs or TIFFs, if you want) in more depth in Chapter 3 of this minibook.

✔ **Apple Aperture:** Apple Aperture is another cool application (Mac only) that marries photo development and management tasks into a single svelte package. I show Aperture 3 running in Figure 1-5. Notice that the left side of the screen is dominated by the Library, Metadata, and Adjustments tabs. The Library tab is where you create projects and organize your photos. Shortcut buttons above the preview window let you change views, identify faces, and geotag.

Figure 1-5: Apple Aperture is a serious alternative to Lightroom.

Aperture revolves around projects contained in a single library rather than in separate collections. (You can use Aperture 3 to create new libraries.) It also has some sample projects you can use to familiarize yourself with how things work in Aperture.

Your main organizational tools, therefore, are projects. When you import photos (or working Photoshop .psd files) into Aperture, you assign them to a project or create a new one. Within the project folder, you can manage subfolders (or *albums*) and individual photos.

As you might imagine, you have all sorts of management tools at your fingertips. You can view, sort, keyword, delete, rate, export, track versions, manage and edit metadata, perform basic photo adjustments, and launch photos to an external photo editor for more advanced editing. Aperture 8 can even send GPS coordinates to Apple so that you can geolocate your photos.

✔ **Capture One, Capture One PRO:** Capture One, by Phase One, isn't well known outside professional circles, but it should be. It comes in two versions: PRO is priced accordingly ($399 new and $299 upgrade from Capture One 5; $99 upgrade from Capture One 4 PRO). It has a ton of features and the standard version, which is well within the reach of casual photo-hobbyists ($129 new, $99 upgrade from Capture One 4). Figure 1-6 shows the classic black interface.

Figure 1-6: I'm in love with Capture One.

The PRO version is pricey, but it's a leading professional-level raw workflow application. It produces photos of stunning quality and has extensive development workflow and organizational tools.

Capture One is comparable to Lightroom and Aperture in that it has a bevy of management features, organized around a Library. Import photos and then sort, rate, preview, organize, tag (add keywords to), develop, and publish them. Capture One also has albums, which are virtual collections.

I can't say enough good things about Capture One. It's fantastic, powerful, and professional, and it focuses on workflow and photo quality.

✔ **Microsoft Expression Media 2:** Never a real powerhouse in the photo management market, Microsoft Expression Media 2 (available for Windows and Mac) was nonetheless bought by Phase One. Phase One is developer of Capture One and Capture One Pro, two powerful and respected photo management and raw development applications.

Each catalog has a number of useful data fields that summarize and organize photos, such as Author, File Type, Keywords, and People. In this sense, Microsoft Expression Media 2 feels a bit like a database program.

The last list in this section contains photo editors that have built-in media management capability. These relatively inexpensive editors are aimed mostly at the cost-conscious photo amateur (don't let that statement deter you — they're quite capable):

✔ **Apple iPhoto:** iPhoto, shown in Figure 1-7, is a nifty little application from Apple that has a number of good organizational tools. You can import and organize photos and then view, rate, tag (add keywords to), title, edit, and publish them. iPhoto is an excellent application for hobbyists.

Figure 1-7: Assigning keywords in iPhoto.

✔ **Adobe Photoshop Elements:** The Adobe entry-level photo editor has a lot going for it, given its price ($99.99 before rebates). It has a photo editor, of course, and the Windows version includes a built-in organizer (Mac users use Bridge). Figure 1-8 shows a photo of a P-51 that I recently geotagged. The building I was in is shown in the map window, and thumbnails are shown in the preview area.

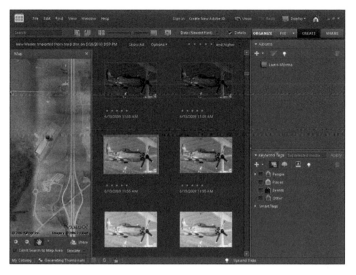

Figure 1-8: Geotagging in Photoshop Elements.

✔ **Corel PaintShop Photo Pro:** PaintShop Photo Pro (originally named Paint Shop Pro) also has two modes: a full editor and an organizer. You can sort, organize, rate, review, keyword, edit, and export photos. The PaintShop Photo Pro Windows-only application lists for $99.99 before instant rebates or price reductions. Figure 1-9 shows the Elements organizer.

Figure 1-9: PaintShop Photo Pro has more power than most beginner-level apps.

✔ **Google Picasa:** Even Google has an entry-level photo editor and organizer that is free and usable on both Windows and Mac platforms. It's *Picasa,* and it's cool. Its interface is shown in Figure 1-10.

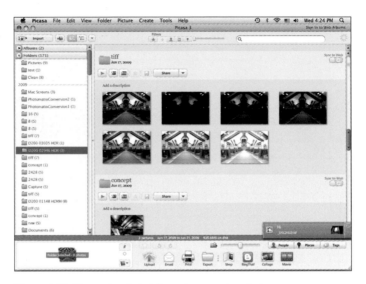

Figure 1-10: Picasa is a helpful way to organize photos.

Picasa scours your hard drive to find your files and then loads them into a library — you don't need to import them unless you want to. (You can add or subtract watch folders or import photos later.) You provide the organizational structure by creating albums and assigning photos to them. You can perform rudimentary editing tasks in Picasa such as rotating, straightening, removing red-eye, and more.

The main management tasks revolve around organizing photos and videos into folders and albums, by people, and then sorting, filtering, tagging, sharing, exporting, blogging, and creating other types of output, such as movies or collages.

The upgrade dance

Suppose that you have Adobe Design Premium Creative Suite 4, Photoshop Lightroom 2, Photoshop Elements 7, Apple Aperture 2, and iPhoto 8. The only problem with this list is that every single application is outdated.

No!

Yes.

Buying software isn't a one-time cost. Companies continually revise their products in light of new technology and then add new features or fix or tweak old ones. So, even when you've found a program you like, you eventually need to upgrade it to stay current.

How often you upgrade depends on a couple of factors:

✔ **Your commitment to the cutting edge:** You might want or need to have the latest software versions — nothing wrong with that. In fact, you get a lot of use from the software you buy if you buy a copy soon after it's initially released. An updated program is also more likely to be compatible with current operating systems and hardware (cameras and raw formats included).

✔ **Your thriftiness:** Just because something has been updated doesn't mean that the old version is rendered useless. Aperture 2 is still going like gangbusters, even though it has been replaced by Aperture 3. (Quick quiz: When Adobe updates its Aperture product from f/2 to f/3, is it stopping down or up? The answer is Down.)

In fact, you may even be able to leapfrog versions. If Aperture 2 works well for you and you don't think you need Aperture 3, see whether you can wait until Version 4 is released.

I don't advise being more than one version out of date. If you decide not to upgrade right away, make sure that you do some research and stay in a valid upgrade path to save money. For example, if you have Version 2 of a program and the company says that you have to have Version 4 to qualify for the reduced upgrade price for Version 5 (which has just been released), you're stuck. You have to buy Version 5 at the full price.

Don't forget to check for operating system (OS) upgrades and program compatibility. If you upgrade your OS, you may have to change or update your applications. In some cases, you have to wait a while for a new OS to be fully supported.

Management tasks

Familiarize yourself with these management tasks as you look at trying out or investing in a particular piece of software. Think about how these tasks fit into your workflow:

- **Grouping:** Creates different structures to hold and organize your photos. It might be called a library, a catalog, a project, an album, or a folder, depending on the application. After it's created, you import photos into this structure, which keeps or separates one set of photos from another. That way, you don't have 10,000 pictures running around with no organization.

- **Sorting:** An active task in which you identify a set of criteria, such as the date or time that a photo was taken or its filename, keyword, or rating, or another parameter, and the program displays the photos or working files in that order.

- **Filtering:** Similar to sorting, but weeds out photos based on the criteria you choose. If you want to see only 5-star photos, all the rest can be hidden.

- **Keywording or tagging:** A straightforward concept that's infuriating in practice. You tag every photo with descriptive keywords that help you organize, sort, find, and otherwise keep track of similar photos.

  The problem is coming up with a list of standard keywords and using them. Don''t get too detailed. For example, you might tag the same photo this way:

  Landscape or D200, landscape, f/8, sunset, Sigma, ultra wide-angle.

- **Geotagging:** Identifies where a photo was taken. Most often, you identify where one or more photos were taken on a map and the coordinates are written to the metadata.

- **Stacking:** Some managers stack different versions of the same photo on top of each other, allowing you to declutter the workspace.

Processing the Good Ones

Even casual photographers rarely have the time or need to process every single photo they shoot. Process good photos, not bad ones. Don't waste your time with them unless you have no other choice.

You can find more details on how to process raw exposures in Chapter 2 of this minibook.

Editing When Necessary

Editing boils down to a balance between time, effort, and quality. Ideally, you shoot photos in raw format, and they need only minimal processing to publish (perhaps a smidgen of sharpness and contrast). Your goal is to go from download to finished product in as little time as possible.

That isn't always the case, for a number of reasons. First, some photos need fixing. That's what photo editors do. You may want to load your best photos into an editor and make adjustments that make them truly stunning. You may be working with panoramas, HDR, black and white, or colorized photos that need the touch of an editor to finish.

No problem. You do that in this step of the workflow, after processing and before publishing. I cover editing more fully in Chapter 3 of this minibook. (And don't forget Chapter 6, where I discuss all things color-related.)

Publishing

You can publish by using just about every type of raw processing, photo editing, or photo management software. The result is normally an 8-bits-per-channel JPEG image if you're going to post it on the Web or a high-quality 8- or 16 bits-per-channel TIFF if you plan to archive the file or send it to a printer. (Check with the printer to make sure that you send a file with the appropriate bit-depth.)

Here's a generalized checklist for publishing final images:

- **Preserve original material:** I can't stress this advice enough. *Never* overwrite original files. Always track names and versions so that when you select Save, you aren't making a big mistake. JPEGs in particular suffer from *lossy* compression — they lose some quality every time you open, edit, and save them.

- **Preserve working copies:** I've flattened Photoshop images to export them and then forgot what I was doing and saved and closed the file. Thankfully, I had the final version even though my work in the middle was lost.

- **Enter copyright and other descriptive information, if you want:** That's what metadata is used for. If you publish your photos to the Web, think about adding this layer of protection to your photos.

✔ **Add copyright or watermark:** This is another way to protect your photos. Whereas copyright and descriptive metadata are invisible, a watermark, mark, or copyright placed on a photo is visible for all to see.

✔ **Strip metadata, if you want:** Conversely, you may want to strip out any metadata to protect your secrets. Not all applications remove data, but you can save final files to a format that doesn't have metadata and then open and save those versions to your final format.

✔ **Resize for the Web:** Unless you want your full-size photos to be posted somewhere online, such as at Flickr or SmugMug, you should resize Web images to make them quite a bit smaller. On the Web, 14 megapixels is serious overkill. (The *pixel count* is the total number of *pic*ture *el*ements, or dots, in a photo; in this case, 14 megapixels stands for 14 million pixels.) Some sites may reduce the size of your photos, anyway.

Pay attention to the resizing method you choose because they're different. For example, Photoshop has these resizing options that appear on a drop-down menu in the Image Size dialog box:

✔ **Nearest Neighbor:** Preserves hard edges. Pay careful attention when you use this method. Examine the edges at 100 percent magnification to see whether the sharp edges cause jaggedness.

✔ **Bilinear:** A good method in which colors are preserved and the image is smooth. You lose a bit of sharpness, however.

✔ **Bicubic:** Works best for smooth gradients; produces results similar to Bilinear, except a bit sharper.

✔ **Bicubic Smoother:** Works best if you're enlarging an image. When you're reducing, this method looks almost indistinguishable from plain old Bicubic.

✔ **Bicubic Sharper:** Works best if you're reducing the image. Distinctly sharper than all other methods, and much better than Nearest Neighbor. It produces sharpness without creating jagged edges. Still, pay attention to whether the level of sharpness suits your needs. If not, resize using Bicubic, and then come back and apply an Unsharp Mask and sharpen the image to the exact degree you want.

For moderately sized Web galleries, 800 pixels wide is a good start. That number is large enough to see detail yet not overwhelming enough to download. If you want a larger size, try 1024 pixels wide or thereabouts.

You often have a plethora of methods to publish photos. Choose the one that best fits your target media requirements. For example, Photoshop Elements and the Photoshop Elements Organizer have more printing and publishing options than you can shake a stick at:

✔ **Save As:** Of course, you can always use this option.

✔ **Save for Web:** In this excellent dialog box, you can save GIF, JPEG, and PNG photos. I resize images before choosing this option.

✔ **Export:** Export the selected file as the same or new file type.

✔ **Share:** Includes Online Album, E-mail Attachments, Photo Mail, Burn Video DVD/BluRay, Burn Data CD/DVD, Online Video Sharing, Mobile Photo and Players, PDF Slide Show, Share with Kodak EasyShare Gallery, Send to SmugMug Gallery, Send to CEIVA Digital Photo Frame, and Share to Flickr.

✔ **Print:** Print single photos, contact sheets, or Picture Packages.

✔ **Order Prints:** Order Shutterfly or Kodak prints from PCs (unfortunately, not part of the current version of Elements for Mac).

On the other hand, you may be working in a professional environment where documents run through Adobe Bridge. You can publish PDF contact sheets or Web Galleries from within Bridge. In Bridge CS5, you can now export JPEGs — a welcome change. If you use Lightroom or Photoshop, you'll likely print, export, or save archive copies from within those applications.

Archiving

Archiving your digital photo collection is in some ways easier than safeguarding photo prints and negatives. The files themselves are, for all intents and purposes, indestructible — as long as you ensure the safety of the medium you store them in. You don't have to worry about prints getting bent or soaked with humidity, or about boxes of them occupying an entire room of storage.

The backup and archiving process doesn't happen by itself. You have to take some time to plan and use diligence to carry out your plans. You can't throw a sleeve of negatives into a cardboard box and tuck them away in a closet.

Playing it safe

First, decide how you want to back up and archive your photos. You have to consider issues such as storage capacity, availability, and organization, in addition to the categories in this list:

✔ **Cost:** You want to pay as little as possible, but you have to strike a balance between being cost-effective and being simply foolish. Don't buy the cheapest (and possibly most unreliable) hard drives known to mankind to protect your valuable files.

✔ **Capacity:** Storage capacity is a true problem. Digital photos take up a lot of space. Choose a storage medium that fits your current and anticipated future workload.

✔ **Access:** Determine whether you can easily access your backups and whether an unforeseen circumstance can prevent you from protecting your work.

✔ **Security:** Assess your security situation to determine how safe (physically, and from a computer networking standpoint) the file are. Put the appropriate safeguards on your home or local network. In addition, files can be easily damaged if you store them at home and your house burns down. If that's your only backup copy, you've lost them.

✔ **The future:** Consider how easy or hard it will be to transfer archived files from one storage device to another. For example, old hard drives may require a connection that will someday be obsolete unless you occasionally update your backup technology. In the very long term, provide thumbnails or a printed index or another form of inventory that, for example, lets your kids or their kids easily figure out what you have stored when you're gone.

Table 1-1 relates my thoughts on specific types of storage media.

Table 1-1	Archival Media Pros and Cons	
Media	*Cons*	*Pros*
CD-ROM/ DVD-ROM	Limited capacity; most camera memory cards have more space; raises questions about longevity.	No moving parts.
Tape backup	Cost for tapes, drive, and software; often uses proprietary storage file formats; may require special software to back up and restore; can be "eaten" by disgruntled machines; data can be erased by strong magnetic fields.	Capacity and longevity.
Memory card or flash drive	Cost per gigabyte makes for an impractical solution; would require 125 8GB digital camera memory cards (an average of $20 to $60 apiece) to match the storage space of a single 1 terabyte drive (a good one is $80).	Easy to use; doesn't occupy much space; no moving parts.

Media	Cons	Pros
Internal hard drive	Moving parts; susceptible to crashing; difficult to swap in or out; data can be erased by strong magnetic fields.	Affordable; high capacity; fast, day-to-day access; useful for temporary backups.
External hard drive	Moving parts; not as accessible as an internal hard drive.	Affordable; fast access; high capacity; portability; can be stored offsite; helpful for long-term storage; uses eSATA for fastest speed.
Online	Time and bandwidth (multigigabyte transfers may initially cripple your camera, but updates are then faster); requires computer with working Internet access; requires service subscription and an account in good standing; company can't go out of business; theoretically vulnerable to unauthorized access.	The ultimate in offsite storage; simplicity; no additional hardware or purchases; can access anywhere and at any time.

Implementing the plan

All the cool storage devices in the world do no good if you never use them. Have a plan in place to back up your files and archive them. Follow these steps to walk through the type of plan I recommend, using a combination of extra internal and external hard drives:

1. **Complete an initial photo backup.**

   Back up new source photos to extra internal hard drives. Repeat this process as often as you download photos so that all your source photos have backup copies. You can't afford to lose the initial download. The photos in it form the basis of your collection and can't be re-created.

   The mechanics of the initial backup are up to you. I simply copy and paste the photo folder to another location. You may want to export photos from your photo management software or use a backup program to perform an incremental copy. This advice applies to each of the following steps.

2. **Perform a weekly backup of edited photo and working files.**

   Back up working files to internal hard drives to keep your work files reasonably safe (remember, you do an initial backup of your photos daily). If you can't afford to lose a single day's worth of productivity, consider daily backups of your working files in addition to source photos.

   For a more relaxed timeline, back up working, edited, and final files monthly.

3. **Complete an end-of-month backup.**

   Back up all working files and source photos to external hard drives, a file server, or a network. This step tidies things up so that each month is a self-contained unit.

   For a more relaxed timeline, back up quarterly or by project.

4. **Perform a biannual backup.**

   Create an off-site backup with all working and source photo files. Put them in a storage barn on your property, rent safety deposit box storage space from a bank, or ask your grandparents to put them in their attic. Just make sure that they're physically separated from your computer and the building you work in. That way, if anything happens to your building, your photos and work files remain safe.

   For a more relaxed timeline, back up annually.

The key to making backups is to balance the time and energy you're willing to invest against the chance of something happening so that you can keep your photos and work files safe and sound.

The plan I suggest may not work for everyone. One alternative, keyed toward a business environment, is to treat every job as a discrete unit and back up photos and work files according to job number. When you transfer the initial photos, back them up. When you finish the job, back up all your work files with source photos and tuck them away on a hard drive devoted to that client. Depending on your workload and client list, you may have one hard drive for many clients or many hard drives for one client. Offset the cost of the extra hard drives by including them in your service fee.

Chapter 2: Deep-Fried Camera Raw

In This Chapter

🖝 **Understanding why you should use raw**

🖝 **Gearing up for raw**

🖝 **Digging into the raw fundamentals**

🖝 **Stepping it up with advanced raw development**

*W*elcome to the wonderful world of raw. You've have taken the leap or are considering moving from a JPEG-only workflow into the realm of raw processing.

dSLR cameras "specialize" in taking raw photos. In other words, they're leading the consumer and professional charge toward shooting in that format — which drives software to support them. This chapter specializes, therefore, in showing you some ins and outs of processing raw exposures taken with a dSLR.

Before I discuss what you can do with a raw editor and your good pictures, I briefly explain what raw photos (sometimes called "camera raw" photos, which is why Adobe Camera Raw was named the way it was) are and why you should bother with them. I then touch on the major software options you have to choose from.

Raw-dy for some deep-fried camera raw?

Raw, Raw, Raw Your Bawt

Camera raw photos (also known as raw exposures or raw photos) are basically "undeveloped" pictures. They contain encoded data from the camera's sensor that hasn't been processed beyond the initial encoding. For example, these photos aren't sharpened and they have no color profile, and their exposure, color, and contrast levels haven't been adjusted. They have metadata, which stores information such as the time the photo was taken and the lens type — just like a JPEG would have.

Raw extensions

The following short list shows many raw file extensions from different manufacturers, including Adobe, which has applied for its Digital Negative raw format to become a potential standard:

Adobe: .dng

Minolta: .mrw

Olympus: .orf

Canon: .crw, .cr2

Nikon: .nef, .nrw

Panasonic: .raw

Pentax: .pef, .ptx

Sony: .arw, .srf, .sr2

Sigma: .x3f

Raw is neither a file format (like .psd) nor an acronym (such as JPEG). Every camera manufacturer creates its own data structure and assigns it a 3-character extension, independent of what other companies do. How the digital SLR stores the data depends on the manufacturer's own sense of design and how they interface the camera's sensor with its internal processor.

Benefits

The advantages of shooting in camera raw mode are numerous. A few of the most critical advantages are described in this list:

- **Fidelity:** The camera sensor captures raw photos — they haven't been processed and saved as JPEGs. The process of converting a raw photo to a JPEG is somewhat subjective and, in the end, data must be "trimmed" to make it fit within the constraints of the JPEG file type. When you process the raw photos yourself, you, not the camera, make the decisions that determine how the JPEG looks.

  When you process camera raw exposures into JPEG files, you still have the raw data to fall back on and reprocess, if the mood strikes you, whether it's tomorrow or next week or five years from now. If you buy a better raw converter, you can go back and reprocess your raw data into new JPEGs to try to make them look better. The possibility always exists that a processing breakthrough can make processing raw photos easier, especially in borderline photos with exposure or another type of problem.

  If you let the camera convert raw data into JPEGs and then discard the raw data (by not saving it), you're forever stuck with that somewhat subjective process. Any additional editing must be done with the JPEG, which is a subset of the original data — not the original data itself.

✒ **Bit depth and dynamic range:** Raw photos have a greater bit depth than JPEG files do. Modern dSLRS range from 12 or 14 bits per channel, which is 4 to 6 bits per channel better than the 8 bits per channel you get from using a JPEG file.

JPEGs aren't useless. It depends on the dynamic range of the scene. If the dynamic range can comfortably fit into 8 bits per channel, a JPEG can capture the scene with little trouble. However, if the exposure or color is off (which may be often), having the extra bit-depth means that you capture more data and can correct problems more easily.

In other words, you blow out fewer raw photos and achieve a greater possible dynamic range because your photos have a greater bit depth.

A greater bit depth also means that you can further manipulate exposure and color in processing as well as preserve and protect shadows and highlights.

✒ **Potential quality:** Camera raw photos have a higher top end, such as in JPEGs. Processing further is similar to making a low-resolution copy of a low-resolution copy: You have little room to mess with exposure and color before you start to make the photo look overprocessed and noisy.

In the end, the JPEG file is a good end product, especially for media on the Web. Where it fails is in not providing you with the camera's sensor data in its original format. If you start with a raw photo, you can push that data in a number of directions (white balance, exposure, saturation, or sharpness, for example) that aren't as effective if you use JPEGs. After all, you're starting with a photo in which those creative decisions have already been made and the remainder of the original data was discarded.

Challenges

Just because a raw photo has a greater upside than a JPEG file does doesn't mean that it's a panacea. In other words, costs are associated with using them. If those costs outweigh the benefits of shooting and processing raw photos for you, don't be afraid to move to (or not change from) a JPEG workflow. You may choose not to shoot raw photos for these practical reasons:

✒ **Limited compatibility:** No industry standard exists for camera raw photo files as it does for JPEG and TIFF files. A camera manufacturer creates its own data file and adds an extension to it and then calls it a camera raw photo. Adobe has championed the independent Digital Negative (.dng) raw file format but hasn't swayed most camera manufacturers to switch to it. In other words, Canon raw photos aren't stored the same as ones from Nikon or Pentax or Sony or anyone else.

Imagine that ten different word processor applications store their documents in a unique, proprietary file format. You would call any file a document, no matter which application created it. That doesn't make them compatible, though. They have different extensions, data structures, and encoding and decoding requirements. With a file format such as JPEG or TIFF, a standard says, in effect, that "every program or camera that saves a file and calls it a JPEG must store the data this way." That's what makes JPEGs compatible, whether it's across computer systems, Web browsers, Web-capable phones, game systems, or e-mail applications.

Compatibility used to be more of a problem. Software developers now pay close attention to new raw file formats and quickly scramble to support them.

However, you can't slap a raw photo directly on a Web page. People won't be able to view it.

- **They take up space:** If your memory card is tight on space, you might not have the room to store camera raw and JPEG files. I would choose camera raw and ditch JPEGs, in that case. Although you can always process JPEG from camera raw shots, the reverse is impossible.

- **Slower shooting speed:** Because raw photos fill a camera's buffer faster than JPEGs do and writing files from the buffer to the memory card takes longer, you produce a faster, more sustained frame rate if you shoot JPEGs with most digital SLRs.

- **Impact on processing time:** If you don't have the time to process camera raw photos, JPEGs are your best solution. In this case, download the JPEGs from your camera, choose the ones you need, and publish them as fast as possible.

- **No need:** You may find that the JPEGs coming from your camera are just as good or better than what you can do yourself with raw. If that's the case, use the JPEGs and don't worry about raw.

If you can set JPEG processing options (color profile, saturation, and sharpness, for example) on your digital SLR, set them the way you want them (take test shots to confirm they satisfy you). Then, as long as you take a well-exposed photo (whatever you may be intending at the time), the JPEG should accurately represent the photo you took. The challenge is that you have to take photos that have little or nothing wrong with them. If you consistently nail the exposure, white balance, and composition within the dynamic range available in a JPEG, you may have little need for camera raw photos.

Workflow

Raw workflow is more flexible than editing JPEGs because you don't make an adjustment, apply it, and move to another adjustment, for example. Raw editors don't apply changes until you export the file.

You should still read your raw application's documentation to see whether it has a preferred workflow, such as tweaking exposure before sharpening.

Most of the time, you can "wing it."

In the case of Adobe Camera Raw, review the tabs on the right and make adjustments along the way. Don't forget the tools above the preview window for tasks such as straightening and spot corrections. The adjustments you select aren't applied until you either save the camera raw file or open it in Photoshop or Photoshop Elements.

In an application such as Lightroom, changes you make on the Develop tab are stored in the Lightroom database. The original files aren't affected *even if you crop the photo.* Press the Reset button at the bottom of the Develop panel to revert to the original photo, if you need to. You can also create virtual copies in Lightroom to try out and compare alternative settings. Only when you export are the settings permanently applied to create the new file, and even then the original is left alone.

Capture One has a recommended development workflow. It suggests working on exposure and high dynamic range, which is its terminology for shadow and highlight recovery and then levels and curves. But if you're working on a Mac with Capture One Pro, you can create your own interface tab and add the tools you want to work with, in the order you want to use them — total customization!

Choosing Raw Software

As long as you shoot raw, choosing the right raw software is one of the most important elements of dSLR photography. Your choice affects your workflow, the specifics of how you manage and process photos, and your sanity.

Choose software that doesn't cause you conniption fits.

As you look through a sampling of available programs, remember that you can use more than one raw converter. You may have a specific need that only one application can fill — such as automatic lens distortion correction for a favorite lens or a CMYK (cyan, magenta, yellow, black) color profile. You can run the majority of your photos through a "standard" raw processor and a select few through an alternate. (In that case, I would use one as a manager and standard processor.)

Your camera's software

Camera manufacturers receive mixed reviews on their raw conversion and image editing software. Some people love what they see, and some people don't.

The following table lists several camera raw software packages by manufacturer, all of which have Windows and Macintosh versions. All are free except for the Nikon Digital Capture NX 2, which costs $179.95 and has a free trial available for download.

Manufacturer	Software Name
Canon	Digital Photo Professional
Nikon	Nikon Capture NX 2
Olympus	OLYMPUS Master 2
Pentax	PENTAX PHOTO Laboratory 3
Sony	Sony Image Data Converter SR

Major photo/raw editing and management software

All the major photo editing and photo management players have raw development integrated into their software to some degree. On the photo editing side, you miss out on a lot of the sophisticated management tools, but even Photoshop Elements and Corel PaintShop Photo Pro have basic organizers built in. Conversely, neither Lightroom nor Aperture (two leading raw processors) have built-in sophisticated photo editing.

More than likely, you use a combination of both types of software. In that case, you can choose in which one to process your camera raw photos.

The Adobe family

Adobe integrates raw development into its two editing applications via Adobe Camera Raw (ACR). Lightroom uses the same basic functionality as ACR but in a different interface.

Adobe Camera Raw

The Adobe Camera Raw (ACR) plug-in works within Adobe Photoshop and Photoshop Elements. It's the nearly universal Adobe raw editor and converter. The popular ACR has a clean and professional interface.

ACR works differently within Adobe Photoshop Elements than in Photoshop. The Elements version has fewer options, bells, whistles, and doodads. The main differences between the Photoshop and Photoshop Element instances of ACR are described in this list:

✔ **Photoshop:** Photoshop has the whole ACR package, as shown in Figure 2-1. In this case, I'm using the HSL / Grayscale tab to selectively boost the saturation of the yellow in the truck. This task isn't one that you can do in Elements.

Figure 2-1: Calling ACR from Photoshop.

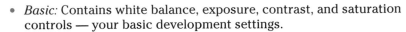

You can choose from nine tabs to do most of your work; from left to right, they're described in the following list.

- *Basic:* Contains white balance, exposure, contrast, and saturation controls — your basic development settings.

- *Tone Curve:* Features a parametric or point tone curve to alter exposure based on specific tonal regions.

- *Detail:* Has sharpening and noise reduction controls.

- *HSL / Grayscale:* Boosts, reduces, or changes hue, saturation, and lightness values according to specific color hues. You can also convert to grayscale on this tab.

- *Split Toning:* Changes the hue or increases the saturation of highlights or shadows. You can also move the mix point.

- *Lens Corrections:* Has controls to correct chromatic aberration, lens vignetting, and vignette characteristics.

- *Camera Calibration:* Lets you assign a camera profile, not to be confused with a color profile, to the photo. This affects how ACR interprets color rendering. You can also alter the tint applied to shadows and the hue or saturation of reds, greens, or blues.

- *Presets:* Lists settings you have saved as presets. You can then create settings based on different cameras, situations, or scenes or an effect you want and quickly apply them to other photos.

- *Snapshots:* Houses a cool tool in ACR. When you save a snapshot, you save the settings you've chosen but can continue developing in ACR. Toggle between two or three alternative to see which one you like best.

You can also choose from several tools at the top of the interface (just above the preview window). When you select the tool (except for rotating and preferences), the cursor changes. It's your cue to do something in the preview window.

- *Zoom Tool:* Zooms in or out.

- *Hand Tool:* Pans around.

- *White Balance Tool:* After you click an element that should be a neutral gray or white in the preview window, loads those settings in the White Balance control of the Basic tab.

- *Color Sampler Tool:* Lets you click and pick as many as nine point samples and monitor their RGB triplets as you modify other settings.

  Although this option may not seem practical, it is if you're photographing a subject that you know is (or has to be) a specific color, such as logos and other carefully designed marketing material.

- *Targeted Adjustment Tool (includes submodes):* Lets you click a color or tone and drag it to alter the hue, saturation, lightness, or grayscale mix.

- *Crop Tool (includes submodes):* Lets you drag a box to identify a crop window on the photo.

- *Straighten Tool:* Establishes one end of a straight line when you click and hold. Continue holding the mouse button and drag to the end point. Release the mouse button to select the end point. You see a rotated crop window based on the angle of the line you chose.

  Zoom in to create good endpoints.

- *Spot Removal:* Removes dust spots and other small blemishes. You can change between Heal and Clone modes, increase the radius, and lower the opacity of the tool.

- *Red Eye Removal:* Removes red-eye.

- *Adjustment Brush:* "Brushes" on adjustments. Choose exposure, brightness, contrast, saturation, clarity, sharpness, and color (to tint).

- *Graduated Filter:* Applies one or more graduated filters to the photo.

- *Preferences:* Presents a list of options you can choose from that are different from the Workflow Options at the bottom.

- *Rotate:* Has two versions (one goes left and one goes right).

✓ **Photoshop Elements:** Adobe Camera Raw from within Photoshop Elements (see Figure 2-2) has only three tabs: Basic, Detail, and Camera Calibration. They work exactly like those in Photoshop. Elements also has fewer tools, such as Zoom, Hand, White Balance, Crop, Straighten, Red Eye, Preferences, and Rotate.

Figure 2-2: Converting in Photoshop Elements.

Among other significant differences are

- *Color profile:* You cannot change the color profile that will be assigned to the converted file. After you open a file in Elements, you can convert it to Adobe RGB, but it would be nice to be able to assign it from ACR on your way into Elements.

- *Limited save:* You cannot save camera raw files in any format other than Digital Negative (.dng).

  Although this limitation is significant, you can work around it by opening the photo in Elements and then saving from there — clunky, yes, but effective.

Adobe Photoshop Lightroom

Except for the style of the interface, Adobe Lightroom shares a lot with ACR. You find all the same controls and tools in Lightroom as in ACR when you launch it from Photoshop. Figure 2-3 shows the interface with the Develop tab active. (This is what happens when kids grow tired of the flash — they cover their eyes every time you come near them.) On the Develop tab, you change your raw development settings to decode and interpret the raw exposures. Notice that I sharpened and increased noise reduction for this photo.

Figure 2-3: Developing in Lightroom.

ACR and Lightroom have a few differences between them. Aside from the overall packaging, Lightroom has a better histogram, a better tone curve, and a snazzy color picker for use when you split tones. That's about it. You should see consistently good results from Lightroom, no matter which camera you have or your other workflow needs.

Apple Aperture

As shown in Figure 2-4, Aperture is a Mac-only image management and editing application that has the same overall functionality as Adobe

Lightroom. I'm in the process of making a sharpness and recovery adjustment to this photo of one of my sons on a swing. Notice that you can select and deselect specific adjustments on the tab.

Figure 2-4: Using Apple Aperture 3.

Apple Aperture is fun to use; it has great compatibility with the Mac OS, nice raw editing capability, and good access to EXIF data; and you can export images to HDR applications. It can do everything except mix drinks while you wait.

Corel PaintShop Photo Pro X3

Corel PaintShop Photo Pro X3 is a full-featured raster (such as a photo or computer graphic that has been "painted") and vector graphics (graphics created from points and lines) editor, complete with a bevy of photo editing tools and features, including a limited raw editor and HDR capability.

The PaintShop Photo Pro Camera RAW Lab (see Figure 2-5) covers the basics: exposure, brightness, saturation, shadow, sharpness, white balance, and noise reduction controls. For this photo, I barely adjusted the exposure, increased the brightness and saturation, and increased the sharpness and noise reduction a bit.

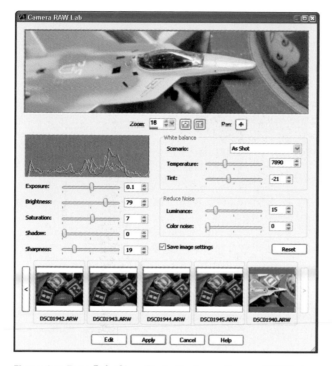

Figure 2-5: Even PaintShop Photo Pro has a Camera RAW Lab.

Taking Care of the Basics

Remember that your goal is to take photos you shoot and *develop* them using raw workflow software. This technical process is guided by your artistic sensibilities. Let me repeat that statement a bit differently. Although raw development is a technical process, it cannot take place without your creative guidance.

For the most part, the force that guides you is your ability to sense what looks good, with the help of right-brained constructs, such as a histogram.

Wanting to provide this guidance is what separates someone who just wants the JPEGs out of the camera and doesn't want to mess with them from someone who wants a say in how the final image looks. Photographers who want to take the trouble to develop their photos often believe that they can do a better job than the camera.

Knowing what you can do before you load a raw converter might help you decide to give it a try. The following list presents some basic tasks that you can do in just about any raw editor. (I show you different programs to prove my point.) By *basic,* I mean the adjustments fundamental to creating the right look, exposure, contrast, and color.

✓ **Read the histogram:** You must be able to read a histogram when you convert raw photos. It tells you how bright, middle, and dark parts of the photo are distributed, which can help you decide whether the exposure is too dark, too light, or just right. You may see a luminance-only histogram, or one with the three color channels distinctly displayed.

Figure 2-6 shows the histogram in Lightroom as I develop a photo of one of my sons sitting on a slide. Notice that the light is concentrated mostly at the low end, which means that the photo may be a bit under-exposed. The problem is that the histogram also shows very bright areas, preventing me from boosting exposure much. Those bright areas are the clouds and sky.

Figure 2-6: Analyzing the histogram in Lightroom.

Never let the histogram tell you what looks good. That isn't its job. It's there to give you information on the balance of lights and darks in the photo, not make decisions for you. There's no perfect histogram that should be applied to all photos.

✓ **Tweak exposure:** An exposure control allows you to push or pull the exposure of the photo down or up. It's measured in exposure value (EV), so your highly developed "photo-sense" should relate to this control.

Raise or lower exposure until the photo looks right. Check the histogram to help you interpret what you're doing, and take care not to blow out highlights or lose shadows. If you do, you can rescue them by tweaking highlights and shadow controls (Adobe calls them Recovery and Fill Light, respectively). If you've gone too far, bring exposure back and readjust shadows and highlights. It's a delicate dance.

In Figure 2-7, I adjusted the exposure upward on a photo of a lake in Apple's entry-level application iPhoto. The floating window shows you that even iPhoto has a lot of adjusting power.

Figure 2-7: Rolling back the sunset in iPhoto.

Read carefully the documentation that comes with your software. For example, the Adobe Camera Raw Brightness slider also affects exposure. The difference between it and the Exposure slider is that it *compresses* highlights whereas the Exposure slider clips them. Big difference! Adobe suggests setting the initial clipping points with the Exposure and Shadow sliders and then setting the overall brightness of the photo with the Brightness slider.

✓ **White balance:** Correcting white balance often means selecting a preset to put you in the ballpark and then adjusting temperature and tint to finish the job. Most programs allow you to choose the camera setting or override it by selecting the application default or to choose a specific lighting condition, such as Outside, Cloudy, or Fluorescent. You may also be able to select a white balance control and click something that should be a white, gray, or black portion on the photo.

Figure 2-8 shows how to correct white balance in Apple Aperture. The first exposure shows the color of the tile with no adjustment. The second shows the process of choosing a neutral gray area, and the final shot shows the correct color, a beautiful blue.

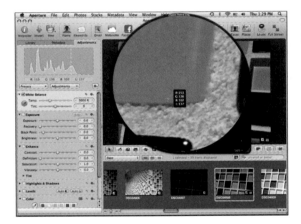

Figure 2-8: Adjusting white balance in Apple Aperture.

Chances are good that the white balance will be good. If you want it perfect, go back in time and set the camera white balance yourself. A more practical solution is to take some time to tweak these controls. If you want absolute certainty, shoot with a gray or white balance card (I use WhiBal), which gives you a known color to use to identify the correct settings (which you then apply to the rest of the photo shoot). You can take a reading from the card to set the camera or include the card in a scene for measurement as you process your photos.

✓ **Improve contrast:** Contrast is the difference between white and black in the photo. Increasing the contrast pushes apart the light and dark regions. Lowering contrast pulls them together so that there's less of a difference.

Figure 2-9 shows a photo of my back porch light after an ice storm in 2008. The first frame is unadjusted. I enhanced the contrast quite a bit in the second. The shadows on the siding and light stand out much more.

Before   After

Figure 2-9: Enhancing contrast in Capture One PRO.

Raise contrast too much, and the photo looks funky. You blow out highlights and push details into darkness. Lower it too much (I'm not sure if I've *ever* lowered contrast), and the photo looks too bland.

Contrast affects exposure, so look at the histogram and, if necessary, retweak exposure, brightness, shadows, and highlight controls.

✔ **Preserve highlights and shadows:** This task is one of the main reasons that raw conversion rocks. I can't tell you how many times I've loaded up a photo and had the sky look so bright that it looks blown out. In raw, I can pull it back so that it's not too bright without ruining the photo. By the same token, I can brighten shadows so that they aren't a uniform black (although you have to watch for noise when you brighten shadows).

I've done this in Figure 2-10, using Adobe Camera Raw. The photo shows a statue of a horse by a housing subdivision north of town. The red and blue highlights reveal bright and dark areas, respectively, that are too bright and dark. I adjusted both Fill Light and Recovery to pull them back into the photo.

Before   After

Figure 2-10: Protecting shadows and highlights (or highlights and shadows?).

You often have a way to highlight blown highlights and shadows in a preview window. It helps you bring problems under control to see immediately how well you're doing.

You don't have to eliminate all bright or dark pixels. Bring them into balance so that the photo looks good.

✔ **Adjust saturation and vibrancy:** These simple controls boost color intensity. Saturation strengthens all colors whereas vibrancy only raises the saturation of weak colors.

In Figure 2-11, I raised the vibrancy on a photo of some cherry tomatoes to boost their color. The first shot shows the original photo, and the second shows the result of the new setting. Notice that the rest of the photo wasn't supersaturated. That's the beauty of vibrancy.

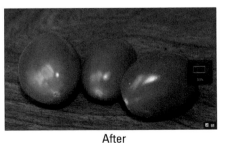

Before   After

Figure 2-11: Nice red(der) tomatoes, courtesy of Aperture.

I like saturated photos, so I don't hold back much. I carefully check noise levels and highlights as I raise it. When possible, I increase vibrancy first to see whether it does the trick.

✔ **Save, open, export:** This isn't an editing task, but it is one that I want to mention. When you use ACR, you have two options to wrap things up: Save Image and Open Image. Save Image saves the converted raw photo to your hard drive as a new image. (To see which options you have, see the earlier sections in this chapter on ACR.) Open Image opens the converted photo in Photoshop or Photoshop Elements. Edit the way you want, and then save the photo in whatever format you like.

Other raw editors may allow you to overwrite the raw photo with your new settings. I can't think of very many situations where this is a good idea. They should also let you save the converted photo as a JPEG or TIFF. I normally choose 16 bits/channel TIFF because I want the highest quality possible. I use that file as my new source image when I am ready to export. If you want to go from raw to JPEG, that's fine, but do so knowing you won't have an interim high-quality file.

You don't save photos in other raw editors such as Lightroom and Aperture — you export them as new files or open them in a photo editor such as Photoshop.

More Advanced Raw Editing

After you get the basics under control, have a look at some of the more advanced raw editing possibilities. As with the more basic choices, you may not need to apply every technique mentioned in this list to every photo (at least I hope you don't):

✔ **Sharpen:** Everybody likes sharp-looking photos. Factors such as the glass you're using (remember that *glass* refers to the lens, in photographer lingo), focus, camera stability, shutter speed, and distance clearly have a large effect on how sharp a photo can be. Within those bounds, you can sharpen a photo quite a bit during raw conversion.

I increased the sharpness of a photo of some ants in Figure 2-12, using the PaintShop Photo Pro Camera RAW Lab.

How, and how well, you sharpen a photo depends on the program you use. Some programs have sharpness controls that are quite

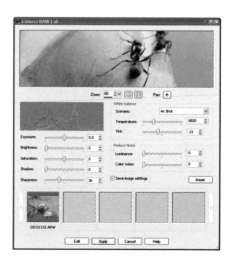

Figure 2-12: Some sharpening during conversion is almost always a good idea.

Book VI
Chapter 2

Deep-Fried
Camera Raw

simple. They don't tell you how they work and give you no options to control the process, other than their overall strength. Other programs give you more control and act similarly to the Unsharp Mask filter in Photoshop.

I generally like "crisping-up" a photo and removing lens softness in raw, but if the photo looks like it has an overall sharpness problem, leave it for editing. You don't want to oversharpen a photo, which can accentuate edges to the point that they dominate the photo, look artificial, and elevate the appearance of noise.

✔ **Noise reduction:** Similarly, most raw converters have some form of noise reduction. Many let you reduce noise in either or both the Luminance channel in the color channels of the photo. Too much noise reduction removes a great deal of a photo's detail.

Figure 2-13 is a close-up of my son's eyeball (the photo is bigger — I zoomed in so that you can see the noise), taken at ISO 900. It's a bit noisy. The second shot shows the effect of applying luminance noise reduction in Lightroom — not bad!

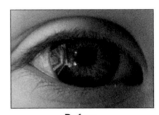

Before

 WARNING!

Be sure to observe how much sharpness you lose when you reduce noise. If it's too much, try backing off and reducing noise in your editor. The internal routines, or third-party noise reduction plug-ins, most often give you much more control over noise reduction and the ability to protect or sharpen details. You can also selectively reduce noise by using layers or masks.

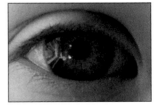

After

Figure 2-13: Noise reduction while converting saves work later.

✔ **Chromatic aberrations:** You know that a photo has chromatic aberrations when you see colored fringe along borders between high-contrast areas. What happened is that your lens wasn't able to focus all wavelengths of light on the same spot. It almost looks like a ghost image.

Figure 2-14 is a great example of chromatic aberration on a flower in my back yard. I zoomed in so that you can see the blue aberration (image on the left). The shot on the right shows the result of the correction in Aperture.

These controls nudge those areas to where they should be — on top of the actual object.

✔ **Lens distortion:** At least one raw editor has a feature to automatically remove lens distortion — the Nikon Capture NX 2. You obviously have to be using a Nikon dSLR and an appropriate lens to use this feature, but it's a useful one to have.

Capture One Pro also has a lens correction tool, oriented toward medium-format cameras, but it also has a generic setting.

Otherwise, you have to remove lens distortion in editing.

✔ **Vignetting:** When you see light falling off in the corners of your photos (they're darker than the center), you have vignetting. Vignetting controls enable you to brighten the corners and even the light across the photo. Some people leave (or even create) vignetting because they think it looks neat. I sort of like it myself.

Figure 2-14: Look for chromatic aberration problems in areas of high contrast.

**Book VI
Chapter 2**

**Deep-Fried
Camera Raw**

Figure 2-15 shows a scene of a bridge at sunset loaded into Capture One Pro. The first shot shows some vignetting in the corners. The effect can be difficult to perceive until you start playing with the controls. The second shot reveals how much I brightened the corners. Although I like vignetting, this correction makes the sky look much more evenly exposed.

✔ **Cropping:** Because you can crop in many raw converters, you don't have to export the photo to an editor to crop. Instead, you can just export your work and be done with it.

✔ **Straightening:** Repeat the preceding bullet but say *straighten* when you see *crop* or *cropping*.

Figure 2-15: Brightening corners in Capture One Pro.

✔ **Spot removal:** Most raw editors nowadays have the capability to remove spots and clone out blemishes. This godsend means that you don't have to load raw photos into an editor just to get rid of a pimple, for example.

Figure 2-16 shows a photo before and after I removed a nasty dust spot in the sky, using Lightroom. You can now easily remove spots in the more advanced raw applications.

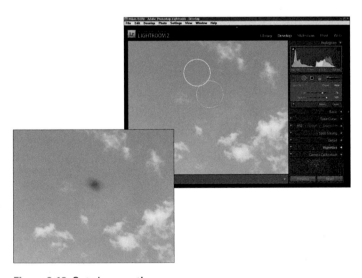

Figure 2-16: Out, darn spot!

✓ **Graduated filter:** Adobe Camera Raw and Lightroom have a cool graduated filter tool that lets you apply one or more ND Grad filters to the raw photo.

Figure 2-17 shows this feature in action. I took this shot just after sunset. I was rushed and had applied all the wrong settings on the camera. Even so, I love this series of pictures. I applied a graduated filter in the water in the second shot to show you an example of brightening an area with this filter. You can also change the contrast and saturation and other parameters.

Figure 2-17: Applying a graduated filter to brighten the foreground.

✓ **Toning:** You can easily and selectively adjust the hue, brightness, and saturation in many raw editors by either using a slider or clicking and dragging in the preview window. You can use this feature artistically, or to correct problems (such as too-bright reds that need to be toned down).

I made a few adjustments in Figure 2-18. First, I used a spot toning tool to darken the shadow on the house to the left. I also brightened the blue bubble blower. These changes are simple yet effective.

✓ **Tinting:** When you add tint, you apply a color to the entire photo, or possibly to specific tonal regions. I cover this topic in Chapter 6 of this minibook.

✔ **Black and white:** Although you can desaturate a photo in all raw editors, some have more complex controls that enable you to add much more input to the black-and-white conversion process. I also cover this topic in Chapter 6 of this minibook.

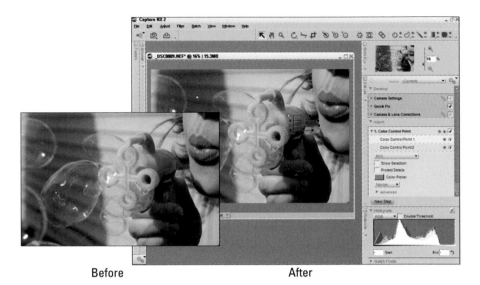

Before   After

Figure 2-18: Spot toning in the Nikon Capture NX 2.

✔ **Working with multiple images:** You can easily work with more than one image at a time in most applications. In others (the more limited raw converters from camera manufacturers), it's essentially impossible. There, you have to save your settings as a preset and apply them to each photo, one at a time.

I have a whole series of photos loaded into Adobe Camera Raw (the Photoshop Elements version) in Figure 2-19 to illustrate how easily you can make uniform adjustments to all shots of a photo shoot at the same time in ACR. I selected the photos in the filmstrip on the left side and increased the Vibrance setting on all of them. Bada-bing, baby!

Using other editors, you can select more than one raw photo and make adjustments to them all in one fell swoop. This helpful time-saver works when you are converting a number of shots from the same photo shoot and they all need the same basic adjustments.

✔ **Presets:** Use presets. They simplify your job tremendously. For example, when I process raw photos for HDR, I use different settings than when I work with normal photos. You can also have different presets based on different levels of sharpening, noise reduction, camera bodies, or lenses.

Figure 2-19: Making identical adjustments to many similar photos is a great time-saver.

Chapter 3: Mad Photo-Editing Skills

In This Chapter

✏ **Following the detailed editing workflow**

✏ **Sharpening**

✏ **Reducing noise**

✏ **Adjusting brightness and contrast**

✏ **Correcting color issues**

✏ **Cloning and retouching**

✏ **Dodging, burning, running, screaming**

✏ **Filtering, distorting, rotating, cropping, scaling, and more**

*I*deally, you should resolve as many brightness, contrast, sharpness, and related problems as possible in your photos during raw processing and then make whatever enhancements you want, such as dodging, burning, saturation, or another creative enhancement.

If you haven't done so, it doesn't mean you should have your head examined. It just means that you should tackle some of these tasks now, during photo editing. Therefore, this chapter shows you how to open your favorite photo editing software (maybe the one you love to hate) and spruce things up.

As usual, I use Photoshop Elements 8 for Windows to demonstrate. It's a good representation of what most other photo editors can do, and it's inexpensive and popular. I've organized this chapter according to the basic workflow I present in the first section.

Let's rock.

Workflow to Go

Most people have questions about the ideal order in which to tackle editing tasks. Believe it or not, part of this process is subjective — the way you like to work. On the other hand, some workflow decisions are more objective. This situation contributes to making workflow a slippery subject.

I've come up with many of my own workflow ideas over time, read many other people's opinions, tested different options, and come to the conclusion that for the most part, workflow doesn't matter as much as you might think.

The dangers of ruining a photo come *much* more from heavy-handed editing than from following the wrong workflow.

The bottom line is to find a process that fits the amount of time you have, your software, and the quality you want. You most likely won't find a *perfect* workflow. Use this chapter as a starting point, an ending point, or a point in between. I think it provides a reasonable balance between competing interests.

As you edit photos, keep these thoughts in mind:

- **Fewer changes are better:** If you're trying to create a realistic interpretation of the photo, the less you mess with it, the better.

  A perfect example is when a portrait looks great — resist the temptation to overdo something just because you can.

- **Pushing too hard often ruins a photo:** You run a greater risk of ruining the photo the harder you push brightness, contrast, color, sharpness, and noise reduction adjustments.

  A perfect example is trying to brighten a photo too much.

- **Knowing when to accept a photo for what it is:** The sensible solution is to find the spot where you can look at a photo and accept it for what it is. Not all photos are perfect. Some have noise; some have exposure problems; some have a bit of distortion.

  Digital photo editing alone cannot turn you into Ansel Adams. You have to take good photos to make that happen.

Don't worry. Within these guidelines are many tasks you can take on to make your photos better. Speaking of which, here's a sample workflow broken into groups:

- **Raw development:** Do what you can here first. See Chapter 2 of this minibook for more information.

- **Color profile:** When opening a photo in your editor, note the color profile (a fancy decoder ring; a color profile helps hardware such as monitors and printers reproduce the same colors) and ensure that it's what you want. If not, change it now (in Elements, use the Image⇨ Convert Color Profile menu) before you do any editing. The two most common color profiles are:

- *sRGB:* The de facto default setting for images and photos and for most printers and commercial kiosks. You have no problems with compatibility when you use it. Its drawback is that it reproduces fewer colors (has a smaller color space) than other profiles. It's often your only choice when using an inexpensive photo editor.

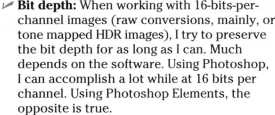

  When I save photos for use on the Web, I always select this profile for the final JPEG.

- *Adobe RGB:* Has a larger color space than sRGB, but not the widest possible one. Use this profile when you want to reproduce the colors in the photo more accurately, such as when printing.

  I usually set my camera to save photos in this profile although it applies only to JPEGs. Raw exposures don't pick up a profile until you save and convert them from raw to TIFF or JPEG (or open them in Adobe Camera Raw into Photoshop or Elements).

  When working with a raw editor, I set the working and final profile to Adobe RBG to ensure that when I edit the photo (if necessary), I have a wide color space.

✔ **Bit depth:** When working with 16-bits-per-channel images (raw conversions, mainly, or tone mapped HDR images), I try to preserve the bit depth for as long as I can. Much depends on the software. Using Photoshop, I can accomplish a lot while at 16 bits per channel. Using Photoshop Elements, the opposite is true.

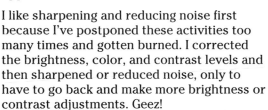

I like sharpening and reducing noise first because I've postponed these activities too many times and gotten burned. I corrected the brightness, color, and contrast levels and then sharpened or reduced noise, only to have to go back and make more brightness or contrast adjustments. Geez!

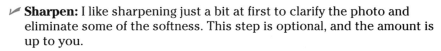

✔ **Sharpen:** I like sharpening just a bit at first to clarify the photo and eliminate some of the softness. This step is optional, and the amount is up to you.

✔ **Reduce noise:** Next, I look to reduce noise. Sometimes, I target specific areas of the photo. I perform more noise reduction later if other edits boost noise.

✔ **Sharpen:** If necessary, I sharpen again (noise reduction tends to soften photo details). Sometimes, I sharpen only select areas of the photo.

The following series of edits often make a huge difference in the overall look of the photo. Good adjustments in this category are worth their weight in digital photos:

✔ **Correct brightness and contrast:** I look at Levels and Curves when working in Photoshop or Levels and Color Curves when using Photoshop Elements. I'm also "getting hip" to Shadows/Highlights, and I sometimes use Brightness and Contrast. (No sense in overthinking everything.)

✔ **Correct or enhance color:** This adjustment includes color casts, hue, and saturation issues. I tend to make black-and-white conversions and other colorization decisions here. Experiment to see what works best for you.

✔ **Recheck noise and sharpness:** Reduce noise and resharpen if necessary, but be careful not to overprocess. Take it easy, young master Jedi!

I wait to make the following types of edits because I think they work better when the photo's noise, sharpness, brightness, contrast, and color levels are set. Believe me: I've done it the other way around and been unhappily surprised when I tried to correct the photo's brightness, only to reveal everywhere that I had cloned (ugly!):

Consider postponing these edits until this point in the workflow:

✔ **Clone and retouch:** Take out specks, dust, skin blemishes, and other distracting elements.

✔ **Dodge and burn:** Dodge and burn to bring out highlights or selectively enhance shadows.

✔ **Other artistic effects:** This category includes filters and effects and other cool artistic treatments.

If you're following along with this workflow, edits that alter everything except the physical properties of the photo are now finished. I've reversed or mixed the order in the past and been unhappy with the remaining options. For example, I've cropped a photo and made other corrections, and then decide that I didn't like the crop. To correct the problem, I had to go back to the beginning. As a result, I would rather have a "finished" photo in hand before I make these types of corrections.

Take better pictures

Taking better pictures lowers your stress level when you edit them because you don't have to do as much editing. Rather than have to continually fix bad-looking areas of your photos, you can devote your time to making good photos great and publishing them.

Here are some tips:

Take your shots at the lowest possible ISO so that you don't have to throw noise reduction at everything you shoot. Support the camera so that it doesn't jiggle or jostle. That way, not every photo is blurry and in need of sharpening. Frame well-designed shots so that you don't have to crop them later. Choose a white balance setting in-camera that matches the conditions you're in. Try to keep distracting objects out of the background. Use the right metering setting for the conditions so that brightness isn't a problem. Hold the camera straight and level. Use lenses with good distortion characteristics (although no lens is perfect). Choose a good color profile from within the camera if you use the JPEGs it saves.

Now, do all that (take better pictures) while you watch your kids and try to avoid getting hit by a car, falling into a river, having an accident, answering the phone, getting into the right position, or getting arrested because you look like a suspicious photographer.

 Finish making brightness, contrast, color, sharpness, cloning, noise reduction, and other types of edits before continuing.

The following types of edits change the physical properties of the photo layer; for example, you might rotate a layer or correct distortion on a single layer or on the entire file, as with cropping:

- ✔ **Correct lens distortion:** If lens distortion is particularly egregious, remove it. Try to avoid this edit, if possible. If the photo looks okay and has no obvious distortion, ignore this task.

- ✔ **Correct perspective:** Correct obvious perspective problems. If they aren't obvious, ignore them.

- ✔ **Rotate:** Rotate after correcting lens and perspective problems to keep the canvas unaltered, which is what those routines like. In other words, it makes no sense to try to correct lens distortion after you rotated, cropped, or scaled a photo. The artificial intelligence behind the lens distortion routine has no way of knowing where the center of the photo was, or is, or how to accommodate your changes.

- ✔ **Crop or scale:** Finally, I either crop the photo or scale my working layer to recompose the photo without changing the photo or canvas size. I like to save my working Photoshop files before I crop and then tackle cropping just before publishing. The conundrum is whether to overwrite your main uncropped editing file with a cropped version. I compulsively try not to lose things, so I save an alternative Photoshop file if I want to preserve the crop or a high-quality cropped TIFF for archiving. For a smooth workflow with maximum production and minimum fuss over tracking changes and as few files as possible, overwrite your working copy with the cropped version.

- ✔ **Publish:** Lastly, I save a TIFF or JPEG for printing or publication. It may be resized or cropped. Please refer to Chapter 1 in this minibook for more information on publishing photos.

Caution: Sharpness Ahead

Sharpness is often equated to quality. Sharper images look better. They tend to be more interesting because you can make out finer details.

Small amounts of sharpening brings an image into better focus and improves its appearance. You can often apply this level of sharpening to the entire image.

You have several ways to sharpen photos in most editing programs. Two of the more interesting routines in Photoshop Elements are Unsharp Mask and Adjust Sharpness.

Unsharp Mask

Select the Enhance⇨Unsharp Mask command to open the Unsharp Mask dialog box, shown in Figure 3-1. It has only three controls to worry about:

- ✔ **Amount:** How much to sharpen. In this case, I have set the Amount to 151, which sounds like a lot but is less than you think. You can't directly equate this setting to Strength because the Radius option plays an important part in sharpening.

- ✔ **Radius:** How wide an area to sharpen around the edge being sharpened. Small amounts restrict the effect to closer edges, and larger radii extend sharpening outward. I have the radius set to 0.6, a small amount. I leave this value low in most cases. Experiment with larger values, which increase the sharpening effect.

✔ **Threshold:** Lets you customize the onset of sharpening. At low values, everything is sharpened; at high values, sharpening still occurs, but not over the entire image. I normally leave Threshold set to 0 because I don't have time to try to figure out the correct amount.

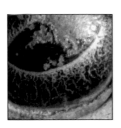
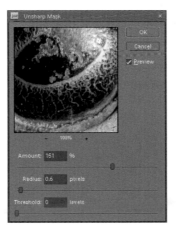

Figure 3-1: Sharpening a modest amount clarifies the photo.

Too much sharpening can ruin a photo by turning low-level noise into a high-level distraction and overemphasizing everything bad about the photo.

Adjust Sharpness

Choose the Adjust⇨Adjust Sharpness command for an alternative sharpening method, as shown in Figure 3-2. This type has a few different options than Unsharp Mask.

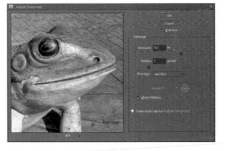

Figure 3-2: Adjust Sharpness is another sharpening tool.

First, select a sharpening type from the Remove list: Gaussian Blur, Lens Blur, or Motion Blur. The former is supposed to be exactly like Unsharp Mask. I can't tell much difference between the three, though. Choose Motion Blur to sharpen an image blurred by camera movement. With this photo (I used the eye from this frog in Figure 3-1), increasing the sharpness better defines the edges. Notice the clarity of the frog's head and the bricks in the background.

Ranting about noise

I'm convinced that most digital SLR photographers worry too much about noise reduction (myself included, but I'm trying to get over it). I'm not saying that you should stand up and cheer yourself over your noisy photos, but the truth is that unless you're blowing up a subject to ridiculous proportions, most noise levels in photos taken under reasonable conditions with anything except the highest ISOs are acceptable.

Photographers often succumb to the temptation to zoom to 400 percent in software and inspect the hair on every person they photograph.

To make matters worse, photographers often use 28-inch, wide-screen, flat-panel plasma monitors that run on nuclear fusion and can light up an entire room, and come with sunscreen so that you don't get burned in the glare. Those monitors reveal every microscopic blemish in photos — and mockingly dare you to do something about it.

Try resisting this situation every once in a while.

The More Refined option is an intelligence test. Either you want the bad version (deselected) or the good version (selected). I vote for the good version. The other controls are basically the same between this option and Unsharp Mask except that you get to choose an angle for Motion Blur.

Experiment with layer blending. Duplicate a layer, sharpen it, and lower its opacity so that it blends in with the unsharpened layer below it. Use the Eraser (or a mask, if you're in Photoshop) to tailor the amount of sharpness even more by erasing areas on the sharpened layer so that they have no sharpness applied to them.

Turning Down the Noise

Sometimes, in the digital photography realm, you just have to get noise under control. This section helps you do that. (To gain some perspective, first read the preceding sidebar, "Ranting about noise.")

Check your camera's documentation to see whether it has either high ISO or long shutter-speed noise reduction built-in and to see whether you like it. I do, but it kicks in when the camera saves the photo to the memory card and makes it impossible to shoot another photo until it's done, which means that I can't use it in every situation.

The obvious route

Apply noise reduction to the entire photo — the massive retaliation option. It's easy to do, too, which is a bonus.

Follow these steps to apply noise reduction in Photoshop Elements:

1. **Choose Filter⇨Noise⇨Reduce Noise to start the process.**

2. **In the Reduce Noise dialog box that opens (see Figure 3-3), choose from these options:**

   - *Strength (0–10):* Determine how strongly you want to seek out and destroy noise. The catch is that the Strength option targets noise (the random, mottled specks of random pixels) that's gray, black, or white — *luminance noise.*

I shot the photo shown in Figure 3-3 at ISO 1400 without a flash, which resulted in more noise than I wanted. Maxing out the Strength option removes much of it.

Look for noise in areas that have a uniform tone. My wife's chin still shows a good deal of

Figure 3-3: Reducing noise.

noise, as does her shirt. My son's face is smoother, a product of the noise reduction.

   - *Preserve Details (0–100%):* Specify how much you want to try to protect edge details in the image. This setting basically allows you to set a high Strength value and have Elements remove noise in larger areas but not overdo it on lines and edges.

     In this case, I wasn't concerned with having sharp edges. I wanted their faces to retain some softness. Therefore, I left this setting at 0.

   - *Reduce Color Noise (0–100%):* Set this strength setting for noise that shows up in the image as variation in color.

     I maxed out this option for the same reason I increased the Strength setting to 10.

- *Remove JPEG Artifact:* If you see JPEG compression artifacts, selecting this check box tries to remove them.

  Find the balance between noise level and softness. Increase the Strength setting until the photo loses detail you want to preserve, and then boost the Preserve Details setting to see whether you can recover those details. If not (or if the result of increasing Preserve Details looks bad), decrease the Preserve Details and Strength settings until the photo looks good.

3. **Select OK to apply noise reduction.**

Although you have other ways to reduce noise in Photoshop Elements, Reduce Noise (no pun intended) is the most practical for photo work because it's customizable and does a good job without blurring the photo. The other options are located on the Filter➪Noise menu.

"Complexifying" noise reduction

You might not need to reduce noise everywhere at the same time and with the same strength. If that's the case, try one of these three options:

- **Select and smack:** Select the noisy areas and apply noise reduction to those specific areas. The drawback to this option is that selecting complex areas with any metaphysical degree of certitude is often difficult, which means that you'll end up with compromises. And, it takes forever.

- **Mask or erase:** The next step up the ladder of sophistication is masked (or erased) noise reduction. Apply noise reduction to an entire layer, and then mask out (hide) or erase areas you don't want the noise reduction on. The un-noise-reduced layer beneath (you have one of those, right?) shows through.

  Note: If your program doesn't have masks, use an eraser.

  Figure 3-4 shows this approach in action for one of my HDR shots. It's an interior shot without a flash in a local bank. I have the file open in Photoshop to show the mask in action. Areas that I masked out are transparent. (Notice the additional work I did as I progressed upward and created new working layers.) The finished, intensely colorful HDR image is also shown.

- **Use multiple masks:** The pinnacle of noise reduction methodology is to apply tailored noise reduction to specific areas of an image by using multiple layers and masks (or the Eraser, in the case of Elements). This time-consuming and often tedious technique works only once because your head explodes afterward. Although the results are fantastic, you can't use the technique on every photo.

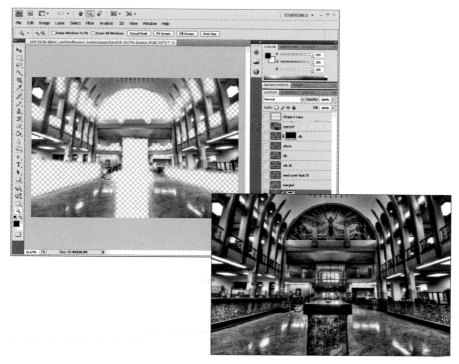

Figure 3-4: Attacking noise with a masked layer.

Fixing Brightness and Contrast Problems

Brightness and contrast are two of the more fundamental editing tasks you should master. You want photos to be bright enough but not too bright, and have enough contrast in them to be clear — but not too much. Got that?

You can correct brightness and contrast in several ways because computer geeks just can't resist the temptation to program the same thing 15 different ways.

Brightness and contrast

Here's the easiest way to adjust brightness and contrast (in Elements, but similar methods are available in most photo editing applications): Choose the Enhance⇨Adjust Lighting⇨Brightness/Contrast command to get started. The controls are simple to use. Raise them to increase brightness and contrast. Lower the controls to decrease. I set the contrast first and then work with the Brightness control to balance everything.

Figure 3-5 shows the open Brightness/Contrast dialog box. I raised both settings to brighten and strengthen this photo of an ice-covered tree.

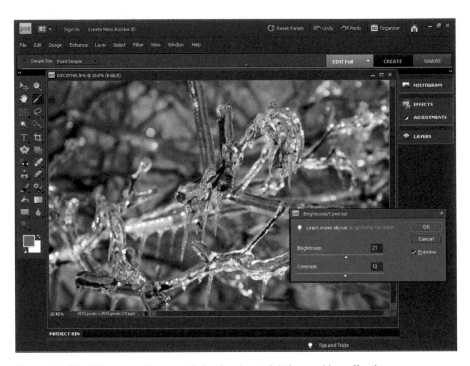

Figure 3-5: The Brightness/Contrast dialog box is straightforward but effective.

Levels

Levels is a step up from using brightness and contrast. It has more controls to master and a histogram to deal with, but the results you can get from Levels are usually worth the extra effort. Don't let the histogram scare you. Its purpose is to show you the distribution of brightness in the photo and help you see the effects of your actions. If you want, ignore it and just look at your photo.

Choose Enhance⊏⟩Adjust Lighting⊏⟩Levels Begin, as shown in Figure 3-6. To lighten an image, drag the white triangle under the main histogram (the graph) to the left, as shown. To darken an image, drag the black triangle to the right. Drag the gray triangle to move midtones up (darkens) or down (lightens).

In Figure 3-6, my wife is blowing out her birthday cake candles with the help of our daughter. I didn't use a flash, but raised the ISO to 1600 and opened the aperture to f/5.6. The photo was still too dark, which makes it a perfect candidate for Levels.

Figure 3-6: Brightening with Levels.

Shadows and highlights

Shadows and Highlights is another brightness and contrast tool. Use it to selectively brighten shadows and simultaneously bring highlights under control. This feature is often immensely helpful.

Select the Enhance⇨Adjust Lighting⇨Shadows/Highlights command to launch it. You have three controls to worry about:

- **Lighten Shadows:** A good tool to have if your shadows are a bit dark
- **Darken Highlights:** Also a good tool, in reverse
- **Midtone Contrast:** The contrast control (affects only midtones)

Figure 3-7 shows the difference that brighter shadows can make in a dark photo. I was looking out my in-laws' garage when I took this shot. Brightening the shadows reveals much more detail than what appears in the original.

Curves

Despite being on the Adjust Colors menu, Curves (see the dialog box in Figure 3-8), is a helpful way to alter brightness and contrast.

Figure 3-7: Using Shadows/Highlights for an interesting effect.

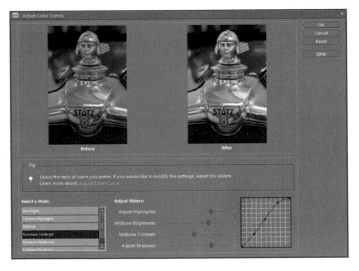

Figure 3-8: Adjusting color curves.

Curves has a simplified interface in Photoshop Elements compared to other programs such as Photoshop or PaintShop Photo Pro. Curves has presets and sliders, whereas the other programs let you plunk points on the curve and move them around. My suggestion is to first select different styles (such as Increase Contrast) and then tweak the sliders to achieve the final effect.

Dealing with Color

When shooting color photos, you must be prepared to correct color problems. For example, the reds might be too bright, or the photo might have an unwanted yellow tint. This happens quite often.

As with brightness and contrast, you have several different tools to choose from. The challenge is finding the right one for the job.

REMEMBER

Don't forget to look for other color routines in your program in addition to the ones I have room to present here. They keep coming up with ways to replace colors, remove colors, automatically adjust color for skin tones, and more.

Saturation

Saturation indicates how strong or pure the colors are in your photo. Shabby or dingy colors make things look dull or prematurely aged. Conversely, overly bright colors can be hard to look at. Your task is to turn the right colors up or down to correct either type of problem.

Broadband attack

The best way to attack saturation is to use the Hue/Saturation dialog box. With it, you can strengthen or weaken the entire range of colors in the photo (or selectively tweak specific hues, but that topic is in the next section).

Select the Enhance➪Adjust Color➪Adjust Hue/Saturation command to open the Hue/Saturation dialog box, shown in Figure 3-9. To increase the saturation, simply raise the level. To lower it, lower the level.

Some editors (Photoshop and PaintShop Photo Pro) have vibrancy controls in addition to saturation. They increase or decrease saturation in unsaturated areas, allowing you to boost muted colors without blasting out the entire photo.

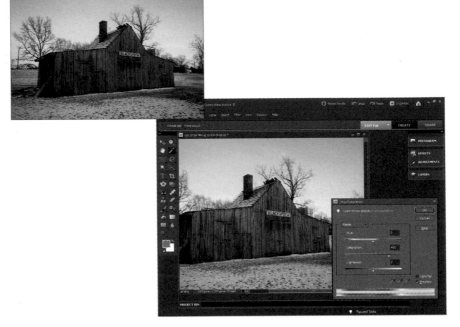

Figure 3-9: Saturating all colors simultaneously.

Targeted color tweakery

It's possible, and often desirable, to selectively saturate or desaturate specific color bands. Use one of the following dialog boxes to try it out:

- **Hue/Saturation:** To target a specific hue, select it from the drop-down list and then raise or lower the saturation (see Figure 3-10). It's as easy as pie.

- **Color Variations:** Another method of selective saturation and desaturation is Color Variations. This series of thumbnails in different colors lets you change the color balance of a photo by clicking a sample you like. (I tell you more about this topic in Chapter 6 of this minibook.)

Using these tricks is helpful when you don't want to blow out an entire image with color.

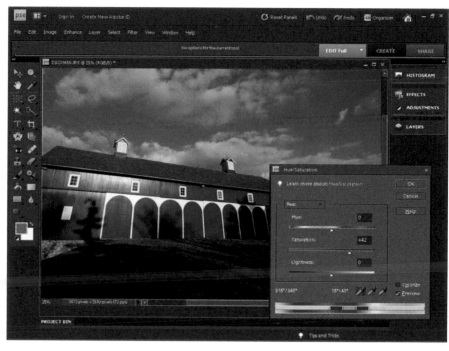

Figure 3-10: Selective saturation.

Color casts

Color cast is a type of color problem that happens a lot, and you may not even be aware of it. Thankfully, you can use these effective methods to combat the problem (which, to be honest, you should handle in raw processing if possible):

- ✔ **Remove Color Cast:** Choose Enhance➪Adjust Color➪Remove Color Cast. Click in an area of the photo that should be black, white, or gray (see Figure 3-11). I clicked the star on the side of the tank's turret. Presto.

- ✔ **Levels:** Similarly, use Levels to adjust white balance and remove a color cast. This option might save you a few steps because you can correct a color cast at the same time as you fix brightness and contrast.

  In the Levels dialog box, click the rightmost eyedropper and click an area in the image that should be white. Anything that wasn't white becomes white automatically. (Theoretically, it's a little like playing the lottery sometimes.)

Figure 3-11: Correcting a color cast in Elements.

✔ **Photo Filters:** Don't forget about photo filters, which I cover next, in barely perceptible depth. Play around with them to remove color cats — er — casts.

Photo filters

I like photo filters. They're the digital equivalent of physical filters put in front of your lens to filter out certain types of light or "filter in" ambiance.

The options in the Photo Filter dialog box are intuitive: Choose a filter type based on the description or a solid color and then choose a density. I'm doing that in Figure 3-12 to cool down the warm photo inside a bank. I wanted the light coming in to be bluer.

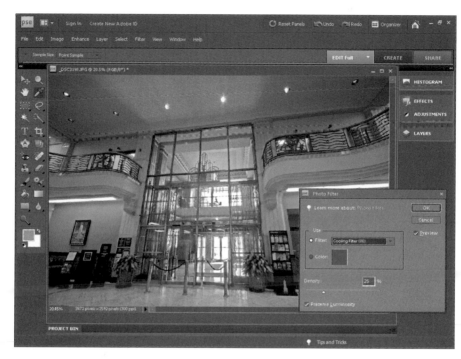

Figure 3-12: Photo filters can warm, cool, or color.

Cloning, Cloning, Cloning, and Retouching

Cloning and retouching are important techniques to master if you want artistic freedom and control over your photos after the fact. Not everyone wants this control to the same degree, however. Wherever you fall on this spectrum, being able to remove dust, wayward camera straps, and other distractions is helpful.

Dust me gently

The occasional dust speck is an irritant to your eyes. Dust can float into your camera body and land on the sensor whenever you change lenses. Even if you're careful about how and where you open it, dust can find a way in. Your camera isn't airtight!

Dust shows up as a big blob in your photo. It's most noticeable in the sky, but also appears in other light, evenly toned areas. I use the Spot Healing Brush as my feather duster in most situations. To remove a dust spot or another small imperfection, follow these steps:

1. **Select the Spot Healing Brush and specify a size large enough to cover the dust.**

2. **Paint over the dust spot with a circular motion.**

   Try the old "wax on, wax off" technique (from *The Karate Kid*), the result of which is shown in Figure 3-13. Notice that I'm brushing just enough to cover the spot. When you release the mouse button, the new material is applied.

 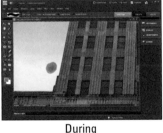 

Before   During   After

Figure 3-13: Dusting with the Spot Healing Brush.

Sometimes, the Spot Healing Brush mangles an area or pulls in unwanted material. When this happens, undo and repeat. Or, if you need more control, switch to the Healing Brush or Clone Stamp tool.

Removing other distractions

Dust isn't the only distraction to remove from your photos. Other objects can divert attention from your subject or make the scene less desirable.

The big difference between the Healing Brush and the Clone Stamp is that the Healing brush blends material you've cloned with the original. The Clone Stamp just plops it down. Aside from this issue, they work similarly.

I prefer using these tools on a separate, empty layer above the photo and making sure that the Sample All Layers tool option is selected. If I don't like how it looks, I'm not stuck. I can erase it or reduce opacity to blend. Here are some handy steps when removing distractions:

1. **Select the Clone Stamp Tool from the Toolbox.**

2. **Change the brush size and hardness.**

   The tool should cover a reasonable amount of space. You don't want it too small, or else it takes forever, and you will have a million potential brush strokes show up. Nor do you want it too large — that also makes your fixes easier to spot. You want it to be ju-u-st right.

   By the same token, a brush that's too hard can clone edges that are easy to spot. Soften it up a bit. Sometimes, you need an edge that isn't totally soft. I've found that when I clone over rocks and similar surfaces, a clone brush that's too soft makes the borders fuzzy and easy to spot. In that case, harden it up a bit.

3. **Check options and select layer.**

   Select the Sample All Layers check box and make sure that the empty clone layer is active. This layer is the one you paint on.

   You have other options (including brush characteristics) that you use in special situations. For example, Aligned returns the source to the same spot after each stroke. This option can be helpful in tight situations, but because you aren't varying the source spot, it can create a discernable, repeating pattern.

4. **Clone, clone, clone, clone, and more clone.**

   Alt+click (in Windows) or Option-click (on the Mac) to set the source location, and then paint over the destination; see this option in action in Figure 3-14, where I'm removing something from the upper left corner of this photo.

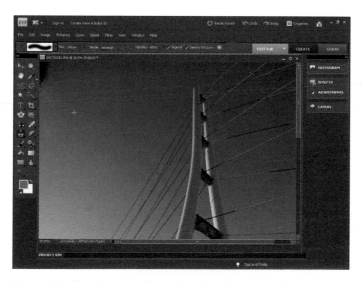

Figure 3-14: Clone away a distracting object.

TIP

Select a new source area regularly. Mix it up, but pay attention. If the texture and tones don't match, the replacement is visible for all to see. You want it to be hidden, and you don't want features to repeat.

Dodging and Burning

Dodging and burning are two (dangerous-sounding!) techniques that you can use to lighten (dodge) or darken (burn) areas with a brush. I use these tools to subtly elevate brightness in areas I want you to look at, to darken areas for drama, or to balance the photo.

Select the Dodge or Burn Tool from the Toolbox, choose a brush size and hardness, and then select a range. The Range option enables you to target specific tones in the image: Shadows, Midtones, or Highlights. All you do is brush it on.

I zoomed in on a scooter light in Figure 3-15. In the second shot, I burned the shadows around the front of the scooter and up into the handlebars. In the third image, I dodged the headlight to bring out the highlights and liven up the scene.

Before   Burn   Dodge

Figure 3-15: Emphasizing the good stuff.

TIP

I have found that dodging and burning work well to emphasize, rather than correct. In other words, I use dodging to brighten highlights in clouds, on water, or elsewhere to accentuate those elements. Quite often, I burn shadows or midtones for the opposite effect.

Using Filters and Effects

Filters (Photoshop Elements and Photoshop) and Effects (PaintShop Photo Pro) are a helpful way to make a photo look artistic. Check out the Filter menu in Elements and play around with some of the more creative filters. I love using them; they add a layer of artistry on top of my photography skills.

Figure 3-16 shows what I mean. It's a photo of a Harley-Davidson motorcycle, taken on a summer day. I took bracketed shots for HDR (see Chapter 4 in this minibook for more info on high dynamic range photography), but this single exposure (not HDR) was converted to a Duotone in Photoshop. (For information on colorizing, flip to Chapter 6 in this minibook and try out a few filters.)

Figure 3-16: Filters are awesome!

Making Distortion, Perspective, and Angle Corrections

Distortion happens when something that should be straight appears curved (or otherwise not kosher) in your photographs. Three types of distortion are caused by lenses, and a few other types are caused by the way you hold the camera:

✔ **Lens**

- *Barrel:* The center of the image bulges outward.

- *Pincushion:* In this most common setting, the center of the image is pinched inward.

- *Combination:* Uneven distortion of either type (barrel or cushion) generally looks worse in the center but tapers off to almost straight by the edges of the image. It's sometimes called *mustache distortion* (but is commonly mistaken for pure pincushion).

✔ **Camera position**

- *Vertical:* When vertical lines aren't straight, you have vertical perspective problems. This problem occurs when you point the camera up or down, which causes vertical lines to either fall away from or fall toward you, respectively.

- *Horizontal:* When horizontal lines aren't parallel to the ground, you have horizontal perspective. This happens when you point the camera left or right of the lines, causing horizontal lines to tilt one way or the other.

To fix lens distortion, choose Filter➪Correct Camera Distortion. The resulting dialog box is shown in Figure 3-17. Pick your poison:

✔ **Remove Distortion:** Repairs barrel distortion (positive values correct bulging by pushing in the center) or pincushion distortion (negative values correct pinching by pulling out the center).

Use the grid lines (select the Show Grid check box at the bottom of the dialog box) to line up elements or turn off the grid to see the image better. You can change the color of the grid and zoom in and out.

✔ **Vignette:** Lightens (positive values) or darkens (negative values) the corners of the image. Use it to correct or cause vignetting. Adjust the Midpoint slider to change how little or how much the vignetting extends into the image.

✔ **Vertical Perspective:** Adjust to make vertical lines vertical. You can also correct perspective problems by using Free Transform.

✔ **Horizontal Perspective:** Adjust to make horizontal lines horizontal. You can also correct perspective problems by using Free Transform.

✔ **Angle:** Straightens the image. I tend not to straighten photos as I correct distortion. I wait until later and then use the Straighten tool.

✔ **Scale:** Enlarges the image. My only caveat here is that unlike transforming the image in the main window, you lose whatever extends beyond the dialog box preview window. In other words, this option crops after it enlarges.

I'm applying two different types of corrections in the photo of a barn shown in Figure 3-17: pincushion and vertical perspective distortion. I also scaled the result so that the corrected photo would occupy the entire canvas.

Figure 3-17: Correcting camera distortion.

Cropping and Scaling

Although everyone wants to be a perfect photographer, framing a scene appropriately isn't always possible. Sometimes, it takes a while to see how a scene should be composed, which makes cropping and scaling (or *recomposing*) a helpful part of finalizing an image.

Elements has the Recompose Tool, which automates some of the process of recomposing a photo. Try it out and see whether you like it. I cover cropping and scaling instead because these techniques work with every photo you have.

Cropping photos

Cropping chops off one or more edges of a photo. You're taking the scissors to it, in effect, so be careful. You have a couple of ways to approach it:

- ✔ **Crop it and forget it:** If you aren't concerned about the final aspect ratio of the photo, just crop it and don't worry about the size or length of the sides. See Figure 3-18 to see the setup for this approach.

- ✔ **Crop it and make it bigger:** If you want the final photo to have the same dimensions as the original, crop using the same aspect ratio and then resize to match. I like this strategy because I have more control over the algorithm used to resize the photo, but trying to remember the photo's original dimensions can be a nuisance.

Figure 3-18: Making a crop.

Scaling layers

I like scaling because even though the layer appears not to fit on the canvas (when enlarging), it's still in the file and available to edit. After I scaled up my working layer, I can move it around, resize it again, or delete it and start over.

To scale the photo layer, select the Image⇨Transform⇨Free Transform command, zoom out so that you can see the photo's edges, and then click and drag a corner handle outward to enlarge the layer. You don't need to hold down the Shift key if Constrain Proportions is enabled. (This shortcut constrains the proportions of the material you're scaling.) I'm in the process of scaling a layer in Figure 3-19.

Notice that the handles extend beyond the canvas and into the gray workspace. That's why you should zoom out.

After you scale the layer, drag it to reposition. When you're done, click the green check mark to accept the recomposed photo.

A limit applies to how far you can reasonably enlarge the layer without reducing the quality of the image dramatically.

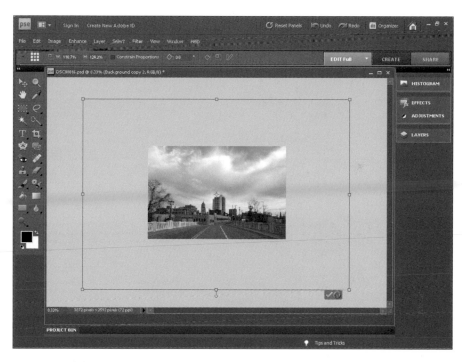

Figure 3-19: Scaling a layer rather than cropping it.

Book VI
Chapter 3

Mad Photo-
Editing Skills

Chapter 4: Home, Home on the High Dynamic Range

In This Chapter

- ✓ **Introducing HDR 101**
- ✓ **Choosing good scenes**
- ✓ **Engaging in bracketology**
- ✓ **Creating HDR images**
- ✓ **Tone mapping HDR images**
- ✓ **Finishing up**

I love high dynamic range (HDR) photography, and I make no bones about it.

I get to go outdoors and shoot landscapes, cityscapes, large and small interiors, still lifes, flowers, vehicles, bridges, buildings, fields, rivers, sunsets, trees, lakes, barns, and other subjects. I can shoot on the move if I want, using fast, handheld autoexposure brackets. I can also capture single raw exposures of people and other moving subjects to create a type of photo known as pseudo-HDR.

dSLRs are ideally suited for HDR photography. dSLR cameras

- ✓ Have large sensors that generate less noise than compact digital cameras
- ✓ Are stable on tripods
- ✓ Readily accept remote shutter release cables
- ✓ Give you the flexibility to change lenses depending on the scene
- ✓ Have a greater shooting envelope (ISO, shutter speed, and aperture)
- ✓ Have a manual shooting mode
- ✓ Often have a good auto exposure bracketing (AEB) feature

HDR photography presents challenges that are different from those in traditional photography. In this chapter, I tell you about HDR, what makes it different, how to shoot it, and how to process your exposures using software.

Understanding HDR Photography

High dynamic range (HDR) photography is an attempt to overcome the dynamic range limitations of current digital cameras and their sensors by taking more than one photo of a scene in the form of exposure bracketed photos. Those photos are merged, using HDR software, to create a high dynamic range image, which is then tone mapped and saved as a low dynamic range image that's more practical and accessible. You can focus on the dynamic range aspect of HDR, if you want, but many people enjoy it simply because it looks good.

You should understand the concept of high dynamic range photography before you begin the technical steps to pursue it. Knowing what you're doing enables you to make better decisions in choosing scenes, shooting brackets, and processing brackets.

If none of that makes sense, keep reading. I continue to explain HDR throughout this chapter.

Defining the definitions

Definitions — ugh. As much as I hate to throw them at you, they help you understand what's happening in the rest of this chapter. If you get confused, check this list:

- ✔ **Exposure value (EV):** EV is a unitless measure of exposure. It's the equivalent of a whole stop (see Book III, Chapter 1 for more information about stops and exposure). For example, the difference between f/8 and f/11 is one full stop, or 1.0 EV.

  (Photography uses *stops* to indicate when light intensity on the sensor doubles or halves. For example, ISO 200 is one stop more than ISO 100, which means that the light is twice as strong. ISO 400 is twice as strong as ISO 200, or four times as much light intensity as ISO 100. In these cases, the stops go "up." When you reduce the exposure by half, you go "down" a stop.)

  In terms of HDR, EV is also used to describe the exposure difference between brackets. For example, a bracketed set of three exposures might have an EV differential of +/–2.0 EV from the center exposure. Assuming that the center exposure is at 0.0 EV (the metered "correct" exposure), the underexposed bracket is at –2.0 EV and the overexposed bracket is at +2.0 EV. In this case, the EV range (from center point to center point) of the brackets is 4.0 EV.

  Don't confuse this range with the total dynamic range that's captured. If your dSLR can capture ten stops of information in one exposure, the total dynamic range of that bracketed set is 15 EV.

Underexposed

Good

Overexposed

Final HDR image

- ✔ **Brackets:** The foundation of HDR. Each bracket is a single photograph, taken as identically as possible except for the exposure. Exposure is intentionally and methodically varied to increase the total dynamic range that's captured. The number brackets can vary widely, from at least two to more than nine exposures. They tend to be separated by +/–1.0 or +/–2.0 EV.

- ✔ **Bracketing:** The process of shooting brackets.

- ✔ **Auto exposure bracketing (AEB):** A special mode where the camera automatically takes a series of photos, each with a different exposure. AEB was originally created to provide photographers with alternative shots of a scene, in the hope that one would have the best exposure. The others could be thrown away.

  AEB, now considered a tool for HDR, frees you from having to fiddle with exposure controls in the middle of a shoot. All you have to do is make sure that your camera is configured correctly, set up the initial shot, and then press the button.

  Most dSLRs have auto bracketing although you will find that every manufacturer implements it somewhat differently. Read the manual that comes with your camera.

- ✔ **Manual bracketing:** The process of shooting brackets by manually adjusting exposure. Most often, you do this by altering the shutter speed and keeping aperture and ISO constant. This approach to HDR keeps the depth of field (constant aperture) and noise level (constant ISO) identical across brackets. Manual bracketing is much slower than AEB because you have to change the shutter speed yourself for every photo.

Dealing in dynamic range

In this context, dynamic range is a range of brightness. In other words, it's the difference between the brightest and darkest areas of the scene. It can be large or small, high or low. Another term for dynamic range is contrast ratio.

Figure 4-1 illustrates a finished HDR image of a mastodon statue. Notice the difference between the dark areas underneath its chin and the brighter areas on the body and sky. The difference between the two areas is the dynamic range of the scene.

Figure 4-1: A trumpeting mastodon in HDR.

Cloudy, dull, misty, or foggy days have less contrast than sunny days with bright features (the sky) and deep shadows. They have a smaller dynamic range. (That doesn't make them completely unsuitable for HDR — it's just that HDR isn't as necessary in those situations.)

What makes it *dynamic* is that the range changes — it isn't the same from scene to scene. As a photographer, that should make a lot of sense to you. You don't set the exposure the same for every photo. Photography is a dynamic exercise, and you have to be flexible and react to changing conditions.

Single-exposure HDR

Many HDR applications let you *tone map* (to convert, or "map," data from a high dynamic range image to a low dynamic range image) a single camera raw photo as though it were a bracketed set. I refer to the practice as *single-exposure HDR* or *pseudo-HDR.* Although it isn't technically HDR, it's closely related.

In effect, you're maximizing the dynamic range inherent (but hidden) in the camera's raw photo, which makes it seem as though there's more dynamic range than there is. You also have different options in HDR software than traditional raw applications, so you can do different things with the photos.

Because of space limitations, I don't explain this aspect of HDR in depth in this chapter. You essentially take a good photo, load the raw file into an HDR application, tone map it like a normal HDR image, and then continue to edit it (if you want) in your favorite photo editing application.

The overwhelming benefit of this technique is that you don't have to set up a tripod or shoot brackets to be able to produce something that, in the end, looks much like traditional HDR.

Sometimes, in fact, shooting brackets fast enough to avoid blurring or significant displacement of the subject is simply impossible. You'll find that single-exposure HDR is a more viable solution in situations in which

- ✔ **You're moving:** In cars, trains, planes, or boats or whenever you're simply walking around.

- ✔ **Your subject is moving:** Most people use this technique for people and moving vehicles.

- ✔ **Your camera can't shoot good brackets:** If your camera has a limited or non-existent AEB function (or maybe your frame rate is too slow), and you don't have time to bracket a scene manually, single-exposure HDR is a solution. Shoot the brackets anyway and use single-exposures as backups.

H + DR = HDR

The relative term high dynamic range (HDR) has come to describe, in part, a genre of photography and certain elements within that genre (file formats, for example). It's relative because the term *HDR* identifies photos with greater dynamic ranges in order to be able to differentiate them from photos with lower dynamic ranges.

Photographers didn't used to make this differentiation — a photo was just a photo. It wasn't identified as a *low dynamic range* (LDR) image. You had no alternatives for comparison.

Achieving the appropriate dynamic range has always been a problem, but past solutions were geared toward metering, exposure, and film processing (à la Ansel Adams and his Zone system). The big issue now is that many scenes have too great a dynamic range for most cameras, including dSLRs, to capture in one photo without making exposure compromises. One end of the histogram or the other gets lost, and possibly data from both ends. Dark areas fade to black and become indistinct. Bright areas *blow out,* or turn to white.

HDR photography tries to avoid losing data by taking more than one photo of a scene. Each photo is exposed differently in order to collect brightness data from different parts of the dynamic range. Although no magic number exists, HDR photographers often take three bracketed exposures, each separated +/–2.0 EV.

I've done a lot of testing (see my book *High Dynamic Range Digital Photography For Dummies*) with different numbers of brackets and different EV ranges, and have come to the conclusion that you receive diminishing returns beyond shooting 3-exposure +/–2.0 EV brackets. Five exposures is better than three, and if they're separated by 1.0 EV instead of 2.0 EV, you see more detail and less noise, but it isn't as though you can tell the difference unless you magnify the images significantly.

The twin pillars of HDR

Like everything else in digital photography, HDR has a process. I call it the "twin pillars of HDR" because it has a photography component and a software component. Both are equally important.

Each aspect of HDR has a unique workflow and requires you to accomplish a different task. Although I explain the two components of HDR in depth later in this chapter, this list summarizes them:

- **Photography:** Take the photos. Take bad photos, get bad HDR. Take good photos, get good HDR.

  HDR requires no special gear, but you'll find that using a camera with a good auto exposure bracketing (AEB) makes HDR much more fun. You can also benefit by having a good tripod and a remote shutter release cable.

  Here's a broad overview of the photographic tasks in HDR:

  1. *Select the scene.*

     Selecting the right scene is important for HDR. Not every scene works equally well, just as not every location is good for shooting portraits. In general, seek out high-contrast scenes with plenty of bright and dark areas.

2. *Configure your camera.*

   Set up your camera to shoot HDR. You use your camera's AEB (use Aperture Priority or Manual Exposure mode) feature or manually set the exposure for each bracket as you shoot.

3. *Shoot the brackets.*

✔ **Software:** Turn your bracketed photos into cool-looking artistic or fantastically realistic images.

HDR requires that you have an application that can merge your brackets into a single, high-dynamic range image and then tone map it. Applications that specialize in this process are *HDR applications*. Some are focused singularly on HDR, such as Photomatix Pro and ArtizenHDR. Others, such as Photoshop, Photoshop Elements, and Corel PaintShop Photo Pro, are also general photo editors.

You can also benefit from having a good raw conversion, photo management, and photo editing software.

4. *(Optional) Convert raw photos.*

   You can throw your raw photos into most HDR applications, and it will work, but using an application that specializes in converting raw photos to TIFFs (ideally 16 bits per channel) produces images with the best quality.

   If you're shooting in JPEG, this step doesn't apply.

5. *Create HDR image.*

   In this step, load your brackets (either converted from raw, unconverted raw, or JPEG) into the HDR application to create an HDR image. This high-bit-depth image combines the data from each bracket into a single shot. By itself, you can't use this image. It exists (in this context) for you to tone map.

6. *Tone map the HDR image.*

   In tone mapping, you turn the impractical high dynamic range image back into a practical low dynamic range image.

   It seems nonsensical, but it isn't. Shooting brackets provides you with a lot of great exposure data — more than you can use in a single non-HDR image. When you tone map, you get to decide (within the limits of the HDR application you use) what data to use, how to blend it, and what to emphasize, for example.

   It's like picking tomatoes at the grocery store. If you walk up and only one remains, you're stuck with it. If you see 50 of them, however, you have a much greater pool to choose from. Chances are good that you'll get a tastier treat!

7. *(Optional) Edit and finish the low dynamic range output.*

Although the tone mapped output from the HDR application is technically done, it's like most other photos — it will benefit from some tweaking in a photo editor.

Selecting the Right Scenes

When I started taking part in HDR photography, I thought I could take a picture of anything and HDR would make it better. I found out that wasn't the case.

Though HDR can flourish in many circumstances (hence, don't hesitate to try it on any scene you like), not every scene is the same. In other words, HDR doesn't contribute the same "oomph" to every set of bracketed photos or single raw exposure.

What's the secret? High contrast, as shown in Figure 4-2. This shot, taken into the setting sun, has very bright brights and dark darks. That's what high contrast means. The final appearance is decidedly artistic. I emphasized both color and contrast as I tone mapped and edited the HDR image.

Figure 4-2: High-contrast scenes work best for HDR.

When I realized how important contrast is, I started seeking out scenes that made sense in HDR. My photography got better, my results got better, and the whole process was more fun and much more rewarding.

If you want to choose scenes more effectively, pay special attention to emphasizing contrast in all its forms. Your HDR will shine!

For more information

If you like this taste of HDR and want more information, pick up my book *High Dynamic Range Digital Photography For Dummies*. In it, I devote much more space to the ins, outs, ups, and downs of HDR, including such topics as choosing the proper equipment, bracketing, converting raw photos for HDR, processing, and more.

Shooting Brackets for HDR

Shooting brackets is the part of HDR that demands the most from you as a photographer. Hey, that's cool. You have a dSLR and want to use it, right?

Set it before you forget it

You have to set up things to shoot HDR. Don't freak out. It's just like most other types of photography. For example, you don't typically use the same camera settings when you shoot still-life macros as when taking photos of kids running around at a birthday party.

Before you leave home

It's never fun to go out shooting and realize at a crucial juncture that you forgot something. (Got your toothbrush packed? Toothpaste? Lens cleaner? Stun gun? Mosquito repellant?)

In addition to packing and preparing, think about setting up your camera for HDR (and cleaning lenses) before you leave. You can do this the night before or just before walking out the door. The point is to save time and lower your stress on location. That's when "you're on," and you should be thinking only about taking the shots.

Book VI
Chapter 4

Home, Home on the
High Dynamic
Range

If you will be shooting using your camera's AEB feature, preconfigure it, if necessary. You might want to do it at home because you don't want to be looking at a sunset that is quickly fading while you're searching your camera's menu system or double-checking a bunch of complicated AEB settings. For example, my Nikon D200 has several AEB settings, as shown in Figure 4-3.

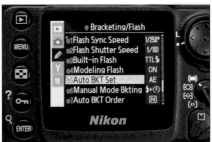

Figure 4-3: Navigating AEB options.

Preconfiguring certain cameras can take a few minutes. After you're done, though, you can leave the settings alone. Check your documentation and read the AEB section until you fully understand the AEB settings on your particular model. In addition to setting up AEB, you should make sure that the file format, size, picture quality, color profile, and other general photo settings are to your liking.

Setting up on location

When you arrive on the scene, unload your gear and pick a vantage point to set up. You have both physical and camera tasks to perform:

✓ **Physical setup:** Connect all devices that need connecting:

- *Lens:* Attach the lens, if necessary. At some point, you should remove the lens cap and make sure that the lens is clean.

- *Tripod:* If you plan to use a tripod, get it out and set it up. Make sure that it's steady and won't tip over. Level it, if you want. Mount your camera securely.

- *Level camera:* Level your camera with a hot shoe bubble level, if you want, or by eyeballing it. I carry around a small level and set it across the hot shoe, but you don't have to be quite as geeky about it.

- *Remote:* Attach your remote shutter release cord or set up your wireless gear. Try not to trip over the remote shutter release cable. (I have done that — ripped it right out of the camera!)

- *Remote flash:* If you're using an external flash, attach it. Don't forget to turn it on when you're ready.

✓ **Power on and configure:** Turn on your camera and complete these basic settings:

- *Batteries:* Double-check your camera's remaining battery power. If necessary, change drained batteries between bracketed sets. Changing them between brackets ruins your composition. Also, confirm that you have enough memory card space to store the photos. Bracketing eats up space!

- *Set Release (Drive) mode:* For AEB, set the release mode to high speed, continuous, or high speed continuous so that you can take the bracketed shots with one press of the shutter release button and in the shortest amount of time.

  If you're manually bracketing, set to single-shot.

- *Flash:* Turn off the flash, if you don't need it.

- *ISO:* Set ISO to a minimum to control noise.

- *White balance:* Set the white balance to match the scene if you're a "striver" (an overachiever who tries hard). Otherwise, leave it on Auto.

Handheld HDR

If you have a fast enough frame rate and AEB, you may want to ditch your tripod and try shooting handheld brackets. However, the shutter speed must be fast enough to avoid blurring.

(I recommend using lens-mounted vibration reduction and image stabilization or a camera body antishake system for handheld HDR. It's good for a few stops of shutter speed if you're on the edge. The HDR software will have to align the photos more than if you were using a tripod, anyway, so a few pixels here and there doesn't matter. If you don't need it, turn it off.)

For example, taking exterior shots in good light allows a fast shutter speed, even at an aperture such as f/8. Interior shooting is another story. It isn't unheard of for the bright end of a bracketed set to take a few seconds indoors at ISO 100. If you can't increase the shutter speed enough to avoid blurring and you don't want to raise ISO, grab a tripod.

Raise ISO as a last resort. HDR tends to multiply noise.

- *Noise reduction (NR):* Turn off in-camera noise reduction to ensure a good frame rate (AEB).

- *Vibration reduction (VR):* If you want to go all-out, turn off vibration reduction, or antishake, if you're shooting brackets and using a tripod. (Camera manuals make a point of telling you to do so.)

   This is if you want to be really nerdy about things. I've made just about every mistake possible shooting HDR, including forgetting to turn off anti-shake or vibration reduction. Forgetting to turn off VR, however, isn't going to make that much of a difference in the final, tone mapped result.

- *Metering:* Choose a metering mode for the best center exposure (the one at 0.0 EV).

   Most often, I use Multi segment (Sony) or 3D Matrix II (Nikon). Other brands have different names for it, and Canon calls it evaluative metering. The point is that the camera considers the entire frame when evaluating the brightness level of the scene.

   (See Book III, Chapter 1 for more information on exposure and metering.)

   If in doubt, look to see whether the center bracket (0.0 EV) is a good photo. (**Hint:** Take some test shots if you're in doubt). If it is, the metering is probably fine, even if it isn't scientifically calibrated and fully verified by the Department of Weights, Measures, and Meters. If the central subject is too bright or in too much shadow, you might consider changing to Spot or Center-Weighted mode.

- *Focus:* Choose a focus mode that works best for the given situation.

  Most of the time, autofocusing is preferred. If the camera has trouble achieving focus, you may have to tell Scotty, down in Engineering, to kick in the manual override and handle it yourself.

- *Confirm the file format, picture quality, color profile, and other photo settings.*

Shooting brackets manually

Whether you have a camera that shoots AEB or not, learning to shoot manual brackets is helpful. After a bit of practice, HDR photography (brackets and exposure and the other aspects or terminology) become imprinted on your brain. You can also get better at working with your camera this way.

Follow these steps to manually bracket a scene with three exposures taken at –2.0, 0.0, and +2.0 EV.

1. **Enter manual shooting mode.**

2. **Compose the scene.**

   Focus manually, if you want.

3. **Meter.**

   Press the shutter release button halfway to see an initial meter reading. You then have the information necessary to set up the camera for the first shot. In other words, the camera shows you what the exposure is (over- or underexposed or perfect), given your current settings.

   If you're using autofocus, make sure to get good focus as you meter.

4. **Set the shutter speed so that the EV meter reads –2.0 EV.**

   The chances are slim that your camera is set up at the perfect exposure before metering. You should have its aperture and ISO dialed in but leave the shutter speed alone. Therefore, when you meter, the reading tells you whether you must, at the current shutter speed, increase or decrease the shutter speed.

   The point of this step is to change the shutter speed so that the exposure index reads –2.0 EV to be able to photograph the underexposed bracket, as shown in Figure 4-4. In that case, in manual mode, I metered at +1.0 EV with an ISO of 100, an aperture of f/8, and an initial shutter speed of half a second.

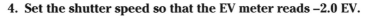

   Figure 4-4: Move the exposure from the first reading to –2.0 EV to set your first bracket.

   For most cameras, three "clicks" of shutter speed equal 1.0 EV. Therefore, if the camera says that you're at +1.0 EV, shorten the shutter speed (remember that faster shutter speeds result in less exposure) by nine increments.

5. Shoot the underexposed bracket.

Figure 4-5 shows an underexposed photo of a nice tree on campus. I had finished shooting for the evening and was walking to my van when the tree caught my attention. The sky and clouds show up well at –2.0 EV and f/8, and none of the highlights are blown out.

Figure 4-5: Pay attention to clouds and highlights in this bracket.

Book VI
Chapter 4

Home, Home on the
High Dynamic
Range

6. Set the shutter speed so that the EV meter reads 0.0 EV.

You're lengthening the shutter speed, as shown by the meter in Figure 4-6. This raises the exposure because the camera lets in more light to strike the sensor.

7. Shoot the center bracket.

8. Set the shutter speed so that the EV meter reads +2.0 EV.

The shutter speed is slowing again. The final bracket is at 1 second — good reason to have a tripod. I could have opened up the aperture or raised the ISO if I needed to shorten the overall speed of these brackets.

9. Shoot the overexposed bracket.

The final sequence of this bracketed set is shown in Figure 4-7. Notice that the sky is completely washed out, but details in the tree and background are brought out. That's what bracketing does.

Figure 4-6: Shadows are brightening, but highlights are, too.

Figure 4-7: Highlights are blown out; it's okay for this bracket.

Over time, you should be able to knock out a bracket of three to five exposures fairly quickly, assuming that the shutter speeds are reasonably fast. You can then overcome some, but not all, cloud movement. The final, tone mapped image is shown in Figure 4-8.

Figure 4-8: The finished image.

Shooting brackets with AEB

Auto bracketing is the bee's knees. It transfers a tremendous amount of workload from you to your camera, making the process more reliable and much faster. (Be sure to tip your camera afterward by giving it a healthy battery recharge.)

Follow these steps to shoot autoexposure brackets. This example consists of five brackets at +/–1.0 EV, as shown on the meter in Figure 4-9.

Figure 4-9: Five brackets selected with a range of +/–1.0 EV between each shot.

1. **Choose a shooting mode.**

   Depending on you and your camera, you may want it to be in fully manual mode, but you can also decide on something a little more automatic. I normally choose Manual mode, even when shooting AEB. That way, I know what's going on. Then I have to set the initial shutter speed to reach 0.0 EV before firing away.

   Double-check your camera's manual to make sure that your shooting mode and AEB are simpatico.

2. **Enable auto exposure bracketing.**

   You have to turn on AEB. For some cameras (such as Sony), AEB may be accessed from the Drive button. Other cameras may have a Bracket or another programmable function button. Still others require you to access and enable bracketing from the menu system.

3. **If possible, select the number of brackets (as shown in Figure 4-9).**

   Many cameras default to three exposures and three exposures only (shades of Sean Connery in *The Hunt for Red October,* where he, as Captain Ramius, requests Vasili to "Reverify our range to target — one ping only.") If you can choose more, your bracketed set will have a greater overall dynamic range.

4. **Choose a bracketing range or increment.**

   From a practical perspective, three brackets separated by +/– 2.0 EV works fine. You may miss some range if the scene has a tremendous contrast between lights and darks. Alternatively, if you're shooting five or more brackets, +/–1.0 EV works well.

5. **Compose the scene.**

6. **Meter.**

   If your camera is in a shooting mode that requires you to set the exposure, do so by adjusting the shutter speed so that the EV index reads 0.0.

   This happens to me because I shoot in Manual mode. If you're in Auto mode or a form of Program mode, the camera should automatically set the exposure.

7. **Press and hold shutter release button (or remote) to take the photos.**

   Bada-bing, bada-boom! One set of brackets coming up, as shown in Figure 4-10. Notice that the difference between each exposure isn't tremendous, because they're separated by +/– 1.0 EV. These brackets cover the same range as three exposures at +/–2.0 EV.

Figure 4-10: Five exposures shot using AEB separated by +/–1.0 EV.

As with manual bracketing, your next steps are in software. Convert raw photos to TIFF at your discretion. Likewise, use JPEG, if you want. Generate the HDR image (I tell you more about this topic later in this chapter), tone map it, and edit. The finished stairwell is shown in Figure 4-11.

Converting Raw Photos

You should read this section if you shoot raw photos and want to create HDR images that take better advantage of the inherent quality of your raw exposures. Then consider taking the time to convert your raw exposures to TIFF files before processing them into HDR images.

Figure 4-11: Even stairwells can be cool in HDR.

Although HDR applications aren't optimized to convert raw photos (the results are acceptable), their bread and butter is HDR.

I typically throw my raw brackets into Photomatix Pro without converting them, to see what I have. If I have a handful of brackets (eight or ten), I use JPEGs and not raw photos to make the "preview" move even faster.

If I like what I see as I tone map the preview, I process the file, save the settings, and use the file as my "concept" file. I then take the trouble to use my raw converter and aim for high quality.

Follow these steps to covert raw photos for HDR using Adobe Camera Raw (in Photoshop Elements; use your chosen raw converter):

1. **Load the bracketed raw exposures into Elements.**

2. **Make a minimum number of tweaks.**

   I normally preprocess as little as possible. The only tasks I recommend are correcting white balance (the same across all brackets) and some sharpening. You're converting, not developing.

3. **Open the photos in Elements.**

   If you're using Photoshop Elements, you can't save a TIFF out of Adobe Camera Raw. Don't panic: Open the raw exposures in ACR, apply the settings you want, and then choose the Open Image command to open the exposures in Elements.

4. **Save each photo and close.**

   You have three choices after you're in Elements. In ascending quality, you can convert the converted raw brackets to a format of 8 bits per channel and save as either JPEG or TIFF, or leave it in 16 bits per channel and save it as a TIFF. The tradeoffs are space (JPEGs are the smallest) versus quality (16 bits per channel TIFFs work best).

If you use Adobe Lightroom or Apple Aperture, you can purchase the Photomatix Pro export plug-in (www.hdrsoft.com) for either application. (Indeed, you can also find a few versions of Photomatix Pro.) It streamlines your workflow by letting you select single exposures or brackets and shoot them over to Photomatix without leaving the friendly confines of your photo management software. You even have the option to automatically import the result into Lightroom or Aperture. The reason I mention it is so that you don't have to convert the raw exposures yourself with this method. Aperture and Lightroom apply your raw development settings to the exposures as they convert them to TIFFs and send them to Photomatix.

Processing HDR in Photomatix Pro

After you shoot bracketed photos, the next step in HDR is to process your brackets (whether they're raw exposures, converted TIFF files, or JPEG files from the camera) into a single high dynamic range image, called (not coincidentally) an *HDR image*.

It's incredibly easy. Follow these steps:

1. **Launch Photomatix Pro.**

2. **Select Generate HDR Image from the Workflow Shortcuts dialog box (see Figure 4-12).**

3. **Select your brackets and continue.**

4. **Set the HDR options.**

   The Generate HDR – Options dialog box, shown in Figure 4-13, has a lot of options, but you click your way through them in no time.

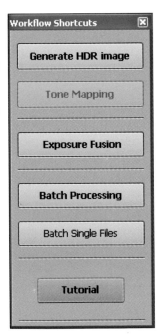

Figure 4-12: Your shortcut to HDR success.

Select from the following options that appear in the dialog box:

- *Align Source Images:* Adjusts for slight movement of the camera.

- *Reduce Chromatic Aberrations:* Reduces red/cyan/blue/yellow fringing.

- *Reduce Noise:* Reduces noise in the combined HDR image.

- *Attempt to Reduce Ghosting Artifacts:* Reduces ghosting artifacts, obviously. Also select either the Background Movement or Moving Objects/ People radio button.

- *Take Tone Curve of Color Profile:* Does its job, but leave it alone. This radio button is available only if you're using images that have a tone curve, such as JPEG or TIFF files.

The following options are visible only if you're using raw photos to generate the HDR image (Figure 4-14 shows how the dialog box changes):

- *Select a White Balance option if needed:* The default setting As Shot should be adequate.

- *Select a color profile:* Choose between sRGB, Adobe RGB, or ProPhoto RGB. You can choose Adobe RGB or ProPhoto RGB now without much concern for portability if you plan to edit the image after tone mapping. Convert down to sRGB when you publish. On the other hand, if you're going to post the result directly to the Web, (that is, save directly from Photomatix Pro as a JPEG), you should choose sRGB.

Figure 4-13: Selecting options for generating the HDR from TIFF or JPEG files.

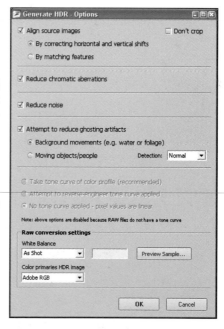

Figure 4-14: Raw conversion options.

5. **Process (or press OK) and prepare to tone map.**

If you use Photoshop, the process is named Merge to HDR. Although it has fewer options, it's similar.

Tone Mapping in Photomatix Pro

When you tone map your HDR images, the software fun starts to happen. The problem is that tone mapping is sometimes so unpredictable that showing you how to do it well is difficult. Every HDR image is different. The key is to experiment with the controls and then practice, practice, practice.

General controls

The first section, shown in Figure 4-15, contains the general controls — they're accessible no matter which section of the dialog box is expanded:

✓ **Strength:** Controls contrast enhancement strength, both local and global. Although it isn't technically the strength of the overall tone mapping effect, it acts like it. For a dramatic effect, raise Strength toward 100. Conversely, to create a more realistic effect, lower strength to 50 or lower.

✓ **Color Saturation:** Controls color strength or intensity (easy).

✓ **Luminosity:** Affects overall brightness by adjusting the tonal compression of the image. Think of this setting, in part, as a shadow brightness control. Raising it brightens shadows, and lowering it darkens shadows.

Figure 4-15: General controls with default settings.

Contrast is also affected when you change the Luminosity setting. Higher luminosity values lower contrast, and lower values have the effect of increasing contrast.

✔ **Microcontrast:** Accentuates local contrast.

Higher settings amplify local contrast and also have the effect of darkening the image. Lower values reduce local contrast and have the effect of lightening the image. The default is 0. Higher settings can increase the "drama" of the image by increasing the local contrast.

✔ **Smoothing:** Controls the level at which contrast enhancements are smoothed out. This setting plays the largest role in determining how the tone mapped image looks, and it's responsible for much of the debate over the "HDR look." Smoothing comes in two modes:

• *Slider mode:* Controls smoothing with a free-ranging slider. Higher values produce more smoothing, and lower values result in less.

• *Light mode:* Shows discrete buttons to control the smoothing strength.

Each smoothing mode has its own, unique algorithm. Think of Slider mode as being beyond the maximum Light mode setting.

Book VI
Chapter 4

Home, Home on the
High Dynamic
Range

Tone settings

One section of the Details Enhancer dialog box contains the Tone settings, shown in Figure 4-16. If the section isn't visible, click the arrow beside the name to expand it.

Figure 4-16: Tone settings with default values loaded.

This section has basic tone controls, as described in this list:

- **White Point:** Sets the white point, or maximum luminosity, of the tone mapped image (the high end of the dynamic range). Higher settings produce more contrast and a brighter image. Lower settings do the opposite.

- **Black Point:** Sets the black point, or minimum luminosity, of the tone mapped image (the low end of the dynamic range). Higher settings result in a darker, more contrasted image. Lower settings do the opposite.

- **Gamma:** Sets the midpoint of the tone mapped image. Higher settings lighten the image, and lower settings darken it. Not every pixel is lightened or darkened by the same amount, however. You're moving the brightness midpoint around, which has the effect of squeezing or expanding highlights or shadows into a smaller or larger space on the histogram.

Color settings

This section of controls contains color settings, as shown in Figure 4-17. The following list describes the controls for the image's color temperature and saturation controls for shadows and highlights:

- **Temperature:** Change the color temperature of the tone mapped image. Moving the slider to the right produces a reddish cast, and moving the slider to the left results in a blue feeling.

Figure 4-17: The Color controls with default settings.

✔ **Saturation Highlights:** Increase or decrease the color strength within the highlights of the tone mapped image.

I often use the Saturation Highlights control as a tool to investigate the tonal regions of an image. Lower the control to the minimum amount, and then raise it to the maximum to see where the highlights are. You can also create different artistic effects.

✔ **Saturation Shadows:** Does the same thing as Saturation Highlights, except as it pertains to the darker areas of the image.

Miscellaneous settings

The Miscellaneous settings section, shown in Figure 4-18, has tone mapping settings related to smoothing and clipping, which I describe in this list:

✔ **Micro-smoothing:** Smoothes details in the tone mapped image.

Higher settings result in a lighter, more realistic appearance and can also reduce image noise. Lower settings perform little or no smoothing.

✔ **Highlights Smoothness:** Smoothes highlights, ignoring the darker parts of the image. Higher values tend to lighten the image. Use this option to blend areas where highlights and shadows meet.

✔ **Shadows Smoothness:** Smoothes shadows and ignores the brighter parts of the image. Higher values also darken the image. Use this option to blend the border where highlights and shadows meet.

**Book VI
Chapter 4**

**Home, Home on the
High Dynamic
Range**

Figure 4-18: Miscellaneous controls with defaults loaded.

Neither Shadows Smoothness nor Highlights Smoothness controls are cure-alls, but they have a good effect if properly used.

✔ **Shadows Clipping:** Sets the dark point where shadows are clipped (discarded). Raising this control can help fight noise in very dark areas by clipping them, which removes them from the tone mapped image.

✔ **360 Image:** If you're shooting a 360-degree panorama, ensures that the left and right borders of an image are tone mapped in relation to each other.

Figure 4-19 shows the settings I chose for this bracketed set and the final edited image. I raised the Strength and Color Saturation, Luminosity, and White Point settings quite a bit. Settings that aren't shown were left alone. In this case, I didn't edit the shot much — I emphasized only the contrast.

Figure 4-19: My tone mapping settings and the final image.

Finalizing Your Images

Tone mapped images don't always look perfect when they leave your favorite HDR application. In fact, sometimes they need more editing. Some images have too much noise (a common problem with HDR), and some may have dust or moving objects or other distracting elements that you want to remove. Many images have lens distortion, which wide angle lenses tend to accentuate. At times, you see color problems — too much, too little, too much of a single color, or the wrong color. On top of all these issues, artifacts can appear in tone mapped images that are the result of movement in the scene.

Use the same techniques I describe in Chapter 3 of this minibook to edit your tone mapped HDR images (see Figure 4-20) and make them shine. In this case, I converted the color, tone mapped HDR image to black and white and then converted it into a tritone image in Photoshop. The old school result makes you believe that you're about to be run over. I love it!

Figure 4-20: Editing is often a vital part of HDR.

Exposure fusion

While writing this chapter, I had an e-mail discussion that I want to share with you.

This person shoots landscapes with ND grad filters. (See Book III, Chapter 5 to find out more about filters, including ND grads.) He wanted to use HDR to capture more dynamic range without the hassle and cost of using filters. The problem he ran into was making his HDR shots look like his filtered shots.

Thankfully, Photomatix Pro also includes the *Exposure Fusion* routine, which happens to fit his needs beautifully. He can use it to shoot brackets the same as with HDR, and rather than tone map them with the Details Enhancer, he can fuse them in Photomatix Pro to create

realistic-looking photos that are closer to the ones he shoots with filters.

Chapter 5: Panoramically Speaking

*T*he results from shooting and processing panoramas are similar in many ways to the results from shooting and processing high dynamic range (HDR) brackets.

Both types of photography require a different setup from traditional photography and benefit from shooting on a tripod with a remote shutter release.

Both involve shooting multiple exposures of a scene.

Both require after-the-fact processing to turn those exposures into a single image.

Both benefit from extra editing.

The key difference is that HDR uses exposure brackets to maximize how much of the dynamic range of the scene you capture. You don't move the camera between shots. The software merges these brackets into a single HDR image, which you tone map to produce a more practical low dynamic range image (such as a JPEG or TIFF file).

In a panorama, you shoot multiple exposures by moving (or *panning*, as in *pan*orama) the camera from frame to frame. You aren't exposure bracketing — you're maximizing the physical coverage of the scene. Afterward, the frames are stitched together in software, which creates a single large image.

It sounds good. Let's do it!

Shooting Pan-tastic Panoramas

I keep this introduction short by minimizing the use of excessively redundant and overly duplicative panoramic words and verbiage and get right to the procedures and steps. Figure 5-1 (cross that one off the list) illustrates why panoramas are so much fun to shoot and create in software. I shot this one at a local university. The weather was great, and the clouds were cooperating nicely. I walked down next to the river (careful not to step in the goose juice and more careful not to fall into the river) with my ultra-wide angle lens and tripod and shot this four-frame panorama.

Figure 5-1: Panoramas bring out the adventurer in you.

Checking your get-ready checklist

The following handy-dandy panorama punch-list gives you a general overview of a panorama workflow and tells you what you need to have with you. Read the list carefully and cross-check yourself against it:

✔ **You have an idea of the tasks involved:**

- *Mount the camera on a tripod.*
- *Pan the camera left, right, up, or down.*
- *Shoot more than one photo so that you photograph more items than a single shot can.*
- *Stitch the frames together in software.*

✓ **You think you have what it takes to shoot panoramas:**

- *You want to try it.* It's not that bad. It's fun to come up with cool panorama ideas.

- *You have a tripod.* Better is better, but even a cheap tripod works.

- *You have a remote shutter release.* Photogeeks use this type of optional equipment — or a self-timer, in a pinch.

- *You have panoramic software.* You can cross this bridge when you come to it, but you need software to combine all individual panorama frames into a single large image. I use Photoshop Elements in this chapter. (Some camera models supply panorama software, such as the free Canon PhotoStitch.)

Shooting the frames

After you're ready to shoot frames, grab your tripod and camera and go find an interesting subject to photograph (the wider or taller, the better). Then follow these steps to set up and shoot frames to create a panorama:

1. **Tweak your camera settings for panoramas.**

   I set up my camera before I set it on the tripod. Then I can more easily look at the top LCD and work some of the controls. Experiment with whatever setup works best for you.

   Ideally, your camera should be in completely manual mode (so that white balance, focus, and exposure don't change willy-nilly), though it isn't always possible. Try these tweaks, at minimum:

   - *White balance:* Change the white balance from Auto to match the conditions you're in (sunlight or cloudy, for example). This way, it doesn't change from one frame to another, even if the lighting is different.

     Strive for consistency across the entire panorama.

   - *Focus:* Consider switching to manual focus if you want to maintain a consistent focal point and depth of field and are concerned that auto-focus might switch to objects that are at different distances.

2. **Mount and level your camera on a tripod.**

   Normally, your camera should rotate about an axis that's as true to vertical as you can get it. Rotate your camera and ensure that it stays level when you point it in a different direction.

If you're like me, you use what you see through the viewfinder to ensure that the scene is level.

3. **Attach the remote shutter release.**

   This step is optional. I use a release as part of my antijostle, dejiggle, and unbump de-seismic-activity strategy.

   I like using a remote shutter release for HDR, in panoramas, and other "tripodded" shots. It keeps my fingers off the camera, which is always a good thing.

4. **Determine your framing strategy.**

   Most people rush this step and just start taking pictures. Relax, take a few minutes, and plan things out.

   Center the scene or your main subject in your viewfinder, and then pan left and right to see how many frames you need in order to fit the entire scene. Plan for a good amount of overlap, and note key landmarks.

   Shooting an odd number of frames works well when you have a central subject (such as a sunset). Put the subject in the center of the center frame and pan out from there to see how many frames you need on each side. You should try to balance the panorama so that it extends equally from the center.

   For less-well-defined subjects, or for scenes where each frame will have equal weight (perhaps a building or general landscape), having an odd number of frames isn't as important.

   Overall, I have found three frames to be a good minimum number, but it depends on the lens I'm using (ultra-wide angle versus standard prime), the amount of overlap I want, and the width of the scene. If you're aiming for a 360-degree megarama, you need more. Conversely, if you're shooting vertically, you may need only two frames.

   As you can see from Figure 5-2, the number of frames you may need can be quite high, even if you're shooting with a wide angle lens. In this example, eight frames was about right. This scene needed more frames because I shot at 180 degrees. In other words, the first and last frames point in opposite directions.

   Try to overlap each frame by about one-third, as shown in Figure 5-3. Overlap helps the panorama program *stitch* (assemble) the frames by providing good reference points. The more reference points, the greater the possibility of a successful stitch in your assembly software.

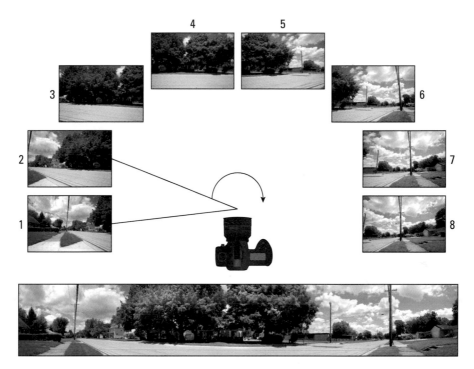

Figure 5-2: Envisioning a framing strategy.

Panoramically Speaking

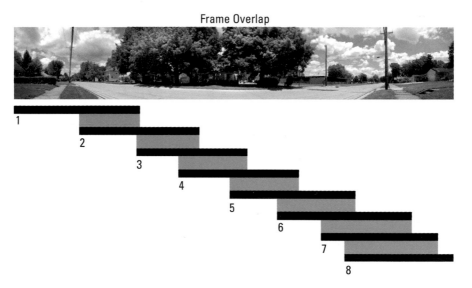

Figure 5-3: Plan for plenty of overlap.

5. Check the alignment of each shot.

This step can be a dry run where you take no photos, or you can go ahead and shoot them. The important task is checking out landmarks that help you identify the boundaries of your frames and how much overlap occurs.

As you can see in Figure 5-4, trees, poles, and buildings make outstanding landmarks. In fact, anything that stands out from the background — and vertical objects seem to work best — serves as a landmark.

If you have a tripod with a compass, you can make a note of the reading for the center point of each frame.

Landmarks

Figure 5-4: Look for landmarks to put in multiple frames.

Take a few meter readings along the way to see whether exposure varies from one side of the panorama to the other. If you like, check your camera's histogram to make sure you're not blowing out any highlights. Decide on a final exposure.

If you're in extreme doubt, shoot a bracketed panorama manually or using AEB. Compare each bracket of each panorama frame against the others and choose the best exposures. You can also turn it into an HDR panorama.

6. Pan to the leftmost frame and double-check the exposure.

Sure, you can start on the right side, if you want. Only personal preference says that you have to shoot one way over another.

Make sure that the exposure you choose is dialed in and set.

I recommend shooting in Manual mode so that the camera can't change the exposure. If you're in semiautomatic or automatic mode, the camera can change settings every time you check exposure.

7. Shoot the first frame of the panorama.

8. **Pan and shoot the second frame.**

9. **Pan and shoot the next frame.**

10. **If necessary, continue shooting frames to complete the panorama.**

The photography task is over after you shoot each frame of the panorama. The remaining task (and the subject of the rest of this chapter) happens in software. Figure 5-5 shows the final panorama after I stitched it together and cropped it in Photoshop Elements.

Figure 5-5: Roads make good 180-degree subjects because they're often linear.

Going the extra mile

Shooting panoramas is a whole 'nother world from traditional photography, with its own set of specialized gear and techniques. If you're not shooting professionally, you don't need to worry about the differences between casual and professional panoramas. If you want the most professional results and the highest-quality images, however, you should do a few things to improve your game.

Buy a dedicated panorama tripod head, which moves the axis of rotation from somewhere in the camera body (where the screw is inserted using a normal tripod head) to a point that is the optical center of the lens. The name of this point is often confusing: the no-parallax point, the entrance pupil, or the nodal point.

Shooting frames that revolve around the no-parallax point reduces or eliminates parallax, a visual side effect where nearby objects move in relation to far objects between frames. You have to dial in this point by taking test shots and moving the camera forward or backward in the panorama head mount.

You can also change the orientation of your camera to vertical (portrait orientation). It's easier to do on certain tripod heads, but it's a breeze if you have a panorama head. The benefit of shooting portrait panoramas is having more photo to use after you stitch the images. You can surely capture enough area so that when you crop the final image, you aren't forced to make incredibly painful decisions on which portions to lose. The downside is that you have to shoot more frames from left to right, but that's easier than shooting two rows or wider frames to capture the same area.

Stitching Frames Together in Photoshop Elements

Panoramas don't merge themselves, you know. You need to use specialized software to combine the separate images into a single image. Photoshop Elements 8 for Windows has Photomerge, which I use to show you how to stitch together these photos. Photoshop has a similar capability (coincidentally, also named Photomerge).

Files and formats

JPEG files from the camera load directly into Elements and require no conversion. You can then start working immediately on your panorama.

If you want to use raw photos for panoramas, you have to convert them to a usable format first. This process is much like converting raw photos in HDR (see Chapter 4 in this minibook for more information), so I don't rehash it here. Simply open the raw files in your favorite raw editor and save them as JPEG or TIFF files. I prefer 16-bits-per-channel TIFF files because they best preserve quality. Photoshop Elements doesn't work well with them, however, so I recommend 8-bits-per-channel TIFFs or JPEGs if you're using Elements.

A stitch in time

Stitching together panoramas in Photoshop Elements isn't difficult. You might need a few run-throughs before you're comfortable, but the process is mostly automated.

Photoshop Elements is a little goofy when you're working with 16-bits-per-channel images. (You might be converting camera raw into 16-bits-per-channel TIFF files.) It prompts you to convert the bit depth before you begin. However, Photomerge gets stuck after the first image and refuses to continue opening and stitching images together (no matter how many times you curse at it), so it's rather pointless. Try this trick: Open 16-bits-per-channel images in Elements and convert them to 8 bits per channel (when you save them, rename the files if you want to preserve the 16-bit images for another purpose), or open and save processed raw photos as 8-bits-per-channel JPEGs or TIFF files.

When you have everything ready, follow these steps to stitch together a panorama:

1. **Open Photoshop Elements and start Photomerge by choosing File⇨ New⇨Photomerge Panorama.**

   As Figure 5-6 shows, the Photomerge dialog box appears, beckoning you toward panoramic greatness.

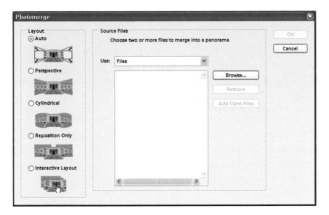

Figure 5-6: The Photomerge dialog box.

2. **Click the Browse button, and in the Open dialog box that appears, browse to the folder containing the tone mapped frames of the panorama, select them, and then click OK.**

   The Open dialog box closes, and the selected files appear in a new, untitled image document as a stitched panorama.

3. **Choose a layout by selecting one of these radio buttons in the Layout section of the Photomerge dialog box:**

   - *Auto:* You're telling Elements to go for it, allowing it to choose between Perspective and Cylindrical layouts.

   - *Perspective:* The center of the panorama remains unchanged, and the outer areas are distorted so that horizontal lines parallel to the ground remain parallel to the ground.

   The major side effect of this layout is the *bowtie effect,* in which the center of the panorama looks normal but the corners are heavily distorted. You lose this area when you crop the final image. Quite often, Perspective is the least attractive option, but in this case it isn't bad (but worse than the next).

   - *Cylindrical:* This projection, shown in Figure 5-7, eliminates the bowtie effect on the corners and results in a panorama where the corners aren't distorted up and out. In fact, the corners are allowed to do the opposite — that is,

   Figure 5-7: Using cylindrical projection.

creep in. Sometimes, the sky bulges upward in the center of the image more than you see here. Everything that isn't a nice, tidy rectangle is cropped out at the end.

- *Reposition Only:* This layout aligns each frame (based again on matching reference points) but doesn't transform them in any way.

The Reposition Only option, contrary to what you might think (photographers often fall prey to the notion that correcting for perspective is always a good idea), can produce good-looking panoramas that don't suffer from undue amounts of distortion. Figure 5-8 shows this method. Overall, it looks good — I like the way the far bridge tower is vertical.

Figure 5-8: Reposition, man.

- *Interactive Layout:* This do-it-yourself option is shown in Figure 5-9. Elements opens a lightbox with your panorama stitched for you (the images it can do so automatically, at any rate) and gives you the control to override the existing layout.

Figure 5-9: Laying it out in the Lightbox.

You can zoom in and out, click and drag frames to reposition them, rotate individual frames, and change the settings from Reposition Only to Perspective. If you select the Perspective radio button, you can even set the vanishing point of the image.

In this case, this method was the only one that enabled me to use the first frame of the panorama. The other methods ignored it. The problem is that I didn't have enough overlap between the first and second panorama frames.

4. **Click OK.**

   Elements aligns and processes the images and eventually creates the panorama as a new image. Each frame occupies a separate layer, with portions *masked* (hidden) to blend together well. ***Note:*** Processing panoramas is one of the few times that Elements allows you to work with masks.

5. **Save your panorama!**

   Save the raw panorama as a Photoshop file (`.psd`) for future reference before you tweak frame blending and make other adjustments. I save the finalized panorama image, shown in Figure 5-10, as a separate file.

Figure 5-10: Fitting the entire bridge into a panorama.

Blending frames with layer masks

Blending allows you to tweak how Elements masked the different layers and then stitched them to create the composite image. This process is useful if an object or area looks better on one frame of the panorama but that spot has been masked by Elements in favor of the same spot in another frame that doesn't look as good. This process requires some experimentation.

Masks in Photoshop Elements (and other image editors) make certain pixels transparent on a layer, allowing what's on the next layer down to show through. Look ahead in this chapter to Figure 5-12 and check out the Layers palette — the black-and-white blobs are the masks on those layers. The black parts are transparent (so that you see through to the layer underneath), and the white parts are "solid."

If you see a strong border around a mask, soften the border by smoothing the mask edge. Or, if you like something on a layer that's masked (a tree looks better in one frame than another, for example), unmask the better tree and mask over the tree in the other frames. You have to practice to get the hang of it because you're working in three dimensions.

Wherever layers overlap each other, you can choose which layer you want to see by virtue of layer order and masking — just follow these steps:

1. **Find the areas that don't look quite right, and click the Eye icon to show and hide the layers to see where the borders are.**

   Hint: You can erase or paint black or white onto the mask to enlarge, shrink, or soften it.

   Figure 5-11 shows a border near my wife's arm (she's sitting on a couch) that looks like trouble. You can see the edge between one frame and the next. This border is a prime candidate for blending.

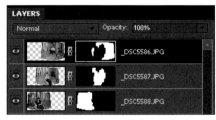

Figure 5-11: This border needs a-blending.

2. **Click the layer mask you want to work with in the Layers palette.**

   Select the mask, not the image. The mask has a white highlight around it when you secure it, as shown in Figure 5-12.

Figure 5-12: Selecting the top layer mask.

3. **Click the small white-over-black box under the main color swatches to select the default foreground and background colors — and then switch them by clicking the color swap arrows above the background color swatch.**

   This step sets the foreground color to white and the background color to black — colors you see when you start painting or erasing.

4. **Select a tool (such as the Brush tool) to paint the mask: Paint with black (making those parts transparent) or white (making those parts solid).**

You can also use the Eraser tool if you don't like switching between black and white — in Figure 5-13, I'm using the Eraser tool with a soft brush tip selected (which is important to keep the edges from being too harsh) to better blend it with the layer beneath. You may find it helps to reduce the Opacity setting to 50 percent or so to avoid abrupt changes in tone.

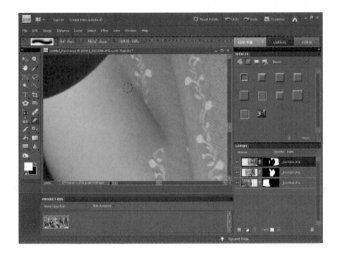

Figure 5-13: Smooth a border by adjusting the mask.

I'm particularly happy with the panorama of my wife, Anne. It's completely unusual. We shot it indoors with a flash. She changed outfits and moved where she was sitting between shots. For this panorama, blending was important. The initial panorama blended one of her poses completely out of the picture! I had to work carefully with the mask to put her back in. Figure 5-14 shows the difference between the panorama I came up with at first and the one I worked to achieve.

Figure 5-14: Sometimes, you have to work at it.

Cropping the final image

Cropping is a final step in creating a panorama, so make sure that you finish other edits first: Blend the transitions, sharpen, correct the color, improve contrast, and reduce noise, for example. This workflow preserves your options longer. If you crop first, you're stuck with it. If you want to go back and crop the panorama in a different way, you have to perform all the edits again to return to the same place.

First make all your edits, and then save the panorama as a working Photoshop Elements file. After you crop, save the image again (with a new name and type) as a final file to publish (for example, as a JPEG if you want to publish the image on the Web, or as a TIFF if you want to print it).

To crop your panorama, follow these steps:

1. **Zoom out to see the entire panorama.**

2. **Select the Crop tool, and drag a border around the area you want to keep.**

   Figure 5-15 shows the crop box positioned over the panorama. In this case, the corners of the panorama bend in and the center bulges out. Unfortunately, you can't do much to rescue transparent areas. Cropping panoramas is a fact of life.

Figure 5-15: Initially positioning the crop box.

3. **Zoom in to see more precisely and then adjust the crop borders to weed out any transparent pixels.**

Figure 5-16 shows the lower-left corner of the panorama at high magnification. The light areas show where the rough crop box was. I'm moving it into the image so that the crop box has no transparent pixels.

Repeat Step 3 on all four corners and ensure that no transparent pixels remain in the middle or on the ends.

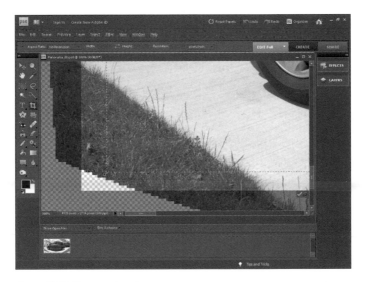

Figure 5-16: Fine–tuning the crop.

4. **Click the check mark to apply the crop.**

    Figure 5-17 shows the finished, cropped panorama of our family's van. I shot this photo with my wide angle lens so that it looks like a fisheye. I moved very close to the van and still had a left-to-right viewing angle of nearly 180 degrees.

Figure 5-17: The Mystery Machine.

PTGui, for panorama lovers

The powerful all-in-one panorama application PTGui is dedicated to supporting specialized panorama features, such as customizable control points and significantly more projection types as Photoshop Elements. If you want to control just about every conceivable part of the panorama process and are considering displaying or selling your panoramas professionally, PTGui is for you. You can enter information about the camera and lens, and then edit the stitched-together frames in the Panorama Editor. PTGui gives you lots of options to control the look of the panorama, the way the frames fit together, and their alignment. PTGui has a developed following and robust support system on the Web. (Visit

www.ptgui.com; the more basic version costs about $100, and PTGui Pro costs about $190.)

Chapter 6: Chroma Chameleon

In This Chapter

✔ Converting color photos to black and white

✔ Colorizing, duotoning, and cross-processing

"Chroma, chroma, chroma, chroma, chroma cha-mee-lee-on" is too large for a chapter title, so I shortened it and will let you look up Boy George on your own.

Allusions to quirky (a vast understatement) 1980s musicians notwithstanding, this chapter walks you through several ways to create black-and-white photos. You also find out how to colorize photos; create duotones, tritones, quadtones, and high-contrast cross-processed photos.

These methods have their historical roots in film photography and printing. People used and adapted the techniques and processes that were available at the time. Sometimes, the result was intentionally unrealistic, and sometimes it was necessarily so. Regardless, you have the tools you need to re-create them by using software. It sounds like fun to me!

What-the?

The following list defines the key terms from this chapter, all in a single convenient location:

✔ **Full color:** A normal color photo. Digital cameras capture colors by wavelength and store the information in three channels: red, green, and blue. You can process, manipulate, blend, separate, or edit all channels together or separately.

✔ **Black and white:** A type of photo taken with a film camera because the negatives are sensitive to light intensity, not to color. The negatives are processed and printed differently from color negatives, and the results are photos in which every object is a complex shade of gray.

Now that our world is computerized and digital, black-and-white digital photos start out as color photos and are *converted* to black and white.

Several of the many ways to do this are conveniently discussed in this chapter.

Some computer geeks use the term *black and white* to describe images that have only black and white pixels — no gray allowed. We photographers think differently.

✔ **Monochromatic:** Consisting of a single color. What makes monochromatic images interesting is that they have many different *shades* of the single color. For a black-and-white image, the color is black, which is expressed in many shades of gray, ranging from black through white.

In certain creative printing circles, the terms *ink* and *color* are sometimes used interchangeably, as in "Monochromes are printed using a single ink."

✔ **Grayscale:** A monochromatic image composed of shades of gray. Also, a color photo whose color information has been omitted, leaving the photo in black and white.

✔ **Colorize:** To add one or more color tints or tones to a photo.

✔ **Sepia-toned:** A photo colorizing that makes it looks old.

✔ **Cross-process:** To use the wrong chemicals to develop color film. A popular technique was to use chemicals normally used to develop color slides to develop standard 35mm film. The result was a greenish yellow photo. Software techniques now commonly duplicate the film effect.

✔ **Duotone:** In the world of Photoshop, a grayscale image "printed" with any number of inks (one: monotone; two: duotone; three: tritone; four: quadtone). After you convert an image to grayscale in Photoshop, you can go to town with duotones (the general term) to colorize them.

Elsewhere, *duotone* refers to the use of two colors in an image.

✔ **Tritone:** Just like duotone, except that you use three colors to colorize the black-and-white photo.

✔ **Quadtone:** A double duotone — four colors. Keep in mind that you start out with a black-and-white photo and then apply four colors to tint the photo. In a quadtone, the result is a complex mixture of shades from four colors.

The rest of this chapter talks about how to covert full-color photos into one of these types of images.

Fade to Black and White

Black-and-white prints evoke different feelings than do their color counterparts. The focus is on tone, texture, and mood rather than on hue and saturation. They can be magical or somber or parts in between. This section shows you many different ways to use software to convert color photos to black and white.

If you shoot JPEGs only, the methods that pertain to raw photos aren't applicable to you.

Working with Lightroom

Use the Develop tab in Adobe Lightroom to convert a photo to black and white. It doesn't matter whether the file is a raw file or a JPEG file: Lightroom handles both with aplomb. Figure 6-1 shows the appropriate section of the Develop tab (I'm split-toning, too, as a way to colorize the photo). This Grayscale method is similar to the one in Photoshop (covered later in this chapter) although the colors along the side are different (red, orange, yellow, green, aqua, blue, purple, and magenta in Lightroom versus red, yellow, green, cyan, blue, and magenta in Photoshop).

Figure 6-1: Grayscale mixing is easy in Lightroom.

Using Apple Aperture

Apple Aperture 3 has some helpful routines to play with color. Activate the Black & White adjustment to show what is essentially a channel mixer, shown in Figure 6-2. Play with the Red, Green, and Blue percentages to mix your black-and-white photo. Notice that I also made a Levels and Color Monochrome adjustment.

Working in-camera

Believe it or not, many dSLRs come with filters that you can apply in-camera to convert your color photos into black and white. For example, the Canon EOS Rebel T2i/550D has the Monochrome Picture Style, which is accessible from the camera's menu system.

If you're shooting JPEG-only with the T2i and other camera models, you create black-and-white photos but no color. What's done is done. The good news is that if you're shooting camera raw (or RAW+JPEG), the camera raw photo preserves the original color information.

Other cameras let you create black-and-white or colorized copies of photos on the memory card. For example, the Nikon D300S has a Retouch menu that copies photos in black and white, sepia, or cyanotype styles. It's like using your camera as a computer!

Please refer to your camera's manual to see whether it has a black-and-white or monochrome Picture Style (sometimes known as Filter, Creative Style, Picture Control, or Picture Mode, depending on the camera manufacturer) and follow your camera's specific steps to activate it.

Figure 6-2: Working on a Friday afternoon in Aperture.

You can also brush black and white in or away (a neat feature) and apply interesting presets. Aperture has dedicated Color Monochrome and Sepia Tone adjustments.

Editing in Photoshop Elements and Photoshop

This section focuses on using many of the tools in Photoshop Elements and Photoshop to convert color photos to black and white. You can use these on JPEGs or converted raw photos (or ones that you open in color using ACR).

Both these program also use Adobe Camera Raw to open and convert camera raw photos. You have the choice when working with raw photos to black-and-white-ify them as you convert from raw or when you open the converted files in Photoshop or Elements.

Adobe Camera Raw (ACR)

Users of Adobe Photoshop and Photoshop Elements use Adobe Camera Raw (ACR) to develop raw exposures. Although its name is the same, ACR behaves differently depending on which of the following programs you're launching it from:

- **Elements:** You have only one option: desaturation.

- **Photoshop:** In Photoshop, the situation is different. In this context, you can desaturate with ACR, but the real treat is located on the HSL/ Grayscale tab. Click the tab icon and explore the panel, shown in Figure 6-3.

Figure 6-3: Going grayscale in Adobe Camera Raw (Photoshop).

ACR (Photoshop) has several options:

- *Convert to Grayscale:* Click to convert the photo to black and white — er, grayscale. The Hue, Saturation, and Luminance tabs disappear and are replaced by the Grayscale Mix tab.

- *Grayscale Mix:* Click Auto or Default (sets values to 0) to apply those presets. Otherwise, drag the sliders to the left or right to change the tonality of the grayscale image. The sliders target specific color ranges and let you completely customize the darkness or lightness of regions based on their original colors.

- *Targeted Adjustment Tool:* Select this tool (or use the T keyboard shortcut) to click and drag the preview and darken or lighten the color region you click.

  This tool is often a *far more* effective way to control the tonality of a photo because you don't have to guess where the colors in the panel are in the photo. Instead, you look at the photo and decide which areas should be darker or lighter directly.

- *Hue, Saturation, and Luminance tabs:* Use these tabs to control the hue, saturation, and luminance of the same color regions. This strategy works if you want to selectively alter the photo based on the original tones. For example, you can increase the saturation on all oranges while leaving the other colors alone.

Zapping color with grayscale

Converting an image to grayscale is a simple procedure. That's the upside. The downside is that you have no control over the process. In Photoshop Elements, choose Image➪Mode➪ Grayscale. When prompted to discard the image's color information, click OK, as shown in Figure 6-4.

Figure 6-4: Throwing away color.

Desaturating photos

Another simple technique to create a fast black-and-white image is desaturation. In Elements, choose Enhance➪Adjust Color➪Adjust Hue/Saturation and then reduce Saturation to 0 in the dialog box, as shown in Figure 6-5.

Figure 6-5: Desaturating an image.

Quick-and-dirty edits

Photoshop Elements has three editing modes: Full (which I'm using in this chapter), Quick, and Guided. Quick Edit includes a saturation control you can use to desaturate photos.

Guided Edit has two options: Enhance Colors (leads to desaturation) and Old Fashioned Photo (guides you through converting a photo to black and white and then colorizing it).

Using Convert to Black and White

Photoshop Elements has a handy Convert to Black and White feature that gives you more creative control than its other methods. To use it, follow these steps:

1. **Finish editing.**

   I like to convert color to black and white close to last in my workflow, so I finish editing the image before processing. This includes noise reduction, contrast enhancements, sharpening, and all other applicable steps. I end up with a working layer ready to convert to black and white.

   This way, if I decide that I don't like how the black-and-white photo turns out, I don't have to redo all my edits. I just pick up the finished color image and go back to the black-and-white drawing board.

2. **Choose Enhance⇨Convert to Black and White.**

   The Convert to Black and White dialog box, shown in Figure 6-6, has these three sections:

   - *Preview:* See the unaltered photo and what it would look like if you applied the current settings.

   - *Select a Style:* Choose from a handy list of styles. Each one blends color information (intensity, not hue) from the three color channels differently. See a comparison in Figure 6-7.

   - *Adjustment Intensity:* Use these sliders to adjust the percentage of each color channel (Red, Green, and Blue) used in the conversion. Alter contrast with the, wait for it, patience, steady now, ready? Alter contrast with the Contrast slider.

3. **Make adjustments to the conversion by moving the Red, Green, Blue, and Contrast sliders.**

   If you don't like the results, click Undo. If you make a mistake, click the Reset button to remove all your changes and start over.

   A little change goes a long way.

Figure 6-6: Converting to black and white in Photoshop Elements.

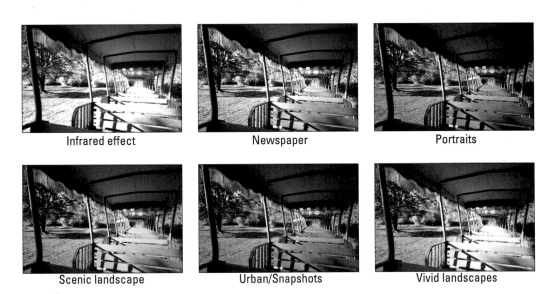

| Infrared effect | Newspaper | Portraits |
| Scenic landscape | Urban/Snapshots | Vivid landscapes |

Figure 6-7: The presets in action.

4. When you're finished and want to approve the conversion, click OK.

The image is converted and appears in the Elements workspace, shown in Figure 6-8.

Figure 6-8: Conversion is complete.

You should save your work, most likely as a Photoshop (.psd) file to preserve the canvas, layers, and other benefits of being a Photoshop file, and then continue editing. In particular, black-and-white images benefit from further contrast enhancements as well as from dodging and burning.

Creating gradient maps

Most people don't think of using gradient maps to convert images to black and white, but the results are quite good. (I happened across it accidentally.) In Photoshop Elements, follow these steps:

1. **Choose Layer⇨New Adjustment Layer⇨Gradient Map to create an adjustment layer.**

   This step opens the New Layer dialog box, shown in Figure 6-9.

2. **Click OK to continue.**

Figure 6-9: Creating a gradient layer.

3. **If necessary, select a gradient from the Adjustments panel.**

   If the gradient runs from black to white, you don't need to change it. (You can see it in the Adjustments panel, shown in Figure 6-10.)

If the preselected gradient isn't black and white (see Figure 6-11), select the Gradient Map drop-down menu and choose the third gradient — Black, White.

4. **Click OK to close the dialog box and apply the gradient map as an adjustment layer, as shown in Figure 6-12.**

A *gradient map* is a mask that turns everything beneath it to grayscale.

 You can create part-color and part black-and-white images in Photoshop Elements by erasing areas of a Grayscale Map mask. Select the Eraser and make sure that the background color is black. (Black areas of the mask allow the lower layer to pass through unaffected.) Click the mask in the Layers panel to select it, and then erase areas on the image that you want to remain in color. If you make a mistake, switch to a paint brush with white as the foreground color and paint white in the mask to reapply the black-and-white adjustment.

Figure 6-10: Find the details in the Adjustments panel.

Going Photoshop

 Not surprisingly, Photoshop has a powerful tool to convert color images to black and white. I use it when I'm photo editing because it gives me a significant degree of control over how the final image looks. I can turn blue skies dark, green grass light, and red features to medium gray, for example. Follow these steps:

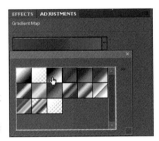

Figure 6-11: Select a black-and-white gradient map, if necessary.

1. **Choose Image➪Adjustments➪Black & White.**

   The Black and White dialog box that opens (see Figure 6-13) has many more options than the Photoshop Elements method.

2. **(Optional) Select a preconfigured preset from the Preset drop-down list.**

   Options include such choices as Darker, High Contrast Red Filter, and Yellow Filter. Scroll the list to find one you like.

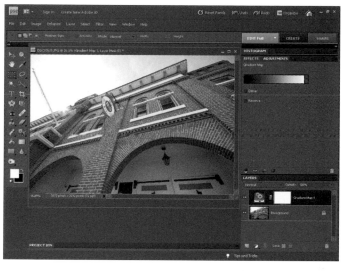

Figure 6-12: The finished adjustment layer.

3. **Use the color sliders to alter color percentages.**

   These six colors create the tonal mixture of the black and white. For example, increasing the amount with the Blues slider increases the intensity of the blue channel during conversion, which lightens the resulting grayscale image. This action makes skies, water, and other blue objects lighter.

   You can, therefore, lighten or darken specific areas of the black-and-white image by increasing or decreasing the color percentage of one of the six colors. Choose the color that's dominant in the area you're working in.

   Be sure to select the Preview check box to see your changes in real time.

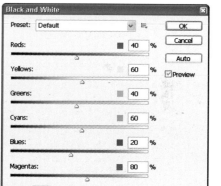

Figure 6-13: The Black and White dialog box, in color.

4. **(Optional) You may also click in the image, as shown in Figure 6-14, and then drag left or right to decrease or increase the color percentage based on the source color of the area you clicked.**

   This method is a fast and effective way to modify tones in a black-and-white image.

   You're not colorizing the image when you make changes to the color sliders. Instead, you're adjusting the gray tone of the specific color you choose. Then you can turn blues dark gray and reds light gray.

Figure 6-14: Click and drag left or right to alter the tonality.

5. **(Optional) Click the Auto button to let Photoshop assign color percentages based on its own best judgment.**

6. **(Optional) Colorize.**

   If you want now to colorize the image, select the Tint check box and then click the Color Picker to select a colorizing tone. Alternatively, control the color by modifying the hue, and control strength with saturation. Then click OK.

7. **When you're happy with the results, click OK.**

   The final photo is shown in Figure 6-15. I'm happy with it. It represents a good example of how black and white can save an otherwise uninteresting color photo. I was able to emphasize contrast, sharpness, and tone.

Figure 6-15: The finished conversion.

Using Corel PaintShop Photo Pro X3

PaintShop Photo Pro has several ways to convert color photos to black and white. The Channel Mixer is most effective, but I like using the Time Machine and Black and White Film effect as well:

- ✔ **Grayscale:** Choose Image⇨Grayscale to discard color information.
- ✔ **Desaturation:** Choose Adjust⇨Hue and Saturation⇨Hue/Saturation/ Lightness to desaturate.
- ✔ **Channel Mixer:** Choose Adjust⇨Color⇨Channel Mixer, choose Monochrome, and then adjust the source channel mixture to create custom black-and-white photos.
- ✔ **Time Machine:** Choose Effects⇨Photo Effects⇨Time Machine to select old photo styles, such as Cyanotype.
- ✔ **Black and White effect:** Choose Effects⇨Photo Effects⇨Black and White Film to create interesting black-and-white film (duh) effects. The dialog box is shown in Figure 6-16. Choose a color, set the brightness, and add clarity to the photo to produce the effect.

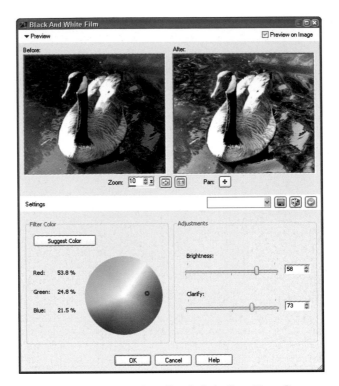

Figure 6-16: Using a creative effect in PaintShop Photo Pro.

Dare to Colorize

Colorizing (or *tinting* or *toning*) black-and-white images overlays one, two, or more colors over the black-and-white image, resulting in aged or other creative effects. For example, sepia-toned images that have the appearance of aging are created this way.

You can approach colorizing images in several ways, depending on the application you use to edit your images.

The infuriating part is that every rule has 15 exceptions in many applications. If you convert color images to black and white in Photoshop Elements by choosing Enhance➪Convert to Black and White, you can't colorize at the same time. If you convert to black and white by desaturating the image using Enhance➪Adjust Color➪Adjust Hue/Saturation (*that's* a mouthful), you can colorize although the desaturation area isn't as good. Hmph.

Colorizing made simple

The easiest way to colorize is to choose Enhance➪Adjust Color➪Adjust Hue/Saturation, reduce saturation to 0, and select Colorize. Choose a hue (color tint), and then adjust the saturation and brightness of the photo. Lower saturation values produce a subtler effect, as shown in Figure 6-17.

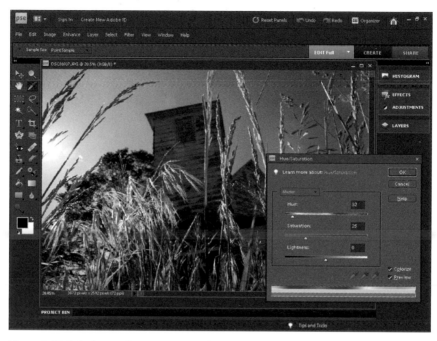

Figure 6-17: Colorize applies a single hue (in this case, number 32) to a photo.

Another way to go about colorizing is to convert the image to black and white, as described in the earlier section "Using Convert to Black and White." Then choose Enhance⇨Adjust Color⇨Adjust Hue/Saturation. When the Hue/Saturation dialog box appears, choose Colorize and then tweak the hue, saturation, and lightness of the photo.

Both approaches are easy.

Using raw processors

Using your camera's software to convert raw photos to black and white is a spotty proposition. Some applications have only rudimentary conversion tools.

Others have a wider variety of gizmos that you can use. For example, Nikon Capture NX 2 has a filter-based Black and White Conversion option. Adjust the filter hue, color filter strength, overall brightness, and image contrast to modify the effect. Or, if you prefer, change the color mode to four black-and-white settings based on different color filters.

Using color layers

An alternative approach to colorizing is to use color layers. Add layers filled with color over the photo layer and blend with opacity and blend modes. You can use more than one color and erase or blend the colors in creative ways. For example, you can create blue-tinted shadows and gold-tinted highlights.

I use Photoshop Elements to illustrate this example, but this trick works in most photo editors that support layers. (A color blend mode helps.) To use color layers, follow these steps on an image already converted to black and white:

1. **Create a color fill layer by choosing Layer⇨New Fill Layer⇨Solid Color.**

2. **In the New Layer dialog box that appears (see Figure 6-18), click OK.**

3. **Choose a color from the Color Picker, shown in Figure 6-19, and then click OK.**

Figure 6-18: Creating a new fill layer.

Choose a basic color from the vertical rainbow and then select a specific hue (light or dark, intense or muted) from the large color box in the middle. Or, enter color values in the HSB, RGB, or Web color boxes. I opted for an orange color in Figure 6-19.

4. **From the Layers palette, open the drop-down list to change the blending mode from Normal to Color; see Figure 6-20.**

Figure 6-19: Choose a colorizing color.

Blending modes affect whether and how layers on top allow other layers to show through. Normally, these layers don't allow other layers to show through because they're opaque. You can change this behavior, which is what you're counting on to colorize the image.

5. **Lower the color layer opacity to blend by using the Opacity slider on the Layers palette.**

   The Opacity slider controls the color intensity, as shown in Figure 6-21. The black-and-white image should show through even at 100 percent because you changed the blend mode to Color.

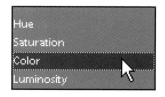

Figure 6-20: Change blending to Color.

   If you have more than one color layer, all except the bottom one must have an opacity of less than 100 percent to allow the bottom layers to show through. You would think that changing the blend mode to Color mode would be enough, but it isn't.

Figure 6-21: Blending with opacity.

6. **Add more color layers, if you want.**

7. **Blend by erasing areas you don't want colorized.**

   This step lets you isolate colors from different layers and have them apply to specific areas of the image.

You can use *adjustment layers* for certain black-and-white and colorizing methods in Photoshop, Photoshop Elements, and Corel PaintShop Photo Pro. These control layers change the way layers beneath them appear but don't change any pixels. After you apply these layers, which preserve the original photo (or *working layer*), you can edit them.

Working with Color Variations

Elements has another colorizing tool — Color Variations. Several controls are available with which to increase or decrease colors in specific tonal regions. In other words, if you want to increase green in the shadows, you can. The downside is that you have only three color options to choose from: Red, Green, and Blue.

 A side effect of decreasing any of the three primary colors is an increase in another color. Red and cyan are thus linked, as are green and magenta, and blue and yellow. Therefore, to increase cyan, decrease red.

To colorize a black-and-white image in Elements using Color Variations, follow these steps:

1. **Choose Enhance⇨Adjust Color⇨Color Variations.**

   The Color Variations dialog box appears, as shown in Figure 6-22.

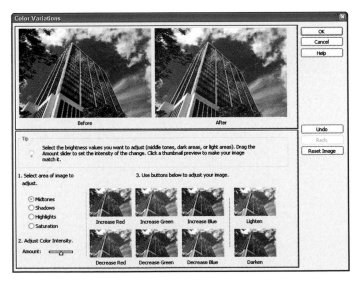

Figure 6-22: Making color variations.

2. **Increase and decrease colors by selecting a radio button (Midtones, Shadows, Highlights, or Saturation), and then adjusting the Amount slider.**

3. **Choose a color to increase or decrease by clicking the appropriate button (Increase Red or Decrease Red, for example). To lighten or darken the image as a whole, click the Lighten or Darken button.**

   Although this method is a simple one, it's sometimes difficult to exercise fine control over the process, and the preview window is tiny. Photoshop also has Color Variations. They are almost identical. One glaring difference is that Photoshop gives you a lot more room to see what you're doing.

4. **When you're satisfied with the results, click OK.**

Duotoning in Photoshop

Photoshop has many of the same colorizing features as Elements (Colorizing, Color Variations, and Color Layers). Where it sets itself apart is in the area of duotones.

Duotoning is powerful yet simple. The greatest challenge you face is deciding what looks best to you, not implementing it. You can choose the number of color tints to apply (one, two, three, or four), create specific toning curves for each color, and choose the colors themselves (by using the Color Picker or browsing the extensive color libraries).

The drawback to creating duotones in Photoshop is that the image must be converted to grayscale, which is 8 bits per channel, and then converted to duotone. You can't stay in RGB, CMYK, or other modes.

Splitsville

Adobe Camera Raw (Photoshop) and Lightroom have split toning, which you use to adjust the hue and saturation of highlights and shadows (refer to Figure 6-1). If you're interested in using unique color effects (perhaps you're making a color correction), check out features like this split toning.

To apply a duotone, follow these steps:

1. **Convert your image to black and white using your favorite method.**

   If you want to quickly colorize an image and not spend a whole lot of time converting it to black and white, jump right into step 2.

2. **If necessary, convert a 16-bits-per-channel photo to an 8-bits-per-channel photo by choosing Image⇨Mode⇨8 Bits/Channel.**

   This step and Step 3 are interchangeable, as long as you end up with an image with 8 bits per channel converted to grayscale. Duotone doesn't work with any other kind of format.

3. **Convert the image to grayscale by choosing Image⇨Mode⇨Grayscale.**

4. **Convert the image to duotone by choosing Image⇨Mode⇨Duotone.**

   The Duotone Options dialog box shows a monotone initially, or the settings from your last application.

5. **In the Duotone Options dialog box, choose a preset from the Preset drop-down list.**

   You might prefer to find some presets you like and possibly modify and save them as your own. (Configure the settings you like, and then select the small drop-down list tucked between the Preset menu and the OK button — within this list are Save and Load Preset menus.) Figure 6-23 shows a preset loaded in the dialog box and the image visible onscreen. I selected the BMY Sepia 4 option in the Preset drop-down list, chose Tritone from the Type drop-down list, and tweaked other details.

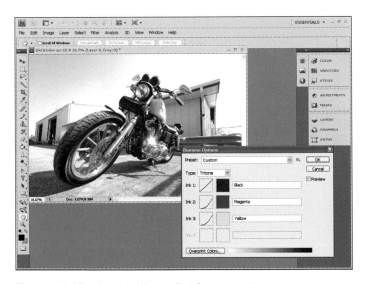

Figure 6-23: Viewing the effects of a tritone preset.

To create your own, colorized image, use these options:

- *Type:* Select Monotone, Duotone, Tritone, or Quadtone.

- *Duotone Curve:* Click the little graph beside each color to control how the tones are applied. Make them darker or lighter, or increase the contrast, for example. The process is similar to adding points on a histogram to brighten or darken, but you're limited to specific ink percentages.

- *Ink:* Click the color swatch to open the Color Picker and choose a new color.

- *Color name:* If you're using a preset, the preset color name appears. If you selected a color from the Color Picker, you can name the color whatever you want.

- *Overprint Colors:* Click the Overprint Colors button to open a dialog box where you can specify the order in which the colors are printed. For example, the result of printing red over blue can look different from printing blue over red.

6. **Click OK.**

   That's it. See Figure 6-24 for my final photo. I recommend saving the colorized image as a separate file because it's now an 8-bits-per-channel duotone image. You can convert it back to RGB if you have other edits you want to make in that color space.

Figure 6-24: Yum — just plain yum.

Cross-processing coolness

You have no direct way to cross-process in applications such as Photoshop Elements, but cross-processing in Photoshop is easy.

Apple Aperture has two good cross-processing presets. The appropriate adjustments appear so that you can edit as you want. Other programs seem to ignore cross-processing. For example, Lightroom has some helpful Quick Develop presets, but cross-processing isn't one of them. You can work around this situation if you split tone. I suppose that it can be an acquired taste.

To cross-process a photo (color or black and white) in Photoshop, follow these steps:

1. **Choose Image⇨Adjustments⇨Curves.**

   The Curves dialog box appears. Photoshop uses curves to alter the in-to-out ratio of each color channel to create contrasted greens and yellows.

2. **Select the Cross Process (RGB) preset from the Preset drop-down list.**

   Figure 6-25 shows the open Curves dialog box with the Cross Process (RGB) preset loaded.

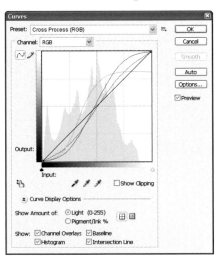

3. **Alter the curve, if you want, by editing the RGB curve or selecting specific channels (R, G, or B) and altering those curves individually.**

4. **Click OK.**

   You're free to continue editing or publishing your image. In this case, I chose the Edit⇨Fade command to reduce the effect to 60 percent. There's nothing wrong with toning it down.

Figure 6-25: Cross-processing is one crazy curve, brother.

Figure 6-26 illustrates both the original color photo and the cross-processed version for you to compare. Notice the otherworldly green tones applied to the image. That's the beauty of cross-processing.

Figure 6-26: Gorgeous cross-processing.

Book VII
Shooting Videos

The 5th Wave   By Rich Tennant

"I've got some new image editing software, so I took the liberty of erasing some of the smudges that kept showing up around the clouds. No need to thank me."

*W*hen I developed the outline for this book, I knew that one minibook had to talk about shooting videos — a relatively new, fun, and exciting topic in the dSLR world.

Not all dSLRs shoot video (yet), so you may not be ready for Book VII. The trend is clear, though: Expect even more digital SLRs to shoot high-definition movies.

With your dSLR, you can shoot movies that are *much better* than the movies you shoot with your compact digital camera. If you compare every benefit of a dSLR against a compact (dSLRs have less noise and larger sensors, and you can change lenses, for example) and apply it to the field of video, the upside is enormous.

Chapter 1 focuses on specific dSLRs that shoot movies, explains movie settings, and walks you through the process of shooting them. In Chapter 2, I discuss movie editing in general and show you specific editing functions and editing software.

Chapter 1: Lights, Camera, Action!

In This Chapter

- ✔ Video killed the radio star
- ✔ Start yourself up
- ✔ Putting videos in context
- ✔ Benefitting from brand-name goodness

Digital SLRs are moving into new territory as they evolve and pick up features that photographers (both consumer and professional) have become accustomed to using on compact digital cameras and digital camcorders.

This evolution is spurred on by a couple of factors.

Compact digital cameras, even the best of them, don't have the same level of flexibility, control, or quality as digital SLRs. Yet compact digital cameras have become test beds for technology. LCD monitors, Live view, digital video, and scenes are all successful features on small cameras. Many people also want to use these features on dSLRs as they make the leap to using more powerful cameras.

The digital camcorder is dedicated to shooting video. What's wrong with that? Not much, really. If you want to shoot video, it's a useful solution. But can you change lenses on a camcorder? Can you shoot super-high-quality still pictures? No. If you want to shoot higher-quality stills and video, you should have to carry around only one powerful yet flexible piece of equipment. Digital SLRs fit that bill.

I use this chapter to show you some of the basic concepts of using digital video and digital SLRs — the mindset you need, which dSLR manufacturers offer digital video on which camera models, and how the models differ.

Vive la Différence

Raise your hand if you've never shot a movie using a compact digital camera.

Okay. Not many. Good.

That means I don't have to give a tedious explanation of what movies are and how they're different from still photographs.

Do you have a television? It has moving pictures. If you've ever seen a magazine, you know that it contains still photographs.

So you know what movies are. Now I want you to think about how the differences between still pictures and movies affect you as a photographer and turn you into a videographer:

- ✏ **Movement:** As a photographer, I have to worry about camera shake for about 1/30 of a second. It ends quickly. Using faster shutter speeds, I don't even have to think about it.

  It's a different story when you're shooting video. Figure 1-1 shows my son rounding the bases. He's moving so fast that he's blurring, and I'm holding the camera with no support — the worst of both worlds.

Figure 1-1: Beware of camera shake and subject blur.

When you shoot handheld videos, you have to continually fight camera movement. Your videos are jumpier and look more "homemade" than if you shoot an award-winning still photo with the same camera.

When you set up your camera on a tripod, camera shake disappears but you still may have to deal with panning if you want to follow the action.

Don't worry about camera shake or following the subject when you set up your camera on a tripod and shoot a stationary object (such as the evening news). Figure 1-2 shows a still from a video where my son reviewed his toy.

Figure 1-2: Sitting still makes shooting videos easier.

✔ **Sound:** Sound adds another dimension to video that isn't possible in still shots. You not only need to concentrate on shooting good videos but also on avoiding the urge to eat crunchy snacks near the camera while it's rolling. All you hear when you play back the movie is the sound of your crunching. Quiet on the set!

Sound is one of the best elements of shooting movies. You can get the flavor of what was happening when a photo was taken, but you never hear children's laughter, for example, or hear them say their first words. Sniffle.

✔ **Memory:** Just when you thought that having a few 8-gigabyte memory cards was a good enough strategy to last through a photo shoot, along came video. If you're like me and you want to shoot the highest-quality videos possible (otherwise, what's the point?), you need more space.

Some cameras limit the amount of time you can shoot at the highest quality settings, so you may not need a 64-gigabyte card. Whether you're limited or not, you can fit far fewer videos on standard memory cards.

✔ **Storage:** When you transfer movies from the memory card to your computer, they take up space — *lots* of hard drive space.

Conversely, I treat digital photos much differently: I take thousands of photos and then don't worry about them.

✔ **Editing:** After buying a raw editor, photo editor, and photo management software, you've plopped down a chunk of change. You've invested all sorts of time and trouble to learn to use the software, and you can organize, tag, sort, print, and upload your photos to Flickr.

And then along came video. You now have to learn how to edit video and add that process to your workflow and your way of life. I don't mean to scare you away from shooting video, but I'm not afraid to point out some differences and encourage you to think about them.

This list describes some good points about shooting movies with a digital SLR:

- **Moving pictures:** Not just still photos, they move. Figure 1-3 shows a still picture from a video I shot of my sons at baseball practice. While watching the whole video, I get to watch their motion and hear them as they catch and throw, which is a far more satisfying experience than looking at a single photograph.

Figure 1-3: Video is all about action.

- **Sound:** Still photos just can't compare with video in this regard. Sound adds a completely new dimension that makes a movie much more memorable.

- **Gear:** Use all your lenses, your tripod, and your filters, bag, and level, for example. Just shoot video instead of photos.

- **The digital SLR difference:** Digital SLRs bring quality to the fight.

    Photographers are all used to shooting videos with smaller compact digital cameras that have poor lenses and small sensors and noisy, high-ISO performance. I would imagine that you're as ready as I am for something better.

If you have a digital SLR, a few lenses, the software to edit movies, and a certain *je ne sais quois* (it's French for "I don't know what"), you can "go indie" and become an independent filmmaker by creating your own *films*, not just home movies.

Getting Started

Shooting video requires that you become familiar with a host of new menu options to set up your camera and prepare for shooting video. In addition, you have other aspects to think about, such as lens choice and what to wear to the Oscars. This list describes the most common movie options:

✔ **Configure a camera for shooting video:** All camera models require you to configure your camera for video and specify certain movie settings:

- *Movie size and aspect ratio:* Set these options as though you're specifying JPEG size and quality for a still photo. (Figure 1-4 provides a graphical comparison.) Most common sizes are in pixels, listed width by height:

  1920 x 1080: At the time I wrote this book, Canon (five dSLRs), Nikon (the D3100), and Sony (three new dSLRs) support 1920 x 1080 movies. They're Full HD 1080 with a 16:9 aspect ratio. They're high-quality movies and have extremely large file sizes.

  1536 x 1014: The largest Pentax video size is a 3:2 aspect ratio.

  1280 x 720: The Canon midsize video is Nikon's previous best (the D3100 shoots 1080) — HD with a 16:9 aspect ratio. Although this size is smaller than for Full HD movies, it's still high quality, and file sizes are larger than the standard (non-HD) movie sizes listed below.

  640 x 480, 640 x 424, 640 x 416: The exact size of this standard 3:2 video depends on the camera brand. These videos aren't high definition, and they have a small file size.

  320 x 216: The Nikon budget size is about as low-definition as they come. It has the smallest file size.

  Look in your camera manual to see the sizes available to you and how long you can record at each size. Some cameras restrict the length of videos, even if you have the space.

- *Frame rate:* All Canon video-capable digital SLRs, except for the T1i, let you specify the speed at which the video is captured. The Canon T1i links frame rate to movie size: The smallest movie (640 x 480) has 30fps, and the largest movie (1920 x 1080) has only 20fps.

  Options depend on the movie size you're capturing. Each size has a low and high-speed frame rate, and may have a third option.

  Higher frame rates capture action and provide smooth playback.

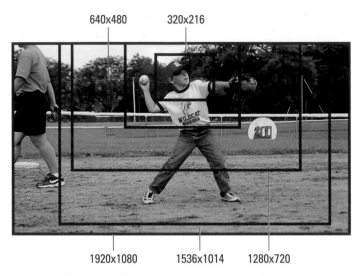

640x480   320x216

1920x1080   1536x1014   1280x720

Figure 1-4: Some vast differences in video sizes exist.

Certain frame rates are standard broadcast speeds for the country you live in, such as 25fps for Europe, which uses PAL, or 30 fps, used in the United States and other National Television System Committee (NTSC) locations. Film is typically 24fps, 50fps is standard for 720 HD, and 60fps is generally the fastest speed you can capture. You can capture at 50 or 60fps and easily edit it to 25 or 30fps, given the proper software.

Figure 1-5 illustrates how the frame rate works. Each slice is a still photo. Put them together and play them back at the rate at which you shot them, and you see a movie.

- *Sound options:* Every video-capable digital SLR has a built-in microphone to record mono (single-channel) audio, the minimum standard. (Sony just upped the bar by releasing three dSLRs with built-in stereo sound.) Because the mic is on the camera body, it picks up your voice more than the subject's. It also records autofocus whirrings and camera clickings.

Figure 1-6 shows the difference between mono and stereo. Just think about being able to hear from one ear versus two. The difference in location gives you directional cues and makes the sound appear three-dimensional.

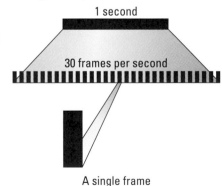

1 second

30 frames per second

A single frame

Figure 1-5: One slice of the frame rate continuum.

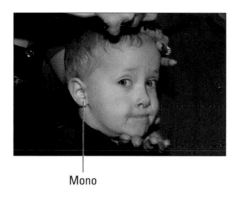

Mono   Stereo

Figure 1-6: Mono versus stereo.

Higher-end video-capable digital SLRs (and all Sony's) have a 3.5mm diameter stereo minijack somewhere on the camera body to raise your audio game. Plug in an external stereo microphone and go to town!

Figure 1-7 shows the Rode VideoMic, a stereo (2-channel) directional video condenser microphone.

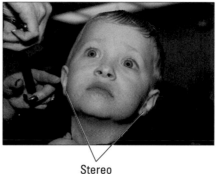

© *Rode Microphones*

Directional means that you have to point at whatever you want to record. Off-axis sound is rejected, which is good in this context. This condenser-type microphone is related to sound interaction and converts physical sound waves to electrical impulses. The long and the short of it are that condenser microphones have to be powered (in this case, by batteries). Because of their design, they're more sensitive than dynamic microphones.

Figure 1-7: Good-looking video mic attached to a digital SLR.

Not all microphones are as cool as the Rode VideoMic. Some just plug in and record sound. I use Rode microphones in my studio, so I was glad to see this one and write about it in this book.

If you want no sound, disable it from the Movie menu.

- *Microphone sensitivity:* Sound levels are generally set by the camera and automatically optimized. Nikon cameras let you adjust microphone sensitivity before you start recording.

- *Live view mode:* Nikon in particular has two types of Live view: Handheld and Tripod. Choose the option that suits your situation.

   Canon has a few different Live view focusing modes: Live mode, Live mode with face detection, and Quick mode.

✓ **Using Live view:** All cameras require you to frame, focus, and manage your shoot using Live view. You cannot look back through the viewfinder.

If you have been using Live view and are comfortable with it, you can quickly adjust to shooting movies.

If you prefer to use the viewfinder, you have to acclimate yourself to viewing the LCD monitor.

✓ **Setting the exposure:** Some cameras give you the freedom to shoot in semiauto (priority modes) or manual shooting modes.

Some cameras let you lock the exposure during a movie by pressing and holding the AE lock (or substitute Canon has you press the ISO button). This feature sounds helpful in theory, but your finger will quickly tire after a few minutes.

✓ **Focusing:** You always have manual. The challenge is seeing the subject well enough on the LCD monitor to create a good focus (*if* it stays still). Some cameras let you zoom in on the LCD and confirm focus before shooting. If that's possible, you create a better focus yourself rather than leave it to the camera.

Autofocus is also available, but may not work the way you expect. For example, the Nikon D300S doesn't autofocus in handheld Live view mode after you start shooting. You get to autofocus once, to set the initial stage — and that's it. After you start shooting, you have to focus manually. Other cameras may support continuous autofocus, but you may find it difficult to track moving objects and keep them in focus unless you resort to Manual mode.

Many cameras have a point-and-shoot preliminary autofocus, which you use to focus the lens for the initial shot. After you begin shooting, you have to refocus manually.

Keeping your subject in focus is one of the more challenging tasks involved in shooting video.

✓ **Choosing a lens:** Choose a lens based on your subject and distance. It's just like taking a still picture.

Realize, though, that longer focal lengths make steadying the image much more difficult.

✓ **Setting up lighting:** You don't have to worry as much about lighting when shooting videos as you do when shooting interior still shots. The lighting basically just works if you leave the camera to expose the movie itself. Unless you're working in Manual mode, the camera operates in a continuous autoexposure mode.

✓ **Playing back videos:** All cameras let you replay and review videos. They have all the same buttons as a VCR (for you old folks) or DVD player: Play, Stop, Rewind, Skip, Slow Motion, and Volume.

Even the largest digital SLR LCD monitor is tiny, compared to a 22-inch widescreen computer monitor or average-size television. It doesn't show you a true representation of the focus of a movie. In fact, the small LCD makes movies look sharper than they are. You can shoot a movie that's completely *out of focus* and not realize it while playing it back on your digital SLR's LCD monitor. (It's a good argument for always reviewing movies on a television or computer monitor before wrapping up your shoot.) I did that for this book — Figure 1-8 is my proof.

Figure 1-8: Beware of previewing focus on a 3-inch LCD monitor.

↳ **Editing in-camera:** Most digital SLRs let you perform rudimentary movie editing while the movie is on the memory card and in the camera. Most often, the process is limited to trimming the beginning or end of the movie.

↳ **Viewing externally:** Use the HDMI or A/V cable to connect your camera to a television and play back or review your movies on a larger screen.

Focusing on a Process

Following a video workflow isn't much different from shooting stills. To shoot movies, follow these steps:

1. **Set up the camera.**

As with still photos, setting up a camera to shoot movies is an important step. If you skip it, you accept the size, sound, and other options that the camera specifies by default.

The "Knowing the Company Line" section has general information to help you complete this process.

2. **Prepare to shoot.**

This step is similar to shooting stills, so I don't belabor the point.

Drag your gear to wherever you want to shoot. Set it up. Take off the lens cap, power on, and enter the correct shooting mode for shooting videos.

Moving back and forth between stills and videos can make your head swim.

3. Frame, focus, and shoot.

Take care of the particulars of framing and focusing, regardless of whether you're shooting handheld or using a tripod.

Make sure that you're truly shooting video (and that it isn't just sitting there idle). Look for a dot on your LCD monitor indicating that you're recording.

4. Review.

Be sure to review your movies for exposure and focus.

5. Repeat until you run out of memory or batteries (or the desire to shoot movies).

Knowing the Company Line

Four of the top digital SLR players now have cameras that shoot movies. Sony is the latest to move into this arena, and it has come on strong.

Similarities occur across brands. The steps you follow to shoot movies are generally the same. However, the buttons and specific options are unique to each camera brand, and sometimes different from model to model.

This overview contains enough information to point you in the right direction. Familiarize yourself with the steps required to shoot movies, and consult your camera's manual for detailed descriptions and explanations of every step in the process.

Canon

Canon sells five camera models that shoot movies. All shoot 1080p full HD video, and all have mono internal microphones. All but the T1i have an optional stereo input jack for an external microphone.

The first three models and the last two share basically the same software and operating functionality. The first batch is:

- **EOS Rebel T1i:** A former top-of-the-line EOS Rebel; still quite capable and a great buy

- **EOS Rebel T2i:** An updated top-of-the-line EOS Rebel

✔ **EOS 7D:** New and powerful; probably the best and most affordable camera that Canon makes (see Figure 1-9)

These cameras shoot videos in a remarkably similar manner. Follow these steps:

© Canon Inc.

Figure 1-9: The incredible Canon EOS 7D.

1. **Set up the camera.**

   Turn the alignment grid on or off; set the metering timer, movie size, autofocus mode, and sound option and enable the remote control.

   If you're using the T2i or 7D and you want to record stereo audio, plug in the microphone.

2. **Set the Mode dial to Movie.**

   This step automatically switches you to Live view and blocks the viewfinder.

3. **Focus.**

   Press the Star button to set the focus when in AF mode. Otherwise, focus manually.

4. **Press the Live View shooting button to start.**

   This step is different from taking a picture. You don't use the shutter button because the shutter is already up!

5. **Press the Live View shooting button to stop.**

The other two cameras I mention operate somewhat differently from other Canon dSLRs:

✔ **EOS 5D Mark II:** The Canon full-frame dSLR with video.

✔ **EOS 1D Mark IV:** A stunner of a cropped-frame camera. You can shoot commercials, short films, and other professional videos with this baby.

You need to finish a little more preparation work to get Live view up and running. You can also shoot in different modes. Follow these steps:

1. **Prepare to shoot.**

   Enable Live view shooting for movies. Set the recording size and other options.

2. **Set the Mode dial to the exposure mode you want.**

The Mark II and Mark IV cameras do *not* have a convenient Movie mode. You're setting their *exposure mode*. The cameras have different modes. You may have more auto exposure options on the 5D Mark II than on the 1D Mark IV. You can also choose Priority mode or Manual mode.

3. **Focus.**

   Focus manually or initiate autofocus.

4. **Press to shoot.**

   If you're using the 5D Mark II, press the SET button. If you're using the 1D Mark IV, press the FEL button.

5. **Press the SET (for 5D Mark II) or FEL (1D Mark IV) button again to stop.**

Nikon

The following Nikon camera models shoot video:

© Nikon Corp.

Figure 1-10: The Nikon D5000, complete with articulated LCD monitor.

- ✔ **D3100:** The newest Nikon dSLR to shoot video. The D3100 improves upon the movie implementation of earlier models. It has a "D-Movie" shooting mode to make things easier and shoots full HD (1080p) video.

- ✔ **D5000:** An exciting, upper-entry-level model and quite a capable camera for the price. Figure 1-10 shows the "vari-angle" LCD screen, a helpful feature for shooting video.

- ✔ **D90:** A midrange digital SLR that doesn't disappoint.

- ✔ **D300S:** The top-of-the-line Nikon cropped-frame camera — quite powerful.

- ✔ **D3S:** The only full-frame digital SLR from Nikon to shoot video. Awesome!

None of the Nikon offerings except the D3100 supports the same high resolution as Canon, and none (again, except the D3100) offers a convenient Movie exposure mode. However, they all shoot in 1280 x 720. The D3100 shoots full HD video at 1920 x 1280 pixels. The D300S and D3S are the only two that support external stereo audio. (Neither the D3100 manual nor the camera were available to me as I wrote this, but expect the D3100 to make shooting videos easier than with the older models. Nikon is getting the message.)

All older Nikons operate in the same basic way:

1. **Configure your movie options.**

   Select a movie size and sound options. Select a Live view mode if you're using the D300S.

2. **Enter the exposure mode.**

   Set the aperture.

3. **Press the Live View button.**

   This step enables Live view and disables the viewfinder. From here on out, you're working with the LCD monitor.

4. **Focus.**

   Choose Manual or Auto.

5. **Press OK to start recording.**

   On the D300S, press the center of the multiselector. You have a different OK button.

6. **Press OK to stop recording.**

   On the D300S, press the center of the multiselector. Your dSLR has a different OK button.

Olympus

Olympus offers no digital SLRs that shoot movies. However, you can take fantastic photographs with your dSLR and not get bogged down by movies. You obviously don't need to know anything in this chapter right away, but if you buy another digital SLR, you'll be more aware of which features and options exist and how you might use them. Cameras in the Olympus Pen series all shoot movies. Though they aren't dSLRs, they're excellent cameras that use the micro four thirds sensor.

Pentax

Both Pentax digital SLRs shoot video:

- ✔ **K-x:** The Pentax entry-level model is shown in Figure 1-11. This great buy competes well with other entry-level dSLRs.

- ✔ **K-7:** The Pentax prosumer digital SLR costs about twice as much as the K-x. You get more of just about everything for the price, except for an increase in video size. The K-7 has an optional stereo input for audio; the K-x doesn't.

The K7 supports 1536 x 1024 video, and both shoot 1280 x 720. The K-7 also supports an external microphone. Both shoot video in the same way. Follow these steps:

1. **Configure the camera.**

   Set the movie size, quality, and sound.

   Set the Movie Aperture Control to Auto (aperture is controlled automatically but fixes during recording) or Fixed (the movie uses the aperture you specify and doesn't change it).

   Enable or disable shake reduction.

2. **Set the Mode dial to movie.**

   This step locks out the viewfinder and displays Live view on the LCD.

3. **Focus.**

   If you're using autofocus, press the shutter button halfway. Otherwise, focus manually.

4. **Set the aperture if the Movie Aperture Control mode is set to Fixed.**

5. **Press the shutter release button all the way to start shooting the movie.**

   Finally, someone uses a shutter button to start a movie!

6. **Press the button all the way down again to stop shooting.**

© PENTAX Imaging Company

Figure 1-11: One of my favorites, the orange K-x.

Sony

Sony has just updated its Alpha dSLRs to shoot full HD video (1080) in AVCHD, the Sony-Panasonic HD video format that Sony now uses in its line of HD camcorders. This combines proven Sony HD video technology and experience with its excellent Alpha lineup.

The movie-capable cameras that were announced in mid-2010 are the Alpha 55, 33, and 560. All shoot full HD (1920 by 1080 pixels) and have built-in stereo microphones. That's right: Stereo from the get-go. Likewise, all these camera have Live view and autofocus improvements to make shooting video easier. As I write this, the cameras have not been released, so full details are unavailable. However, Sony has a history of making new features friendly and accessible to all users. I expect shooting movies will be an easy proposition with these cameras.

Chapter 2: The Video Editing Bar and Grill

In This Chapter

- Getting to know your software
- Editing videos
- Adding effects and other elements of cool
- Exporting a movie
- Deciphering camera movie formats
- Finding video editing software

After you shoot some movies with your digital SLR camera, you'll want to do something with them. Exactly what that "something" is depends a lot on your desire and motivation.

The good news is that you can scale your efforts to whatever level suits you. If you want to post an unedited movie on YouTube — no problem. If you want to edit out some of the bad parts before you upload it to the world, that's okay, too. You can even go as far as to shoot and produce your own professional-level videos, if you want.

Whatever level you aspire to, you need the help of a digital video editor. I introduce you to digital video editors as a class and show you how they operate. Then I walk you through some editing basics and then how to produce a video.

For this task, I'm using Corel VideoStudio Pro X3, an excellent program (Windows-only, unfortunately) that is reasonably priced and has all the features I want you to know about. It isn't the only video application out there, of course — I devote the last half of this chapter to reviewing other available products so that you can make your own choices.

Basic Software Operations

Most video editors work the same way: You import video clips into a project; cut, trim, edit, and apply text, titles, and other effects; and then export the result as a finished video file (that can be in a different format from the originals). Producing that finished file is what this chapter talks about. But first this section gives you an overview of the video editing process.

Understanding the project paradigm

Before you read any further in this section, repeat after me:

"Video editing revolves around projects. Projects can include one or more video clips, audio clips, special effects, graphics, or other objects."

(Okay, you can stop.)

A *project* is a container. It collects and holds media. It stores all your editing decisions and settings. You can associate a project with a single video you shot with your camera, but you really start to take advantage of the power of digital video editing when you realize that you can use *multiple* videos in a project.

You can shoot a 30-second commercial and use 100 separately shot video clips as your source media and then export the finished product as a seamless whole. By approaching video with an eye towards projects as opposed to individual clips, you're freed from thinking you have to shoot a video that is perfect from start to finish. If you run into trouble, shoot the video in three or four takes and then edit the clips together. Watch television and movies to see how professional directors cut between scenes (DVD commentaries are a gold mine of movie-making tips and tricks if you find a talented and talkative director). Projects have video and audio properties and compression schemes that are independent of their source media. You choose the properties of the final, exported video most often when you export your finished project file as a final movie. (Look for instant projects or project templates to help you get started.)

Understanding the interface

Digital video editors don't look like word processors. They don't act like them, either. I remember the first time I looked at a professional digital audio workstation (which was similar in many ways to the video applications I describe in this chapter). I felt helpless. I was clueless about where to start. Part of my dilemma was the interface — it had too many unfamiliar elements.

Begin by mastering the interface of whichever application you use. Look it over and make sure that you understand where things are and what they look like. Hover the mouse over screen elements to see whether context-sensitive help pops up. Right-click screen elements to see what happens. Read the manual.

Figure 2-1 shows Corel VideoStudio X3 in action. I have created a project and imported videos and done some editing. Notice that the project is divided into distinctly different areas.

Preview Window   Library

Navigation Panel   Timeline   Toolbar

Figure 2-1: Video editors are intimidating at first — but you get used to them.

Several main areas are fairly consistent across all video applications, and you should become familiar with them:

✔ **Preview window:** Shows you what your final video will look like, including transitions, text, effects, audio — the whole shootin' match.

✔ **Navigation panel:** Contains the video controls to play, stop, rewind, mute, and repeat. Most often, they're located near the preview window.

A timer near this panel tells you the timecode — in other words, exactly where you are on the timeline. Programs may display the timecode differently, but the last little section of it in VideoStudio X3 indicates the frame number for each second.

✔ **Timeline:** The big enchilada — your roadmap to what's going on in the project. Because you can't "see" everything at once in a video, tracking it by time makes sense. Some programs also track every frame of the movie.

The timeline contains one or more *tracks*. Each track is independent of the others and all play at the same time. They may contain audio, video, text, effects, or nothing.

Some programs let you create multiple video and audio tracks. Some, such as VideoStudio, limit the number of audio and video tracks you can use in a project. In this case, you're allowed one video track, one voice track, two title tracks, three music tracks, and six overlay tracks (which are sort of like extra video).

Figure 2-2 shows the Track Manager dialog box from Corel VideoStudio. Checked tracks show up on the timeline. Unchecked tracks are hidden.

✔ **Storyboard:** The storyboard is an alternative way of looking at the project and usually replaces the timeline when it is visible. Rather than seeing every second of the project and every track, you see thumbnails of every video clip and the overall sequence of events. This is a good view to manage scenes and transitions in.

Figure 2-2: The track concept can be a critical one to grasp.

Figure 2-3 shows the storyboard. Notice that it has three clips. Though you can see the transitions between them, it's hard to see the effects, text, and audio.

Storyboard

Figure 2-3: The Storyboard provides an alternate view of the project.

- ✔ **Library:** Contains a visual reminder of all media clips you've added to the project. VideoStudio Pro organizes the library by media type. Access media, transitions, title templates, and other elements from the Library panel.

- ✔ **Options:** The VideoStudio Options panel opens when you select an effect you can alter. Enter your options to customize.

  Figure 2-4 shows the options for a title (end credit) effect. Options are the meat-and-potatoes of customization. Don't always settle for the default settings. Change things up to suit your style and the purpose of your video.

- ✔ **Toolbar:** Most programs have one or more toolbars with different tools on them. The tools may change, depending on which program mode you're in.

Options

Figure 2-4: Showing the Options panel for the credit roll.

Creating a project

Most often, you have to create a project to get started. Even if you can start working immediately with a blank project, you'll want to save it at some point. Create a project just as you would create a new word processing document. Start with the File➪New Project command.

You can access project properties at any time, as shown in Figure 2-5, and control certain project options from your preferences settings.

Adding movies to a project

You should be able to drag and drop movies into your project. If not, find the File➪Import command or a similar

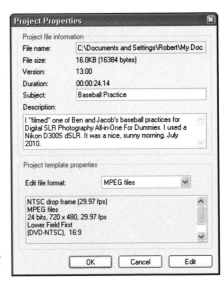

Figure 2-5: Project properties in VideoStudio Pro.

one. VideoStudio Pro has a couple of different import options, both located on the File menu:

- ✓ **Insert Media File to Timeline:** You have five options: Video, Audio, Digital Media, Photo, and Subtitle.

- ✓ **Insert Media File to Library:** You have four options: Video, Audio, Digital Media, and Photo.

The difference between these two options is that the former inserts whatever element you're inserting directly on the timeline. In other words, it's drafted into action right away by snuggling up next to the last clip or the beginning of the timeline.

The latter command inserts the media into your library, which makes the video accessible but keeps it off the timeline until you need it. When you're ready to use the clip, drag and drop it onto the timeline. This technique is the best one to use if you're adding a number of clips at the same time and haven't yet decided where to use them.

Dragging clips to tracks

After you've imported your movies into a project, they're accessible to the editor and ready to be used on the timeline. The important part: You have to get them there. Do this task by dragging and dropping clips directly on the track you want to use them on, as shown in Figure 2-6. The track snaps to the timeline and moves to the beginning of any empty space.

Figure 2-6: Drag and drop clips onto tracks on the timeline.

Previewing the movie

Previewing is easy: Press the control you want to operate, just like on a DVD or Blu-ray player. Play plays. Stop stops. Rewind returns to the beginning. Repeat repeats the entire movie or the area you have selected (if possible) from the timeline.

Scrubbing

Scrubbing involves moving back and forth in the video by using your mouse. Scrub to check transitions and other effects. You can also scrub to look for and examine the action in the video. VideoStudio has two ways to scrub.

The first method involves using the Scrubber just below the Preview window. Click the Scrubber and hold down the mouse button, and then drag the Scrubber back and forth to "scrub" (it's like moving a record back and forth with your hand) the video. It's fun. Although it's hard to see from a static screen shot, I'm scrubbing in Figure 2-7.

Scrubbing

Figure 2-7: Scrubbing isn't as hard as it sounds.

The other way to scrub is on the timeline. It has a marker that shows the position of the video as shown in the Preview window. Click and scrub with it, just like the other Scrubber.

Measuring video in time and frames

Video is measured in time and frames. If you shoot a video at 30 frames per second, for example, it contains 30 still images per second. Switching back and forth between the Preview and the timeline can be a little confusing if you've zoomed in far enough on the timeline to see the "blank space" between the frames. Recognize that each frame is displayed for a certain length of time and then replaced with the next one. That's the essence of video. Figure 2-8 shows how VideoStudio Pro displays the time.

Hours:Minutes:Seconds.Frame

Figure 2-8: Knowing where you are on the timeline is important.

Editing (The World's Most Boring Section Title)

Most photographers want to be able to make basic edits of their videos. Maybe you started recording and it took a few seconds for the action to start. Maybe you want to excise a flub from the middle — no problem. Most editors can handle these simple edits with aplomb.

Trimming video

The task of trimming video involves cutting off from either end any video that isn't worth keeping. You establish new starting and ending points and then trim. It's an easy way to edit a movie to the essential element of what you want to show.

In "full-featured" editors, just split a movie wherever you want to trim it and then delete the clips you don't want to keep.

Splitting video

Splitting video is a fundamental task if you want to cut bad sections from your movie or just separate the movie into different clips. The good news is that it's easy:

1. **Using the timeline or preview window, find in the video the first point you want to split, as shown in Figure 2-9.**

   In this step, scrubbing helps you find the exact frame you want to cut at. You can also advance by single frames to choose your spot.

2. **With the timeline cursor placed at the proper location, choose Edit⇨Split Clip.**

Timeline cursor at split point

Figure 2-9: Select the location where you want to split.

The clips are split, as shown in Figure 2-10. You see a new thumbnail, which designates the beginning of a clip.

Another method is to right-click and choose Split Clip from the context-sensitive menu.

Figure 2-10: The clip has been split in two.

3. **Find the second spot as you did the first.**

   This step is necessary only if you want to cut something out of the middle.

4. **Clip it as you did the first cut.**

5. **Select and delete the middle clip, if you want.**

   To trim the beginning or end, select the appropriate clip instead of the middle and delete.

If necessary, click and drag a clip on the timeline to reposition it, whether you just split it or inserted a new video on the timeline.

Separating the audio track

If you have shot a movie and hate the audio, don't fret. You can separate the audio track from the video and do whatever you want to the isolated audio track: delete it, record over it, replace it — whatever.

Suppose that you have an audio track filled with camera noises. Delete the track and replace it with a voiceover or music. Normally, it's a simple menu operation. In VideoStudio Pro, right-click the video clip in the timeline and choose Split Audio. The movie audio appears on the voiceover track, as shown in Figure 2-11. At this point, the audio that was shot with that video clip behaves like an independent track, not tied to the video.

Audio split from video

Figure 2-11: The audio track appears as a separate entity when you split it out.

Adding a voiceover or music track

Recording a voiceover is easy in VideoStudio Pro. Follow these steps:

1. **Make sure that you have an empty spot on a voiceover track.**

2. **Navigate to the timecode you want to start.**

   Most of the time, you click the timeline to establish a new cursor location. Choose a starting point before you plan to start talking so that you have time to catch up and begin.

3. **Select the Record/Capture Option button and choose Voice-over, shown in Figure 2-12.**

4. **Speak into the microphone and test your audio level. Turn up the input volume from the Windows audio mixer if the sound being recorded is too weak.**

5. **Press Start and begin your voiceover.**

6. **Press Stop to end the recording.**

   Figure 2-13 shows that I did two voiceovers, end to end. They appear on the voiceover track.

   You can now edit the track just like any other resource in the project.

Figure 2-12: Choose Voice-over to record narration.

Figure 2-13: New clips show up on the timeline where you recorded them.

If you would rather use music, drag and drop music from Windows Explorer directly into your project or to the track you want to add it to. You can also import music into your project and drag it from the media area, as shown in Figure 2-14.

Figure 2-14: Drag and drop music just like videos.

Adding Effects to Clips

It's one thing to cut bad parts out of your movie. It's another thing to add transitions, titles, credits, and other special effects. They polish your presentation and make it more than a rudimentary recording.

Adding scene transitions

Transitions join scenes and segments and ease the transition from one shot to the next. Instead of the scene jumping instantly to the next one, you can fade out, fade in, or insert a different, creative transition. George Lucas loves transitions. He uses them quite a bit in all the *Star Wars* movies.

Drag a transition to the border between two clips, as shown in Figure 2-15. It's that easy.

Figure 2-15: Place transitions between clips.

Adding effects

Add effects to create interest, humor, and action. You can also correct jitter, color, lighting, and sound with effects. Here's a list of the some of the effects (or *filters*) that VideoStudio offers:

- **Anti Shake:** Tries to smooth out your achy shaky videos.
- **Auto Exposure:** Automatically adjusts the exposure for a clip.
- **AutoSketch:** A creative filter that turns the clip into a sketch.
- **Blur:** Blurs the clip.
- **Color Shift:** An interesting special effect where a color channel flies through the frame.
- **DeNoise:** Reduces noise in the video clip.
- **Detail Enhance:** Enhances details in the video clip.
- **Duotone:** Converts the clip into a two-toned image, just like you would create a sepia-tinted photo.
- **Flip:** Flips the clip.
- **Old Film:** Another creative filter that turns the new, color, digital video clip into something that looks old, black and white, and grainy.
- **Picture-In-Picture:** Turns the clip into a small picture-in-picture.
- **Sharpen:** Sharpens the clip.
- **Video Pan and Zoom:** Enables you to zoom in and pan around a video clip.
- **Vignette:** Adds a matte around the video clip, like a school portrait of old.

Drop effects on clips to apply them, as shown in Figure 2-16. I'm applying the DeNoise effect to the first clip on the timeline.

Adding titles and credits

Titles show up at the beginning of movies. Credits appear at the end. The process is the same — you simply add the elements to different locations.

In VideoStudio, titles and credits are effects you add to the title track (you can have two title tracks). These are the steps:

1. **Select the Titles tab.**
2. **Select a template.**
3. **Drag the template to a title track, as shown in Figure 2-17.**
4. **Enter your titles in the options.**

For end credits, drag the effect to the end of your timeline.

Figure 2-16: Place effects on clips.

Figure 2-17: Titles are placed at the beginning.

Exporting Your Videos to the World

YouTube has made directors and producers out of millions of people. To get your video uploaded and online, you have to export it — a true statement even if you just want to see your video on your computer.

The trick to exporting successfully is to choose the right file type, audio options, and compression scheme.

In Figure 2-18, I'm exporting my project to a single Microsoft .avi video file.

Figure 2-18: Exporting a single movie file.

A professional tip

For professional results, many people convert Canon .mov files (compressed using the H.264 codec) to the ProRes codec by Apple, using MPEG Streamclip (see www.squared5.com) or other software. The reason is that the highly compressed files from the camera require a lot of processing power to "scrub" the timeline (going back and forth) during advanced editing. For playback, it's just fine.

The same statement applies to many Nikon and Pentax users, who convert their .avi files compressed with Motion JPEG into .mov or other formats compatible with (and faster in) their editors.

If you want to create a disc to pop in your Blu-ray or DVD player, look for options in your program to export to those formats.

Of Mice and Movie Formats

Like any computer files, movies have a certain format. For most normal folks (such as yourself), what happens inside the file is meaningless. As long as a movie comes out of the other end, who cares!

The most important thing is to consider the format the digital SLR gave you and ensure that the software you use supports it. This table summarizes the movie formats that each camera brand produces.

Brand	*Movie Format*
Canon	MOV
Nikon	AVI/MOV (D3100)
Pentax	AVI
Sony	AVHD

A Cornucopia of Video Software

The remainder of this chapter looks at a full collection of popular video editing tools now available. I encourage you to download free trial versions, if available, and try these programs for yourself. I give you an idea of what each one is like and describe its strong points.

Table 2-1 summarizes different software packages. More information is contained in the sections that follow. The Web links are available in the book's eCheat Sheet at Dummies.com. (Find more info in the book's inside cover.)

Table 2-1		Video Editing Software	
Name	*Platform*	*Price*	*Notes*
Google Picasa	Mac or Windows	Free	For people who don't have a lot of money to spend; good organization; limited editing
Adobe Premier Elements	Mac or Windows	$99.99	On the same level as Photoshop Elements
Adobe Premier CS5	Mac or Windows	$799	Professional product; excellent capabilities
Apple iMovie	Mac	$79	Consumer-level movie editing
Apple Final Cut Express	Mac	$199	Acceptable if you don't need the full version of Final Cut Pro
Apple Final Cut Pro (part of Final Cut Studio)	Mac	$999	Professional product.; beware of sticker shock, but if you need it, you need it
Pinnacle Studio HD and Ultimate	Windows	$49.99 $99.99	A new discovery; I use Avid Pro Tools audio software often and have heard of its superadvanced video tools; the line from Pinnacle is for consumers
Corel VideoStudio Express	Windows	$39.99	A scaled-down version of VideoStudio X3
Corel VideoStudio Pro X3	Windows	$79.99	A robust package at a good price
Sony Vegas Movie Studio HD	Windows	$44.95	Entry-level movie editing, but good
Sony Vegas Movie Studio Platinum	Windows	$94.95	More advanced
Sony Vegas Pro	Windows	$599.95	Fantastic audio timeline and integration with video
CyberLink PowerDirector 8	Windows	$99.95	A powerful package for a good price
Camtasia Studio	Windows	$299	Helpful options to produce videos; good integration with slides and other graphics
Windows Movie Maker	Windows	Free	Good basic package

Book VII Chapter 2

The Video Editing Bar and Grill

Mac/Windows

The applications described in the following sections are available to both Macintosh and Windows users. Though the pickings are slim, they cover a broad range of prices and capabilities: one free, entry-level product (Picasa), a more powerful consumer-level product (Premier Elements), and a professional video editing suite (Premier CS5).

Google Picasa

Managing your photos and videos doesn't get much simpler than this: free to download, free to install, free to use. Picasa works well with the Internet and has a fantastic organizational interface. It doesn't do a lot of video editing, but it lets you trim your clips from either end and then export the new movie. Figure 2-19 shows the interface. I have a clip loaded into the editor. There's not much to it.

Figure 2-19: Easy splitting and uploading to YouTube by way of Picasa.

Adobe Premier Elements

The price point of Adobe Premier Elements, the popular video-editing software package, is affordable for nonprofessionals, yet its feature list is beefy. You can do a lot more in Premier Elements than trim scenes.

Aside from managing files, Premier Elements offers a multitude of editing and effects features:

✔ **Motion graphics:** Insert graphics, text, and other objects in the scene and add motion to them — they follow you around.

✔ **Static and animated artwork:** Add either type to your movies. Place them where you want.

✔ **InstantMovie:** Automatically edit and combine clips, music, titles, effects, and transitions.

✔ **Themes:** Find instant satisfaction with movie themes.

✔ **Problem-solving:** Correct shakiness, color, and lighting problems.

✔ **Auto-trim:** Premier Elements cuts unwanted material for you.

✔ **Audio:** Balance audio automatically.

Figure 2-20 shows the Premier Elements interface. Does it remind you of anything? Right — all the interfaces look reasonably similar. They aren't necessarily copying each other; it's just that the process of video editing dictates a common approach to designing the programs that perform it.

Figure 2-20: Premier Elements has a lot of powerful functionality.

Adobe Premier CS 5

Adobe Premier, the super-über-brother of Premier Elements, is aimed at professionals. It has more of the video management tools and options that professionals need, such as

✔ **Performance:** Programmed to be faster and stronger than Elements

✔ **Support:** Supports more video camera models than you can shake a stick at

✔ **Authoring:** Tools to produce Blu-ray and DVDs

✔ **Cooperation:** Works with Final Cut Pro and Avid video software (the more advanced applications that I don't cover in this minibook)

Mac-only

Apple has cornered the market on Mac-only video editing products; that's not much of a surprise. As with Mac/Windows software, each level is covered: entry (iMovie), midrange (Final Cut Express), and professional (Final Cut Pro).

Apple iMovie

iMovie, which is part of iLife, is iGood. I'm not sure about the iApple ifixation with putting the letter *I* in front of everything. The Apple practice of "i-naming" its products (such as the iPod) started with the initial iMac and has yet to run out of steam. The company's newest i-gizmos are iPad and the latest version of the iPhone.

Don't get me wrong: My family and I use and love our iMac. It's useful for audio and video tasks and is quite portable — which has nothing to do with editing movies. I call it "bonus coverage."

Anyway, iMovie adds basic elements, such as titles, transitions, and effects. Add menus and export your movies with a side of popcorn. Figure 2-21 shows the interface of (the slightly outdated) iMovie 8.

Figure 2-21: iMovie is a good application for the Mac that doesn't break the bank.

Apple Final Cut Express

Final Cut Express, a more serious application than iMovie, bridges the gap between iMovie and Final Cut Pro, and it has a lot of power to it.

Final Cut Express has the standard array of editing tools, and it features a new open-format Timeline, which enables you to mix different video formats all at one time. Express has great compositing tools that help you create multilayered video with filters and effects.

You can recognize a more serious video application by the way it treats audio. Basic apps don't let you do much with it. Final Cut Express lets you mix multiple audio tracks, apply professional filters such as reverb, delay, echo, and equalize audio to eliminate obnoxious frequencies or enhance the sound.

Sounds like good stuff to me!

Apple Final Cut Pro

Using this premier video editing suite from Apple isn't for the faint of heart, though it handles everything you need for it to handle (which makes it easier to describe and explain than handle). Here's how it works:

Put video in.

Edit like a pro.

Feature-rich, immersive multimedia comes out.

Windows-only

Windows users have more Windows-only software titles to choose from (and more are out there, if you want to find them). Corel and Sony carry a broad range of products at varying prices. PowerDirector is comparable to many of the other consumer-level editing options. Camtasia also makes a powerful editor. Finally, Microsoft Movie Maker fills in the entry-level niche and is comparable to Apple iMovie or Google Picasa.

Pinnacle Studio HD and Ultimate

Pinnacle has a couple of cool products in its lineup: Pinnacle Studio HD and Studio Ultimate.

The software lets you add such elements as animations, effects, sound, music, stop-motion capture, and templates. You can fix shakiness. The program has a number of export options that match sites where you might want to upload your movies.

The Ultimate version adds Blu-ray and HD-DVD support.

Corel VideoStudio Express

VideoStudio Express 2010 is a simple package with a lot of features. It's priced affordably too. You can perform basic editing tasks easily with VideoStudio Express, use templates, and share videos online.

Corel VideoStudio Pro X3

VideoStudio Pro is the more advanced video editing software from Corel. It has a workflow more compatible with HD video and supports graphics processor acceleration to speed up the process. The program has lots of premade templates and other content to help you get started. You can add effects, images, text, and other doodads, not to mention clip, cut, and export. VideoStudio Pro supports Blu-ray and DVD burning.

Sony Vegas Movie Studio HD and Platinum

The two programs Sony Vegas Movie Studio HD and Platinum are the Sony entry-level and mid-level video editing suites. They look much like Vegas Pro, except that they aren't quite as powerful.

Anything Sony does has fantastic support for audio, such as multiple tracks, effects, levels, mixing, formats — you name it. Vegas Movie Studio specializes in HD video, DVD, and Blu-ray creation.

You can use the editing tools to generate text, titles, and backgrounds. Fix shaky video, correct color and lighting, remove red-eye from photos, animate text, roll titles, and scroll credits. Cool beans!

Figure 2-22 shows the interface. Sony uses lots of gray rather than dark gray or black. You can see the media panel, preview window, track list, and timeline, all similar to the ones in other programs.

Sony Vegas Pro

Vegas Pro is the bee's knees from Sony. I have used their music software (mostly Acid Pro) extensively, in addition to using Vegas. They share the same paradigm, except that one deals with video (Vegas Pro) and the other with audio (Acid Pro).

The interfaces take a little getting used to if you're not familiar with them, though I can directly attest to the power and supercoolness of Vegas.

Figure 2-23 shows Vegas Pro up and running. If you cut your teeth on Platinum, moving to Pro should be easy for you (a common theme). Notice that most companies produce both an entry-level video editing application and a professional version.

Figure 2-22: Not for the faint of heart.

CyberLink PowerDirector 8

PowerDirector has a nice-looking interface with access to loads of tools. For
editing videos, you can add effects,
text, titles, multiple tracks, optimized
rendering, and upscaling. And, you can
fix video problems. PowerDirector also
features the Particle Effects Designer,
which lets you create special effects
like the ones you see in movies.

PowerDirector give you access to DVD
menus, templates, effects, and picture-
in-picture objects. The software lets
you easily export HD video to Facebook
and YouTube, or you can create Blu-
ray discs for viewing at home. Not bad!

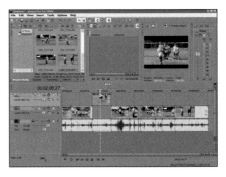

Figure 2-23: Similar to Platinum but with
more power.

Camtasia Studio

I've used Camtasia Studio to produce video tutorials, Though it's a little
clunky at times, it is also very powerful. Its strengths lie in producing and
exporting videos — you have lot of options! The timeline is less impressive
than, say, Sony Vegas Pro, but it works.

Windows Movie Maker

Windows Movie Maker is the Microsoft answer to Apple iMovie. It has the basics, and maybe a little more. Add transitions between clips, special effects to clips, titles, end credits, music, and narration. When you're done, save the movie to your My Videos folder on your computer. Movie Maker suggests video and audio compression settings suitable for online or DVD playback.

Book VIII

The dSLR Reference

The purpose of Book VIII is to show you a broad selection of digital SLRs from different manufacturers and start you thinking about capabilities, price, and performance. I have devoted a chapter apiece to Canon, Nikon, Olympus, Pentax, Sony, and notable non-dSLRs. Each chapter addresses specific cameras and specific benefits or drawbacks of each model.

If you're shopping for a digital SLR, you need this type of information — and the knowledge to use it — so that you can analyze and compare camera specifications and then make the best choice possible for you.

Chapter 1: Clicking with Canon

In This Chapter

Canon (www.canon.com), a premier dSLR and dSLR accessory manufacturer, builds and sells cameras, lenses, and flashes as well as, or better than, anyone else. Along with Nikon, Canon dominates the dSLR market; both have great name recognition among consumers.

Taste has a lot to do with which camera camp you join and invest in. And yes, it's an investment. After you buy a $900 camera (see Figure 1-1) and $1,500 worth of lenses, switching teams can be difficult.

This chapter describes the current lineup of Canon dSLRs, with information on lenses and flashes. The chapter ends by presenting lists of detailed camera specifications organized into tables.

© *Canon Inc.*

Figure 1-1: The newest *Rebel* flagship from Canon, without flags or ships.

The Extensive Canon dSLR Lineup

Canon offers an extensive lineup of dSLR cameras. It has something for everyone, whether your budget is large or small and whether you need a professional-level camera or are just beginning your adventure.

Full-frame

Sensor size sets apart the cameras in this group. These *full-frame* dSLRs have a sensor the size of a 35mm piece of film. Although the full-frame sensor has definite advantages, some are debatable. Most involve the perception of better-quality pictures that have lower noise than other dSLRs.

Canon has two full-frame camera models: EOS-1Ds Mark III and EOS 5D Mark II (for specs, see Table 1-1). Both have built-in vertical grips that add considerably to their size and weight — and cool factor.

Table 1-1	Canon Full-Frame dSLR Specifications	
	EOS-1Ds Mark III	*EOS 5D Mark II*
Year announced	2007	2008
Price (may vary)	$$$$$	$$$
Megapixels (effective)	21.1	21.1
Full or cropped	Full	Full
Built-in flash	No	No
Maximum FPS	5	3.9
Video	No	1080 FHD
Audio (built-in/input)	N/A	Mono/stereo
RAW+JPEG	Yes	Yes
P/Tv/Av/M modes	Yes	Yes
Full auto	No	Yes
Creative auto	No	Yes
Scenes	No	No
AEB (exp; total range)	3; 6.0 EV	3; 4.0 EV
Base ISO (not equivalent)	100–1600	100–6400
Viewfinder coverage	100 percent	98 percent
LCD size (in)	3	3
LCD dots	230,000	920,000
Live view	Yes	Yes
Tilt LCD	No	No
HDMI	No	Yes
Maximum shutter speed	1/8000	1/8000
Autofocus	45-point	9-point
Metering	63-zone	35-zone
Image stabilization (body)	No	No
Memory card	CF (I/II); SD/SDHC	CF (I/II)
Weight (g)	1205	810
Weight (in cans of soda)	3.54	2.38

Each camera model has its own, unique character:

- **EOS-1Ds Mark III:** It's the pinnacle of the Canon EOS camera line — as reflected in its price. Only well-funded photographers with serious intentions can afford it. It comes with a full-frame sensor and 21.1 megapixels, and enough metering and autofocus control to shake a stick at.

  On the downside, the aging and complex EOS-1Ds Mark III is heavy (at approximately 1210 grams, you could use it to train for an Olympic shot put event), and it doesn't shoot video or deliver on other features that many less expensive cameras have.

- **EOS 5D Mark II:** The Canon full-frame camera for a limited budget. You can buy it for about 35 percent of the cost of the EOS-1Ds Mark III. At that price, the EOS 5D Mark II costs less than the more advanced cropped-frame dSLR.

  The Mark II features 21.1 megapixels, full HD video with mono audio or stereo input, more autoshoot modes than the Mark III, a greater ISO range, and better LCD in a package that weighs about one-third less than the EOS-1Ds Mark III.

  The Mark II doesn't have many negatives although it has fewer autofocus and metering points and zones and it can't shoot as fast as the Mark III. But, if you must have a full-frame camera and budget is a consideration, the Mark II is the one for you.

High-end cropped frame

A dSLR with a sensor smaller than a 35mm frame of film is a *cropped frame* model. The term *crop factor* doesn't directly tell you how much smaller the sensor is than a 35mm frame of film. It indicates how much larger a 35mm frame of film is than the camera's sensor. A crop factor of 1.5 tells you that a frame of 35mm film is one and a half times larger (normally measured diagonally) than the sensor.

For more information on cropped versus full-frame sensors, please flip to Book I, Chapter 1.

Cropped Canon cameras may have one of two sensor sizes: APS-H and APS-C. The -H models (EOS-1D Mark IV and EOS-1D Mark III) have larger sensors with crop factors of approximately 1.3 as opposed to a crop factor of 1.6 for APS-C (EOS 7D and EOS 50D) cameras.

The following four cameras, whose detailed specs are listed in Table 1-2, offer a wealth of discriminating options:

- **EOS-1D Mark IV:** At almost $5,000, this model is serious business. Although it isn't full-frame, its sensor is APS-H, which is sized between the smaller APS-C sensor and a 35mm film frame.

The Mark IV is quite possibly the best camera Canon offers. True, its sensor size matters to some people, but in almost every other category, this camera meets or beats its full-frame siblings. It's newer, shoots at ten frames per second (fps), supports full HD video, and has an outstanding ISO range. It has a top-notch LCD, 100 percent viewfinder, fast shutter, and built-in vertical grip and excellent autofocus and metering capabilities. And, it doesn't weigh nearly as much as a Volkswagen Beetle.

Compared to Canon's full-frame cameras, the Mark IV has 16.1 megapixels versus 21.1 and has limited auto-shooting modes (compared to the EOS 5D Mark II). Although it's a bargain, it still costs a tremendous amount of money.

✔ **EOS-1D Mark III:** Knock off $1,000 and a few features from the EOS-1D Mark IV, and you have its progenitor, the Mark III. Although it's an outstanding camera in its own right, it doesn't shoot video, and it has fewer pixels, a smaller ISO range, and fewer LCD dots than the Mark IV.

Keep in mind that the full-featured Mark III is still a $4,000 camera that takes outstanding photographs. I'm only talking about *relative* differences.

The high-end EOS 7D and EOS 50D are priced dramatically less than the EOS-1D Mark III and IV, which signifies they are being marketed and sold as semiprofessional/high-end enthusiast cameras and not professional dSLRs. Although you can become a successful professional by using these cameras (priced between $1,000 and $2,000), your camera is considered appropriate for semiprofessional and serious amateur photographers.

Cameras you may think are expensive or powerful enough to be super-professional models may in fact be described as semiprofessional. The truth is cameras are cameras, no matter what the advertising copy says.

✔ **EOS 7D:** At 18 megapixels and hosting a bevy of cool features, the EOS 7D is a serious contender for best semiprofessional dSLR. It can shoot an outstanding 8 fps, and in full HD video, and it has a decent ISO range, good shutter speed, and auto shooting modes. It's also new, has the latest Canon image processor, a high-resolution LCD, and good autofocus and metering capabilities. It's also the first camera we've seen with a built-in flash — all for $1,699.

Compared to more expensive cropped-frame dSLRs, this one uses no built-in vertical grip, contains fewer autofocus points, shoots marginally slower, and has a bit less ISO than the EOS-1D Mark IV.

✔ **EOS 50D:** The EOS 50D is a bit older than the EOS 7D, which shows in its price and features. This one costs just over $1,000 (a good price), but doesn't shoot video and has fewer megapixels, less ISO, and fewer autofocus points and metering zones.

Compared to cameras in the same class (apples to apples), the EOS 50F suffers a bit because it's older.

Table 1-2	Canon High-End Cropped dSLR Specs			
	EOS-1D Mark IV	*EOS-1D Mark III*	*EOS 7D*	*EOS 50D*
Year announced	2009	2007	2009	2008
Price (may vary)	$$$$	$$$$	$$$	$$
Megapixels (effective)	16.1	10.1	18	15.1
Full or cropped	Cropped	Cropped	Cropped	Cropped
Built-in flash	No	No	Yes	Yes
Max FPS	10	10	8	6.3
Video	1080 FHD	No	1080 FHD	No
Audio (built-in/input)	Mono/stereo	N/A	Mono/stereo	N/A
RAW+JPEG	Yes	Yes	Yes	Yes
P/Tv/Av/M modes	Yes	Yes	Yes	Yes
Full auto	No	No	Yes	Yes
Creative auto	No	No	Yes	Yes
Scenes	No	No	No	Yes
AEB (exp; total range)	3; 6.0 EV	3; 6.0 EV	3; 6.0 EV	3; 4.0 EV
Base ISO (not equivalent)	100–12800	100–3200	100–6400	100–3200
Viewfinder coverage	100 percent	100 percent	100 percent	95 percent
LCD size (in)	3	3	3	3
LCD dots	920,000	230,000	920,000	920,000
Live view	Yes	Yes	Yes	Yes
Tilt LCD	No	No	No	No
HDMI	Yes	No	Yes	Yes
Maximum shutter speed	1/8000	1/8000	1/8000	1/8000
Autofocus	45-point	45-point	19-point	9-point
Metering	63-zone	63-zone	63-zone	35-zone
Image stabilization (body)	No	No	No	No
Memory card	CF (I/II); SD/SDHC	CF (I/II); SD	CF (I/II)	CF (I/II)
Weight (g)	1180	1155	820	730
Weight (in cans of soda)	3.47	3.40	2.41	2.15

The Rebels

The Rebel is a model that most people can afford. All of them cost less than $1,000, including a kit lens (EF-S 18-55 f/3.5-5.6 IS). All have cropped sensors, are smaller, and have fewer features than the more professional-level cameras. The Rebel is also a good starter, enthusiast, or entry-level professional camera. Table 1-3 highlights the specs, and the list that follows has the details.

Cameras in this class are updated frequently. None of these Rebels was "born" before 2008. Technology keeps marching on. The four cameras in the Rebel class are

- **EOS Rebel T2i (550D):** The newest Canon dSLR sports quite a few features: 18 megapixels, video shooting, the greatest ISO range in its class, and all the auto modes you could ask for. It also has a large, high-resolution LCD (the best of any Canon dSLR) and decent autofocus and metering capabilities.

  I can't think of anything to dislike about this camera.

- **EOS Rebel T1i (500D):** The T1i is a bit older than the T2i (but not by much), has a little less of everything (again, not by much), and costs a bit less than the T2i (you guessed it — not by much).

  If you're on the line about which camera to choose, spend the extra money on the newer T2i, especially if you find a good deal. You won't lose out on much.

- **EOS Rebel XSi (450D):** Its megapixel count is still good (in fact, over 200,000 pixels more than my older Nikon D200 dSLR — a much more serious camera), and it has a reasonable frame rate, auto modes, bracketing, and other features.

- **EOS Rebel XS (1000D):** Don't let this model's spot on the low end of the scale deter you from buying it. It has features and capabilities at a price that was unheard of just a few years ago.

The preceding two other cameras are decidedly entry-level models. They sport fewer megapixels, don't shoot video, have a lower ISO range, and feature less-capable LCD monitors. If you're decidedly budget-conscious, however, buying one makes a great initial investment into photography. You can buy these camera bodies with a kit lens and begin learning how to take good photographs. As time goes on, build a lens collection. Don't worry about upgrading the camera's body until you're ready. When you do, you can take the lenses with you — as long as you buy a compatible Canon camera. If you never upgrade, you still get your money's worth — despite buying at the entry level, you can take a lot of great photos with these cameras!

Table 1-3	Canon EOS Rebel dSLR Specifications			
	EOS Rebel T2i (550D)	EOS Rebel T1i (500D)	EOS Rebel XSi (450D)	EOS Rebel XS (1000D)
Year announced	2010	2009	2008	2008
Price (may vary)	$$	$$	$	$
Megapixels (effective)	18	15.1	12.2	10.1
Full or cropped	Cropped	Cropped	Cropped	Cropped
Built-in flash	Yes	Yes	Yes	Yes
Max FPS	3.7	3.4	3.5	3
Video	1080 FHD	1080 FHD	No	No
Audio (built-in/input)	Mono/Stereo	Mono	N/A	N/A
RAW+JPEG	Yes	Yes	Yes	Yes
P/Tv/Av/M modes	Yes	Yes	Yes	Yes
Full auto	Yes	Yes	Yes	Yes
Creative auto	Yes	Yes	Yes	Yes
Scenes	Yes	Yes	No	No
AEB (exp; total range)	3; 4.0 EV	3; 4.0 EV	3; 4.0 EV	3; 4.0 EV
Base ISO (not equivalent)	100–6400	100–3200	100–1600	100–1600
Viewfinder coverage	95 percent	95 percent	95 percent	95 percent
LCD size (in)	3	3	3	2.5
LCD dots	1,040,000	920,000	230,000	230,000
Live view	Yes	Yes	Yes	Yes
Tilt LCD	No	No	No	No
HDMI	Yes	Yes	No	No
Maximum shutter speed	1/4000	1/4000	1/4000	1/4000
Autofocus	9-point	9-point	9-point	7-point
Metering	63-zone	35-zone	35-zone	35-zone
Image stabilization (body)	No	No	No	No

	EOS Rebel T2i (550D)	EOS Rebel T1i (500D)	EOS Rebel XSi (450D)	EOS Rebel XS (1000D)
Memory card	SD/SDHC/SDXC	SD/SDHC	SD/SDHC	SD/SDHC
Weight (g)	530	480	475	450
Weight (in cans of soda)	1.56	1.41	1.40	1.32

Through the Looking Glass

As a full-service imaging and optical products manufacturer, Canon builds and sells a complete line of lenses to complement its cameras: standard zoom, ultra-wide zoom, telephoto zoom, wide-angle, standard/medium telephoto (35mm through 100mm), telephoto (135mm through 300mm), super telephoto (400mm through 800mm), macro, and tilt-shift lenses.

You can distinguish some, but not all, Canon lenses by the light color on the lens barrel. The Canon lens on many cameras also sports a red stripe near its front end. When you see either of these features, you're looking at a professional, "L" series lens. Figure 1-2 shows the EF 70-200mm f/2.8L IS II USM, which has both distinctive features. The manual focus and zoom rings are dark. Other Canon lenses are available in black and without the red stripe.

© Canon Inc.

Figure 1-2: Look for this type of lens at sporting events.

Canon, like all manufacturers, uses different nomenclature (a set of terms or symbols, such as the extra letters and doodads around the name of the lens) to describe its lenses. In addition to the focal length and maximum aperture range, look for these acronyms:

- ✔ **EF:** The name of the lens mount in Canon cameras since 1987. Don't buy an older, non-EF lens and expect it to be compatible with your newer dSLR.

- ✔ **EF-S:** APS-C Canon cameras sport the EF-S mount. A lens with the EF-S designation is not compatible with an EF body. However, EF lenses *are* compatible with EF-S bodies, such as the EOS 7D.

✔ **L:** Indicates superior-quality lenses — the best Canon makes. People drool over them.

✔ **IS:** Helps you control camera shake, especially when taking handheld photos. Canon puts image stabilization in the lens and not in its camera bodies.

✔ **USM:** Features an ultrasonic autofocus motor, designed to reduce noise and camera shake when focusing. The USM motor is also designed to be fast.

Speedlite Flashes

Canon offers several types of Speedlite flashes that are compatible with its line of dSLRs. *Speedlite* is the Canon term for its line of external flashes that mount on a camera's hot shoe. The Speedlite 580EX II is shown in Figure 1-3.

Most Canon dSLRs have built-in flashes, so you don't need to automatically run out and buy an extra. You may have a number of reasons to buy a Speedlite flash, however. Aside from the most obvious one (if your camera has no flash), many lenses cast a shadow if you use the camera's built-in flash. You may also want to take advantage of the stronger flash that these units have over in-camera flashes, with the added flexibility of bouncing. (For more information on bouncing flash, refer to Book IV, Chapter 2.)

Canon offers the following flash models:

© *Canon Inc.*

Figure 1-3: Bounce that flash.

✔ **Speedlite 580EX II:** This top-of-the line Speedlite has it all: power, bounce, swivel, and wireless master or slave. You pay for that level of versatility, but if you're working with complicated flash setups and multiple units, you should have at least one of these.

🖊 **Speedlite 430EX II:** This one comes in a close second to the 580EX II. Although you lose some power and versatility, you don't pay as much.

If you're in doubt, buy the flash with more features. Then, if you need them, you already have them and don't have to feel like you've wasted your money.

Alternatively, buy the 430EX II first and become comfortable using it. When you want to add a unit, buy the 580EX II and use it as the master — problem solved!

🖊 **Speedlite 270EX:** This budget model doesn't swivel, can't go wireless, and doesn't have an LCD screen or configuration buttons. However, it's inexpensive and compact, and it bounces.

🖊 **Macro Twin Lite MT-24EX:** On this flash unit, two flash heads mount on a ring that encircles the lens. The heads can be rotated, swiveled, and aimed separately, which is helpful for close-up macro work.

🖊 **Macro Ring Lite MR-14EX:** It's similar in concept to the Twin Lite (see the preceding bullet), but rather than use smaller flash heads (or *flash tubes*) on opposite sides of the lens, this one virtually encircles the lens — very cool.

The Bottom Line

Aside from offering two full-frame dSLRs, Canon has some serious performers in the high-end cropped class, a few affordable midlevel cameras, and quite a few inexpensive Rebel dSLRs. Regardless of the camera class, Canon puts image stabilization (IS) in its lenses. Therefore, if you don't have an IS lens, you have no IS.

You may notice the Canon EOS Rebel line has two numerical designations. For example, the EOS Rebel T2i is also the EOS 550D. You may see one name or the other, depending on the material you're looking at.

Finally, Canon emphasizes shooting full High Definition video. Canon leads all other camera manufacturers in this area — the videos are larger and you have several options to control both video and sound. (Refer to Book VII for more information on shooting video with digital SLRs.)

**Book VIII
Chapter 1**

Clicking with Canon

Chapter 2: Naturally Nikon

In This Chapter

✔ **dSLRs to dazzle you**

✔ **Lenses to look through**

✔ **Flashes to blind you**

✔ **Notes to end on**

✔ **Tables to sift through**

*T*he Nikon (www.nikon.com) reputation for building high-end professional cameras is evidenced in part by its having no fewer than four full-frame, professional-caliber dSLRs for sale at the same time. That's twice as many as some companies have in their entire catalogs, and twice as many as Canon and Sony, their leading competitors.

As I say in Chapter 1 of this minibook (in regard to Canon), you can't go wrong with Nikon and its fantastic dSLRs that take great-looking pictures.

Nikon cameras have their own look and feel (see Figure 2-1), their own, internal software to run the cameras, their own button layouts, their own terminology, their own strengths, and their own shortcomings.

In short, they're *Nikons*.

The secret is that all digital SLRs are pretty similar, but each company — Canon, Nikon, Olympus, Pentax, Sony, and others — finds ways to individualize its cameras and impart its own sense of style. The more you pick them up and compare, the more you sense it.

Although I can't mind-meld with you to share my own experience with my Nikon D200, I can walk you through the current lineup of Nikon dSLRs and tell you a little about each one in the following section.

The Nikon Stable of dSLRs

Nikon emphasizes the top end and doesn't apologize for it. It has four top-end, full-frame dSLRs, a single top-end, cropped-frame dSLR (the D300S), and a handful of good entry- and mid-level cropped-frame options (the D90, D3000, D3100, and D5000).

With Nikon, you don't see a large middle ground.

© Nikon Corp.

Figure 2-1: The glorious Nikon D300S.

Shopping for full-frame Nikon dSLRs

Nikon offers four full-frame dSLRs, three of which are D3 variants with the built-in vertical grip, and have so many cool features that the short lists I present in this part of the book simply don't do them justice. Nonetheless, that's what I have to work with. See Table 2-1 for the specs of Nikon's full-frame dSLRs.

Table 2-1	Nikon Full-Frame dSLR Specs			
	D3X	*D3S*	*D3*	*D700*
Year announced	2008	2009	2007	2008
Price (may vary)	$$$$$	$$$$	$$$$	$$$
Megapixels (effective)	24.5	12.1	12.1	12.1
Full or cropped	Full	Full	Full	Full
Built-in flash	No	No	No	Yes

	D3X	D3S	D3	D700
Maximum FPS	5/7	9/11	9/11	5/8
Video	No	Yes	No	No
Audio (built-in/input)	N/A	Mono/stereo	N/A	N/A
RAW+JPEG	Yes	Yes	Yes	Yes
P/S/A/M modes	Yes	Yes	Yes	Yes
Full auto	No	No	No	No
Creative auto	No	No	No	No
Scenes	No	No	No	No
AEB (exp; total range)	9; 7.0 EV	9; 7.0 EV	9; 7.0 EV	9; 7.0 EV
Base ISO (not equivalent)	100–1600	200–12800	200–6400	200–6400
Viewfinder coverage	100 percent	100 percent	100 percent	95 percent
LCD size (in)	3	3	3	3
LCD dots	920,000	921,000	920,000	920,000
Live view	Yes	Yes	Yes	Yes
Tilt LCD	No	No	No	No
HDMI	Yes	Yes	Yes	Yes
Maximum shutter speed	1/8000	1/8000	1/8000	1/8000
Autofocus	51-point	51-point	51-point	51-point
Metering	1005-segment	1005-segment	1005-segment	1005-segment
Image stabilization (body)	No	No	No	No
Memory card	CF (I/II); microdrive	CF (I)	CF (I/II); microdrive	CF (I)
Weight (g)	1220	1240	1240	995
Weight (in cans of soda)	3.59	3.64	3.64	2.92

When shooting full-frame (FX, as Nikon calls it), each of these cameras shoots the slower of the two speeds listed in the table. To use the higher speed, you have to be shooting in DX, or Cropped, mode.

Here are some short write-ups on Nikon's full-frame dSLRs:

✔ **D3X:** The Nikon digital flagship costs the most and carries the greatest level of prestige. It has an absurdly large megapixel count (24.5) and good speed, AEB, and LCD; it also has professional-level autofocus and metering control.

The D3X is probably the finest dSLR now available. If you must have unparalleled quality and price is no option, this camera is for you.

✓ **D3S:** Think of the D3S as a more responsive D3X with fewer pixels (12.1 versus 24.5), Movie mode, and vastly superior low-light capability (ISO 12800). It's not bad for almost $3,000 less than the D3X.

✓ **D3:** The oldest and cheapest of the three D3-type Nikons, the D3 launched the original Nikon FX-format sensor. It's full-frame, and only in Nikon style. It shoots fast and has better ISO performance than the D3X, but has no Movie mode and not as much sensitivity (ISO) as the D3S.

There's some debate as to whether the D3 has been discontinued. There's been no official announcement from Nikon, and the D3 appears on its Web site as part of the dSLR lineup. However, it isn't universally available.

✓ **D700:** The D700 is the Nikon "bargain" full-frame dSLR, for only $2,699. It has outstanding ISO performance, shoots as fast as the D3X, and has as many pixels as the D3 and D3S (12.1 megapixels) all in a smaller, lighter body.

Inquiring about cropped-frame Nikon dSLRs

Nikon has five cropped-frame (DX) dSLRs, running the gamut from the fairly expensive but quite capable D300S to the entry-level D3000. I cover both in this section as well as in Table 2-2.

Table 2-2	Nikon Cropped dSLR Specs				
	D300S	**D90**	**D5000**	**D3100**	**D3000**
Year announced	2009	2008	2009	2010	2009
Price (may vary)	$$$	$$	$	$	$
Megapixels (effective)	12.3	12.3	12.3	14.2	10.2
Full or cropped	Cropped	Cropped	Cropped	Cropped	Cropped
Built-in flash	Yes	Yes	Yes	Yes	Yes
Maximum FPS	7/8	4.5	4	3	3
Video	Yes	Yes	Yes	Yes	No
Audio (mic/input)	Mono/stereo	Mono/none	Mono/none	Mono/none	N/A
RAW+JPEG	Yes	Yes	Yes	Yes	Yes
P/S/A/M	Yes	Yes	Yes	Yes	Yes

	D300S	D90	D5000	D3100	D3000
Full auto	No	Yes	Yes	Yes	Yes
Easy shooting modes	No	No	Yes	No	No
Scenes	No	Yes	Yes	Yes	Yes
AEB (exp; total range)	9; 7.0 EV	3; 6.0 EV	3; 1.0 EV	N/A	N/A
Base ISO (not equivalent)	200–3200	200–3200	200–3200	100–3200	100–1600
Viewfinder coverage	100 percent	96 percent	95 percent	95 percent	95 percent
LCD Size (in)	3	3	2.7	3	3
LCD dots	920,000	920,000	230,000	230,000	230,000
Live view	Yes	Yes	Yes	Yes	No
Tilt LCD	No	No	Yes	No	No
HDMI	Yes	Yes	Yes	Yes	No
Maximum shutter speed	1/8000	1/4000	1/4000	1/4000	1/4000
Autofocus	51-point	11-point	11-point	11-point	11-point
Metering	1005-segment	420-segment	420-segment	420-segment	420-segment
Image stabilization (body)	No	No	No	No	No
Memory card	CF (I); SD/SDHC	SD/SDHC	SD/SDHC	SD/SDHC/SDXC	SD/SDHC
Weight (g)	840	620	560	455	485
Weight (in cans of soda)	2.47	1.82	1.65	1.34	1.43

Although the D300 is in a class of its own, I want you to see the side-by-side comparison:

✔ **D300S:** The D300S is truly a professional camera. The best-performing cropped-frame Nikon dSLR shares many features and characteristics of the awesome D700. The D300S has marginally more pixels, and it shoots faster and shoots movies. Aside from its cropped-frame, it suffers in ISO performance compared to the D700.

When you compare the D300 to other high-end dSLRs, it finishes evenly or ahead in most areas.

✔ **D90:** The D90 is slightly older and less capable than the D300S. It isn't exactly top-of-the-line, but neither is it entry-level. It's perfect for mid-range photographers who want a better product than is possible at entry-level but aren't ready to spend the money for a semiprofessional- or professional-level camera.

The D90 shoots slower than the D300S and has a marginally worse AEB mode, a 96 percent viewfinder, a slower maximum shutter speed, and fewer autofocus points and metering segments.

Although not as good as the D300S, the D90 compares quite favorably to other cameras in its price range.

The next three cameras are on the low end of the Nikon dSLR spectrum. Though all are good cameras, they don't carry the features or performance of the D90 and D300S. Here's a comparison:

✔ **D5000:** The best entry-level Nikon dSLR shoots video and has a good frame rate (4 fps), better ISO performance, and more pixels than the D60 and D3000, and an articulated LCD with Live view. It definitely holds its own against other upper-entry-level dSLRs.

✔ **D3100:** Of the three entry-level dSLRs from Nikon, the D3100 (which replaces the aged D60) is the newest; it was announced in mid-2010. The D3100 is similar to the D3000, but it has been upgraded in several areas — most notably in its ability to shoot full 1080-pixel HD movies (something that's lacking in the other Nikon dSLRs that shoot movies). It also adds Live view, a boost in ISO performance, and the addition of an HDMI port and support for SDXC memory cards.

The D3100 has some great new features for beginners, including a Guide Mode (which walks you through a series of menu screens to help you set the camera up to take the pictures you want) and a Scene Auto Selector mode.

✔ **D3000:** This solid entry-level dSLR has 10.2 megapixels, shoots 3 fps, and has decent ISO performance compared to others in its class. It is by far the least expensive Nikon dSLR by more than $150.

NIKKOR Lenses

Nikon lenses, or *NIKKOR* lenses, aren't part of a separate company. NIKKOR (or Nikkor, even in Nikon documentation) is a brand name, just as the F-150 is a brand of Ford pickup truck. The F-150 is a Ford, and Ford makes the F-150. Similarly, NIKKOR is the brand name that Nikon applies to its lenses. When referring to a specific lens model, use *NIKKOR* because it's part of the name (see Figure 2-2).

Nikon manufactures its own lenses and has quite a selection. It's a veritable alphabet soup at Nikon when it comes to lens nomenclature. I won't list every possible combination here, but you should be familiar with a few designations:

© Nikon Corp.

Figure 2-2: My Nikon AF-S DX NIKKOR 35mm f/1.8G prime lens.

- ✔ **DX:** Lenses designed for DX (cropped-frame) bodies. DX lenses fit on and work with all current FX models, which automatically recognize the DX lens and cut down the image size to accommodate them. That is, although they work, DX lenses convert your FX camera into a DX camera.

- ✔ **FX:** If the lens doesn't have the DX label, it's designed for both full-frame (FX) and cropped-frame dSLRs.

- ✔ **ED:** Extra-low Dispersion lenses have the highest quality glass that Nikon offers. They are designed to capture sharp photos with little or no chromatic aberrations.

- ✔ **VR:** Vibration Reduction. Some lenses have VR II.

- ✔ **AF-S:** Stands for Auto Focus, Silent. Has Nikon's Silent Wave Motor (SWM).

- ✔ **D:** The D series is a bit older. Cameras in this series have an aperture ring. Also called a *CPU lens* because a chip inside transmits distance information to the camera body.

- ✔ **Micro:** It's the new Nikon term for *macro*.

- ✔ **G:** The G series is a newer series than the D series, which the Gs are slowly replacing. G-series lenses have no aperture ring. The camera controls the aperture of the lens.

Don't Forget the Flash

Nikon has several off-camera flashes to choose from, named *Speedlights*. This list describes Nikon's current Speedlight models:

- ✔ **Speedlight SB-900:** A powerful, top-of-the-line Speedlight from Nikon with LCD, controls, wireless, master or slave operation, bounces, and swivels. Very good but pricey; replacing the SB-800 (although Nikon continues to market the SB-800 on its Web site).

- ✔ **Speedlight SB-600:** Less capable than the SB-900, but priced accordingly. It bounces and swivels, and operates wirelessly, but only as a slave unit. Figure 2-3 shows my SB-600 from a vantage point that illustrates the LCD screen and buttons on the back.

✐ **Speedlight SB-400:** The smallest and cheapest Speedlight isn't wireless. Bounces. This model is good enough if you want to buy an external flash but don't need esoteric setups, such as off-camera wired or wireless.

✐ **Remote Wireless Speedlight SB-R200:** Bypass the camera's hot shoe entirely with this wireless unit. It's suitable for macro work, but not large photo shoots.

✐ **Wireless Speedlight Commander SU-800:** It serves as a wireless trigger for remote flashes and mounts on the camera's hot shoe.

✐ **Nikon Close-up Speedlight Kits:** The Nikon Close-up Speedlight Commander Kit (RC1C) comes with everything you need for close-up work: a Wireless Speedlight Commander SU-800, two wireless Speedlight SB-R200 units, and an attachment ring. The SB-200 unites are placed on either side of the lens, and the commander placed on the camera's hot shoe. The Nikon Close-up Speedlight Remote Kit (R1) comes with everything except the Commander.

Figure 2-3: My Nikon SB-600 flash.

The Bottom Line

Nikon dSLRs have no onboard image stabilization. Nikon puts image stabilization in the camera lens and calls it Vibration Reduction (VR). Nikon dSLRs generally sport fewer megapixels than ones from Canon. Additionally, with the exception of the D3100 (anounced in mid-2010), Nikon dSLRs that shoot video shoot at a lower resolution than Canon, and shooting the videos feels a bit clunky at times (the D3100 is a serious attempt to rectify this situation). My second dSLR, the Nikon D200, is the predecessor of the D300. The D200 has been a pleasure to use and a joy to hold. It's powerful, flexible, rugged, and it takes great-looking photos. Because of the D200's size and controls, I felt like a real photographer the moment I received it. At times, it has made me work harder to take those good photos, though: It has no Live view, Auto mode, or video, and its ISO performance is somewhat poor.

The Nikon implementation of AEB *rocks* on its higher-end cameras but is curiously weak or absent from the low end of its dSLR range.

Chapter 3: Olympus Rocks

*Q*uietly, it seems, Olympus (www.olympus-global.com) is delivering the dSLR goods. It isn't the biggest camera company, and it doesn't offer the largest number of cameras, but when you start looking at its line of products, you realize that is has developed its own niche in the dSLR market by making some snazzy dSLRs.

Among other qualities, Olympus prides itself on being *small*. Figure 3-1 illustrates the diminutive (a large word to describe a small item, if I've ever seen one) E-420, which is, along with the E-450, the world's teeniest, tiniest, littlest, smallest, and cutest dSLR. Although there is nothing to compare the camera to in the photo, it is a hair over 5 inches (129mm) wide and just over 3.5 inches (91mm) high.

Another Olympus claim to fame is that it's one of the few dSLR manufacturers to sell sensors that have aspect ratios of 4:3 instead of 3:2. I explain that topic in the next section.

dSLRs of the Gods

All Olympus dSLRs have *four thirds* sensors and lenses, which means that they have a 4:3 aspect ratio — the same as on a traditional TV screen. Most other dSLRs, whether they're full-frame or cropped, share the same aspect ratio as a 35mm film frame, which is 3:2. Because four thirds sensors have a crop factor of 2, they're much smaller than cropped-frame sensors with crop factors from 1.3 to 1.6, and much smaller than full-frame sensors, which have no crop factor.

What all this means is that Olympus has chosen the smaller sensor to control costs and reduce size and weight, among other factors. One unfortunate side effect is that the sensor is a tad more susceptible to noise than larger varieties are. In a practical sense, *how much* more noise is debatable and not always apparent, which means that you shouldn't reflexively fear the four thirds system or the sensors.

© Olympus Corp.

Figure 3-1: The tiny Olympus E-420 dSLR, attractively presented.

If you want to take a look at a camera that sports the *micro four thirds system* (whose sensors are even smaller than the four thirds digital SLRs), I cover the Olympus Pen in Chapter 6 of this minibook.

Megaphotonic

Two Olympus dSLRs stand apart from the others in the Olympus dSLR stable in price, size, and such capabilities as shutter speed and frames per second: the E-3 and the E-30. This list describes them for you:

- **E-3:** The Olympus flagship dSLR.

  If you're concerned only with specs, the E-3 doesn't deliver the same punch as other mid- to high-end, cropped-frame dSLRs. It has a below-average pixel count (10.1 megapixels); shoots a little slower (5 frames per second, or fps) than the Pentax K-7 (5.2 fps), Canon EOS 50D (6.3 fps), and Sony Alpha 550 (7 fps); lacks snazzy autoshoot modes; has a smaller LCD than other dSLRs in its class; and is growing old (it was announced in 2007).

  The E-3 in-body image stabilization (IS) supplies IS wherever you go, no matter which lens you put on the camera. The E-3 also sports a large viewfinder, a cool LCD that swings out from the camera back, and a great-looking Live view implementation. It also has a fast top shutter speed (1/8000 second), decent AEB, and good autofocus and metering qualities.

- **E-30:** If you like the E-3, you'll love the E-30. Similar to the E-3 but costs about $300 less. The E-30 has more pixels (12.3 versus 10.1 megapixels), more auto modes, and a slightly larger LCD. The E-30 weighs less than the E-3 and has essentially the same specs elsewhere, except for the viewfinder.

The cool art filters and multiple exposure modes on the E-30 let you process artistic shots in-camera and, as the marketing copy says, "on the fly." Sounds like fun!

Table 3-1 gives you a look at the specifications for the top Olympus dSLR models.

Table 3-1	Top Olympus dSLR Specs	
	E-3	*E-30*
Year announced	2007	2008
Price (may vary)	$$	$$
Megapixels (effective)	10.1	12.3
Full or cropped	Cropped	Cropped
Built-in flash	Yes	Yes
Maximum FPS	5	5
Video	No	No
Audio (mic/input)	N/A	N/A
RAW+JPEG	Yes	Yes
P/S/Av/M modes	Yes	Yes
Full auto	No	Yes
Easy shooting modes	No	Yes
Scenes	No	Yes
AEB (exp; total range)	5; 4.0 EV	5; 4.0 EV
Base ISO (not equivalent)	100–3200	100–3200
Viewfinder coverage	100 percent	98 percent
LCD size (in)	2.5	2.7
LCD dots	230,000	230,000
Live view	Yes	Yes
Tilt LCD	Yes	Yes
HDMI	No	No
Maximum shutter speed	1/8000	1/8000
Autofocus	11-point	11-point
Metering	49-point	49-point
Image stabilization (body)	Yes	Yes
Memory card	CF (I/II); microdrive; xD	CF (I/II); microdrive; xD
Weight (g)	810	655
Weight (in cans of soda)	2.38	1.93

There's no Achilles heel here

The less expensive end of the Olympus dSLR lineup appears not to have weaknesses, as dSLRs go. However, the one knock on all Olympus dSLRs is that they don't shoot video. If you don't mind carrying around a camera for stills and a video camcorder for movies (you could also just not shoot movies), you won't miss a beat.

These cameras compete well in the entry-level, sophisticated amateur category. They feature good resolution and good shooting speed. (All are as good as or better than most of the Canon Rebel line, the inexpensive Nikon dSLRs, and the three least expensive Sony cameras.) These cameras have a plethora of autoshooting, creative, and scenic modes, and they have decent AEB, Live view, and good LCD shutter speeds. Also, most have in-body IS, and all feature wireless flash technology that triggers compatible Olympus external flashes — not bad for the entire *low end* of the Olympus lineup:

This list describes Olympus's budget dSLR lineup:

- ✓ **E-620:** The cream of the inexpensive Olympus dSLR crop, with features that rival others in its class and then some. It even has illuminated buttons so that you can lurk in the shadows and see which one you're about to press. The articulated LCD and art filters are cool, too.

- ✓ **E-600:** The same as the E-620 but with a few changes to make it less expensive. Illuminated buttons on the body that make it easier to operate in low-light conditions were removed, and a few art filters have disappeared. You might not even be able to tell the difference.

- ✓ **E-520:** Similar to the E-450, with in-body image stabilization and wireless remote flash control (a feature found on more expensive bodies).

Table 3-2 lists the Olympus entry-level, sophisticated amateur camera specs.

Table 3-2 Plus Lineup				Olympus Entry-Level	
	E-620	E-600	E-520	E-450	E-420
Year Announced	2009	2009	2008	2009	2008
Price (may vary)	$	$	$	$	$
Megapixels (effective)	12.3	12.3	10	10	10
Full or cropped	Cropped	Cropped	Cropped	Cropped	Cropped

	E-620	E-600	E-520	E-450	E-420
Built-in flash	Yes	Yes	Yes	Yes	Yes
Maximum FPS	4	4	3.5	3.5	3.5
Video	No	No	No	No	No
Audio (mic/input)	N/A	N/A	N/A	N/A	N/A
RAW+JPEG	Yes	Yes	Yes	Yes	Yes
P/S/Av/M	Yes	Yes	Yes	Yes	Yes
Full auto	Yes	Yes	Yes	Yes	Yes
Easy shooting modes	Yes	Yes	Yes	Yes	Yes
Scenes	Yes	Yes	Yes	Yes	Yes
AEB (exp; total range)	3; 4.0 EV	3; 4.0 EV	3; 4.0 EV	3; 4.0 EV	3; 4.0 EV
Base ISO (not equivalent)	100–3200	100–3200	100–1600	100–1600	100–1600
Viewfinder coverage	95 percent	95 percent	95 percent	95 percent	95 percent
LCD size (in)	2.7	2.7	2.7	2.7	2.7
LCD dots	230,000	230,000	230,000	230,000	230,000
Live view	Yes	Yes	Yes	Yes	Yes
Tilt LCD	Yes	Yes	No	No	No
HDMI	No	No	No	No	No
Maximum shutter speed	1/4000	1/4000	1/4000	1/4000	1/4000
Autofocus	11-point	7/11-point	3/11-point	3/11-point	3/11-point
Metering	49-point	49-point	49-point	49-point	49-point
Image stabilization (body)	Yes	Yes	Yes	No	No
Memory card	CF (I/II); Micro-drive; xD	CF (I/II); Micro-drive; xD	CF (I/II); Micro-drive; xD	CF (I/II); Micro-drive; xD	CF (I/II); Micro-drive; xD
Weight (g)	475	475	475	380	380
Weight (in cans of soda)	1.40	1.40	1.40	1.12	1.12

Shopping for a dSLR

Shopping for a dSLR can be a stressful experience, especially the first time. Many variables are involved: price, manufacturer, quality, lenses and other accessories, the cool factor, and of course, the specifications of the cameras.

I give you an overview of all available dSLRs from the biggest name brands. Although that discussion is important, knowing how to put it all together is critical. I offer you this methodology as someone who has gone through it himself, made mistakes, learned from them, and, in the process of writing this minibook, visited every manufacturer's Web site, looked at every available dSLR specification, downloaded every manual, and then pored over them to give you good indicators of which dSLRs can meet your needs.

To shop for a digital SLR, follow these general steps:

1. **Set a budget.**

    There's no sense in looking at a $2, 500 camera if you can't afford it. Seriously, people will tell you (or you will read) how much better a $2,500 camera is than one that sells for $800 until you're sick of it. Although they may be right, that information is *entirely irrelevant* to you and your decision. Your budget depends on you and is probably based largely on factors unrelated to photography. Don't forget to factor in items such as lenses, bags, tripods, filters, flashes, extra batteries, and remote shutter releases.

2. **Identify your needs.**

    This step can be difficult, and you should know that your needs may change over time. What you need today may not be what you need in two years (then it's time to buy another camera). After buying my first dSLR, I realized that I needed a camera with these three items: a good Live view implementation, the ability to save every photo in both raw and JPEG formats, and Auto mode. Your needs may be video, a robust AEB mode, ultra-high ISO capability, or uncompromising full-frame quality.

    Completing this step points you to a class of cameras that you can afford.

3. **Start adding cameras to a list of possible matches.**

    Compare camera models from one or more manufacturers to see whether any of them meets your needs (you may need to reevaluate), and add them to your list. If something is on the line, add it.

    Completing this step points you to one or more cameras within a class that meet your general criteria.

4. **Narrow your search by weeding out cameras.**

    Compare each camera's specs against your needs and against each other. Does a clear winner emerge? Look for reviews and see whether you can find a store where you can hold the camera. Ultimately, you want to find the "sweet spot" where your needs meet the price you can afford and the performance you desire.

    Completing this step points you to your camera.

As the smallest dSLRs in the world, the E-450 and E-420 are remarkable. Each one weighs slightly more than a 12-ounce can of soda, and is small enough (with the proper lens) to fit into a pocket or purse. If you're on the go and need a camera that's far more powerful and flexible than your average compact digital camera, either of these is a strong choice.

You have to make some compromises, though. Both cameras lack true in-body image stabilization, instead featuring digital IS. Although digital IS isn't as capable as mechanical methods (such as a sensor shift in the camera body or a lens with mechanically stabilized optics), at least it's *something*.

✓ **E-450:** The E-450 is essentially an E-420 with art filters. My glowing review of the E-420 is in the next bullet.

✓ **E-420:** The E-420 is a fantastically small, light, and capable camera. Although it's not a professional model, it's not intended to be. If you need something better than a compact digital camera but don't want the bulk of owning a larger dSLR, look no further.

What's more, the E-420 is less expensive than most high-end digital compact cameras. The Canon G-11 (arguably one of the best-performing non-dSLRs) now lists for $50 *more* than the E-420, which is truly an entry-level dSLR. The significance is this: You get better photos, more flexibility, lower noise, swappable lenses, and all-around dSLR power that beats the performance of most or all compact digital cameras for about the same price. Marry this inexpensive body with the lens of your choice.

Prices change, and my analyses may not hold for the life of this book. In a larger sense, I hope you understand how I am analyzing prices and features. That way, when the prices and features change, you'll be able to compare them on your own.

Lenses of the Titans

Olympus features a full range of Zuiko Digital lenses, shown in Figure 3-2 and arranged in these three tiers:

✓ **Super High Grade:** Tend to be pricey (between $1,799 and $6,999) wide angle or fixed-focal-length telephoto lenses. Yeah, that's *super* high-grade.

✓ **High Grade:** Easier on your wallet or purse and tend to be standard zoom lenses, with one fisheye and a 50mm macro.

**Book VIII
Chapter 3**

Olympus Rocks

© *Olympus Corp.*

Figure 3-2: A group shot of Zuiko lenses.

✔ **Standard:** A compromise between price and performance, with lots of variety — wide-angle, macro/prime, and zoom.

Flashes of Brilliance

Olympus has the standard array of flash units available. The Olympus wireless flash RC system features a lot of in-camera control over compatible wireless Olympus flash units. The system uses the camera as the flash commander, alleviating the need for either of these models to act as the master flash unit.

The top two units from Olympus, the FL-50R and FL-36R, are summarized in the following list. Both are compatible with all dSLRs listed in this chapter.

✔ **FL-50R:** A wireless unit that bounces and swivels; a bit bigger than, and with more power than, the FL-36R.

✔ **FL-36R:** Not as powerful as the FL-50R, but adequate for the price (see Figure 3-3). It's the eternal trade-off between price, power, and size. More power equals more size and results in a unit that costs more.

© *Olympus Corp.*

Figure 3-3: Cool dual-external flash setup on an E-30.

✔ **Ring flash:** A combination of ring flash and controller collectively named Ring Flash Set SRF-11. It's helpful for macro work because it prevents the lens from casting a shadow.

Chapter 4: The Syntax of Pentax

*P*entax (www.pentaximaging.com) isn't the biggest dSLR manufacturer, nor does it have the most models. In fact, its lineup is quite small compared to those of Canon, Nikon, and Sony. Figure 4-1 illustrates their top dSLR model — the K-7.

Pentax, which has been in the business for nearly a century, has a history of encouraging innovation and quality and has snappy products and happy customers (known as *Pentaxians*). The Pentax story shows you that you don't have to be the biggest manufacturer around in order to have excellent cameras and lenses.

Don't let the limited Pentax product line intimidate you. The company simply doesn't attempt to fill every possible market segment with two or more options. Its two camera models have features designed to meet most needs of most entry-level or midrange or semi-professional photographers.

The Pentax dSLR Lineup

The Pentax dSLR line now features two models, each representing a different class of camera: the K-7 midlevel semiprofessional camera and the entry-level K-x consumer model. Both cropped-frame dSLRs (the crop factor for both cameras is 1.5, even though the sensor for the K-x is fractionally smaller than the K-7) have features that compare well against other brands. Table 4-1 lists the specs for both cameras.

© PENTAX Imaging Company

Figure 4-1: The K-7 is a nice-looking Pentax camera.

Table 4-1	Pentax dSLR Specs	
	K-7	*K-x*
Year announced	2009	2009
Price (may vary)	$$	$
Megapixels (effective)	14.6	12.4
Full or cropped	Cropped	Cropped
Built-in flash	Yes	Yes
Maximum FPS	5.2	4.7
Video	720 HD	720 HD
Audio (built-in/input)	Mono/stereo	Mono/none
RAW+JPEG	Yes	Yes
P/S/Tv/Av/M modes	Yes	Yes
Full auto	Yes	Yes
Picture mode	No	Yes
Scenes	No	Yes
AEB (exp; total range)	5; 4.0 EV	3; 6.0 EV
Base ISO (not equivalent)	100–3200	200–6400
Viewfinder coverage	100 percent	96 percent
LCD size (in)	3	2.7

	K-7	*K-x*
LCD dots	921,000	230,000
Live view	Yes	Yes
Tilt LCD	No	No
HDMI	Yes	No
Maximum shutter speed	1/8000	1/6000
Autofocus	11-point	11-point
Metering	77-segment	16-segment
Image stabilization (body)	Yes	Yes
Memory card	SD/SDHC	SD/SDHC
Weight (g)	751	482
Weight (in cans of soda)	2.21	1.42

This list describes both digital SLRs available from Pentax:

- **K-7:** The top-of-the-line Pentax dSLR, roughly comparable to the upper end of the Canon Rebel line or the low end of its midlevel dSLRs.

  For the price you pay for the K-7 ($1,099.95), you get quite a bit of camera: It has 14.6 megapixels and shoots at a respectable speed (5.2 fps) with a fast top-end shutter speed (1/8000 second). The K-7 shoots 720 HD video in mono with the built-in mic or in stereo using a microphone terminal. The LCD measures three inches wide and has plenty of dots (921,000), which is comparable to the current crop of dSLRs, regardless of class. Its weight is similar to most midlevel-cropped dSLR bodies.

  The characteristics that prevent the K-7 from being able to compete with more expensive dSLRS is shooting 720 HD versus 1080 full-HD video and having a low maximum ISO (3200) and fewer autofocus points (11). With the possible exception of video, none of the items is worse than cameras in its class. However, you can't buy a K-7 and expect it to have the same features or capabilities as a Canon EOS 7D or a Nikon D300s.

  All in all, the K-7 stacks up well against cameras in its class.

- **K-x:** The K-x story is remarkably similar to the K-7 story except that K-x aims at the entry-level market. It compares well against other cameras in its class, such as the Canon Rebel XS/XSi and Nikon D3000. The body and a kit lens (DA L 18-55mm lens) lists for about $650. On an artistic note, the K-x is the only dSLR that is available in no less than eight colors (five of which are vibrant): black, white, red, navy, orange, bright blue, green, and purple.

In many ways, the K-x is a better value. It shoots video, whereas the low-end Canon doesn't, nor does the Nikon D3000. The K-x has a higher top ISO than these cameras with faster maximum shutter speeds.

Looking at Lenses

Despite only having two digital SLRs, Pentax manufactures several types of lenses to fit them — wide-angle, standard, zoom (see Figure 4-2), telephoto, and macro.

© PENTAX Imaging Company

Figure 4-2: The smc PENTAX DA 17-70mm F4 AL (IF) SDM. Got it?

By the way, the letters *smc* stands for *Super Multi Coating* — the Pentax lens-coating technology designed to eliminate reflections and flares. The other designations in this lens name are: AL (hybrid aspherical optical elements), IF (internal focusing), SP (super protect coating to repel dust, water, and grease), and SDM (built-in supersonic autofocus motor).

Pentax lenses are separated into these categories:

- **DA Star:** The best Pentax lenses, including Supersonic Drive Motor (SDM) focusing motors, a distinctive bronze ring near the business end of the lens, and a green ring near the mount.

- **DA:** A line that balances price and performance. This type of lens has a distinctive green ring. A few are weather resistant, and at least one has an SDM focusing motor.

- **DA Limited:** The Pentax high-quality prime lenses — sharp and small and offering uncompromising quality. Focal lengths range from 15mm to 70mm.

- **D FA:** Full-frame lenses designed for digital photography but that are backward-compatible with Pentax 35mm film cameras.

- **FA:** D FA in reverse — full-frame lenses designed for film SLR cameras but compatible with modern dSLRs.

Adding Flash with Pentax

The prices and features of the four flashes that Pentax offers for its dSLRs correspond to those of most other manufacturers:

© *PENTAX Imaging Company*

Figure 4-3: The AF 540FGZ flash.

- ✔ **AF 540FGZ:** The premier Pentax flash, shown in Figure 4-3. It has Auto and Manual modes, an LCD display, lots of buttons, and wireless capability, and it can be the master or slave.

- ✔ **AF 360FGZ:** The not-quite-premier Pentax flash. It has bounce, wireless slave mode, lots of on-flash controls, and an LCD display.

- ✔ **AF 200FG:** The Pentax budget model — small and simple.

- ✔ **AF 160FC:** The Pentax ring flash, designed to mount on the lens and illuminate close subjects with a flash ring rather than a blocky flash head.

Chapter 5: Sony-Sony, Bo-Bony

In This Chapter

↙ **Alpha dog dSLRs**

↙ **Lenses to howl over**

↙ **Flashes that pierce the night**

The story of Sony (www.sony.com), one of the big three dSLR manufacturers now in operation, is unique. Konica Minolta (Konica and Minolta, two storied names in camera history, merged in 2003) decided to get out of the camera business in 2006. They transferred all their camera assets to Sony, which continued to develop the Konica Minolta dSLR line under the Sony Alpha brand name.

So, with Sony's resources and business sense, the Konica Minolta vision lives on. The Sony Alpha dSLRs (Figure 5-1 shows the Alpha 55, which was announced in mid-2010) has become a viable alternative to the established and successful brands of Canon and Nikon.

Enough business, more cameras. This chapter is devoted to showing you the current Sony Alpha lineup in all its glory.

Examining Sony dSLRs

Sony has some excellent dSLRs, all priced quite competitively. It has two full-frame models and several low-to-midrange cropped dSLRs.

Sony doesn't compete for the ultra-high-end market in either case. It tends to focus on budget-conscious professionals and amateurs. As the book was going to press, Sony announced several new mid-range and budget camera models: the Alpha 55, 33, 560, 390, and 290. The 55 and 33 are fairly revolutionary in design. They have a fixed mirror that is semi-transparent. It doesn't have to move out of the way when taking photos. That boosts frame rate and has other technical advantages. (A fixed translucent mirror was introduced to SLRs in 1989 by Canon and the Canon EOS RT, which lasted until 1992, and again on the EOS-1N RS, from 1994-2000. This type of mirror is also called a pellicle mirror because it splits the beam of light entering the camera.)

Sony also has joined the movie fray with these additions. The 55, 33, and Alpha 560 all shoot full HD video with built-in stereo microphone. The 390 and 290 are updates of the budget class.

Looking at the full-frame variety

To put the full-frame digital SLR marketplace into perspective, Sony has as many full-frame models as Canon, and both have competitive price points.

If you have to use full-frame and are on a budget (who isn't?), look closely at these two cameras:

© Sony Corp.

Figure 5-1: The revolutionary Alpha 55.

✔ **Alpha 900:** The Sony flagship camera — the top of the heap. The Alpha 900 has the highest megapixel count (24.6) of any digital SLR available today, decent frame rate for this class (5 fps — full-frame dSLRs shoot slower than cropped-frame dSLRs, which means 5 fps is about average), standard controls, and even full auto shooting mode.

The combination of a reasonable AEB (Sony skimps on it across the board), ISO, LCD, maximum shutter speed, and light weight makes this camera a steal at $2,699. Although its weight is undoubtedly cut by its lack of a built-in vertical grip, it isn't much to gripe about.

✔ **Alpha 850:** The Sony budget full-frame dSLR, which means a great deal because the Alpha 850 doesn't cost much more than many high-end, cropped-frame dSLRs. It's priced considerably less than the cropped-framed dSLRs that lead the class.

The Alpha 850 doesn't give much ground, either. It shoots a bit slower (3 fps), and the viewfinder covers only 98 percent of the frame. In all other ways (that I can determine), this camera is identical to the Alpha 900.

Table 5-1 details the Sony full-frame dSLR specs.

Table 5-1	Full-Frame Sony dSLR Specs	
	Alpha 900	*Alpha 850*
Year announced	2008	2009
Price (may vary)	$$$	$$$
Megapixels (effective)	24.6	24.6
Full or cropped	Full	Full
Built-in flash	No	No
Maximum FPS	5	3
Video	No	No
Audio (built-in/input)	N/A	N/A
RAW+JPEG	Yes	Yes
P/S/Av/M modes	Yes	Yes
Full auto	Yes	Yes
Creative/Easy modes	No	No
Scenes	No	No
AEB (exp; total range)	3; 4.0 EV	3; 4.0 EV
Base ISO (not equivalent)	100–6400	100–6400
Viewfinder coverage	100 percent	98 percent
LCD size (in)	3	3
LCD dots	921,600	921,600
Live view	No	No
Tilt LCD	No	No
HDMI	Yes	Yes
Maximum shutter speed	1/8000	1/8000
Autofocus	9-point	9-point
Metering	40-segment	40-segment
Image stabilization (body)	Yes	Yes
Memory card	CF I/II; microdrive; Memory Stick Duo	CF I/II; microdrive; Memory Stick Duo
Weight (g)	850	850
Weight (in cans of soda)	2.5	2.5

Comparing numbers

As you look through the tables and interpret the numbers in this minibook, remember that it's all relative. In five years, 5 fps will be irrelevant. The proper way to analyze and compare camera specifications won't be.

For example, Sony might have a full-frame dSLR that shoots 12 fps by then. Fine. How does it compare with the others in its class? Is it better, worse, or the same? Does the camera cost more, less, or the same? Are there other mitigating factors that make it stand out from the crowd, even if it suffers when comparing frame rates?

Examining the Sony cropped-frame class

Splitting the Sony cropped-frame class (all weigh in with a crop factor of 1.5) into subcategories is difficult. The company has no fewer than six cropped-frame dSLRs for less than $1,000 and, based on price (not on capability), they all belong in the budget class. As the prices of these cameras rise, their capabilities fall more in line with other midlevel to high-end cropped-frame dSLRs.

Sony has the peculiar practice of basing two cameras on a single body (if not identical, virtually indistinguishable), making the features slightly different (on both the high end and the low end), and pricing them accordingly. For example, the Alpha 500 and 550 are paired this way, as are the lower-level Alpha 290/390 and the exciting new Alpha 33/55.

Cropped-frame Sony Alphas are described in this list (check Tables 5-2 and 5-3 for their specifications):

✔ **Alpha 550:** This model is priced competitively, which is somewhat surprising considering its several features put it in the same ballpark with cameras from Canon and Nikon that retail for hundreds of dollars more. For example, its megapixel count (14.2), shooting speed (7 fps), and excellent ISO characteristics (200-12800) are comparable to the Nikon D300S, making the 550 a nice dSLR to own.

Where the Alpha 550 *doesn't* deliver is in its lack of a Movie mode (like all Sony dSLRs), the less-than-full coverage of its viewfinder, and its top shutter speed of only 1/4000 second. When you compare those specifications against other, higher-end cropped bodies, the Alpha 550 doesn't match up well. However, if you consider it a midlevel to high-end entry-level camera, it outpaces most budget-oriented cameras.

Both the Alpha 550 and 500 (its low-end counterpart) have tiltable LCDs, which enhance the Live view feature considerably.

✔ **Alpha 560:** This model is similar to the Alpha 550, except that it supports full HD video with stereo audio. The 560 also has a marginally better low ISO range and improved metering and autofocus capabilities. All for less money than the 550! I wouldn't expect the 550 to last long given these realities; it may be replaced by the Alpha 580, which is an Alpha 560 with 16 megapixels.

✔ **Alpha 55:** The Alpha 55 is Sony's splash into new dSLR territory. It has a translucent mirror that doesn't have to move out of the way to take a photo. This breakthrough gives the Alpha 55 a much greater frame rate (10 fps) than other cameras in its class when shooting still photos and gives the camera a boost when shooting videos. (It has to do with allowing phase-detection autofocus at the same time the camera is exposing the sensor.)

The Alpha 55 also shoots full HD video with stereo microphone built into the camera body, has a nice 16.2 megapixel count, and 100 percent coverage through an electronic viewfinder. The traditional pentaprism and optical viewfinder have been eliminated because the mirror doesn't split enough light for direct viewing to be practical. The 55 also has built-in GPS time stamping and features improvements in autofocus and metering segments.

This is a stunning camera for under $1,000 if you don't mind looking through an electronic viewfinder (which is large and bright) or using Live view constantly.

✔ **Alpha 33:** The Alpha 33 is very similar to the 55. The key differences: fewer megapixels (14.2MP) and a slightly slower frame rate (7fps). That's it.

The Alpha 33 has the same revolutionary translucent fixed mirror design as the 55 and costs just a little bit less.

✔ **Alpha 390:** The Alpha 390 stacks up well against other budget dSLRs. It has plenty of megapixels (14.2), Live view, and an articulated LCD. The exceptions are shooting speed (only 2.5fps) and its meager AEB capability. High dynamic range photography is a challenge to shoot using AEB if all you have to work with is 3 exposures +/– 0.7 EV.

Given the price (just over $500), though, it's a strong entry-level contender for budget-minded consumers.

✔ **Alpha 290:** The Alpha 290 is an Alpha 390 without Live view or an articulated LCD monitor. That's basically it. If you don't want or need Live view, save yourself a little bit of money and get the 290. Conversely, the 390 isn't that much more expensive than the 290 and so is well worth the price of the extra features.

If you're struggling to afford a dSLR with decent features and you need to shave the cost a little, this dSLR is a perfect choice. Although Sony budget models tend to shoot slower and have pitiful AEB features, they have good ISO characteristics, comparable shutter speeds, LCDs, and shooting modes.

Book VIII
Chapter 5

Sony-Sony,
Bo-Bony

Table 5-2 details the Sony midrange cropped dSLR specs. Table 5-3 details the entry-level cropped specs.

Table 5-2	Sony Midrange Cropped dSLR Specs			
	Alpha 550	*Alpha 560*	*Alpha 55*	*Alpha 33*
Year announced	2009	2010	2010	2010
Price (may vary)	$$	$	$$	$
Megapixels (effective)	14.2	14.2	16.2	14.2
Full or cropped	Cropped	Cropped	Cropped	Cropped
Built-in flash	Yes	Yes	Yes	Yes
Maximum FPS	7	7	10	7
Video	No	Yes	Yes	Yes
Audio (built-in/ input)	N/A	Stereo/ Stereo	Stereo/ Stereo	Stereo/ Stereo
RAW+JPEG	Yes	Yes	Yes	Yes
P/S/Av/M modes	Yes	Yes	Yes	Yes
Full auto	Yes	Yes	Yes	Yes
Creative/Easy modes	No	No	No	No
Scenes	Yes	Yes	Yes	Yes
AEB (exp; total range)	3; 1.4 EV	3; 1.4 EV	3; 1.4 EV	3; 1.4 EV
Base ISO (not equivalent)	200-12800	200-12800	200-12800	200-12800
Viewfinder coverage	95 percent	95 percent	100 percent	100 percent
LCD size (in)	3	3	3	3
LCD dots	921,600	921,600	921,600	921,600
Live view	Yes	Yes	Yes	Yes
Tilt LCD	Yes	Yes	Yes	Yes
HDMI	Yes	Yes	Yes	Yes
Maximum shutter speed	1/4000	1/4000	1/4000	1/4000

	Alpha 550	*Alpha 560*	*Alpha 55*	*Alpha 33*
Autofocus	9-point	15-point	15-point	15-point
Metering	40-segment	1200-segment	1200-segment	1200-segment
Image stabilization (body)	Yes	Yes	Yes	Yes
Memory card	Memory Stick PRO Duo/Pro-HG Duo; SD/SDHC	Memory Stick PRO Duo/Pro-HG Duo; SD/SDHC/SDXC	Memory Stick PRO Duo/Pro-HG Duo; SD/SDHC/SDXC	Memory Stick PRO Duo/Pro-HG Duo; SD/SDHC/SDXC
Weight (g)	599	599	492	492
Weight (in cans of soda)	1.76	1.76	1.45	1.45

Table 5-3	Sony Entry Level dSLR Specs		
	Alpha 500	*Alpha 390*	*Alpha 290*
Year announced	2009	2010	2010
Price (may vary)	$	$	$
Megapixels (effective)	12.3	14.2	14.2
Full or cropped	Cropped	Cropped	Cropped
Built-in flash	Yes	Yes	Yes
Maximum FPS	5	2.5	2.5
Video	No	No	No
Audio (built-in/input)	N/A	N/A	N/A
RAW+JPEG	Yes	Yes	Yes
P/S/Av/M modes	Yes	Yes	Yes
Full auto	Yes	Yes	Yes
Creative/Easy modes	No	No	No
Scenes	Yes	Yes	Yes
AEB (exp; total range)	3; 1.4 EV	3; 1.4 EV	3; 1.4 EV
Base ISO (not equivalent)	200-12800	100-3200	100-3200
Viewfinder coverage	95 percent	95 percent	95 percent

(continued)

Table 5-3 *(continued)*

	Alpha 500	Alpha 390	Alpha 290
LCD size (in)	3	2.7	2.7
LCD dots	230,400	230,400	230,400
Live view	Yes	Yes	No
Tilt LCD	Yes	Yes	No
HDMI	Yes	Yes	No
Maximum shutter speed	1/4000	1/4000	1/4000
Autofocus	9-point	9-point	9-point
Metering	40-segment	40-segment	40-segment
Image stabilization (body)	Yes	Yes	Yes
Memory card	Memory Stick PRO Duo/ Pro-HG Duo; SD/SDHC	Memory Stick PRO Duo; SD/ SDHC	Memory Stick PRO Duo; SD/ SDHC
Weight (g)	597	497	456
Weight (in cans of soda)	1.75	1.46	1.34

Deciphering the Lens Situation

Sony uses a number of different lenses in its Alpha line of dSLRs, ranging from standard zoom lenses to fixed-focal length prime lenses. The line includes macro lenses and even *teleconverters*, which increase the focal length of any lens they're attached to. For example, a 2x teleconverter turns a 100mm lens into a 200mm lens — doubling its power.

Alphas users can also take advantage of the large stable of Minolta lenses.

Sony lenses are divided into these categories:

- **Standard Sony:** Sony has an extensive lens collection for its Alpha dSLRs, covering every necessary focal length and category.

  Digital Technology (or just *DT*) lenses were designed for cropped-frame digital cameras with APS-size sensors. If you have a full-frame Alpha, be sure not to buy an incompatible lens.

- **Carl Zeiss:** Although Zeiss isn't exclusively associated with Sony, Sony markets and sells Alpha-compatible Zeiss lenses in one of its two high-grade lens categories (see Figure 5-2). Zeiss lenses have a long history and have generally high quality.

✔ **G Series:** The Sony native, high-grade lens category was created by Minolta as a "gold standard" in performance and quality.

Carl Zeiss lens' autofocus motor technology is named Super Sonic Wave Motor, or SSM. Sony lenses use SAM, or Smooth Autofocus Motor. Additionally, Sony Alpha dSLRs rely on in-camera image stabilization (IS). It makes the lenses lighter and less expensive than their counterparts that have in-lens IS.

Choosing the Right Flash

Sony has just the flash for you, whether you want the top-of-the-line model to set up one or more off-camera flashes or simply an inexpensive alternative (like the HVL-F20AM) to your camera's pop-up flash. This list describes your options:

© Sony Corp.

Figure 5-2: The Carl Zeiss, from Sony, with the 24-70mm f/2.8 zoom lens.

✔ **HVL-F58AM flash:** The premier Sony flash has good output, wireless capability (master or slave), bounces, an LCD and external controls, and other cool features. Quick Shift Bounce, for example, lets the head orbit to the left or right. If you want to buy the best flash from Sony, this is the one.

✔ **HVL-F42AM flash:** Buy this model, the next best thing to the F58AM, if you need an excellent flash but not all the extras that come with the HVL-F58AM. This one bounces and swivels and can act as a wireless slave.

✔ **HVL-F20AM flash:** This budget model moves the flash off the camera. Even budget external flashes are more powerful than pop-up flashes, have a larger flash, and if they bounce, are more flexible. The F20AM is designed to be light and easy to use; the flash bounces based on whether you specify the indoor or outdoor setting.

✔ **HVL-RLAM Alpha Ring Light:** The Sony ring flash unit (see Figure 5-3) is useful for macro and close-up shots.

✔ **HVL-MT24AM Macro Twin Flash Kit:** The Sony twin flash unit is useful for macro and close-up shots.

Book VIII
Chapter 5

Sony-Sony, Bo-Bony

Sony incorporates the flash's guide number (in meters) into the product number, which makes figuring out their power easier. For example, the F58AM has a guide number of 58. That means it has a distance of 58 meters at ISO 100 and f/1.0 when operating at full power. The practical distance is often much less and depends on the aperture you are shooting at. For example, at f/8 and ISO 100, the F58AM has a range of only 7 meters. Also, remember that Sony's top dSLRs don't have built-in flash. You have to choose an external model or work with other types of studio lighting.

© Sony Corp.

Figure 5-3: The HVL-RLAM Alpha Ring Light, looking quite round.

Summing Up

✔ Coming on strong, Sony has made great leaps in the video category and has introduced a significant new wrinkle to the dSLR design: a semi-transparent, fixed mirror combined with an electronic viewfinder.

✔ Sony isn't shy about updating models. Look for camera numbers and capabilities to continue to change at a rapid pace.

✔ Compare apples to apples. My first dSLR was the 10-megapixel Alpha 300, which has Live view and a tilt-screen LCD. I love that camera — it takes great-looking photographs. Despite my affection for it, I wouldn't put it in the same league as a $2,500 camera.

✔ The hot shoe on Sony dSLRs is a different size from the industry standard (Canon and Nikon), which can be a pain because not all flash accessories are compatible (for example, spirit levels that fit in the hot shoe). Sony makes a hot shoe adapter, in case you need one.

✔ Because Sony puts image stabilization in-camera rather than in-lens, every lens you buy is supported by image stabilization (unlike other brands).

Chapter 6: Notable Non-dSLR Digital Cameras

In This Chapter

✓ Checking out the cream of the compact digital crop

✓ Looking into using nontraditional formats

✓ Exploring medium-format digital

Despite the topic of this book (dSLR cameras), let me spend a few pages showing you a few notable non-dSLRs. They range from high-end compacts such as the Canon G-11 to the medium-format cameras such as the Hasselblad H4D-40.

Despite the loads of power that premium compact digitals have, they cannot stand toe-to-toe with dSLRs in terms of responsiveness and image quality. On the other end of the spectrum, medium-format cameras take far better photos but are too expensive for many professionals, not to mention semipros and amateurs, to own. In the middle of the spectrum is the developing category of digital cameras that put a cropped-frame-size sensor in a compact body. This technology represents the greatest challenge to traditional dSLRs because it does away with the clunky mirror system that defines SLR cameras. (See Book I, Chapter 1 for an explanation of mirrors and SLRs.)

Powerful Compacts

The compact digital camera is a threat to the dSLR in only one area: size. The compact digital, which is small and easy to carry and often has simplified shooting modes, typically doesn't let you change lenses. In fact, most compact digital cameras don't support raw photo formats and have eschewed manual shooting modes.

Despite this situation, a market exists for high-end compacts as backups to dSLRs. They have manual modes and take good-looking photos, and they support the raw format and are easy to stick in your camera bag.

Canon G11

The Canon G11, shown in Figure 6-1, packs as much goodness as possible into the body of a compact digital camera. It shoots raw, has an articulated LCD, and a nice heft, and (as far as compacts go) it shoots nice-looking pictures.

A compact is a compact, so no matter how expensive it is or how many nice features it has (like movie and manual modes, a large LCD monitor, a view-finder, and so on), its sensor is small, noise is a problem, and you have little or no ability to change lenses, like you can on a dSLR.

Having said that, manufacturers try their best to resolve image-quality problems. Canon cut the sensor resolution for the G11 to reduce image noise by two stops compared to the G10.

Figure 6-1: The beefy Canon G11.

Panasonic Lumix DMC-LX3

Panasonic makes a top-end compact in the same class as the Canon G11. The LX3, shown in Figure 6-2, has a good feature set and a 2.5x optical zoom with an f/2.0 Leica lens. (Most compacts have f/2.8 or greater.) It shoots a good wide angle for this class (24mm in 35mm equivalent terms, wider than normal for compact digitals), reaches a maximum ISO of 3200, and has manual and scene-shooting modes.
Additionally, it's light, it looks good, and it supports raw photos.

As with other premium compacts, the LX3 shoots slow (2.5 fps) and has a small sensor — you just can't work around it.

Panasonic makes a few dSLRs, too. Have a peek at its Web site (www. panasonic.com) for more information. You should also browse Leica's snazzy non-dSLRs at www.leica.com.

Figure 6-2: The high-end Panasonic LX3 compact camera.

Sigma DP series

Sigma (http://sigma-dp.com) makes an excellent series of compact digital cameras, including DP1, DP1s, DP1x, DP2, and D2s. The DP1 claim to fame, as shown in Figure 6-3, is that it's the first compact digital camera with a dSLR-size sensor (just smaller than APS-C but larger than four thirds).

The Sigma DP1 doesn't have the specs to compete with most high-end digital cameras, but if you like the bare-bones approach to photography, you'll love

Figure 6-3: The well-respected Sigma DP1.

the DP1. Sigma is also pioneering the FOVEON image sensor that uses three color-sensing layers instead of the alternating grid layout of traditional Bayer sensors used in most digital cameras.

Sigma (www.sigmaphoto.com) also makes two dSLRs: the SD-14 and SD-15. Give them a look-see to compare them with the other cameras described in this minibook.

Curious New Camera Formats

New-format cameras try to put as much dSLR-like power into as small a format as possible without being tied to the single-lens reflex design. (Boy, that's a mouthful.)

The dSLR evolved from the SLR — which is, ultimately, a mechanical design. The mirror and shutter inside your dSLR must move up and down and open and close to work, and do so perfectly at blazingly fast speeds. (I think 1/8000 of a second qualifies.)

This concept is elegant, but not mandatory in the digital age. People are trying to invent better ways to take digital photos than to use the dSLR. (One of these new designs could be the wave of the future.)

Samsung NX10

Although the Samsung NX10 isn't a dSLR, it has an APS-C dSLR sensor inside. The difference between it and a dSLR is that the NX10 eliminates the traditional dSLR viewfinder-and-mirror system and implements an electronic viewfinder. The specs for the NX10 show good ISO performance (100–3200), a reasonable maximum shutter speed (1/4000 second), plenty of shooting modes, a three-inch LCD, HD video shooting, and raw shooting. That sounds like a dSLR to me!

Samsung makes a powerful dSLR, the GX-20. Head over to the Samsung site at www.samsung.com to see photos of both cameras.

Panasonic Lumix G Micro System

The Panasonic G Micro System has championed the micro four thirds system. Cameras include the G1, G2 (with a nice-looking touchscreen LCD — see Figure 6-4), G10, GF1, and GH1. These cameras are essentially dSLRs without the traditional viewfinder and mirror. They act like dSLRs, look like dSLRs (except for the GF-1), and have sensors the size of dSLRs.

Panasonic also makes the DMC-L10 dSLR.

Figure 6-4: The cool-looking Panasonic Lumix G2.

Olympus Pen series

The Olympus Pen series features exciting cameras. The E-PL1, E-P1, and E-P2 (see Figure 6-5) are all interchangeable lens cameras with micro four thirds lenses and in-body image stabilization. They do away with the traditional viewfinder and SLR mirror. Don't let the interchangeability fool you: Olympus's dSLR lenses are not compatible with the Pen series (it has to do with how shallow the Pen cameras are compared to deeper dSLRs). The sensor is the same size as the ones used in the larger dSLR bodies. (That's hot, baby!)

Figure 6-5: The E-P2, with a few of its lenses and an electronic viewfinder.

Medium-Format Digitals

Despite what you may think, the dSLRs described in the other chapters of this minibook aren't at the high end of the digital camera world. As good as they are, their sensors are, at most, the size of a 35mm frame of film as though that isn't as large as they come, in either film or digital.

For all practical purposes, the honor of top dog in the digital camera world goes to the medium format (whether it's a dSLR-type medium format camera or not). These cameras have large sensors and huge megapixel counts. For example, the sensor on the Hasselblad H4D-40 (see Figure 6-6) measures 33.1 x 44.2mm and can capture 40 megapixels. The downside to this perfection is that the camera costs about $20,000.

Figure 6-6: The Hasselblad H4D-40 medium-format dSLR.

Mamiya also makes medium-format digital cameras, and Pentax announced one in the summer of 2010.

Book IX

Practical dSLR Tips

*I*n the chapters in this minibook, I show you how to set up a camera for specific shooting situations. I discuss the photos, describe how I shot them, specify the parameters I used, and provide other helpful tips that relate to shooting those subjects.

I reviewed my entire photo collection to choose good examples of photos I shot with my digital SLRs, and then I organized them by category. You'll find in this minibook photos of fireworks, people, lightning, sunsets, bridges, construction projects, more people, landscapes, animals, bugs, corn, rivers, birthday cakes and parties, eggs, ants, trucks, planes, people, bigger trucks, motorcycles, race cars, fire engines, large buildings, small buildings, interiors, gravestones, guitar amplifiers, and trash.

That's *a lot* of photos, and I didn't even list them all.

Chapter 1: Working with Light and Time

In This Chapter

- ✔ Shooting into the sun
- ✔ Working with low contrast
- ✔ Putting the sun to the side
- ✔ Fading with the last glowing embers
- ✔ Working with shadows
- ✔ Going out in a storm
- ✔ Framing creatively
- ✔ Photographing fireworks

*Y*ou shouldn't be surprised to read that light and time are important aspects of photography.

Different situations with different lighting conditions at different times of the day (or night) combine to make an incredible palette that you as the photographer get to try to capture.

If you're tired of shooting the same old scenes, make the effort to go out at different times of the day. Try shooting at dusk and at night, into the sun and away from the sun, with the sun shining sideways, or from shadow or into shadow, for example.

High-Contrast Sunset in HDR

This set of photos was taken after a long afternoon of shooting. I shot quite a few bracketed shots of the area while my family visited the park. While driving home, we noticed that the sunset started to look *incredible,* so I made a quick turn and went where I knew I could capture the sunset without letting too many obstacles get in the way.

Stay on the lookout for clouds as the sun sets. They can transform a scene into an incredible display of color and detail as they show highlights and shadows and capture the color of the setting sun.

(ISO 100, f/8, 1/320 second, Sigma 10-20mm F4-5.6 at 10mm) 2009

Bracketing the scene allowed me to point directly into the sun to capture detail and color in the foreground. If I had approached this shot normally, the sunset and sky (and, to some degree, the river) would have looked good, but everything else would have been in silhouette.

For more information on HDR, turn to Book VI, Chapter 4.

Option	Setting	Notes
ISO	100	HDR shot with ISO 100 to reduce noise; shutter speed generally not a problem
Aperture	f/8	My "go-to" aperture for most scenic shots for depth of field
Shutter speed	1/320 second	For the 0 EV exposure
Brackets	9 (+/− 1.0 EV)	AEB; 9 exposures at 4/−3/−2/−1/0/+1/+2/+3/+4 EV
Camera	Nikon D200	Semipro dSLR; cropped body (FX)
Lens	Sigma 10-20mm F4-5.6	Ultra wide-angle zoom; useful for wide landscape shots
Focal length	10mm	35mm equivalent: 15mm
Processing		Nikon Capture NX 2 (raw); Photomatix Pro (HDR); Photoshop
Other		Manual exposure mode; tripod; remote shutter release; pattern metering

Low-Contrast Cloudy Evening

This scene presents the opposite challenge from shooting at sunset in HDR. In this photo, the sun is setting, and the light is hidden behind the cloud cover on the edge of the horizon. The sky lacks dramatic contrast, and the scene as a whole has a limited color palette.

Sometimes, less than optimum conditions can contribute to producing fantastic shots. Results matter — not our preconceived notions. In this case, I processed the photo artistically by adding a vignette in Photoshop to emphasize the silhouetted bridge and clouds.

*(ISO 100, f/8, 1/60 second,
Sony DT 18-70mm f/3.5-5.6 at 20mm) 2009*

Option	Setting	Notes
ISO	100	Outside shooting toward the setting sun; even though this is a darker scene, you don't need to raise the ISO because the shutter speed was more than reasonable
Aperture	f/8	My "go-to" aperture for most scenic shots for depth of field
Shutter speed	1/60 second	No need to go faster; nothing is moving in the scene, and I used a tripod
Camera	Sony Alpha 300	Entry-level dSLR; cropped body (FX); built-in Super SteadyShot image stabilization
Lens	Sony DT 18-70mm f/3.5-5.6	General-purpose zoom; budget kit lens; good value
Focal length	20mm	35mm equivalent: 30mm
Processing		Adobe Camera Raw (raw); Photoshop
Other		Manual exposure mode, tripod, remote shutter release, pattern metering

Sunlit from the Side

You never know when you're going to get a truly nice-looking photo. I realize that my statement sounds strange in a book that describes how to take good photos in different conditions, but it's true.

(ISO 100, f/5, 1/160 second, Sigma 10-20mm F4-5.6 at 16mm) 2008

I took this shot at a local zoo. My family was riding a small train that circles around the lake. As the train chugged back to the station, I leaned out and took the shot, looking ahead. The sun was low and off to the right, which is a key element of the photo. You don't capture shadows like this when you point your camera at the sun or directly away from it.

I was momentarily in the right place at the right time, ready to take the photo. Sometimes even landscape shots can be spontaneous.

Know how your camera works and practice using it. Be ready for every situation so that can you can literally just "point and shoot."

Option	Setting	Notes
ISO	100	Outdoors in strong daylight
Aperture	f/5	An action shot in the sense that I was moving and used a larger aperture to get a faster shutter speed, an approach I chose over raising the ISO
Shutter speed	1/160 second	Fast enough shutter speed for a blur-free shot from a slow-moving train
Camera	v	Entry-level dSLR; cropped body (FX); built-in Super SteadyShot image stabilization
Lens	Sigma 10-20mm F4-5.6	Ultra wide-angle zoom
Focal length	16mm	35mm equivalent: 24mm
Processing		Photomatix Pro (pseudo-HDR); Adobe Camera Raw (raw); Photoshop Elements; in this case, I overlaid a semitransparent pseudo-HDR layer (created from Photomatix Pro) on top of the normal photo to enhance the contrast and color
Other		+1.0 EV exposure compensation; center-weighted metering; aperture priority; shot handheld while moving on a train

Just Past Dusk (Or Thereabouts)

Unlike the photo in the earlier section "Sunlit from the Side," this shot was completely set up. I set up camp on the east side of the lake so that I could frame the water, trees, and light all at the same time as the sun went down.

(ISO 100, f/4, 1/13 second, Sigma 10-20mm F4-5.6 at 10mm) 2008

Don't waste your time going out and setting up your equipment, shooting five or six shots, and then wrapping up and going home. Go out and stay a while. Take extra batteries and one or two extra memory cards.

To capture the photo shown in this section, I arrived early, chose my position, examined different framing options, and started taking photos during the golden hour. I continued until dark so that I would have a wealth of options to choose from when I returned home and analyzed the photos. Although they show the same scene, they're completely different pictures because of the ever-changing light.

Option	Setting	Notes
ISO	100	Maintain a low setting to reduce noise; originally part of an HDR bracketed set that didn't look good in HDR, so I selected a single exposure and processed it
Aperture	f/4	Opened, to let in more light
Shutter speed	1/13 second	Fast shutter speed not as important; no moving objects and using a tripod
Camera	Sony Alpha 300	Entry-level dSLR; cropped body (FX); built-in Super SteadyShot image stabilization
Lens	Sigma 10-20mm F4-5.6	Ultra wide-angle zoom; useful for scenic shots, such as this one, where no distortion is detected
Focal length	10mm	35mm equivalent: 15mm
Processing		Sony Image Data Converter SR (raw)
Other		Manual exposure mode, tripod; remote shutter release; mosquito repellent; snacks; pattern metering

Casting a Shadow

This shot from my local zoo (again) takes advantage of the setting sun, which is highlighting the trees on the far side of the lake. I couldn't find a vantage point to take the photo without my shadow getting in the way, but then I realized that purposely making the shadow an element of the photo would be interesting. (The rocks in the foreground weren't exciting, anyway.)

My wide-angle lens helped capture the lake and made it feel large.

(ISO 100, f/8, 1/200 second, Sigma 10-20mm F4-5.6 at 20mm) 2008

Option	*Setting*	*Notes*
ISO	100	Shot outdoors in strong daylight
Aperture	f/8	My "go-to" aperture for most scenic shots
Shutter speed	1/200 second	Fast; stop down to reduce, if necessary, when shooting at ISO 100
Camera	Sony Alpha 300	Entry-level dSLR; cropped body (FX); built-in Super SteadyShot image stabilization
Lens	Sigma 10-20mm F4-5.6	Ultra wide-angle zoom
Focal length	20mm	35mm equivalent: 30mm
Processing		Adobe Camera Raw (raw); Photoshop Elements
Other		Manual mode; pattern metering; tripod; remote shutter release; exhausted family in a van (out of frame to the left) waiting to return home

Lightning Crashes

One good thing about storms, unlike other exterior subjects such as mountains or the ocean, is that they're everywhere. I took this shot from the front porch of our house.

(ISO 100, f/5.6, 16 seconds, Sony DT 18-70mm f/3.5-5.6 at 20mm) 2008

Photographing lightning is a matter of being in the right place at the right time with your camera set up and *already shooting* when the lighting strikes. (Notice the taillights on the car in the lower left corner.) That's right: The shutter must be open if you want to capture lightning — it's too fast otherwise. Close the shutter when you think you're on the verge of overexposing the photo or after the strike.

I had to choose a focal length that provided good coverage of the sky and, more importantly, choose which direction to point the camera. To do that, I observed the storm to see where it was moving and tried to predict its action.

In this case, an intense storm cell had just passed, and the rain had eased, so I was able to set up my camera on the porch without fear of getting it wet. I quickly oriented the camera at the trailing edge of the storm, plugged in the remote shutter release cable, and switched to Bulb mode. Then I triggered the first exposure and waited. And waited. When I wasn't waiting, I missed several lightning strikes because they were behind me or on the other side of the house. Then I saw an incredible strike hit, just up the street. I got it!

Do *not* take unnecessary risks for a photograph. Shooting during storms, especially when lightning is present, can be incredibly dangerous.

I took the shot in this section when the storm was moving away, and even then, the lightning strike scared me silly. I went inside soon afterward.

Option	Setting	Notes
ISO	100	No need for high ISO with extended shutter times
Aperture	f/5.6	I didn't consider setting an optimum aperture at the time, proving that you can sometimes choose questionable settings and still produce good-looking photos
Shutter speed	16 seconds (Bulb)	Bulb setting, much like the one for fireworks; open the shutter and wait for the "zap!"
Camera	Sony Alpha 300	Entry-level dSLR; cropped body (FX); built-in Super SteadyShot image stabilization
Lens	Sony DT 18-70mm f/3.5-5.6	General-purpose zoom; budget kit lens; good value
Focal length	20mm	35mm equivalent: 30mm
Processing		Sony Image Data Converter (raw), Photoshop
Other		Tripod; remote shutter release; pattern metering; change of underwear

Inside-Out Bobcat

The following photo shows a creative way to take advantage of light and shadow. As I stood outside our garage, looking through the window, as a Bobcat tore out the existing concrete.

I used center-weighted metering because a lot of things were happening that could confuse the camera. The interior of the garage was much darker than the outside, and the driver was in shadow. It was just after 2 p.m., and the sun was beating down brightly from almost directly overhead.

You can change metering modes whenever you need to.

I switched to center-weighted metering to try to properly expose the Bobcat, but even then had to address some of the shadows in processing.

(ISO 100, f/4, 1/1000 second, Nikon Nikkor 28mm f/3.5 AI) 2009

Option	*Setting*	*Notes*
ISO	100	Subject shot in strong light
Aperture	f/4	Used older lens to experiment with wider apertures; sharp with good depth of field, mostly because of the distance
Shutter speed	1/1000 second	A bit of overkill, dictated by the wide aperture
Camera	Nikon D200	Semipro dSLR; cropped body (FX)
Lens	Nikon Nikkor 28mm f/3.5 AI	Used an older manual-focus lens on my Nikon FE2 SLR. Although it's compatible with my D200, it supports only manual focus. This focal length is used on cropped bodies. AI lenses were introduced by Nikon in 1977 and allow the camera to automatically index the maximum aperture of the lens
Focal length	28mm	35mm equivalent: 42.0mm
Processing		Photoshop Elements; from JPEG (proving that you don't always need to use raw)
Other		Aperture priority, manual focus; center-weighted metering; handheld

Fabulous Fireworks

Don't skimp when you take photos of fireworks — take as many pictures as you can. Bring extra memory cards, too, if you have them. Take longer exposures of a few blasts and shorter ones of a single burst. If you leave your shutter open too long, light reflecting off the smoke from the display becomes more visible.

Bring along your tripod and (cable or electronic) remote shutter release. The tripod is a necessity because you'll leave the shutter open (use the Bulb setting to press and hold open the shutter), and you want blurry photos. If you use the remote shutter release, you can sit back and have some fun as you watch the fireworks without having to manhandle the camera during every exposure. Use a locking cable so that your finger doesn't cramp up from endlessly holding down the shutter release button.

(ISO 100, f/8, 2 seconds, Sigma 10-20mm F4.5-5.6 at 12mm) 2008

The secret to shooting fireworks is using the Bulb shutter speed in Manual exposure mode. The exact timing is up to you. Your camera will pick up the light from the fireworks just fine. You have to decide whether you want to freeze a burst (as I did here) or catch an extended display.

You can't physically move closer or further away easily, so bring a multipurpose zoom lens. Experiment with different focal lengths so that you get the coverage you want at your current distance. Previewing photos in the heat of a noisy fireworks display is difficult. Check a few photos first, and then trust your settings. Set the manual focus to infinity, turn off long-exposure noise reduction, and set the ISO to 100.

Take snacks, beverages, a blanket, and possibly a lawn chair to sit on while you watch the show and take your photos. And don't trip over the shutter release cable!

Option	Setting	Notes
ISO	100	No need for a high ISO, even in the dark; the fireworks, combined with the Bulb shutter speed, are plenty bright
Aperture	f/8	My "go-to" aperture for most scenic shots
Shutter speed	2 seconds (Bulb)	To use the special shutter speed Bulb, press and hold the shutter release button to open the shutter and then release the button to close it; your finger appreciates your use of a remote shutter release with a locking button
Camera	Sony Alpha 300	Entry-level dSLR; cropped body (FX); built-in Super SteadyShot image stabilization
Lens	Sigma 10-20mm F4-5.6	Ultra wide-angle zoom; a good general-purpose kit lens with reasonable wide-angle capability would work well, too
Focal length	12mm	Used this decidedly wide-angle focal length to cover a good portion of the sky and not leave fireworks outside the frame; cropped to the fireworks blast (35mm equivalent: 18mm)
Processing		Sony Image Data Converter SR (raw), Photoshop Elements
Other		Manual exposure mode (because of the Bulb shutter speed), tripod; remote shutter release; pattern metering; candy; family

Chapter 2: Embracing People

In This Chapter

- ↙ Taking a Mother's Day portrait
- ↙ Shooting action shots
- ↙ Photographing birthday parties
- ↙ Surviving a family self-portrait
- ↙ Capturing close moments
- ↙ Having fun at events
- ↙ Shooting street photography
- ↙ Photographing construction workers

*P*hotographing people can be quite challenging. Unlike sunsets, people can be indoors, outdoors, in action, at rest, posed, or acting goofy. The settings you use when you photograph them, therefore, are different.

My number-one concern is to keep the shutter speed fast enough to avoid blurring. When the speed is set, I work the other settings to come up with the best exposure. Often, I use a flash or raise the ISO to accommodate a fast shutter speed.

Knowing the right range of settings helps you faster and better create the effect you want. As you read this chapter, pay special attention to the settings to see how I've set up these shots. They represent a good cross-section of the types of photos most people take.

Mother's Day Portrait

I took this semiformal portrait of my wife, Anne, right around Mother's Day 2009.

(ISO 100, f/4.5, 1/180 second, Nikon AF-S DX NIKKOR 35mm f/1.8G) 2009

When you want to find a good photo of someone, look for a good background first. It's more important than you might think. An attractive setting makes the person in the photo stand out because unsightly distractions are removed from the viewer's mind.

Unfortunately, *ugly* is all around, and finding the right setting takes some work. You might find a park or an attractive tree, bush, or building. One of my favorite spots is out in the back yard, in front of the fence.

Aside from my having to ensure that the shutter speed was fast enough to avoid blurring, taking this photo was fairly straightforward. The ISO was low for noise control with a reasonably wide aperture. I took a few shots with a flash for comparison, but ended up liking this one (sans flash) better.

Option	Setting	Notes
ISO	100	Achieved good shutter speed without raising ISO, even in muted light
Aperture	f/4.5	Wider aperture for aesthetic reasons and for low light; could go wider with a faster shutter speed
Shutter speed	1/180 second	Keep portraits fast so people's faces don't blur; could go faster with a wider aperture
Camera	Nikon D200	Semipro dSLR; cropped body (FX)
Lens	Nikon AF-S DX NIKKOR 35mm f/1.8G	A standard prime lens for DX bodies
Focal length	35mm	35mm equivalent: 52mm
Processing		Adobe Camera Raw (raw); Photoshop
Other		Aperture priority; handheld; spot metering

Jake in Action

When you take action shots, you need to focus on shutter speed. (See Book III, Chapter 3 for more examples of action and shutter speed.) One of my sons is playing swingball in this photo, and he's giving it his best shot.

I use Shutter Priority mode and set the speed as fast as possible, given the ISO and aperture I'm using. For this photo, it was 1/500 second, a short enough length of time to capture my son in action without blurring.

(ISO 400, f/3.2, 1/500 second, Nikon AF-S DX NIKKOR 35mm f/1.8G) 2009

The other settings (ISO and aperture) are balanced against the needed shutter speed to get the right exposure. I could have raised the ISO but didn't want to deal with extra noise (which is almost more than I would want at ISO 400). I could have widened the aperture to f/1.8 (I was using a good, low-light prime lens), but didn't want a microscopic depth of field. As it is, f/3.2 is a bit limited. I could also have used a fill flash, but I wanted to use the natural light in this photo.

Options, options, options. Good rules of thumb exist in photography (keep the shutter speed fast, for example), but it also has room for personal choices and preferences.

Option	Setting	Notes
ISO	400	ISO raised to achieve fast shutter speed
Aperture	f/3.2	Opened to compensate for fast shutter speed
Shutter speed	1/500 second	Required for fast action; notice that the tennis ball is sharp, in addition to Jake's face and the racket
Camera	Nikon D200	Semipro dSLR; cropped body (FX)
Lens	Nikon AF-S DX NIKKOR 35mm f/1.8G	A standard prime lens for DX bodies
Focal length	35mm	35mm equivalent: 52mm
Processing		Adobe Camera Raw (raw); Photoshop
Other		Shutter priority; handheld; pattern metering

Birthday Boy

With four children in our family, it seems that we're always celebrating someone's birthday. That's a good thing because I love taking pictures of everyone opening their presents and eating their cake. In this 2010 photo, one of my sons is preparing to blow out the candles on the cake celebrating his third birthday. It was the only fraction of a second during which he sat still all day.

(ISO 400, f/5.6, 1/100 second, Sony DT 18-70mm f/3.5-5.6 at 60mm) 2010

The key elements to getting good photos in these situations are described in this list:

- **Raise the shutter speed:** You're photographing kids, not sloths. They move, twitch, jump, and otherwise don't sit still. The only way to take photos that aren't blurry is to raise the shutter speed. Just make your other exposure controls (ISO, aperture, flash) work around it.

- **Increase the ISO:** I keep the ISO to a minimum level when I shoot because I don't want to deal with noise. However, you probably can't leave it set to 100 and be able to raise the shutter speed. It's a trade-off. In this case, trade ISO for speed.

- **Use a flash:** If you're having problems taking well-lit, crisp photos, use a flash. To soften shadows (almost always a problem), use some form of flash diffuser or softener.

Although I pull out my 35mm or 50mm primes for portraits at our family parties, multipurpose zoom lenses are the best overall lenses. You can move around the room, zoom in on the action, or zoom out and shoot wide-angle.

Option	Setting	Notes
ISO	400	Often must be raised when shooting inside, even if you're using a flash because it helps maintain fast shutter speeds
Aperture	f/5.6	A reasonably large aperture provides artistic bokeh and lets more light into the camera, which eases pressure to a slow shutter speed
Shutter speed	1/100	This speed is probably on the slow side; I normally set the shutter speed to somewhere around 1/250 when photographing kids in motion

Option	Setting	Notes
Camera	Sony Alpha 300	Entry-level dSLR; cropped body (FX); built-in Super SteadyShot image stabilization
Lens	Sony 18-70mm f/3.5-5.6	General-purpose zoom; budget kit lens; good value; I sometimes use a 50mm prime for parties to maximize quality and close-ups; but I use this lens for flexibility
Focal length	60mm	Being able to zoom in is critical when shooting at parties so you can stand back a ways and still take close-ups; 35mm equivalent: 90mm
Processing		Photoshop Elements; I took the camera JPEG and barely adjusted the contrast to illustrate that you don't always have to superprocess every photo you take
Other		Program AE exposure mode; pattern metering; in-camera flash (pop-up); handheld

Family Portrait

In this family portrait, taken on my and wife's tenth wedding anniversary, we all sat on the couch while I used a long, remote shutter-release cable (that I have since tripped over and ripped from the camera) to trigger the shutter. Our oldest child then took the photo.

Sitting still can be challenging for children, especially when you're doing something as fun as taking a family portrait (insert tongue in cheek). We let them take turns with the shutter release although one son tried to escape occasionally.

(ISO 200, f/8, 1/80 second, Sony DT 18-70mm f/3.5-5.6 at 20mm) Ben Correll, 2008

The camera settings reflect a straightforward flash photo. I raised the ISO slightly, kept the aperture small enough for a good depth of field, and made sure the shutter speed was fast enough to avoid blur. For a "sit still" portrait, shutter speeds don't need to be superfast, and the flash tends to stop the action, anyway. The camera was stabilized, and we used the remote to take photos. If you have no remote, use the camera's built-in timer.

Option	Setting	Notes
ISO	200	Even with a flash, ISO sometimes needs to be raised, especially indoors in low-to-moderate lighting conditions; I could have gone to ISO 400 but was trying to keep the noise down
Aperture	f/8	A dependable, all-around aperture that results in a good depth of field and shutter speeds
Shutter speed	1/80 second	Decent shutter speed; needed to keep humans looking sharp; if I wanted something faster, I could have opened up the aperture
Camera	Sony Alpha 300	Entry-level dSLR; cropped body (FX); built-in Super SteadyShot image stabilization
Lens	Sony DT 18-70mm f/3.5-5.6	General-purpose zoom; budget kit lens; good value
Focal length	20mm	35mm equivalent: 30mm
Processing		Adobe Camera Raw (raw); Photoshop
Other		Manual exposure mode; pattern metering; external flash (hot shoe); tripod; remote shutter release (triggered by my son)

Mother and Son

This close-up photo of my son and my wife was taken on my wife's birthday. I wanted to get good shots of her and all our kids. I use my best 50mm prime (the Nikon 50mm F1.4G) on my cropped-body dSLR for portraits such as this one. This fantastic lens takes great-looking photos yet lets me stand at a reasonable distance to still frame things tightly.

(ISO 560, f/4, 1/125 second, Nikon AF-S NIKKOR 50mm f/1.4G) 2010

This 50mm lens also helps me focus exclusively on faces. I don't even try to capture the background or bodies. The lens lets me concentrate on taking beautiful pictures regardless of the room or what's happening around my subjects.

I raised the ISO in this shot to avoid having to use the flash. The natural light, coming from the left, is soft and casts a more attractive shadow than a flash smacking my family in the face would have done.

Option	Setting	Notes
ISO	560	I fired a few exposures with flash but this one, without, looks best; higher ISO to shoot indoors without flash and maintain higher shutter speed
Aperture	f/4	Artistic; close-up subjects and wide aperture limit depth of field; notice that Anne is in it but Jake is just outside
Shutter speed	1/125	Fast, to keep them from blurring
Camera	Nikon D200	Semipro dSLR; cropped body (FX)
Lens	Nikon AF-S NIKKOR 50mm f/1.4G	Nikon's flagship standard prime lens; compatible with full-frame and cropped-frame camera bodies (although the field of view will differ, based on the crop factor of the camera)
Focal length	50mm	35mm equivalent: 75mm
Processing		Adobe Camera Raw (raw); Photoshop Elements
Other		Spot metering; Manual exposure mode; handheld

Monster Truck Girls

This shot is another one taken with my 50mm F1.4 lens, except that the whole family is outdoors, at a monster truck rally. My wife and daughter sat together, and our boys sat between us.

I was there, of course, to take pictures of the action, but I looked over and saw my wife laughing. I swung the camera around and took a few shots of the girls.

(ISO 100, f/2, 1/125 second, Nikon AF-S NIKKOR 50mm f/1.4G) 2009

I was shooting in Shutter Priority mode because I was taking action shots of trucks, motorcycles, and quads. I kept the ISO down but was shooting wide open.

You can "trade" stops of ISO, aperture, and shutter speed to maintain the same exposure. For example, if you want to reduce the size of the aperture *(stop down),* increase the ISO. I call this "trading ISO for aperture." In this case, you can lower the aperture to F4 and raise the ISO to 400 while maintaining the same overall exposure.

See Book III, Chapter 1 for more information on exposure and trading aperture, shutter speed, and ISO.

Option	Setting	Notes
ISO	100	Shot outdoors with adequate lighting; wide aperture helps keep ISO down
Aperture	f/2	Wide open to keep ISO down and achieve a nice bokeh, which you can't do with all lenses
Shutter speed	1/250	Fast to keep photos sharp and catch the action, such as my wife's laughter
Camera	Nikon D200	Semipro dSLR; cropped body (FX)
Lens	Nikon AF-S NIKKOR 50mm f/1.4G	Nikon's flagship standard prime lens
Focal length	50mm	35mm equivalent: 75mm
Processing		Nikon Capture NX 2 (raw); Photoshop
Other		Shutter priority; handheld

Festival Photography

When I took my camera to a local fall festival, I was able to catch the fife and drum corps in action. This festival celebrates frontier life and the pioneer spirit of the United States in the early 1800s.

I followed along the parade route, careful not to get in the way, and took many good shots. I was tempted to crop out bystanders and trash on the ground, but wanted you to see the scene the way it was.

(ISO 100, f/8, 1/125 second, Sigma 10-20mm F4-5.6 at 15mm) 2008

I stooped low to create an interesting angle and captured the honor guard just as they were about to pass. Speed was important because I was unable to remain completely steady and the men were marching across the camera field, which tends to cause more subject movement problems.

Although my camera was in Aperture Priority mode, I was able to monitor its shutter speed. Had it been too low, I would have raised the ISO or widened the aperture. When you start thinking this way at the time you take a photo, you'll become a much better photographer because you will be able to match the right exposure with your artistic sensibilities and the practical matter at hand.

Option	Setting	Notes
ISO	100	Shot outdoors in strong daylight
Aperture	f/8	A dependable, all-around aperture that results in a good depth of field and shutter speeds
Shutter speed	1/125 second	Speed is always important when photographing people; in this case, they were moving; even this setting is on the slow side
Camera	Sony Alpha 300	Entry-level dSLR; cropped body (FX); built-in Super SteadyShot image stabilization
Lens	Sigma 10-20mm F4-5.6	Ultra wide-angle zoom
Focal length	15mm	35mm equivalent: 22mm
Processing		Adobe Camera Raw (raw)
Other		Aperture priority; handheld; pattern metering

Overseeing the Job

This photo is another casual portrait: this time, of the contractor installing our new driveway. He's standing, shovel in hand, and surveying his crew as they spread out the new concrete being delivered by the mixer in the background.

As usual, shutter speed is the key element to pulling off photos with people casually moving around or working. I didn't use a flash, so getting the right exposure was important. I used my 35mm prime lens, which is fantastic for medium-range portraits such as this one on a cropped body. My 50mm model would have focused on the contractor's face, whereas pulling back too far would have resulted in a less-than-photogenic background.

When taking photos of people, backgrounds matter — often, critically. Poor backgrounds turn a great-looking photo into a so-so photo. Keep this concept in mind when choosing the lens, the focal length, and the composition.

(ISO 100, F8, 1/160 second, Nikon AF-S DX NIKKOR 35mm F1.8G) 2009

Option	*Setting*	*Notes*
ISO	100	Shot outdoors in strong daylight
Aperture	f/8	A dependable all-around aperture that results in a good depth of field and shutter speeds
Shutter speed	1/160 second	Nice and fast to capture him without blurring
Camera	Nikon D200	Semipro dSLR; cropped body (FX)
Lens	Nikon AF-S DX NIKKOR 35mm f/1.8G	A standard prime lens for DX bodies
Focal length	35mm	35mm equivalent: 52mm
Processing		Apple Aperture (raw); Photoshop Elements
Other		Aperture priority; handheld; pattern metering

Chapter 3: Framing Landscapes and Nature

In This Chapter

- ✔ Photographing gorgeous rivers
- ✔ Working with pets
- ✔ Capturing flowing water
- ✔ Working with bees
- ✔ Going out in the field
- ✔ Getting close to the action
- ✔ Photographing ice
- ✔ Catching the first signs of spring

The challenge of capturing landscapes lies in getting out and finding the right landscape to photograph. It doesn't come to you. You don't generally have a birthday party for it, nor can you set it on a table and take a studio still life of it.

Look for great-looking landscapes where you live. They don't have to consist of mountains or oceans or rainforests. After all, we don't all live in the Alps or in Hawaii. Get in your car or on your bike, or put on your hiking boots and get outside to find it.

The other challenge is to make the scenes you find memorable. Anyone can walk out in a field or on a beach and take a picture. Can you do it so that it's interesting and tells a story? Does it evoke an emotion? Is it captivating? Which settings should you use to help you achieve your goals?

Ask yourself similar questions as you frame shots and sort out the technical details of choosing the right settings for your camera.

Scenic River in HDR

(ISO 100, variable aperture, 1 second, Sigma 10-20mm F4-5.6 at 20mm) 2009

I shot this scene in late spring during a particularly stunning sunset. The problem was that I was at home when the sun began to set. I looked outside and said, "Man, what a pretty sky!" only to realize that I was at home, my camera was packed up, and the sky wouldn't last.

I threw everything in my van and rushed off to the river to set up my camera for one set of brackets. One set — that's all I got before the sun dipped down and the light changed.

The other problem is that I left my camera in the wrong mode for HDR. It had been in Shutter Priority mode the last time I used it, and I forgot to change it. Because I shot auto brackets (for more information on HDR photography, turn to Book VI, Chapter 4), I didn't realize what had happened until I was home, and it was too late to do anything about it.

Rather than change the shutter speed to bracket the scene, the camera kept the shutter speed constant throughout the five exposures and changed the aperture instead. When the camera ran out of aperture (the lens could reach only as wide as 5.6 at the given focal length), the camera switched to exposure compensation.

REMEMBER

The result? A hare-brained HDR session, but still a stunning sunset. Go figure.

Reset your camera between sessions. Even accidents can produce great-looking photos.

Option	Setting	Notes
ISO	100	I shoot HDR at ISO 100 to reduce noise; shutter speed generally isn't a problem
Aperture	variable	I accidentally left my camera in Shutter Priority mode to bracket; apertures for brackets are f/5.6, f/9, and f/13
Shutter speed	One second	The "wrong" way to shoot HDR is to keep shutter speed constant across all exposures; oh, well — the photos turned out great!
Brackets	5 (+/–- 1.0 EV)	AEB; five exposures at –2/–1/0/+1/+2 EV (from an accidental combination of changing aperture and exposure compensation)
Camera	Nikon D200	Semipro dSLR; cropped body (FX)
Lens	Sigma 10-20mm F4-5.6	Ultra wide-angle zoom
Focal length	20mm	35mm equivalent: 30mm
Processing		Nikon Capture NX 2 (raw); Photomatix Pro (HDR); Photoshop
Other		Shutter Priority mode; pattern metering; tripod; remote shutter release

Scenic Rover

I don't normally shoot — er, *photograph* — pets. Most of the time, my family's cats are resting comfortably on the back of the couch, on the floor, on the table, on the bed, or at our feet. Get the picture? See cat loaf. Repeat.

To make matters worse, the backgrounds aren't normally conducive to creating pet calendars.

*(ISO 100, f/3.5, 1/250 second,
Nikon AF-S DX NIKKOR 35mm f/1.8G) 2009*

Once in a while, though, you find a situation where everything works, such as this photo of a dog at the birthday party for a member of our extended family. I was snapping pictures of the party when I looked down and noticed him looking playfully at me.

Thankfully, I shot with a fast shutter speed, so the photo is crisp. (He didn't pose for long.) I also used a flash, which helps bring out the details in the dog's otherwise low-contrast fur.

Option	Setting	Notes
ISO	100	A higher ISO not necessary because of the flash
Aperture	f/3.5	Fairly wide, to create nice bokeh and work with ISO 100
Shutter speed	1/250	Fast to keep everything crisp, especially animals, because they're always moving
Camera	Nikon D200	Semipro dSLR; cropped body (FX)
Lens	Nikon AF-S DX NIKKOR 35mm f/1.8G	A standard prime lens for DX bodies
Focal length	35mm	35mm equivalent: 52mm
Processing		Adobe Camera Raw (raw); Photoshop Elements
Other		In-camera flash (pop-up); handheld

Falling Water

This is a photo of the fountain at our local mall. I was there to shoot photos of the carousel when I decided to walk down the hall to see how the fountain looked. As a result, I got better shots. The color of the tile and flowers, not to mention the movement of the people and water, makes for an interesting photo.

(ISO 100, f/22, 2 seconds, Sigma 10-20mm F4-5.6 at 10mm) 2008

The key was extending the shutter speed so that the water flows and blends in with itself. This 2-second exposure was stopped down to f/22 and at ISO 100 to keep from becoming too bright.

REMEMBER

Don't forget to ask permission to shoot pictures on private property (even if it seems like a public place). I was escorted to the main office not long after I set up the camera. After I explained my purpose, the authorities released me, but I was shadowed until I left.

Option	*Setting*	*Notes*
ISO	100	Low ISO to compensate for long shutter speed, which was needed to smooth the water
Aperture	f/22	Stopped down to compensate for long exposure in a relatively bright room
Shutter speed	2 seconds	Long shutter speed to get smooth water
Camera	Sony Alpha 300	Entry-level dSLR; cropped body (FX); built-in Super SteadyShot image stabilization
Lens	Sigma 10-20mm F4-5.6	Ultra wide-angle zoom
Focal length	10mm	35mm equivalent: 15mm
Processing		Sony Image Data Converter SR (raw); Photoshop Elements
Other		Manual mode; spot metering; tripod, remote shutter release

Buzzing Bee

While in the back yard, photographing flowers, I looked up and realized that I was being swarmed by large bees. I decided to try and capture them in the act of doing whatever bees do.

Composition is critical because you can't pose bees. Normally, you can move around, but I was glued to my tripod. I picked one side of a flower and caught one walking to my side.

*(ISO 100, f/5.6, 1/320 second,
Sony DT 18-70mm f/3.5-5.6 at 70mm) 2008*

My camera was set to ISO 100 because of the strong light, and I used a relatively wide aperture for a nice bokeh around the flowers. Thankfully, the shutter speed was fast enough, given those settings, to capture the bees walking without any blurring. Had I needed to, I would have switched to Shutter Priority mode, dialed in a fast shutter speed, and then compensated with a higher ISO or flash to get the right exposure.

Option	Setting	Notes
ISO	100	Shot outdoors in strong daylight
Aperture	f/5.6	I wanted to blur the background; limited depth of field, especially at this distance
Shutter speed	1/320	Fast, for bugs
Camera	Sony Alpha 300	Entry-level dSLR; cropped body (FX); built-in Super SteadyShot image stabilization
Lens	Sony DT 18-70mm f/3.5-5.6	General-purpose zoom; budget kit lens; good value; I wanted to be able to zoom in
Focal length	70mm	35mm equivalent: 105mm
Processing		Photoshop
Other		Aperture priority; tripod; pattern metering; remote shutter release

Children of the Corn

Ah, yes — a cornfield. You can't live in Indiana without taking pictures of corn or soybeans (or fast cars or basketball). They're a part of the scenery for most of the year.

To make this photo look more compelling than a plain old cornfield, I didn't just walk to the middle of the field and take the photo. Heavens, no! I worked it like a pro: I walked out, *knelt down,* and took the photo.

Unique angles or perspectives make otherwise uninteresting photos interesting. Try to remember this statement when you're setting up shots.

(ISO 100, f/8, 1/160 second, Sigma 10-20mm F4-5.6 at 10mm) 2008

Option	Setting	Notes
ISO	100	Shot outdoors in strong daylight
Aperture	f/8	My "go-to" aperture for most scenic shots
Shutter speed	1/160 second	In some cases, a setting is bound by other elements that determine exposure. Because I set ISO and aperture first, the shutter speed had to be 1/160 second to reach the right exposure
Camera	Sony Alpha 300	Entry-level dSLR; cropped body (FX); built-in Super SteadyShot image stabilization
Lens	Sigma 10-20mm F4-5.6	Ultra wide-angle zoom
Focal length	10	35mm equivalent: 15mm
Processing		Photoshop Elements
Other		Manual mode; handheld; pattern metering; the camera's implementation of Live view and tilt-screen LCD made composing this shot far easier than if I had to look through the viewfinder

Silhouette in HDR

This sht was a challenge to get because I had to position myself beside the river and not fall in. The ground wasn't level, and I had to fiddle with the tripod legs to set them to the proper length for a stable, level shooting platform.

After shooting away from the sun for a while, I turned the camera toward the sun and took several shots with different compositions.

What makes this shot work best for me is that the tree on the left anchors the photo. This element, plus the other nearby branches, make the whole thing interesting. The paradox is that your eyes don't rest on the trees; they move on to look at the water and sky beyond. There's a feeling of space to this photo.

(ISO 100, 1/320 second, Sigma 10-20mm F4.5-5.6 at 18mm) 2009

Technically speaking, I shot this photo in HDR to include more detail from the river and its far bank, but I processed it realistically in Photoshop. I left the trees in the foreground in silhouette for dramatic effect.

Option	Setting	Notes
ISO	100	Low ISO for outside shooting in daylight, plus HDR noise control
Aperture	f/22	Small aperture for shooting directly into the sun
Shutter speed	1/320	For the 0 EV exposure
Brackets	5 (+/– 1.0 EV)	Manual; five exposures at –4/–3/–2/–1/0 EV; skewed intentionally dark
Camera	Sony Alpha 300	Entry-level dSLR; cropped body (FX); built-in Super SteadyShot image stabilization
Lens	Sigma 10-20mm F4.5-5.6	Ultra wide-angle zoom
Focal length	18mm	35mm equivalent: 27mm
Processing		Photoshop (HDR and photo editing)
Other		Center-weighted average metering; tripod; remote shutter release

Ice, Ice, Baby

Sometimes, scenic or interesting nature photos are right in front of you.

My family was in the midst of the worst ice storm in our area in a decade, and I literally walked out our front door and across the street to take this shot of ice measuring an eighth- to a quarter-inch thick on the trees.

(ISO 100, f/8, 1/320 second, Sony DT 18-70mm f/3.5-5.6 at 60mm) 2008

The key elements in this photo are the strong light and focal length of the lens. The light makes the ice shine. A cloudy or dull day wouldn't have produced an identical photo. It has a liveliness that's hard to describe. The focal length of the lens allowed me to zoom in tightly on a specific ice-covered branch to make it the central subject of the photo, as opposed to the tree as a whole.

Option	Setting	Notes
ISO	100	Shot outdoors in strong daylight
Aperture	f/8	A dependable, all-around aperture that results in a good depth of field and shutter speeds
Shutter speed	1/320 second	In some cases, a setting is bound by other elements that determine exposure. Because I set ISO and aperture first, the shutter speed had to be 1/320 second to reach the right exposure
Camera	Sony Alpha 300	Entry-level dSLR; cropped body (FX); built-in Super SteadyShot image stabilization
Lens	Sony DT 18-70mm f/3.5-5.6	General-purpose zoom; budget kit lens; good value
Focal length	60mm	Nice and zoomed in; 35mm equivalent: 90mm
Processing		Adobe Camera Raw (raw); Photoshop
Other		Aperture priority; pattern metering; handheld

Spring Springs

Oddly enough, this photo shows the same tree as in the photo in the preceding section, except that I photographed it during the spring instead of in the dead of winter and covered in ice.

*(ISO 100, f/5.6, 1/320 second,
Sony DT 18-70mm f/3.5-5.6 at 55mm) 2009*

The settings are remarkably the same; only the aperture differs substantively. The ISO and shutter speed are the same, and the focal length is only 5mm off.

The result? The same idea, but completely different. The tree recedes into the background much more because of the different aperture, and the focus is on two blooms.

Why two blooms? Because they're more interesting. A single bloom looks nice, but shooting the pair allowed me to offset them from the center of the photo and balance the frame well.

Option	Setting	Notes
ISO	100	Shot outdoors in strong daylight
Aperture	f/5.6	Open for nice bokeh
Shutter speed	1/320 second	In some cases, a setting is made because it's bound by other elements that determine exposure. Because I set ISO and aperture first, the shutter speed had to be 1/320 second to reach the right exposure
Camera	Sony Alpha 300	Entry-level dSLR; cropped body (FX); built-in Super SteadyShot image stabilization
Lens	Sony DT 18-70mm f/3.5-5.6	General-purpose zoom; budget kit lens; good value
Focal length	55mm	A little gentler zoom, but I was closer; 35mm equivalent: 82mm
Processing		Adobe Camera Raw (raw); Photoshop
Other		Aperture priority; pattern metering; handheld

Chapter 4: Capturing Everyday Life

In This Chapter

- Celebrating birthdays
- Getting a new driveway
- Turning kids into excellent subjects
- Drooling over food
- Capturing important moments
- Documenting your activities
- Getting out in the back yard
- Living together

Everyday life — everyone has one. We don't all work as internationally renowned magazine photographers whose subjects show up to our studio or have jobs with *National Geographic* magazine and travel the world, taking pictures. We go places, do things, and experience the life *we* have. Part of the fun is taking photos of these activities.

Sometimes, we take pictures in our backyard or when we go for a walk. Maybe you're thinking of taking a trip to the zoo, doing fun things in the kitchen, throwing lots of parties, or when humongous space monsters attack your large metropolitan area (similar to the movie *Cloverfield*). Photos of these types celebrate life; take your camera along for the ride.

Opening Presents

One of the best times to pull out the old camera is during parties of any sort. If there are people and presents, there's good pictures to be had. I don't mean to imply that it's easy. This photo represents a tamer shot from my collection.

My family is gathered at the table, surrounding my wife, and she's about ready to start. I sat across the table, directly in line with the kids. Photographing them head-on is always a challenge because they tend to open presents sitting on the floor. I normally have to get down there with them to avoid taking photos of the tops of their heads.

(ISO 100, f/1.8, 1/125 second, Nikon AF-S DX NIKKOR 35mm f/1.8G) 2010v

I used a flash with bounce on this shot. Check out the side effects:

- **Dark background:** Flash photography can make backgrounds look darker than they are. In this case, the far background (to the right) is extremely dark, and the middle background (just to the right of my wife) is dark but not to the extreme. The closer you move to a subject, the worse this effect seems. I've backed off a little for this photo (it's the 35mm lens), so the background isn't that bad.

- **Sharp shadows:** Notice the shadow coming off the green present as it lands on my son's arm. The shadow is harsh.

Some of the best techniques to keep harsh shadows out of your pictures are to bounce the flash, use a diffuser, or move the flash off-camera and use a shoot-through or bounce umbrella. (See Book IV for more information on flash photography.)

Aside from these things, it helps to have all your photo subjects be on the same plane, relative to the camera. They won't cast shadows on each other. Also, keep the background in the background. Notice that you can't see any shadows from anyone falling on it. If I were off to an angle, or a break appeared between people, you would see the shadows.

Option	*Setting*	*Notes*
ISO	100	Remained low because of the flash
Aperture	f/1.8	Wide open for artistically shallow depth of field
Shutter speed	1/125 second	Fast, for handheld photography of people who move
Camera	Nikon D200	Semipro dSLR; cropped body (FX)

Option	Setting	Notes
Lens	Nikon AF-S DX NIKKOR 35mm f/1.8G	A standard prime lens for DX bodies; this lens is great for everyday events like this one
Focal length	35mm	35mm equivalent: 52mm
Processing		Adobe Camera Raw (raw); Photoshop
Other		Manual exposure mode; pattern metering; handheld; external flash (hot shoe); LumiQuest flash bouncer; presents; fun family

Pouring Concrete

This photo is the third in the Great Driveway Construction project, undertaken by my family in 2009, to appear in this minibook. I got some great shots of the action and the people involved.

(ISO 100, f/8, 1/125 second, Sigma 10-20mm F4-5.6 at 20mm) 2009

In this photo, I knelt (often a key element of photography) to gain a good vantage point on the chute delivering the concrete into the form. I used my Sigma ultra wide-angle lens and moved close to the chute, yet was able to include the side of the house and the truck in the background.

I zoomed in so that the focal length was at 20mm instead of 10mm to focus the attention on the chute and prevent all other distractions. This is one case where the lens makes all the difference in the world.

Option	Setting	Notes
ISO	100	Shot outdoors in strong daylight
Aperture	f/8	A dependable, all-around aperture that results in a good depth of field and shutter speed
Shutter speed	1/125 second	Fast enough to catch the action
Camera	Nikon D200	Semipro dSLR; cropped body (FX)
Lens	Sigma 10-20mm F4-5.6	Ultra-wide-angle zoom
Focal length	20mm	35mm equivalent: 30mm
Processing		Adobe Camera Raw (raw); Photoshop
Other		Aperture priority; pattern metering; handheld; cement truck and concrete

A Budding Photographer

In this photo, our youngest son has a Panasonic Lumix LZ8 compact digital camera in hand and is taking pictures with me in the backyard. I was set up to shoot his siblings at play, so my camera was in Shutter Priority mode with a fast shutter speed.

I looked down and there he was, smiling because he had just taken my picture (he's not quite 2½ years old in this shot), so I decided to take his photo, too.

(ISO 400, f/2.8, 1/500 second, Nikon AF-S DX NIKKOR 35mm f/1.8G) 2009

The settings are all wrong for this type of shot, but it works. The aperture opened wide, and the ISO elevated automatically to be able to take the picture at 1/500 second. I could have put it on Aperture priority and set the f-number to f/8 or so, lowered the ISO (or ensured that it wasn't too high), and maybe had a technically better shot.

The problem is that sometimes you have no time to make changes. You have to react to a moment that's in front of you one instant and gone the next. This was the 1/500th of a second where my son looked up at me, smiling, eyes wide open. I had to take the shot then or lose it entirely.

Option	Setting	Notes
ISO	400	High ISO to compensate for fast shutter speed
Aperture	f/2.8	Artistic depth of field; also helps set up fast shutter speed
Shutter speed	1/500 second	Camera was on Shutter Priority because I was taking action shots of my kids playing outdoors
Camera	Nikon D200	Semipro dSLR; cropped body (FX)
Lens	Nikon AF-S DX NIKKOR 35mm f/1.8G	A standard prime lens for DX bodies
Focal length	35mm	35mm equivalent: 52mm
Processing		Photoshop Elements
Other		Shutter priority; pattern metering; handheld

Yummy Birthday Cake

I love taking photographs of our family's birthday cakes and candles. It locks in the memories of the parties we have and the cakes we make. In this case, you can hardly experience anything yummier.

(ISO 400, f/5.6, 1/160 second, Sony DT 18-70mm f/3.5-5.6 at 55mm) 2009

On one son's fifth birthday, he chose a chocolate cake with chocolate icing, and my wife added the candies on top to round out the nutritional value per serving. Quite accidentally, they also make the photo visually compelling because of the added color.

I shot this photo at ISO 400 and f/5.6 to be able to use a fast shutter speed on the kids. I also used a flash and diffuser to keep the shadows from becoming too harsh.

The candles are being lit, and we're almost ready to go!

Option	Setting	Notes
ISO	400	Used Shutter Priority to photograph children and didn't switch it off to photograph the cake, so the ISO jumped to compensate for the fast speed
Aperture	f/5.6	Artistic depth of field and increased light for indoor photography
Shutter speed	1/160 second	Relatively fast because I was taking photos of the birthday party
Camera	Sony Alpha 300	Entry-level dSLR; cropped body (FX); built-in Super SteadyShot image stabilization
Lens	Sony DT 18-70mm f/3.5-5.6	General-purpose zoom; budget kit lens; good value
Focal length	55mm	35mm equivalent: 82mm
Processing		Photoshop Elements
Other		Shutter Priority; pattern metering; external flash (hot shoe); handheld

Getting a Pony Ride

My family visits the zoo often. Our kids love the animals and the other fun attractions. We love to ride the train, the log ride, the lift that carries you over part of the zoo, the pony rides, and more. You can't take a pony ride without someone taking pictures, which is why my wife took this one (among others).

(ISO 100, f/10, 1/80 second, Sony DT 18-70mm f/3.5-5.6 at 24mm)
Anne Correll, 2009

The settings reflect a basic setup. The ISO is low because my wife was outside in the sun, and there's no need to add unnecessary noise. The aperture was stopped down a little because of the light, but also to create a good depth of field. The far background is blurred, but the pony, which is larger from front to back than you might think, is perfect. The shutter speed isn't blazing but good enough to get a handheld photo of a slow-moving subject.

Notice the shadow pattern from the tree leaves. They complicate the scene and make it a bit harder to get the right exposure on the subject, but they also add a good deal of visual interest.

Option	Setting	Notes
ISO	100	Shot outdoors in strong daylight
Aperture	f/10	Good depth of field to cover the pony
Shutter speed	1/80 second	Fast enough for a slow pony
Camera	Sony Alpha 300	Entry-level dSLR; cropped body (FX); built-in Super SteadyShot image stabilization

(continued)

Option	Setting	Notes
Lens	Sony DT 18-70mm f/3.5-5.6	General-purpose zoom; budget kit lens; good value
Focal length	24mm	35mm equivalent: 36mm
Processing		Adobe Camera Raw (raw); Photoshop
Other		Program AE mode; pattern metering; handheld

That's Egg-Zactly How It's Done

My family colors Easter eggs in our house for Easter, and then we have zany, candy-assisted, fun-filled Easter egg hunts before calling it a day. As the resident photographer, it's mostly my job to capture these moments.

(ISO 360, f/4, 1/125 second, Nikon AF-S NIKKOR 50mm f/1.4G) 2010

I took this close-up of my wife dipping a blue egg into a coffee cup with my 50mm lens. It's perfect for those moments when you want to move in close to see details yet not have to hover over the action. I opened up the aperture a little for a depth-of-field effect. The ISO needed to be raised, and I ensured that the shutter speed was fast enough to prevent blurring.

Option	Setting	Notes
ISO	360	Higher than normal to avoid using flash
Aperture	f/4	Wider for artistic bokeh
Shutter speed	1/125 second	Fast for handheld photography with some action in it
Camera	Nikon D200	Semipro dSLR; cropped body (FX)
Lens	Nikon AF-S NIKKOR 50mm f/1.4G	The Nikon flagship standard prime lens
Focal length	50mm	35mm equivalent: 75mm
Processing		Adobe Camera Raw (raw); Photoshop
Other		Manual exposure mode; pattern metering; handheld

A Bloom with a View

This shot is another one taken from my backyard. In this case, I lurked out by the peonies, taking pictures of ants on the blooms. The way ants gather on them is somewhat creepy; like a sort of science fiction movie.

(ISO 100, f/6.3, 1/100 second, Sony DT 18-70mm f/3.5-5.6 at 60mm) 2008

Good magnification is important for photos such as this one. I used my general-purpose zoom lens and set it at 60mm, which is strong. That made it possible to frame the scene so that the bloom occupies most of the center of the photo. As a result, the ants are nicely visible.

Other parameters weren't difficult to achieve. I chose a low ISO to keep the noise down, a reasonable shutter speed for handheld photography, and a wider aperture to make the background blur.

When you're first starting out in photography, thinking simultaneously about the major exposure settings can be difficult (not to mention keeping track of metering and autofocus modes). With practice, you can check them off your list so fast that they become second nature.

Option	Setting	Notes
ISO	100	Shot outdoors in reasonably strong daylight
Aperture	f/6.3	Wider to keep the shutter speed up and create a nice bokeh
Shutter speed	1/100 second	Fast enough for handheld photography
Camera	Sony Alpha 300	Entry-level dSLR; cropped body (FX); built-in Super SteadyShot image stabilization
Lens	Sony DT 18-70mm f/3.5-5.6	General-purpose zoom; budget kit lens; good value
Focal length	60mm	35mm equivalent: 90mm
Processing		Adobe Camera Raw (raw); Photoshop Elements
Other		Shutter priority; pattern metering; handheld

We Survived the Ice Storm

In the real-life moment shown in this photo, my family was in the midst of experiencing the worst local ice storm in a decade. The power was out. We decided to stay at home and take care of our house and pets, but we had ourselves to take care of, too. We set up camp in the kitchen, and the kids turned the table into a small car-and-truck playground.

(ISO 100, f/8, 1/60 second, Sigma 10-20mm F4-5.6 at 10mm) 2008

The light in the room comes from the sun outside; it's shining directly at me, which is why I pulled out an external flash and used it to light my kids. If I hadn't, they all would have been in shadow, with the window the only element properly exposed.

When using my ultra-wide-angle lens, I have to rely on an external flash, not the in-camera pop-up flash. The lens gets in the way of the pop-up flash and casts a horribly obvious shadow. I bounced the flash off the ceiling, which give the room a good deal of diffused light. This is a great technique to avoid harsh shadows or a flash that's too harsh (right in the face).

I'm working at a wide angle in this photo, enough that the distortion is more apparent than in a landscape photo, for example.

Option	Setting	Notes
ISO	100	Could have been increased to create a faster shutter speed, but the flash was good enough to get the right exposure, even at f/8.
Aperture	f/8	A dependable, all-around aperture that results in a good depth of field and shutter speed.
Shutter speed	1/60 second	Good enough for normal action; notice that the kids aren't blurred.
Camera	Sony Alpha 300	Entry-level dSLR; cropped body (FX); built-in Super SteadyShot image stabilization.
Lens	Sigma 10-20mm F4-5.6	Ultra-wide-angle zoom.
Focal length	10mm	Vertical distortion readily apparent in a small room with people and the camera pointing downward; 35mm equivalent: 15mm.
Processing		Adobe Camera Raw (raw); Photoshop.
Other		Aperture priority; bounced external flash (hot shoe); handheld.

Chapter 5: Showing Off Vehicles

In This Chapter

✓ **Going to an air show**

✓ **Gettin' down and looking up**

✓ **Looking at shapes and angles**

✓ **Shooting HDR**

✓ **Picturing the entire car**

✓ **Focusing on color and texture**

✓ **Staying flexible**

✓ **Photographing small features**

*V*ehicles are captivating subjects to photograph. (I love them.) They can be new or old, shiny or rusty, colorful, dark, moody, friendly, or just plain fun.

The helpful thing about most vehicles is that you can walk around them to find the best vantage point for the time and light, as well as look up or down on them. You have quite a bit of control over it.

However, you may have *no* control and be required to shoot the best photo from the only angle you can find.

This chapter has a wide range of photos of vehicles that I've had the pleasure of photographing over the past few years. I've heavily processed some of them and left others essentially alone. Have fun!

P-51, Cadillac of the Skies

As my family returned home from an errand one afternoon, I looked out the window and saw a Consolidated B-24 Liberator flying off to the side — not something you see every day.

I later saw a news story describing an air show that would take place nearby over the coming weekend. Bingo! I knew that the location had to be the destination of the B-24. After looking up the schedule, we attended the show a few days later.

(ISO 100, f/8, 1/400 second, Sony DT 18-70mm f/3.5-5.6 at 70mm) 2008

Most of my photos of the aircraft were, frankly, disappointing. Because we arrived after the flight line closed, I had to stand behind a chain-link fence. After lunch, the P-51 returned from flying a few people around and parked facing away from us. I was able to position the front of the lens just right so that I could shoot through the fence and not have it appear in the photo.

Converting the photo to black and white in Photoshop is the icing on the cake. For more information on converting photos to black and white, plus tinting them, please look at Book VI, Chapter 6.

Option	Setting	Notes
ISO	100	Shot outdoors in strong daylight
Aperture	f/8	A dependable, all-around aperture that results in photos with good depth of field and shutter speeds
Shutter speed	1/400 second	Strong daylight often dictates fast shutter speeds, even when you don't necessarily need them for other reasons (for example, a moving subject)
Camera	Sony Alpha 300	Entry-level dSLR; cropped body (FX); built-in Super SteadyShot image stabilization
Lens	Sony DT 18-70mm f/3.5-5.6	General-purpose zoom; budget kit lens; good value
Focal length	70mm	I stood behind a fence some distance away; 35mm equivalent: 105mm
Processing		Photoshop
Other		Manual mode; pattern metering; handheld

Now, This Is a Monster Truck

While driving to dinner one evening, I happened to look over to the right of the van and saw a behemoth of a truck sitting beside the road at a rental store.

(ISO 100, f/8, 1/160 second, Sony DT 18-70mm f/3.5-5.6 at 18mm) 2009

TIP I was able to stop and grab a few pictures because I had my camera with me. (That's a hint.) In addition to getting good photos, the kids erupted in cheers and proclaimed me the "Best Dad Ever" for stopping.

I enter the Aperture priority in many shooting situations in order to set the camera's aperture first. It locks in the depth of field and determines whether I need to raise the ISO setting from 100. After quickly checking to see whether the shutter speed is fast enough for handheld shooting, I'm off to my destination.

I knelt near the ground for this photo and used the Sony tiltable Live view LCD screen, which helps me compose and shoot off-angle shots tremendously.

Option	Setting	Notes
ISO	100	Shot outdoors in strong daylight
Aperture	f/8	A dependable, all-around aperture that results in a good depth of field and shutter speeds
Shutter speed	1/160 second	Shutter speed bound by other parameters
Camera	Sony Alpha 300	Entry-level dSLR; cropped body (FX); built-in Super SteadyShot image stabilization
Lens	Sony DT 18-70mm f/3.5-5.6	General purpose zoom; budget kit lens; good value
Focal length	18mm	35mm equivalent: 27mm
Processing		Adobe Camera Raw (raw); Photoshop
Other		Aperture priority; pattern metering; handheld

Finding Beauty in the Details

My family was, oddly enough, out at our storage unit when I took this shot of part of an abandoned truck. Though the truck itself is interesting, I have found that close-up shots bring out elements that a traditional shot cannot. In this case, the orange turn light is the center of attention — an element that surely would have been lost otherwise.

(ISO 100, f/10, 1/125 second, Sony DT 18-70mm f/3.5-5.6 at 60mm) 2008

The key to this photo was ensuring that the shutter speed was quick enough not to blur and that the aperture gave me the depth of field I wanted. In the latter case, you might think that f/10 is too small to create a nice bokeh (the part of the photo that is out of focus). This photo shows that if you're close enough to the subject, the depth of field is shallow enough that you'll see the effect.

Option	Setting	Notes
ISO	100	Shot outdoors in strong daylight
Aperture	f/10	The blurred background shows you that even a relatively small aperture can produce a limited depth of field if the focal plane is close enough to the camera
Shutter speed	1/125	Chosen for handheld stability
Camera	Sony Alpha 300	Entry-level dSLR; cropped body (FX); built-in Super SteadyShot image stabilization
Lens	Sony DT 18-70mm f/3.5-5.6	General-purpose zoom; budget kit lens; good value
Focal length	60mm	This focal length compresses the background, making objects appear closer than they are; in this case, that effect makes the photo even better; 35mm equivalent: 90mm
Processing		Sony Image Data Converter SR (raw); Photoshop
Other		Shutter-priority mode; pattern metering; handheld

Serendipity in HDR

After searching for good HDR subjects one day, I decided to photograph some construction equipment. I asked for permission to shoot in the lot at my local equipment rental establishment, and the owner agreed.

(ISO 100, f/8, 1/250 second, Sigma 10-20mm F4-5.6 at 10mm) 2008

Before I could make my way to the front-end loaders, backhoes, graders, and Bobcats, I spied a gorgeous Harley-Davidson Sportster. Ah, serendipity.

This was the first series of shots I took that day, and they were by far the best. Go figure. I could have packed up and saved myself an hour or so of work! I was *stunned* by how good the HDR looked when I processed the files in Photomatix.

Buy yourself some good kneepads. When you kneel in gravel, rocks, or on hard surfaces, your knees will thank you. I bought some, as a direct result of this photo shoot, after stooping in the gravel on my hands and knees to set up the tripod for a dramatic angle.

Option	Setting	Notes
ISO	100	Shoot HDR with ISO 100 to reduce noise; shutter speed generally not a problem; bright daylight conditions for this shot
Aperture	f/8	A dependable all-around aperture that results in a good depth of field and shutter speeds
Shutter speed	1/250 second	For the 0 EV exposure
Brackets	3 (+/− 2.0 EV)	Manual; three exposures at −2/0/+2 EV
Camera	Sony Alpha 300	Entry-level dSLR; cropped body (FX); built-in Super SteadyShot image stabilization
Lens	Sigma 10-20mm F4-5.6	Ultra-wide-angle zoom
Focal length	10mm	Not obviously distorted; 35mm equivalent: 15mm
Processing		Sony Image Data Converter SR (raw); Photomatix Pro (HDR); Photoshop
Other		Manual mode; center-weighted average metering; tripod; remote shutter release

Three-Quarter Car Portrait

At the Kruse Automotive and Carriage Museum in Auburn, Indiana, I took a photo of Michael Andretti's 1991 CART/ PPG championship IndyCar. It's a more traditional car portrait, taken from a tripod without a flash.

Cars make great-looking subjects, but you have to be careful about the background if you aren't zooming in. In this case, the museum makes a great backdrop. Dale Earnhardt's number-3

(ISO 100, f/4, 1/2 second, Nikon AF-S DX NIKKOR 35mm f/1.8G) 2009

NASCAR vehicle is off to the left, and a purple car is further back and to the right. Neither car distracts from my photo.

Because I was shooting HDR that day, I didn't have my flash, which limited my shots to long exposure times. When nothing is moving in the scene, longer exposure times are okay (although they can add noise if they're longer than a few seconds). In fact, relying on natural light can look better — or at least be more practical. A small flash wouldn't have been able to light this scene, other than to provide a fill flash on the immediate subject. I could have raised the ISO, but that action introduces noise.

Option	Setting	Notes
ISO	100	Shot in HDR, so I set up without a flash and wasn't concerned with longer shutter speeds
Aperture	f/4	Wider aperture for shallower depth of field
Shutter speed	1/2 second	Bound by other settings, which would be a problem if this were handheld
Camera	Nikon D200	Semipro dSLR; cropped body (FX)
Lens	Nikon AF-S DX NIKKOR 35mm f/1.8G	A standard prime lens for DX bodies
Focal length	35mm	35mm equivalent: 52mm
Processing		Nikon Capture NX 2 (raw); Photoshop
Other		Manual mode; pattern metering; tripod; remote shutter release

Engine 78

This close-up of the front of Engine 78 at our local fire station highlights the grill, lights, and engine number.

TIP

Background, background, background. When the background is distracting, zoom in or move closer.

You can't know how many great shots are ruined because the background stinks. When you zoom in, you in effect crop out the far background and can concentrate on details. I would rather

(ISO 100, f/8, 1/160 second, Sony DT 18-70mm f/3.5-5.6 at 20mm) 2008

repeat that process a thousand times than to sit at the computer in Photoshop or Photoshop Elements and try to mask out an ugly scene or clone over a distraction.

Option	Setting	Notes
ISO	100	Shot outdoors in strong daylight
Aperture	f/8	Dependable, all-around aperture that results in a good depth of field and shutter speeds
Shutter speed	1/160 second	Bound by other settings, but nice and fast, resulting in a crisp handheld photo
Camera	Sony Alpha 300	Entry-level dSLR; cropped body (FX); built-in Super SteadyShot image stabilization
Lens	Sony DT 18-70mm f/3.5-5.6	General-purpose zoom; budget kit lens; good value
Focal length	20mm	Wide angle to get the subject because I was close; 35mm equivalent: 30mm
Processing		Photoshop Elements
Other		Aperture priority; pattern metering; handheld

Simplicity

You can file this single-shot HDR photo in the file labeled Something Completely Different. I took this photo at the same air show where I photographed the P-51C, described earlier in this chapter. I wasn't able to shoot freely, I walked around the parking lot and found an old Cushman Scooter parked in the grass next to the airport building. I shot a few photos of it that helped make the day productive from a photography perspective.

(ISO 100, f/5.6, 1/500 second, Sony DT 18-70mm f/3.5-5.6 at 50mm) 2008

I love the simple look of the chrome, but a great deal is happening to make this photo compelling. Check out the tire texture and details, smooth chrome, damaged fender, and interesting colors: gray, green, blue, orange, yellow, white, and silver.

Option	Setting	Notes
ISO	100	Shot outdoors in strong daylight
Aperture	f/5.6	Wider aperture for artistic depth of field
Shutter speed	1/500 second	Very fast shutter speed because of the bright day
Camera	Sony Alpha 300	Entry-level dSLR; cropped body (FX); built-in Super SteadyShot image stabilization
Lens	Sony DT 18-70mm f/3.5-5.6	General-purpose zoom; budget kit lens; good value
Focal length	50mm	35mm equivalent: 75mm
Processing		Photoshop Elements
Other		Aperture priority; pattern metering; +0.7 EV exposure compensation; handheldv

Pontiac

One of my favorite shots is of an old, abandoned Pontiac Executive sitting between a building and an abandoned truck. The vehicle even has a hole in its front window and a battery sitting in front.

(ISO 100, f/8, 1/60 second, Nikon AF-S NIKKOR 50mm f/1.4G) 2008

I tried several angles in this scene, and none seemed to work well. When I knelt and oriented the camera up a bit, at an angle off the front of the car, I knew that I had hit pay dirt.

This photo was processed as HDR, but has the dramatic effect of being converted to black and white, with a little tint to it. The HDR brought out details in the grille that were impossible to see in a normal photograph without blowing out the highlights. The black-and-white conversion in Photoshop focuses all your attention on details and contrast.

Don't be afraid to process your photos. Depending on your style, it might simply involve sharpening or improving the contrast. At the other end of the spectrum are HDR and black and white.

Option	Setting	Notes
ISO	100	Shot outdoors in strong daylight; my standard HDR ISO
Aperture	f/8	A dependable, all-around aperture that results in a good depth of field and shutter speeds
Shutter speed	1/60 second	For the 0 EV exposure
Brackets	4 (+/– 2.0 EV)	Manual; four exposures at –4/–2/0/+2 EV; skewed dark because of the bright conditions and some reflections off the left side of the car
Camera	Sony Alpha 300	Entry-level dSLR; cropped body (FX); built-in Super SteadyShot image stabilization
Lens	Sigma 10-20mm F4-5.6	Ultra wide-angle zoom
Focal length	18mm	35mm equivalent: 27mm
Processing		Sony Image Data Converter SR (raw); Photomatix Pro (HDR); Photoshop
Other		Manual mode; center-weighted average metering; tripod; remote shutter release

Chapter 6: Photographing Buildings and Cities

In This Chapter

- Walking in the park
- Going downtown
- Looking up
- Shooting the skyline
- Photographing houses
- Looking for great skies
- Working in small rooms
- Capturing large interior spaces

*P*hotographing buildings and cities is similar in many ways to shooting landscapes: You're generally dealing with very large subjects — much larger than the average flower, car, truck, person, amplifier, camera, or birthday cake. Neither can you move these objects, although it's easier to move *around* or *inside* a building than a mountain.

The big difference between a building and something like a landscape is that buildings are manmade. They have different textures, surfaces, angles, and colors, and they evoke different emotions than landscapes do. Play with that difference. Accentuate it.

Buildings come in different sizes and shapes, so be flexible. Take photos of skyscrapers and cities, or your own house. Take pictures indoors and out. As when you're shooting landscapes, you don't use a flash most of the time. You might use a flash on the inside, but your in-camera or external flash is generally too underpowered for whole buildings. (Exceptions always exist.)

Pavilion in the Park

I took this shot in a park that has an open-air pavilion with a reflecting pool. The structure, a popular wedding location, is surrounded by flowers of different types.

(ISO 100, f/10, 1/320 second, Sony DT 18-70mm f/3.5-5.6 at 20mm) 2008

Because the shot is handheld, I had to ensure a shutter speed fast enough to prevent shake and blur. The aperture created a nice depth of field, but at this distance (the focal distance is essentially infinity), even a wide aperture would have worked. As always, when I shoot outdoors, I try to keep the ISO to 100.

Option	*Setting*	*Notes*
ISO	100	Shot outdoors in strong daylight
Aperture	f/10	Smaller aperture because of the bright conditions
Shutter speed	1/320 second	Shutter speed bound by other parameters
Camera	Sony Alpha 300	Entry-level dSLR; cropped body (FX); built-in Super SteadyShot image stabilization
Lens	Sony DT 18-70mm f/3.5-5.6	General-purpose zoom; budget kit lens; good value
Focal length	20mm	35mm equivalent: 30mm
Processing		Sony Image Data Converter SR (raw); Photoshop
Other		Landscape scene mode; pattern metering; handheld

One Summit Square

The more than 400-foot-tall skyscraper shown in this figure is positioned so that you can take some isolated shots of it, as shown here.

(ISO 100, f/5.6, 1/500 second, Sigma 10-20mm F4-5.6 at 10mm) 2009

On the day I shot this photo, I was experimenting with wider apertures and cityscapes in HDR. This single exposure is from a bracketed set and shows the difficulty of setting the proper exposure when you take shots of buildings that rise into the bright sky. Buildings tend to look like they're in shadow unless the sun is hitting them face-on. You can walk around to the other side, but if your best vantage point isn't oriented properly to the sun, you're stuck.

Aside from performing extensive or convoluted processing after the shoot, my suggestion is to shoot buildings in HDR if you can't find the right light. You can be creative and shoot buildings in silhouette or try to use a neutral, density-graduated filter to keep the sky from blowing out, but ND grad filters are best suited for flat horizons.

I just threw a lot of stuff at you in that paragraph. I cover the specifics of the different techniques throughout the book. HDR is in Book VI, as are other software processing solutions. Book III, Chapter 5 has information on different types of filters and how to use them.

This type of shot exposes and accentuates vertical distortion, where buildings appear to lean away from you. Combat distortion, if you can, by first leveling the camera so that it doesn't tilt up at the building and then zooming in. I did neither in this case — proving that necessity often wins the battle over idealism.

Option	*Setting*	*Notes*
ISO	100	Outdoors in strong daylight
Aperture	f/5.6	Experimenting with a wider aperture than normal for buildings and landscapes; at this distance, depth of field isn't a problem
Shutter speed	1/500 second	Fast because of the bright light and larger aperture
Camera	Nikon D200	Semipro dSLR; cropped body (FX)
Lens	Sigma 10-20mm F4-5.6	Ultra-wide-angle zoom
Focal length	10mm	35mm equivalent: 15mm
Processing		Photoshop Elements
Other		Manual mode; pattern metering; −2.0 EV exposure compensation (to avoid blowing out the sky); tripod; remote shutter release

Monumental Building

The shot of a courthouse shown in this photo was taken from just across the street, looking up at the dome with Lady Liberty on top. In this example, you can see the benefit of being on the same side of the building as the sun. Setting the correct exposure is much easier than trying to brighten it in software. The building looks good, the sky isn't blown out, and the trees add a nice touch to the composition.

(ISO 100, f/11, 1/160 second, Sigma 10-20mm F4-5.6 at 20mm) 2008

I've tried taking good photos from the other side of this building and have yet to be satisfied. It has a nice-looking lawn, and you can see other tall buildings in town. The problem is that although the other side is quite scenic in person, it's almost impossible to shoot without blowing out the sky, leaving buildings in the dark, creating too much vertical distortion, or working around buildings that are in your way. Sometimes buildings are in places where taking a good photo is virtually impossible.

Option	Setting	Notes
ISO	100	Shot outdoors in strong daylight
Aperture	f/11	Smaller aperture (stopped down) because of the light
Shutter speed	1/160 second	Fast for handheld shooting
Camera	Sony Alpha 300	Entry-level dSLR; cropped body (FX); built-in Super SteadyShot image stabilization
Lens	Sigma 10-20mm F4-5.6	Ultra wide-angle zoom
Focal length	20mm	35mm equivalent: 30 mm
Processing		Photoshop Elements
Other		Handheld

Skyline

The key to shooting skylines is the same as for single buildings: You simply have to find the right vantage point. If you don't, your photos, even if they're technically correct and properly exposed, will be uninteresting.

I shot this photo from a road bridge leading toward my local downtown area. The presence of the road meant there were no obstructions directly in my way, and I had a clear view with a good sense of depth. (Roads leading into the distance have that effect.) At sunset, the sun glowed softly from the right side of the scene. The clouds, like the buildings, are lit from the side, not from the top.

(ISO 100, f/8, 1/125 second, Sigma 10-20mm F4-5.6 at 11mm) 2009

Option	*Setting*	*Notes*
ISO	100	Though the light is not overpowering, the low ISO is more than adequate; you have no reason to raise it unless necessary
Aperture	f/8	The "go-to" aperture for most scenic shots to provide a good depth of field
Shutter speed	1/125 second	Having set the ISO and aperture for other reasons, shutter speed was set to reach the right exposure
Camera	Sony Alpha 300	Entry-level dSLR; cropped body (FX); built-in Super SteadyShot image stabilization
Lens	Sigma 10-20mm F4-5.6	Ultra wide-angle zoom

Option	Setting	Notes
Focal length	11mm	35mm equivalent: 16mm
Processing		Photoshop Elements
Other		Manual mode; center-weighted average metering; tripod; remote shutter release

From the Driveway

You can photograph buildings on a smaller scale than skyscrapers. I took this photo from the end of my driveway, looking back at the house. A storm had passed, and clouds were moving past. I was looking west, toward the setting sun.

(ISO 200, f/4.5, 1/30 second, Sigma 10-20mm F4-5.6 at 12mm) 2008

This shutter speed is on the slow end of what I like to work with when shooting handheld. The light isn't strong, and I didn't want to raise the ISO by much to avoid increasing noise. Even after opening the aperture to f/4.5, I ended up having to raise the ISO some in order to be able to shoot at 1/30 second. I then brightened the house and grass in processing to make them stand out more.

This is an example of something you could use as a real estate photo. It shows off the house, yard, and neighbors in one shot.

Option	Setting	Notes
ISO	200	Outdoors in reasonable light, but ISO 200 still necessary in order to keep shutter speed fast enough to shoot handheld and not blur
Aperture	f/4.5	Larger aperture for more light to keep shutter speed reasonable
Shutter speed	1/30 second	Fast enough for handheld of a stationary subject
Camera	Sony Alpha 300	Entry-level dSLR; cropped body (FX); built-in Super SteadyShot image stabilization

(continued)

Option	Setting	Notes
Lens	Sigma 10-20mm F4-5.6	Ultra wide-angle zoom
Focal length	12mm	35mm equivalent: 18mm
Processing		Photoshop Elements
Other		Aperture priority mode; patter metering; handheld

Big Red Barn

This photo shows the effect of positioning yourself with the sun behind you when you photograph a building. In this case, it's the archetypal red Indiana barn. The photo has strong reds, greens, and blues, and the white in the clouds and the white highlights on the barn break up larger areas and make the scene more interesting — almost active.

(ISO 100, f/8, 1/400 second, Sigma 10-20mm F4-5.6 at 11mm) 2009

My settings are fairly standard: I used ISO 100 because I was outdoors with good light. I set the aperture to f/8 to provide a good depth of field.

TIP

If you have no tripod, consider buying a nice one (something sturdy that costs more than $20) if you shoot any landscape or cityscape photography. Setting up the camera on a sturdy platform frees you from having to worry about it moving and shaking. You can then concentrate on composing and taking the photo. Or, if you don't want to lug around a tripod, check out a monopod.

You *can* use image stabilization, but for landscape shots, I'm always happier with the camera attached to the earth.

Option	Setting	Notes
ISO	100	Outdoors in strong daylight
Aperture	f/8	My "go-to" aperture for most scenic shots
Shutter speed	1/400 second	Determined by other parameters
Camera	Sony Alpha 300	Entry-level dSLR; cropped body (FX); built-in Super SteadyShot image stabilization
Lens	Sigma 10-20mm F4-5.6	Ultra wide-angle zoom
Focal length	11mm	35mm equivalent: 16mm
Processing		Photoshop Elements
Other		Manual shooting mode; pattern metering; tripod; remote shutter release

In the Kitchen

I took this photo, an interior photograph of a kitchen, for the realtor selling the house. You need three key items in order to set up shots like this one:

✔ **Level tripod:** Frees you from having to use fast shutter speeds and helps you compose the photo and take several identical shots with different settings. Use a tripod with a level, or mount a level on the camera's hot shoe. (They make small bubble levels that slip right on.) Taking level photos minimizes vertical distortion and reduces processing time.

(ISO 400, f/8, 1/6 second, Sigma 10-20mm F4-5.6 at 10mm) 2008

✔ **Remote shutter release:** Lets you take a photo without making you stand in a particular spot behind the camera. This strategy also keeps your fingers off the camera and helps prevent camera-shake. Using the release, you can sometimes place the camera in a corner and simply get out of its way.

✔ **Wide-angle lens:** A must-have for interior photography if you want to truly show off a room. In this case, you can see the rangetop in front and the sink, counter, refrigerator, and door to the garage — about 80 percent of the kitchen in a single shot. (A standard lens cannot even hope to compete.)

I don't use a flash for interior shots like this photo because I want even lighting from front to back and from side to side. (And I don't want to mess with the lighting gear necessary to light each room like it were a movie studio.) Although that requirement means longer shutter speeds, the room looks more natural without the flash causing harsh shadows. This approach (no flash) limits me to daytime photography and higher ISOs because I rely on the ambient light — an acceptable trade-off.

Option	Setting	Notes
ISO	400	Indoors without a flash; no concern about shutter speed because of the tripod
Aperture	f/8	An all-around aperture useful in many situations that results in a good depth of field and shutter speeds; in this case, I didn't want to open the aperture and reduce the depth of field because the point was to show the kitchen
Shutter speed	1/6 second	Slow but acceptable because of the tripod; nothing in the frame was moving
Camera	Sony Alpha 300	Entry-level dSLR; cropped body (FX); built-in Super SteadyShot image stabilization
Lens	Sigma 10-20mm F4-5.6	Ultra wide-angle zoom
Focal length	10mm	35mm equivalent: 15mm
Processing		Photoshop Elements
Other		Manual mode; pattern metering; tripod; remote shutter release

Sanctuary in HDR

This photo is an HDR image of the sanctuary of The Chapel, a large church in my family's local area. I took seven photos, separated by one stop of exposure (1 EV) and combined them in my favorite HDR software, Photomatix Pro. Afterward, I edited the image in Photoshop.

Using bracketed exposures (which is a staple of HDR) to shoot large interiors lets me find the best exposure in an entire scene using no extra lighting but keeping highlights from becoming too bright and blowing out.

(ISO 100, f/8, 1 second, Sigma 10-20mm F4-5.6 at 10mm) 2009

In the photo, I'm at one end of a large space; the far end, as you can see, is well lit. In addition, the darker areas in the pews and ceiling are properly dark, and the lights and ceiling aren't blown out, which is what a single, long exposure would do.

Option	Setting	Notes
ISO	100	Shooting HDR with ISO 100 reduces noise; shutter speed generally not a problem
Aperture	f/8	My "go-to" aperture for most scenic shots, including large interior spaces
Shutter speed	One second	For the 0 EV exposure
Brackets	7 (+/– 1.0 EV)	AEB; seven exposures at –3/–2/–1/0/+1/+2/+3 EV
Camera	Nikon D200	Semipro dSLR; cropped body (FX)
Lens	Sigma 10-20mm F4-5.6	Ultra wide-angle zoom
Focal length	10mm	35mm equivalent: 15mm
Processing		Nikon Capture NX 2 (raw); Photomatix Pro (HDR); Photoshop
Other		Manual mode; pattern metering; tripod; remote shutter release

Chapter 7: Picturing Odds and Ends

In This Chapter

- ✔ In memoriam
- ✔ Choosing odd subjects
- ✔ Looking for interesting perspectives
- ✔ Keeping your other interests in mind
- ✔ Photographing decorations
- ✔ Understanding that even trash can be interesting
- ✔ Taking a traditional product shot
- ✔ Sizing up an odd still life

This chapter showcases photos that don't fit into the traditional categories of landscape, cityscape, party, pet, or interior.

If you're in a same-subject rut — such as when you notice that you're taking too many pictures of your backyard — you have to point your camera at a different subject to get out of that rut. Simply walk around to the *front yard,* for example, to see what you can find. You might take a shot of your amplifier rather than the musical instrument you play, or shoot some trash you see in the park instead of its beautiful landscaping. Other examples are the eggs you just colored, a frog at the zoo, your Christmas tree, a drum set, a camera, or a gravesite.

Regardless of whether you're looking at a brand-new subject or an old one from a different angle (hint!), be sure to have some fun!

Resting Place in HDR

Taking a photograph of a loved one's final resting place may seem odd, but it's practical, for a number of reasons. Even putting aside the emotional aspects, it provides you and your family with a visual record of the grave site. Take photos of recent relatives and those from the distant past to create photographic support for your genealogical records. Then pass on these mementos to your descendants.

(ISO 100, f/4, 1/1000 second, Sigma 10-20mm F4-5.6 at 11mm) 2009

I took this photo of my mother's gravestone in 2009 as part of a photographic expedition to my hometown to shoot bracketed HDR. I had to get close to the ground, and the stone, to create this angle, which is the element that makes this photo stand out from the others I shot that day. The large aperture blurs the background nicely.

Get the job done right the first time — don't rush when you shoot important photos. Choose a day with nice weather, if you can, and set up your equipment with the expectation to stay a little while. Experiment with angles and orientation as well as distance to the subject.

Option	Setting	Notes
ISO	100	Shot outdoors during daylight hours with low noise because of working with HDR
Aperture	f/4	Depth of field limited to the near side of the headstone
Shutter speed	1/1000	For the 0 EV exposure
Brackets	5 (+/− 1.0 EV)	AEB; 5 exposures at −2/−1/0/+1/+2 EV
Camera	Nikon D200	Semipro dSLR; cropped body (FX)
Lens	Sigma 10-20mm F4-5.6	Ultra wide-angle zoom
Focal length	11mm	35mm equivalent: 16mm

Option	Setting	Notes
Processing		Nikon Capture NX 2 (raw), Photomatix Pro (HDR), Photoshop
Other		Manual exposure mode; pattern metering; tripod; remote shutter release; use a tripod or monopod to stabilize this type of shot even if not shooting HDR

Ribbit

My wife took this funky shot of a frog statue at the zoo. It's odd, which is why it's in this chapter.

I processed the raw exposure in Photomatix Pro as *pseudo-HDR* to bring out details and enhance contrast. (It isn't HDR because it has no bracketed exposures to increase the dynamic range that the camera captured — it's more of a software trick.)

(ISO 100, f/11, 1/320 second, Sony DT 18-70mm f/3.5-5.6 at 18mm)
Anne Correll, 2009

Keep your camera ready, wherever you are. Take photos of odd-looking statues, signs, people, animals, or whatever else you see, wherever you are. You might be able to turn your subject into a truly cool photo, like the one in this section.

Option	Setting	Notes
ISO	100	Outdoors in strong daylight
Aperture	f/10	Smaller due to the light
Shutter speed	1/320 second	Fast, for crisp, handheld shots
Camera	Sony Alpha 300	Entry-level dSLR; cropped body (FX); built-in Super SteadyShot image stabilization
Lens	Sony DT 18-70mm f/3.5-5.6	General-purpose zoom; budget kit lens; good value
Focal length	18mm	35mm equivalent: 27mm
Processing		Photomatix Pro (pseudo-HDR); Photoshop
Other		Program AE mode; pattern metering; handheld

Drum Set in HDR

This HDR image of a drum set is from the sanctuary of The Chapel (also mentioned in Chapter 6 of this minibook). I took several bracketed sets of photos from different vantage points around the room, both high and low. I was ready to wrap up when I realized that I could position the camera and tripod so that it looked like you were sitting at the set, looking out into the audience.

(ISO 100, f/8, 1/2 second, Sigma 10-20mm F4-5.6 at 10mm) 2009

The unique vantage point, combined with the colors and shapes of the set and contrasted with the room, make this photo a keeper.

Option	Setting	Notes
ISO	100	I shoot HDR with ISO 100 to reduce noise; shutter speed generally is not a problem
Aperture	f/8	My "go-to" aperture for most scenic shots, including large interior spaces
Shutter speed	1/2 second	For the 0 EV exposure
Brackets	9 (+/– 1.0 EV)	AEB; 9 exposures at –4/–3/–2/–1/0/+1/+2/+3/+4 EV
Camera	Nikon D200	Semipro dSLR; cropped body (FX)
Lens	Sigma 10-20mm F4-5.6	Ultra wide-angle zoom
Focal length	10mm	35mm equivalent: 15mm
Processing		Nikon Capture NX 2 (raw); Photomatix Pro (HDR); Photoshop
Other		Manual exposure mode; pattern metering; tripod; remote shutter release

Loud Is Good

You might call the photo in this section a product shot. I took a photo of one of my amps, a Marshall Vintage Modern 2266 50W Valve (tube) Amplifier head. I zoomed in because I didn't want to see the room beneath, behind, beside, and above, and I set the camera off at an angle to hide some of the distortion of the lens.

(ISO 100, f/8, 2 seconds, Sony DT 18-70mm f/3.5-5.6 at 35mm) 2009

When you take photos of any subject that has a straight line, lens distortion can stand out like a sore thumb. Most often, a bulge appears in the middle of the photo, which makes lines bow out in the center. Even expensive, high-quality lenses suffer from some amount of distortion.

Rather than try to delete distortion in software, which isn't always feasible, orient your camera so that you can't see it in the first place.

Option	Setting	Notes
ISO	100	Shooting indoors normally dictates higher ISOs, but I shot this one with a tripod and ignored long shutter speeds
Aperture	f/8	A dependable all-around aperture that results in a good depth of field and shutter speeds
Shutter speed	Two seconds	Slow, but not a problem with a stationary subject and a tripod
Camera	Sony Alpha 300	Entry-level dSLR; cropped body (FX); built-in Super SteadyShot image stabilization
Lens	Sony DT 18-70mm f/3.5-5.6	General-purpose zoom; budget kit lens; good value
Focal length	35mm	35mm equivalent: 52mm
Processing		Adobe Camera Raw (raw); Photoshop
Other		Manual exposure mode; pattern metering; tripod; remote shutter release

Diorama

At the National Military History Center in Auburn, Indiana, I shot this close-up photo of a diorama illustrating the Battle of the Bulge. Because most of the center's presentations involved full-scale equipment, getting good shots of specific pieces of gear without including everything else in the frame was difficult. My 50mm lens was invaluable in zeroing in on a single tank driving on the street. Had I used a wide-angle lens, the effect would have been completely off.

(ISO 100, f/8, 1/5 second, Nikon AF-S NIKKOR 50mm f/1.4G) 2009

I processed the brackets as HDR but then overlaid the result on the 0 EV exposure in Photoshop. I reduced the HDR layer's opacity to 36 percent. This effect accentuated the details and contrast in the traditional photo without going "full-bore" into HDR.

Be flexible when you process your photos. Use whatever tools and techniques you have at your fingertips to create whatever look you're after.

Option	Setting	Notes
ISO	100	Shot in HDR with ISO 100 to reduce noise; shutter speed generally not a problem
Aperture	f/4	Although photo was shot in HDR, I opened the aperture for a shallow depth of field, which has the effect of making it appear to be shot from a distance
Shutter speed	1/2 second	For the 0 EV exposure
Brackets	5 (+/− 1.0 EV)	AEB; 5 exposures at −2/−1/0/+1/+2 EV
Camera	Nikon D200	Semipro dSLR; cropped body (FX)
Lens	Nikon AF-S NIKKOR 50mm f/1.4G	The Nikon flagship standard prime lens
Focal length	50mm	35mm equivalent: 75mm
Processing		Nikon Capture NX 2 (raw); Photomatix Pro (HDR); Photoshop.
Other		Manual exposure mode; pattern metering; tripod; remote shutter release

Trash

On a photo walkabout, I struggled to take "nice" photos of the general scenery of a park I was visiting.

(ISO 100, f/5.6, 1/500 second, Sony DT 18-70mm f/3.5-5.6 at 18mm) 2008

When I saw a bit of trash on the ground, I realized that it set up a focal point near the camera and added contrast to the beauty of the landscape that immediately made the photo interesting.

When you're looking for something to photograph, look for *subjects,* even if it's trash in the foreground. Shots of "nothing" tend to be boring.

Option	Setting	Notes
ISO	100	Outdoors in strong daylight
Aperture	f/5.6	Artistic depth of field
Shutter speed	1/500 second	Extremely fast because of the strong daylight
Camera	Sony Alpha 300	Entry-level dSLR; cropped body (FX); built-in Super SteadyShot image stabilization

(continued)

Option	Setting	Notes
Lens	Sony DT 18-70mm f/3.5-5.6	General-purpose zoom; budget kit lens; good value
Focal length	18mm	35mm equivalent: 27mm
Processing		Photoshop Elements
Other		Program AE mode; pattern metering; handheld

A Classic SLR

This photo shows my Nikon FE2 with three older, manual focus lenses, in a classic product shot. I set up a miniature studio with a white paper backdrop draped underneath the camera and extending off the near side of the table, with a flash reflector to one side and on the other a remote flash on a tripod triggered by the in-camera flash. The remote flash had a small, soft box on it to diffuse the light.

(ISO 100, f/11, 1/60 second, Nikon AF-S NIKKOR 50mm f/1.4G) 2009

This sort of setup isolates the subject and provides good lighting from any angle you want. I used my Nikon D200 and Nikon SB-600 Speedlight (with an Opteka Soft Box), but could have easily used my Sony Alpha 300 with Sony HVL-F36AM flash. Both have wireless modes, which frees me from having to run sync cords between my camera and its flash.

Though the white backdrop wasn't perfect, it let me extract the camera from the background fairly easily in software.

Option	Setting	Notes
ISO	100	Dual flashes and tripod kept this down
Aperture	f/11	Deeper depth of field for product shot
Shutter speed	1/60 second	Good for normal still life or product-type shots; no need to wait around on long shutter speeds
Camera	Nikon D200	Semipro dSLR; cropped body (FX)

Option	Setting	Notes
Lens	Nikon AF-S NIKKOR 50mm f/1.4G	The Nikon flagship standard prime lens
Focal length	50mm	35mm equivalent: 75mm
Processing		Corel PaintShop Photo Pro
Other		Aperture Priority; pattern metering; dual flash: in-camera flash (pop-up) and external flash (remote); remote triggered by pop-up flash; remote flash on tripod with soft box; tripod; remote shutter release

A Study in Eggs

This photo is included in this book because I took it at ISO 1600 although I rarely stray to a setting higher than 400. In fact, I most often shoot at ISO 100.

I was near the eggs to eliminate the background as much as I could. I also didn't want to use my pop-up flash or try to set up a remote flash unit on the spur of the moment. I opened the aperture a little and set the shutter speed, and then increased the ISO in order to take the shot.

(ISO 1600, f/5.6, 1/160 second, Nikon AF-S NIKKOR 50mm f/1.4G) 2010

Photography almost always involves a compromise between the camera settings you want and the ones you have to choose in order to make the shot work. In the end, not many people will care that you chose f/5.6 over f/4 or ISO 1600 over ISO 400. What people want to see (except for photographers, who may be interested in studying *how* you took a photo) are compelling photos.

Option	Setting	Notes
ISO	1600	Shooting handheld photos inside without a flash dictates high ISOs (often incredibly so), even with a decent aperture
Aperture	f/5.6	A wider aperture for handheld shooting in low light with no flash

(continued)

Option	Setting	Notes
Shutter speed	1/160	Adequate for shooting handheld and could even be slower
Camera	Nikon D200	Semipro dSLR; cropped body (FX)
Lens	Nikon AF-S NIKKOR 50mm f/1.4G	The Nikon flagship standard prime lens
Focal length	50mm	35mm equivalent: 75mm
Processing		Adobe Camera Raw (raw); Photoshop
Other		Manual mode; pattern metering; handheld

Index

Notes

Notes

Notes

Apple & Macs

iPad For Dummies
978-0-470-58027-1

iPhone For Dummies,
4th Edition
978-0-470-87870-5

MacBook For Dummies, 3rd
Edition
978-0-470-76918-8

Mac OS X Snow Leopard For
Dummies
978-0-470-43543-4

Business

Bookkeeping For Dummies
978-0-7645-9848-7

Job Interviews
For Dummies,
3rd Edition
978-0-470-17748-8

Resumes For Dummies,
5th Edition
978-0-470-08037-5

Starting an
Online Business
For Dummies,
6th Edition
978-0-470-60210-2

Stock Investing
For Dummies,
3rd Edition
978-0-470-40114-9

Successful
Time Management
For Dummies
978-0-470-29034-7

Computer Hardware

BlackBerry
For Dummies,
4th Edition
978-0-470-60700-8

Computers For Seniors
For Dummies,
2nd Edition
978-0-470-53483-0

PCs For Dummies, Windows
7 Edition
978-0-470-46542-4

Laptops For Dummies,
4th Edition
978-0-470-57829-2

Cooking & Entertaining

Cooking Basics
For Dummies,
3rd Edition
978-0-7645-7206-7

Wine For Dummies,
4th Edition
978-0-470-04579-4

Diet & Nutrition

Dieting For Dummies,
2nd Edition
978-0-7645-4149-0

Nutrition For Dummies,
4th Edition
978-0-471-79868-2

Weight Training
For Dummies,
3rd Edition
978-0-471-76845-6

Digital Photography

Digital SLR Cameras &
Photography For Dummies,
3rd Edition
978-0-470-46606-3

Photoshop Elements 8
For Dummies
978-0-470-52967-6

Gardening

Gardening Basics
For Dummies
978-0-470-03749-2

Organic Gardening
For Dummies,
2nd Edition
978-0-470-43067-5

Green/Sustainable

Raising Chickens
For Dummies
978-0-470-46544-8

Green Cleaning
For Dummies
978-0-470-39106-8

Health

Diabetes For Dummies,
3rd Edition
978-0-470-27086-8

Food Allergies
For Dummies
978-0-470-09584-3

Living Gluten-Free
For Dummies,
2nd Edition
978-0-470-58589-4

Hobbies/General

Chess For Dummies,
2nd Edition
978-0-7645-8404-6

Drawing
Cartoons & Comics
For Dummies
978-0-470-42683-8

Knitting For Dummies,
2nd Edition
978-0-470-28747-7

Organizing
For Dummies
978-0-7645-5300-4

Su Doku For Dummies
978-0-470-01892-7

Home Improvement

Home Maintenance
For Dummies,
2nd Edition
978-0-470-43063-7

Home Theater
For Dummies,
3rd Edition
978-0-470-41189-6

Living the
Country Lifestyle
All-in-One
For Dummies
978-0-470-43061-3

Solar Power Your Home
For Dummies,
2nd Edition
978-0-470-59678-4

Internet

Blogging For Dummies,
3rd Edition
978-0-470-61996-4

eBay For Dummies,
6th Edition
978-0-470-49741-8

Facebook For Dummies, 3rd
Edition
978-0-470-87804-0

Web Marketing
For Dummies,
2nd Edition
978-0-470-37181-7

WordPress
For Dummies,
3rd Edition
978-0-470-59274-8

Language & Foreign Language

French For Dummies
978-0-7645-5193-2

Italian Phrases
For Dummies
978-0-7645-7203-6

Spanish For Dummies,
2nd Edition
978-0-470-87855-2

Spanish For Dummies,
Audio Set
978-0-470-09585-0

Math & Science

Algebra I For Dummies,
2nd Edition
978-0-470-55964-2

Biology For Dummies,
2nd Edition
978-0-470-59875-7

Calculus For Dummies
978-0-7645-2498-1

Chemistry For Dummies
978-0-7645-5430-8

Microsoft Office

Excel 2010 For Dummies
978-0-470-48953-6

Office 2010 All-in-One
For Dummies
978-0-470-49748-7

Office 2010 For Dummies,
Book + DVD Bundle
978-0-470-62698-6

Word 2010 For Dummies
978-0-470-48772-3

Music

Guitar For Dummies,
2nd Edition
978-0-7645-9904-0

iPod & iTunes
For Dummies,
8th Edition
978-0-470-87871-2

Piano Exercises
For Dummies
978-0-470-38765-8

Parenting & Education

Parenting For Dummies,
2nd Edition
978-0-7645-5418-6

Type 1 Diabetes
For Dummies
978-0-470-17811-9

Pets

Cats For Dummies,
2nd Edition
978-0-7645-5275-5

Dog Training For Dummies,
3rd Edition
978-0-470-60029-0

Puppies For Dummies,
2nd Edition
978-0-470-03717-1

Religion & Inspiration

The Bible For Dummies
978-0-7645-5296-0

Catholicism For Dummies
978-0-7645-5391-2

Women in the Bible
For Dummies
978-0-7645-8475-6

Self-Help & Relationship

Anger Management
For Dummies
978-0-470-03715-7

Overcoming Anxiety
For Dummies,
2nd Edition
978-0-470-57441-6

Sports

Baseball
For Dummies,
3rd Edition
978-0-7645-7537-2

Basketball
For Dummies,
2nd Edition
978-0-7645-5248-9

Golf For Dummies,
3rd Edition
978-0-471-76871-5

Web Development

Web Design
All-in-One
For Dummies
978-0-470-41796-6

Web Sites
Do-It-Yourself
For Dummies,
2nd Edition
978-0-470-56520-9

Windows 7

Windows 7
For Dummies
978-0-470-49743-2

Windows 7
For Dummies,
Book + DVD Bundle
978-0-470-52398-8

Windows 7 All-in-One
For Dummies
978-0-470-48763-1

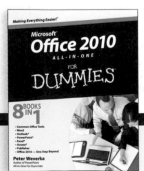

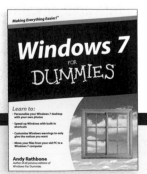